YOUR OWN WORDS

2nd edition

JACKIE EAMES & JUDITH WAINWRIGHT

Nelson

6/04

Nelson
Nelson House
Mayfield Road
Walton-on-Thames
Surrey KT12 5PL
United Kingdom

First published by Thomas Nelson & Sons Ltd 1992
Second edition published 1999

ISBN 0-17-490053-8

9 8 7 6 5 4 3 2
03 04 05 06 07

Designed and typeset by Jordan Publishing Design

Printed in Croatia, by Zrinski d.d., Čakovec

CONTENTS

INTRODUCTION TO THE SECOND EDITION

Since *Your Own Words* was published English teaching and syllabuses have changed substantially. Three particular developments seemed of especial importance as we wrote this new edition:

- The (regrettable) diminution in the coursework element of A-levels, which has placed a greater focus on exam technique and on investigating language and creating original writing in exam circumstances.

- The unitising of English A-levels, enabling students to do a genuine combination of literature and language, which has blurred the distinction – perhaps always artificially constructed – between the two disciplines and brought more ex-literature teachers and learners into contact with language. This has made us look carefully at our division between 'literary' and 'non-literary'.

- The identification of a subject core which will constitute the new AS.

We have also had a good deal of feedback from colleagues in addition to the often bizarre experience of teaching from our own textbook! Again three key facts have emerged:

- There are benefits to literature students and teachers in adopting a more systematic and precise approach to analysis – or what has been traditionally called practical criticism. This is important to the new tranche of students taking English Language and Literature A-level as well as those doing straight Literature.

- Teachers and students would appreciate different analysis-related activities such as writing in various styles and re-presenting.

- Even in the short space of time since the publication of *Your Own Words* (5 years as we write) many textual references have become dated. Mrs Thatcher may still be famous but many other figures have disappeared into the mists of history.

Other practical facts needed taking into account as we took a fresh look at the book. We have both taught and examined for the NEAB Language A-level whilst teaching the AEB Literature. We have also designed and taught a modularised NEAB Language and Literature A-level. Pursuing this course, students have far less time to focus on stylistics in isolation but can benefit from the techniques of analysis in their study of literary texts. The AEB have introduced a new A-level in Language. It places a major emphasis on stylistic analysis and also, significantly, demands that students re-present material. We have looked at exam papers and talked to colleagues of syllabuses we do not teach and our intention in the 'How to use this book' section is to clarify for teachers of different syllabuses which sections of the book might be most useful for them.

How to use this book

English Language teachers and students were and remain our major audience. The division of the book into theory and practice has been seen as useful so we have retained it. However, the bridge chapter, Chapter 5, seemed to us almost too schematic and not focused enough. We have identified three key questions to ask of any text and applied them to one particular piece, providing an example of what we mean by an analysis, which was lacking in the first edition. Building on the three key questions, we have simplified the approach to texts by introducing three headings, 'Context', 'Audience' and 'Purpose', under which we have grouped texts in the central 'Language in Action' section of the book, using some familiar and some new examples. We hope this will reinforce the approach to analysis we are suggesting without losing the usefulness of referring to the book when studying particular varieties. At the end of the chapters in 'Language in Action' we have included a range of possible activities, some for individuals and some for pair and group work. This is in response to feedback to our inservice sessions where teachers have repeatedly asked for teaching suggestions. We hope you find them useful. When creating the tasks we have tried to strengthen the link, which we see as central to the course, between the student as analyst and as writer.

Increasingly, Language students consider texts without designating them literary or non-literary. Examiners likewise seem often to blur the distinction.

We have written an entirely new section of the book relating to that grey area between clearly literary and non-literary texts – such as travel writing and genre fiction – entitled 'Take me away from all this'. All NEAB students must now do a third exam in lieu of coursework. Those who opt for language investigation can refer to the three chapters about coursework language investigation but we have also added a new section on the Language Investigation exam. Our experience is that students need precise guidance for this, from which they benefit enormously. It appears to be an exam where 80/80 is awarded. We have likewise re-written the final chapter of the book to include advice for writing creatively in timed conditions (though we feel that this is not frankly to be recommended).

We anticipate that Language and Literature students will find the theory and action sections of the book useful. They will all have to do the Issues and Stylistics elements of A-level Language so the terminology and approaches which the book suggests will be of value to them. Many Dual students opt for the Original Writing as their coursework so the final chapter of the book, 'Original Writing', will give them some guidance.

Finally, we hope that Literature students will employ the approaches of the book to establish a more rigorous and systematic approach to practical criticism. While they may wish to retain a separate vocabulary and thus eschew the glossary of terms, they definitely benefit from scrutinising texts in a more systematic way. Of the 'Language in Action' section, the literary and quasi-literary 'Take me away from all this' may provide the best starting points. 'Purpose' is often a focus of practical criticism questions so this section is also worth their perusal. Many literature students struggle with the more creative coursework assignments that teachers like to set; others are keen to find their own voices and do the ancillary creative writing option. For both types of student the final chapter will give some useful pointers.

To summarise

Language students: the whole book

Language and Literature students: all but either the ultimate or the penultimate chapter

Literature students: Chapters 1 to 5, Chapters 8 'Purpose', 9 'Take me away', 10–15 literature chapters, and final chapter.

The activities have icons to indicate the type of task and number of students:

Thinking   Individually

Discussion   In pairs

Writing   In groups

Section One

LANGUAGE IN THEORY

This section provides a vocabulary for describing language.

Chapter 1
In the Beginning Was the Word . . .

In every piece of speech or writing we find words, words, words, and any consideration of language ought, reasonably, to start with them. Their selection is by no means random; every user of words, consciously or otherwise, weighs several possibilities before plumping for the chosen word. Slips of the tongue such as 'blix the ingredients' betray the fact that we are selecting from options – here 'blend' and 'mix'.

The fact that our language, English, has the largest wordstock of any language means that English users have a particularly large range of possibilities to choose from:

▶ Are you drinking from a mug, beaker or cup?

▶ Do you say the dress is scarlet, crimson or just plain red?

▶ Is the man hurrying, dashing or rushing?

▶ Is he hurrying impatiently, desperately or determinedly?

Notice that in each case the three alternatives are interchangeable because they all do the same job. Depending on the job they are doing, words in their context are ascribed to WORD CLASSES* such as NOUN, ADJECTIVE, VERB and ADVERB. As a native speaker you do not need to be familiar with these terms to know that you would never say 'Are you drinking from a scarlet?' or 'Is the dress mug?' If, however, you want to analyse or describe language as well as use it, you need explicit terms in addition to implicit knowledge.

Implicit knowledge tells us that not only do we need a certain sort of word, we also need to combine words in certain ways. In English, we place adjectives before nouns, for example, although this is not always the case in French. The importance of word order (SYNTAX) will be discussed in a later chapter when we consider phrases, clauses and sentences. To begin with, we will look at the four major word classes and what makes us choose one word from the numerous options available within each class.

* Terms whose first occurrence in the text is in capitals are defined in the Glossary.

WHAT FACTORS AFFECT OUR WORD CHOICE?

Sometimes the need to be precise, to label correctly and describe accurately is what motivates us. Sometimes a desire to praise or blame will push us toward emotive adjectives (inspiring emotion) like willowy or skinny (the first complimentary, the second pejorative) rather than the more neutral 'thin'. Sometimes a desire to impress makes us select the longest possible LATINATE word where an ANGLO-SAXON one would serve just as well – consider 'perambulate' and 'walk'. Of course, down-to-earth Anglo-Saxon can be speciously sincere.

Our word choice is affected by context, audience, intellect… a whole host of factors. It is a useful exercise to try to 'read between the lines' of a text in order to discover what linguists call the SUBTEXT. Some things you might consider include:

What is the SENDER up to?

What is he trying to tell the RECEIVER about himself?

What is he actually telling the receiver about himself?

Why are words so important to us all anyway?

NOUNS: MAKING SENSE OF THE UNIVERSE

Most of us remember very little about learning our own language – it just occurred as if by magic. This is not the time or place for a lengthy digression about child language acquisition, but the first words children use tell us a lot about what words mean to, and do for, us all.

The first words children use are nearly always not only nouns but CONCRETE NOUNS. Children do not want to discourse upon love, loyalty or other abstractions. They have quite enough to cope with learning labels for the really important things in life like 'juice' and 'biccies'. When you comfort a child who is afraid of a big alsatian you cut it down to size by saying 'It's only a dog.' Give it a label and it isn't so frightening any more, because it's placed in the universe. The names for things allow us to talk about them when they aren't there. This gives us the ability to talk about other times and places, indeed unreal ones. Names have enormous potency: some stand for something so disturbing that we come to avoid the word itself. This explains the numerous euphemisms for cancer, 'the big C', and for death. As one child remarked, 'Death wouldn't be so bad if it was called hig.'

It isn't only children who have an obsession with labelling (giving something a name and thus getting control over it). Many adults take great pride in knowing a pippit from a peewit, a spitfire from a hurricane, an elm from an oak. Clearly, this is partly a practical matter – it takes far longer to describe the differences between two birds/planes/trees than to attach to them a generally agreed label. Knowing lots of labels is useful in terms of precision as well as ego-boosting! More and more precise labels become necessary among specialist groups, be they drug traffickers saying what's available or ornithologists discussing the mating habits of guillemots and puffins.

Concrete nouns seem to be eminently practical things, giving useful or interesting information. All English speakers above a certain age and intellectual level share a set of mental pictures ready to be conjured up by words like snow, boy and bucket.

ACTIVITY ◻

As an experiment, draw now on a piece of paper a sun, a house and a flower. Turn to the end of the chapter to see if your pictures and ours coincide.

Concrete nouns, however, are not so straightforward as they appear. Consider the following options:

1   Bird
2   *Troglodytes troglodytes*
3   Wren
4   Teeny Brown Birdie

All are labels for the same thing – they have the same DENOTATION or dictionary meaning – but they do not have the same CONNOTATIONS (associations). 1 is very general; 2 likely to seem unnecessarily technical except among true specialists; 3 is precise and workaday; and 4 could be patronising or appropriate, depending on the age of the receiver.

To judge their efficiency as labels you'd need to consider context. Quite often people deliberately go up or down the scale of specialism for their own purposes. Some men oversimplify technical terms in order to convey to women that they don't expect them to understand such things; doctors, lawyers and even teachers use specialist terms to exclude and intimidate non-specialists. In such a situation you have to be either very confident or very close to the speaker to say 'Don't talk to me as though I'm an idiot,' or 'What the hell are you talking about?' Your worry stems from the fact that (if the speaker plays it convincingly enough) you feel that the fault is with you. You feel that everyone else in the room understands and it's just you who is dense, or that the speaker is not meaning to talk down to you and means it kindly, so you mustn't be rude. Choice of labels, then, can be significant in the power politics of conversation.

In the wider political arena choice of label indicates a point of view. Sometimes this point of view is deliberately expressed and received: we would expect to hear of 'the rationalisation of the Health Service to improve its efficiency' from one side of the House, but of 'an attack on the Welfare State to drain its lifeblood' from the other. It is interesting to note whose version of the truth a particular reporter chooses to report, since we would not expect a deliberate expression of viewpoint from a reporter.

Many noun choices reflect the word-user's stance, consciously or not. In what contexts or from what speakers might you expect to hear the following sets of labels, which could all denote the same two things?

house	home	property	place	abode
girl	woman	lady	tart	female

Labels seem to matter to us. You only need to think of the frustration of not being able to remember a name, or the awful feeling of powerlessness engendered when trying to get what you want in a foreign country, to realise that words for things are vital to us all.

What of labels for the intangible — abstracts such as joy, justice and truth? Could these concepts exist if we did not symbolise them in words? What exactly do they represent? Such words certainly carry a massive emotional weight, perhaps the greater because each individual will have their own interpretation of each of them. 'Love' and 'freedom' will probably not carry precisely the same mental pictures for any two people: the words are nevertheless hugely suggestive. ABSTRACT NOUNS like these are of little use in imparting information, but for discussing possibilities and ideals they are invaluable.

So what is the implication of all this for analysis of language? To summarise, we might say that a communicator who wants to be precise, specific and to convey facts will lean heavily on concrete nouns. This will enable the receiver to have a clear mental image and it will lend an air of realism to the TEXT (either written or spoken). A communicator who wants to discuss ideas, to philosophise and suggest without stating, will employ more abstract nouns.

It is always worth looking at the selection of nouns that a writer uses. If they are predominantly concrete, are they related to a similar field of life or activity? You often find that a tone is established by clustering related words, or words within the same SEMANTIC FIELD. For example, in the first paragraph of *A House for Mr Biswas* by V. S. Naipaul, dollars, interest, money and rent concentrate the reader's mind on Mr Biswas's financial problems:

> Ten weeks before he died, Mr Mohun Biswas, a journalist of Sikkim Street, St James, Port of Spain, was sacked. He had been ill for some time. In less than a year he had spent more than nine weeks at the Colonial Hospital and convalesced at home for even longer.
>
> When the doctor advised him to take a complete rest the Trinidad Sentinel had no choice. It gave Mr Biswas three months' notice and continued, up to the time of his death, to supply him every morning with a free copy of the paper.
>
> Mr Biswas was forty-six, and had four children. He had no money. His wife Shama had no money. On the house in Sikkim Street Mr Biswas owed, and had been owing for four years, three thousand dollars. The interest on this, at eight per cent, came to twenty dollars a month; the ground rent was ten dollars. Two children were at school. The two older children, on whom Mr Biswas might have depended, were both abroad on scholarships.
>
> V. S. Naipaul: *A House for Mr Biswas*

A cynic might feel that the use of abstract nouns makes it more difficult to pin down meaning. Advertisers can promise that you'll be 'at peace with your pipe' and it's well-nigh impossible to disprove them. When the next political conference takes place, count the abstract nouns in the party leader's big speech. Let's look at the literary writer using abstract nouns:

> ... thanks to the occult tyrannies of those blandly saluting clocks I had been mysteriously handcuffed to history, my destinies indissolubly chained to those of my country.... I ... had become heavily embroiled in Fate.
>
> Salman Rushdie: *Midnight's Children*

Notice here the predominance of abstract, somewhat mysterious nouns. Also notice the cluster of words in the semantic field of fate. Neither of these things are accidental: they create an aura of mystery about the central character. They also make us suspect that he is rather pleased with himself!

What's in a name?

We all have a large number of labels stuck onto us in the course of our existence. They can signal our relationship with the speaker, be it familial (Auntie), affectionate (luv) or formal (Madam). What we are called helps to establish the right tone, on a scale from the totally formal to the intimate. Deliberately using an inappropriate name signals that something is wrong: thus the angry parent lengthens Sam to Samantha; the boss on his dignity reintroduces the surname which had been dropped as you'd become more friendly. A secretary would not expect the boss's spouse to ring up and ask for Chubby-poos, and if you're unfortunate enough to be taught by your mother, you'd certainly avoid calling her Mum at school. Very young children, naturally, break the rules, embarrassing the milkman by called him Dad or mortifying their older sister by calling the next-door neighbour Snoopy Sam to his face.

Nicknames are an interesting phenomenon: used overtly they're a matter of peer group identity; used covertly they are often a harmless rebellion against authority.

Look at the following greetings. How would you scale them in terms of intimacy?

1   Wotcher, Cock.

2   Hi, Fred.

3   Morning, Linda.

4   Good-day, Madam.

5   How's things?

6   Good morning, Mrs Brown.

Could you make any guesses about the age of speaker five, the regional background of speaker one, or the sort of context within which speaker four is operating? Of course you could: we all recognise such differences fairly easily. What you need to do is raise this intuitive knowledge to the surface when doing analysis.

We all know that the first name is friendlier than a surname – otherwise 'Call me John' would be a pointless utterance – it is seen as a marker of favour. Similarly, we all know that surnames mark formality or respect (but they can also mark hostility, which is important to remember). If two people are speaking to each other, one using the first name and one the surname, the surname-user is almost certain to be younger or inferior in status.

Sometimes our liking for someone, which predisposes us to use their first name, clashes with a social duty to show them respect by using their surname. Many people solve this problem by referring to the person by both their names, thus signalling respect and affection. Older students often do this when talking about teachers. Do you? It's usually younger pupils who have relatively less power who use nicknames (often beginning with 'old'!). Meeting people in a different context can be difficult, too. You can't really say 'Would you like a drink, Miss?' but would you sound over-familiar using her first name?

Names, then, are clear indicators of role, status and intimacy in conversation. They are equally significant in writing. Journalists' terms for politicians make their allegiances quite clear. Is Tony, The P.M., Bambi, Tony Blur, Mr Blair or Tony Blair? Could you make an intelligent guess as to which newspaper would use which appellation?

If someone you've never met writes to you using their first name, aren't they certain to be selling you something, be it a cause or a course?

Writers of fiction, Charles Dickens for example, sometimes use names to indicate the character of a person (Gradgrind in *Hard Times* and Bumble in *Oliver Twist*) or the nature of an institution (Dotheboys Hall in *Nicholas Nickleby*). Funny, memorable names are a stock-in-trade of comic writers (in both meanings of the word comic: consider Billy Bunter and Olive Oyl as well as Podsnap and Toby Belch in Shakespeare's *Twelfth Night*). Alliteration in names is often used by writers to catch the reader's attention.

You will have noticed that large incidence of capital letters at the beginning of words in the last few paragraphs. They are the typographical markers of PROPER NOUNS. They are those nouns which are most truly 'naming words'. They stress particularity and individuality, and as such they are numerous in news reporting, realistic fiction and guide books, to name but a few! However, not all writers want to be precise and informative – some prefer to make their creations mysterious.

The man with no name

Storytellers sometimes avoid giving their characters names, as these would endow them with identity. Names can give clues to racial and social background. You don't find many Alexandras or Henrys in inner city Manchester, for example, and there are no prizes for guessing the origins of Jacob Epstein or Michael O'Flaherty. When anonymity is necessary a pronoun is used. But more of this in the next chapter.

Normally, pronouns are used to replace a previously named thing or person and thus to avoid useless repetition. This is their straightforward grammatical function.

However, when they are favoured above a name, you can be sure that writers have their reasons. One character in a novel may refer to another only as 'him' or 'her' because of their disgust: they cannot even humanise the person with a name. John Fowles uses this technique when Miranda talks about her captor in *The Collector*. This is not such a surprising effect when you remember that pronoun use is generally regarded as rude: we have all been told that 'she's the cat's mother'. Feminists, entirely reasonably, object to the use of 'he/him' as generic pronoun, and calling anyone older than a small baby 'it' is a terrible insult. Personal pronouns can be just that.

Possessive pronouns are often interesting, too. Do couples refer to 'our' or 'my' house, car or children? How often do they feel the need to mark ownership anyway? (Again, if children are anything to go by, this impulse is very basic – 'That's mine' and 'That's not yours' are early favourites!) Why do adults sometimes replace the possessive pronoun with the definite article? Is referring to 'the wife' more, or less, offensive than talking about 'my wife'? Is it true to say that 'the' distances and makes you less responsible than 'my'? It is easier, certainly, to give 'my' an intonation suggesting pride, affection etc. whereas 'the' sounds very matter-of-fact.

I hope that by now you are beginning to see that all word choices can give us clues about a communicator's intentions and emotions. Try to train yourself to notice whether a writer uses a lot of proper nouns, or many concrete ones, or numerous abstracts. When you have noticed what is there, don't leave it at that: ask yourself why. Who is the writing or speaking aimed at? Does the writer seem confident/patronising/ironic? The answer will be there in the words and structures chosen. It is not a mystery, available only to a privileged few; it's there for all to see if only you look carefully and thoughtfully enough.

ADJECTIVES: MODIFICATION – DIRECTION OR INFORMATION?

When we first start writing, we are soon encouraged by our teachers to make our writing more colourful or precise by adding adjectives. In response to the request 'Tell us more about it: what sort of man? What kind of house?' we might transform the sentence 'The man walked up to the house' into 'The tall, thin man walked up to the old, ruined house.' It's still not exactly inspired but the picture is already coming into sharper focus: extra qualities are being added to the nouns. More information makes the reference more specific. The nouns 'man' and 'house' have been MODIFIED. Since, in English, adjectives precede the nouns they modify unless separated by a verb, they can condition our response to them, and most of us capitalise fully upon the opportunity adjectives give us to direct the response of the reader or listener. A few adjectives do add strictly factual information to the noun, but more reflect some personal judgement of the speaker or writer.

One of the most neutral, factual ways of adding information to a noun is to use another noun as an adjective: 'plastic spoons', 'brick wall' and 'safety catch' are all examples of phrases in which the modifier, in other contexts, is a noun.

....

ACTIVITY ◼ ▨

List six other examples of 'nouns' modifying other nouns.

....

Other purely physical visual properties can be similarly added — take 'woollen rug' and 'luminous signs'. There is much PRE-MODIFICATION in technical writing since it allows you to pack in lots of information.

ACTIVITY ◐ 💭

Pick out nouns being used as modifiers and visual adjectives from this extract:

> The parallel current flow through the metallic coils allows the relay logic operation to be followed precisely.

Other words which add physical properties to nouns might seem at first sight to be similarly factual, but a moment's thought will make us realise that 'large' and 'tall' are purely relative. Such adjectives as 'fat', 'thin' and 'pretty' are value judgements: your viewpoint depends on your own starting point. From a height of five feet, five feet nine is tall, and many people consider themselves fat because they are comparing themselves with an ideal. Children think you are old at thirty – in fact the older you become, the farther away 'old' seems! To people in developing countries, we in the West would all seem rich, and even the question of whether or not human beings are mortal depends on religious viewpoint.

It is actually very difficult to choose adjectives which are not highly personal, even when we are trying not to be emotive. How we describe other things and people is intimately linked to our attitudes, tastes and personal attributes. Not only might one girl describe a lad as 'hanging' (Lancastrian dialect for 'ugly') and another girl describe him as 'handsome', or more likely 'fit', but the same two girls could describe the same shade of dark red as 'maroon' or 'plum'. It is well-nigh impossible to ensure that your listener will DECODE (interpret) your message in the desired way.

In short, adjectives are frequently subjective and imprecise: in different contexts this can be an advantage or a disadvantage. Adjectives clearly express personal, cultural and political bias, but they are unclear guides to action: how much should I spend on a 'reasonable' present? Do I really give her a 'teeny drop' of sherry? When he refers to his son-in-law as 'dark' is he referring to his hair or his skin? All these confusions can be, and are, exploited by writers, who often use deliberately ambiguous words. The rest of us rarely realise how biased and misleading our words can be.

We may not intend to mislead, but there is little doubt that the chocolate manufacturer who sells 'fun-sized bars' is being 'economical with the truth': a more dispassionate observer might call them plain 'small'. Advertisers generally exploit the unspecific nature but powerful impact of adjectives: thus Ford tell us that the Fiesta is 'strong and sophisticated, potent and practical'. Emotive adjectives (wonderful, happy, sad, tragic and many more) and evaluative ones (good, bad, stupid, brilliant, wrong) are heavily used by advertisers and journalists to attribute praise or blame. In argument, we have all been guilty of piling one emotive or extreme adjective upon another to vent our spleen.

Sorting the fact from the opinion

....

ACTIVITY

Find and list the adjectives in the following article.

First, select those which are factual. Then divide the others into 'favourable', 'neutral' and 'unfavourable'. It might help if you scale them from one (very favourable) to five (very unfavourable). For example:

1   mature   experienced   elderly   old   decrepit   5

> The bombing of the Pan Am flight 103 with the loss of 259 passengers and 11 local people in Lockerbie was a sickening atrocity. It could not conceivably serve the interest of workers or oppressed nations. If it proves to be true that a Palestinian group was responsible for the appalling bombing then it will have done nothing whatsoever for the cause of the Palestinian people. It could undermine the gains made by the magnificent intifada, the biggest Palestinian mass movement for 50 years.
>
> In 13 months there have been countless demonstrations, strikes and general strikes as the mass of the population become involved in this vital struggle. Even the atrocious brutality of the Israeli army which has resulted in over 400 deaths has failed to dampen the courageous struggle for democratic and national rights.
>
> The great sweep and scale of the mass uprising has had a profound effect upon the working class in Israel.
>
> *The Militant*

....

ACTIVITY

Now find your own examples to analyse in the same way.

....

Politicians are not averse to using the same technique, even if the Speaker tells them it is unseemly (a pretty emotive word in itself). An easy way to get some practice in spotting loaded adjectives is to listen to Radio 4's parliamentary summary programme, which includes recordings of politicians in action.

Sow's ear or silk purse?

Adjectives also allow us to be euphemistic. Asked what we think of a dress we might say 'It's very nice.' 'Nice' has become little more than a polite noise. We say someone is 'poorly' when we cannot face their being really ill; and it is more socially acceptable to be 'affluent' than 'rich', more desirable to be 'curvaceous' than 'well-padded'.

Any stretch of reading or listening can provide countless examples of the ways in which adjectives are used and abused. In the second part of this section we shall look at some more.

Post-modification – justice for all?

As we have seen, the usual place for an adjective is in front of the noun, unless of course it is the COMPLEMENT in the sentence, as in 'The tea was too hot' or 'She seems very clever'. It is extremely unusual to find an adjective directly after a noun – 'the body beautiful' is the only example that springs to mind. When it does occur it's usually for literary or stylistic effect, and thus well worth noticing.

However, adjectives are not the only way to modify nouns. A word-user can, instead, POST-MODIFY using a group of words.

Consider the following pair of sentences:

> The starving children crowded into the refugee camp.

> The children, who were starving, crowded into the refugee camp.

- What is the difference between them?
- Is there a difference in emphasis in that 'starving' is stressed in one and 'children' in the other? To what effect?
- When might you choose to use each sentence?

Some would argue that if the adjective comes before the noun it colours your impression before you hear or see the noun itself, whereas if the modification comes afterwards it is separable from the noun – almost an afterthought. It is impossible to make blanket rules about what form of modification is most effective or noticeable, but in looking at language it's worth noticing which method has been used and suggesting why.

Look at another example. Is there a difference in emphasis between these two sentences?

> The dying man wrote his will.

> The man, who was dying, wrote his will.

Of course, it isn't always a straightforward either/or choice. If you want to pack in lots of information, you are likely to use both pre- and post-modification as in 'The new and innovative theatre complex, which is almost complete, will open in May.'

You have probably noticed that post-modification sounds more formal, and it is more typical of the written mode. In conversation, you would never say 'My dentist, a portly, middle-aged stock-car racing enthusiast, is moving to a new surgery' but you surely recognise where you might read it.

Post-modification is often more precise than a single adjective can hope to be. 'The pink flower' paints a far less precise picture than 'The flower, which was tinged with the palest possible shade of pink'. Using an adjectival or RELATIVE CLAUSE to follow a noun rather than butting in also has the advantage of seeming fairer.

Certain varieties of language are either more, or less, likely to make use of post-modifiers. They are seldom used by advertisers and frequently used by legal writers. Method of modification sometimes divides the broadsheets (*The Times*, the *Guardian*, the *Daily Telegraph* and the *Independent*) from the popular press (the *Sun*, *Daily Star*,

Mirror and the rest). Writers seeking to make a direct emotional impact are likely to lean heavily on adjectives. They will talk of 'terrorised pensioners', 'macho men' and 'sexy starlets'. If, conversely, they want to give detail, they might well prefer to use adjectival and relative clauses. We are being somewhat simplistic here for the sake of clarity. This topic is covered in more detail in the 'purpose' section.

A final word on adjectives

The range of choice of adjectives is enormous. The right shade of meaning can be differentiated by selecting just the right adjective, and the hallmark of a good writer is an unerring success in doing this. If inspiration fails the rest of us, there's always Roget's *Thesaurus*!

As readers, we likewise make precise judgements: 'wealthy', 'affluent', 'rich' and 'comfortable' do not mean exactly the same thing, though they are in the same range of meaning (or, to put it more technically, the same semantic field). Expressions like 'well-heeled' and 'well off' are separated from the others by being more informal (COLLOQUIAL), which is another factor writers need to consider. How sophisticated and formal a writer chooses to be will depend largely upon AUDIENCE.

'Audience' is the term linguists use to describe language receivers, whether they are listening or reading. If an audience is relatively uneducated, there is little point in using a word like 'quintessential'. Children's writers have to edit out sophisticated LEXIS (vocabulary) in order to be understood. A word which is simply too difficult cannot fulfil another of the two functions of an adjective – to inform or move. All the same, constant use of the simplest, most common and therefore somewhat meaningless words such as 'nice' and 'lovely' is equally ineffective and has the added disadvantage of insulting the receiver's intelligence.

VERBS: THE MUSCLES OF SENTENCES

Language can't get very far without verbs. They are the muscles of sentences, and give them direction and point, telling us what all these sundry things and people are doing – or having done to them.

ACTIVITY

Try to imagine a diary entry without verbs:

> Out of bed. Breakfast. Letters. Car. At the Bistro. Home.

At first glance this might appear to make sense in the way that telegrams or notes make sense. Supply the verbs that the other words suggest, to make a complete narrative.

Have you used 'got', 'ate', 'read', 'washed', 'dined' and 'went'? Some are easier to predict than others – for instance 'car' would most regularly be COLLOCATED with 'drove', 'mended' or 'started'. The point is that there are very many possibilities and that verb choice greatly affects meaning. Consider this alternative diary entry:

> Leapt out of bed. Skipped breakfast. Wrote letters. Crashed car! Drank at the Bistro. Staggered home.

This depicts a rather more dramatic day! It also gives an impression of a more dynamic character.

Since the context of this writing is a diary, the assumption we have made is that the subject of the verbs is first-person – most probably the singular 'I' but possibly the plural 'we'. If we gave ourselves the freedom to change the subject governing the above verbs, we could produce a different story:

> John leapt out of bed. The rest of his family had skipped breakfast. His sister was writing some letters when their neighbour crashed his car. He had been drinking at The Bistro. His friends had staggered home.

In this version, there are more characters. Each subject has its own verb, and this has to be a FINITE one. In its infinitive form (e.g. to leap, to skip) the verb is NON-FINITE and has not been activated or made sense of by a subject. Once subject and verb have been brought into relation, you have a meaningful grammatical unit: the CLAUSE or SIMPLE sentence. We will discuss these larger units in Chapter 3.

Let us now return our attention to the verb itself. There are two broad types of verb, STATIVE and DYNAMIC. Stative verbs such as 'to be', 'seem', 'appear' and 'know' tell us what *is*. They can sound extremely matter-of-fact. However, if they are clustered, their subject is seen as passive, ineffective and even victimised.

The effect is very different when the subject is followed by numerous dynamic verbs. Dynamic verbs tell us what the subject does. This person, it seems, is active, effective and in charge of their own destiny, making things happen as opposed to allowing things to happen to them. Consider this brother and sister:

> He knew he would never be a success. He was too unambitious. He appeared apathetic. He seemed made for failure.
> She told him to pull his socks up. She insisted that he needed confidence, suggested therapy and nagged him to visit a psychiatrist.

The verbs associated with the brother – 'was', 'appeared' and 'seemed' – are stative ones, but those associated with the sister – 'told', 'insisted', 'suggested' and 'nagged' – are all dynamic.

We might not like the sound of the sister – doers are often a nuisance – but we recognise her dynamism. We may pity the brother, but we suspect that he is a lost cause.

In our writing we can explore verbs in different ways. Chosen carefully, they can carry a lot of meaning within a text by adding to the descriptive effect. How many verbs can you think of as an alternative to the relatively neutral 'walk'? To replace it with 'stroll' or 'amble' enables the reader to see the scene (and character) more clearly. We need not explicitly state that a character is violent if many of the verbs associated with him/her suggest violence.

ACTIVITY

Write a paragraph employing ten violent verbs. Get a friend to rank order them in terms of forcefulness.

Verbs don't necessarily draw attention to themselves in the way that unusual adjectives might because they are such an integral part of the sentence structure. In analysis, it is easy to overlook them. Don't – they are frequently very significant.

ACTIVITY

Take a close look at the verbs in the following passage.

- What meaning do they seem to carry?
- What effect do they have on you?

> The first thing the midwife noticed about Michael K. when she helped him out of his mother into the world, was that he had a hare lip. The lip curled like a snail's foot, the nostril gaped. Obscuring the child for a moment from its mother, she prodded open the tiny bud of the mouth and was thankful to find the palate whole.
>
> To his mother she said, 'You should be happy, they bring good luck to the household.' But from the first Anna K. did not like the mouth that would not close and the living, pink flesh it bared to her. She shivered to think of what had been growing inside her all these months. The child could not suck from the breast and cried with hunger. She tried a bottle; when it could not suck from the bottle, she fed it with a tea-spoon, fretting with impatience when it coughed and spluttered and cried.
>
> 'It will close up as he gets older,' the midwife promised. However, the lip did not close, or did not close enough, nor did the nose come straight.

J. M. Coetzee: *The Life and Times of Michael K*

When and how did it happen?

Apart from choosing particular verbs carefully, the TENSE of those verbs may also be varied for different purposes. A little earlier when you were asked to add the verbs to the diary entry, you almost certainly used the past tense. This is because you were describing events which had already occurred. People automatically use the past tense for storytelling, for reporting and, of course, for diary-writing. If a writer deliberately selects another tense, for example the present, this will be for a particular effect.

Here is an extract from *David Copperfield* by Charles Dickens, in which David is describing the house in which he was brought up. Why, do you think, does he use the present tense?

Looking back, as I was saying, into the blank of my infancy, the first objects I can remember as standing out by themselves from a confusion of things, are my mother and Peggotty. What else do I remember? Let me see.

There comes out of the cloud, our house – not new to me, but quite familiar, in its earliest remembrance. On the ground-floor is Peggotty's kitchen, opening into a back yard; with a pigeon-house on a pole, in the centre, without any pigeons in it; a great dog-kennel in a corner, without any dog; and a quantity of fowls that look terribly tall to me, walking about in a menacing and ferocious manner. There is one cock who gets upon a post to crow, and seems to take particular notice of me as I look at him through the kitchen window, who makes me shiver, he is so fierce. Of the geese outside the side-gate who come waddling after me with their long necks stretched out when I go that way, I dream at night; as a man environed by wild beasts might dream of lions.

Charles Dickens: *David Copperfield*

This is a literary example, but the usage is also familiar from speech: consider 'I'm walking down the street and he comes up to me and says...'. More expected uses for the present tense would include the stating of opinion, commenting, describing a habitual action or state, or summing up a situation. Examples of these usages would be

I think she's very talented.

He is a fool to himself.

I go dancing every Monday.

He belongs to the Scout Movement.

The Muslim world is in ferment.

If any of these verbs were changed to the past tense, for example 'He was a fool to himself' or 'The Muslim world was in ferment' we would immediately have the action placed in time. The SIMPLE past describes completed action whereas the present is timeless. You can talk about someone who is dead and nevertheless use the present tense, for example 'Mozart is the greatest composer of all time.'

If you want to describe the past but sequence events within it, you would have recourse to the PLUPERFECT. This is the verb form which includes the word 'had' and it precedes the simple past. An example will make this much clearer:

When I had told him off (pluperfect) he began to cry (past or perfect).

By using those particular verb tenses, I have made it clear that the telling off occurred before the crying. In narrative, this sort of information is vital and is usually referred to as SEQUENCING.

Non-native speakers often confuse tense, unaware of subtle differences. They may use the pluperfect 'had' too often, thus going too far into the past. Or they may use 'used to' instead of the simple past, not appreciating that 'used to' implies past HABITUAL action and not one self-contained act. Consider the difference between 'I used to smoke when I was younger' (subtext 'But now I don't) and 'I smoked when I was younger', which is a statement of fact and has no clear subtext.

There is yet another complication in verb forms and that is the difference between the simple and the CONTINUOUS. The simple present and past we have already mentioned: they deal with what is always true or what happened once. 'I write' and 'I washed the glasses' will serve as examples. Consider the change in meaning if we use the continuous forms 'I am writing' and 'I was washing the glasses'.

···

ACTIVITY

What words might you add to either clause? Jot them down.

···

To 'I am writing' most people would add 'at the moment' or 'a book' because the continuous suggests a very precise moment in time, not an activity which is habitual but may not be happening at this very moment. A speaker whose first language is English would not say 'I am writing every day' or 'I write now', but a second- or foreign-language speaker could be forgiven for not recognising the difference. As analysts, you need to be aware of these subtle differences.

Taking our second example, most English speakers would follow 'I was washing the glasses' with the word 'when...'. We use the past continuous to suggest interrupted action. This use helps to sequence: you were doing one thing when something happened. Notice the interruption occurs once, so the simple past is used. Perhaps the telephone rang; perhaps the light went out. Either way you were interrupted. You find a good many 'past continuous plus simple past' formations in mystery and horror stories. They are useful for narration and atmosphere creation: 'I was sleeping peacefully when I heard a strange sound' is far more effective and clear than 'I was asleep. I heard a strange sound.' The terseness of the two simple forms would be very appropriate in other contexts, for example action-packed narratives: 'He dashed in. Furiously, he searched the drawers. He could not find it.' By now, you will see that one tense is not as good as any other. Nor is it just a matter of past, present or future.

Before we leave tense let us look quickly at the future. It would seem self-explanatory: it describes that which is yet to occur. Either 'going to' or 'will'/'shall' can be used, but it is worth noticing that the future can also be marked by use of an adverb, as in 'Tomorrow I meet my fate.' Some languages and dialects prefer to use a function word rather than a tense change: for example, in Black English you find 'mi go yisede' not 'I went'. Language gives us enormous creative flexibility: something you should remember as a sender and receiver of it.

It is not the case that once you pick your tense you have to stay with it: very often it is more interesting or subtle to alter tense. A change from the predominant tense of a narrative – past to present or continuous to simple past – can indicate a change of perspective or mode. The CONDITIONAL tense, for example, might indicate an interior monologue, daydreaming or a speculative passage. We could continue on this subject forever: let's leave tense for now and look at the *voice* of verbs.

Passivity means lack of responsibility

An interesting phenomenon is the way writers use the ACTIVE and PASSIVE forms of the verb, referred to as the voice. Before we go any further let's clarify what these are.

In an active sentence the subject is followed by the verb, then the sentence is completed by an object or complement, for example 'The dog bit the man.'

In a passive sentence the recipient of the action becomes the subject of the verb. The verb is followed by 'by' plus the AGENT, which is the person or thing which performed the action. For the example above, the passive form would be 'The man was bitten by the dog.'

Here is another example:

Active: Lee Harvey Oswald shot President Kennedy.

Passive: President Kennedy was shot by Lee Harvey Oswald.

• •

ACTIVITY ◼ 💬

Turn these active sentences into the passive:

Michelangelo painted the Sistine Chapel.

Blackburn Rovers won the FA cup.

Prime Minister sacks Home Secretary.

• •

What difference does it make?

As in the last example above, journalists and literary writers use the active form of dynamic verbs to make responsibility for actions abundantly clear. 'Doctor slams her critics' and 'Chief Constable blasts Archbishop' are both headlines from a newspaper. In both cases it's very clear who is doing the slamming and blasting. These are active verbs. The subject or agent is clear, and we can praise or blame the agent accordingly.

Suppose, however, that the journalist had wanted to suggest that the Archbishop or his opinions were unpopular with the police force, but couldn't quote the Chief Constable directly on it. He might then have written 'Archbishop criticised in police circles'. In this headline the Archbishop is made the subject of a passive verb rather than as previously the object of an active one. The source of the criticism therefore remains mysterious.

Look at these two further examples:

The Captain fought the blaze all night. He sent women and children to safety then set about tackling the problem.

Dutton attacked Emma viciously. He broke six of her ribs, burnt her body and knocked out her front teeth.

In either of the above cases a switch to the passive would make a significant difference. The second example above will probably have shocked you, whereas the passive version makes the horrible truth more palatable:

> All night the fire was fought. After women and children were sent away, the problem was tackled.

> Terrible injuries were sustained. The child was viciously attacked. Six of her ribs were broken, her body burnt and six of her teeth knocked out.

In the passive versions emphasis is placed on what occurred, not who was responsible for what occurred. A reader may well wonder who did this terrible/wonderful thing, but the writer chooses not to give this information. The sentences include no agents, so we can only guess at their identity; the hero and the culprit have both disappeared. How did you respond to the two versions?

Use of the passive is also typical of reports and technical and scientific writing. In all these, what is done is more important than who is doing it:

> The test tube was heated to a temperature of 100 degrees.

> When the material is exposed to light...

Use of the passive is more frequent in formal, written English than in speech. A straightforward spoken narrative or account of events will usually be delivered in the active voice, because we are interested in the personalities involved: 'Then do you know what he did?' We may, of course, use the passive to describe a state of affairs:

> When I got home (active – personal interest) the door had been broken and the window smashed.

We do not know who did the breaking and smashing, so we are forced to use the passive.

When we are looking at verbs within a text or transcript, or are thinking of ways to exploit them in our own writing, there are three main things to look for:

1   The choice of the verb itself – dynamic or stative, general or precise
2   The tense(s) used – especially any shifts in tense
3   The voice that has been used – active or passive.

As an analyst, remember that use of the passive voice is relatively sophisticated. It is one of the last structures we acquire as we learn to use language.

ADVERBS: WHERE, WHEN, HOW AND WHY?

Just as the adjective functions as additional information to a noun, an adverb goes with a verb to tell us more about it. It clarifies where, when, how or why something was being done. Some critics would argue that adverbs are really a sign of careless choice of verb. If the writer had troubled to use 'whisper' and not 'speak' he would not need the how-adverb 'quietly'. Most how-adverbs would, in fact, join the ranks of the unemployed if writers were more willing to vary their verbs. Writing dialogue is a case in point. You cannot shout quietly or stammer fluently, and good writers of dialogue eschew adverbs as 'unnecessary letters'.

The adverb comes into its own when it is answering the more factual questions 'when' and 'where'. You cannot include the notion of 'yesterday' or 'nearby' in a verb, and these clarifications are sometimes vital. Try to give someone instructions without using adverbs and you will discover how valuable they can be. 'How often?' must be answered by adverbs like 'repeatedly', 'seldom' or 'often' – where would the writers of questionnaires be without them?

There are clearly times when the use of ADVERBIALS gives necessary precision. This is true whether the adverb is a single word or a group of words. As we found with adjectivals, there is more room for clarification in clauses than in single words. In answer to the question 'Where did he go?' the reply 'Out' is positively unhelpful; an adverbial phrase is much better. You might say 'To the park' or 'Up the pub' (if you're a Cockney).

Helpful, informative adverbials are very common in factual writing, be they 'when' ones in history writing or 'where' ones in directions. When we tell a story, sequencing – getting things in clear order – is vital, and adverbs enable us to do this:

> First he noticed the silence. Next the unpleasant odour assailed his nostrils. Then he saw it. Finally, he knew.

Notice in this extract how the writer has placed the adverbs in initial position in the sentences for greater emphasis and drama. As children we are taught that adverbials come after the verb they modify. However, there is actually far more flexibility in the placing of adverbs than of adjectives. Novelists and journalists like initial adverbials; novelists for the sake of drama, journalists for re-establishing the important facts in the readers' minds:

> Yesterday, the Prime Minister...

> In Regent's Park last night, police arrested...

All writers can see the virtues of where- and when-adverbials; there is less unanimity of enthusiasm for the 'how' and 'why' ones. The reason for this is that how- and why-adverbials are far more subjective. All the how-adverbs of manner, most of which end in -ly, are matters of personal opinion, just like evaluative adjectives. One observer may feel that the miners' leader 'unreasonably refused to talk to the Coal Board chief'; another commentator would replace 'unreasonably' with 'bravely' or 'resolutely'.

Bias, then, can very often be signalled by adverbs: 'He washes his hair daily' is a statement of fact but 'He washes his hair obsessively' is a very different matter.

Clearly (like 'obviously' a rather assertive, dogmatic adverb with which to start a sentence) one can see that, for a speaker or writer trying to establish mood or character, how- and why-adverbials are extremely valuable:

> Tenderly, she picked up her child and, cradling it lovingly in her arms, softly hummed a lullaby.

> Gradually, the light faded. The water lapped repeatedly but gently against the boat, making it sway rhythmically, in tune with its surroundings.

The next time you are looking at a text, look especially carefully at the adverbials. Are they there to move us or to clarify for us? Keep asking yourself what the writer's purpose was, using the adverbials as a clue. They can reverse the impact of the verb – 'She held him to her, frigidly' – or create a paradoxical effect – 'The child smiled sadly.' Sometimes their use is blatantly persuasive – 'insincerely', 'cruelly' and 'generously' make the writer's intentions quite apparent – at other times a little more thought is required to decide what the subtext is really saying. The only way into the subtext is through careful and systematic consideration of the text.

Chapter 2
Stringing Words Together

In the previous chapter we looked at the four major word categories (sometimes called as a group LEXICAL WORDS), words which seem directly to carry meaning. In this chapter we go on to look at other words which are vital when we begin to string words together. As soon as we do this, FUNCTION WORDS become very important.

Within this 'umbrella' term there are several different kinds of function word, but what they have in common is that usually they only come into play when we want to combine words into sentences or utterances. They are very important, although almost impossible to discuss in terms of what they mean in isolation. For example, we could all begin to try to describe what 'car' or 'happy' or 'walk' or 'sleepily' mean, either by using other words of similar meaning, or by mime or drawing. Could we do the same of 'the' or 'of' or 'but'? It would be wrong to imply that such words do not contribute significantly to meaning, as 'Do you want it cut and washed?' is clearly very different from 'Do you want it cut or washed?', but the significance of such words arises from their position in the string.

There are relatively few of these sorts of words. We have a limited stock of them, and they change very little. We are constantly adding to our stock of lexical words by coinings and borrowings for many different reasons. For example, when television was invented we needed a name for it, and one was created. The four major word classes are therefore called 'open'. It would be unlikely, however, for us suddenly to need a new function word, and these are therefore closed word classes. We use them all the time and they provide the 'cement' between the bricks of language. Any kind of language structure would be impossible without them.

The importance of function words in our language is made clear when we consider small children's language use. At the two-word stage they frequently use one lexical word and one function word. Thus 'Mummy up' means 'Pick me up, please, mummy' and 'Sock off' would be a request to go bare-footed.

We are going to look at four types of function words. There are more, but these are possibly the most frequently used: determiners, pronouns, prepositions and conjunctions.

DETERMINERS

DETERMINERS introduce nouns, or noun phrases. They 'modify' them in the sense that they give us information about the noun or noun phrase, before we hear or read the noun itself. The most common ones are the indefinite and definite ARTICLES 'a' and 'the'.

Indefinite and definite articles

The indefinite article is 'a', or 'an' before a word which begins with a vowel. It comes before a noun – 'a house', 'a holiday', 'an orange' – or before a noun phrase – 'a new house', 'a long hot holiday', 'a rotten orange'. In English, adjectives almost always come between the article and the noun.

You may not think that such an apparently insignificant word is giving us much information, but when its use is compared with that of the definite article, 'the', then we can see that the choice can be crucial. If we say 'the house' it means something very different from 'a house'. 'The long hot holiday' seems to carry references to or comparisons with other holidays – brief wet ones perhaps – built into it, as 'the rotten orange' implies the existence of other, ripe ones. Normally we are only able to use 'the' in writing if there has been a previous reference to the noun, or in speech if it is obvious from the context or from shared experience which particular thing we are referring to.

If, for example, we say 'Pass me a book' we can deduce either that all the possible books are the same, so that it doesn't matter which is given, or that the purpose for which the book is required (to prop up a broken chair leg?) means that it doesn't matter whether the book is a novel or a chemistry textbook, the important thing is that it's a book.

If, on the other hand, we say 'Pass me the book' we know that either it's the only book available, or it's a book we've been discussing: the important thing is that it's that book – using 'the' relies on shared knowledge. Often the use of 'the' functions as a linking device carrying an automatic reference back to an earlier sentence or utterance.

Or the definite article can be used to exclude, to insist: 'the method we could adopt is…' rather than 'a method we could adopt is…'. A politician's fate has depended on whether she has declared in a speech 'I do not want to belong to *a* racist Labour party' or 'I do not want to belong to *the* racist Labour party.' What is the difference between these two statements?

There is no need to list exhaustively the implications or uses which choice of the definite or indefinite article might have – your intuitive understanding of language will tell you once you start to think about it. Sometimes the definite article indicates uniqueness – 'the sun', 'the moon', 'the queen'. It would be unusual, but perfectly possible, to use the indefinite article with these nouns, and this would alert us to a particular effect. When a character in Shakespeare's *Timon of Athens* says 'Men shut their doors against a setting sun' it is not only context which tells us that this has a metaphorical as well as a general, literal meaning; it is also the use of the indefinite article 'a'.

It is surprising, given that we have said that use of the definite article implies a shared reference between addresser and addressee either from context or from previous reference, how often writers begin with the definite article. Look at this opening from an article in a magazine about medicine in the Third World:

> The health workers were eager. They demonstrated their 'baby-weighing' scheme, complete with animated health talks. Then, sitting down under a giant fig tree with the mothers and children of the village, they boasted of the dramatic fall in child deaths and reduction in malnutrition over the past two years.
>
> *New Internationalist*

If you chose to begin a story with 'The sunlight streamed through the broken window' rather than 'Sunlight streamed through the broken window', why would you have made that choice? You may not even have been aware that you were making a choice but it seems to us that in both these cases 'the' adds a greater sense of personal involvement and observation.

As you can see from the preceding example, nouns or noun phrases do not have to be preceded by an article or determiner: 'Cars drive too fast through busy streets' means something different from 'The cars drive too fast through the busy streets.'

To leave out these function words before nouns gives a statement a more general meaning. If we say 'School is boring' or 'Swimming is good for you' we are making general pronouncements. Circumstances in which these words are consciously omitted are newspaper headlines – 'MP in Scandal' – and notices in personal columns where space costs money (literally), and such words can be omitted without seriously affecting meaning:

> Petite, Pretty Brunette – Slim, warm, intelligent, 36, 5'2". Seeks professional man, 30s–mid 40s, with good sense of humour and a kind heart. Photo/note/phone, please.

● ●

ACTIVITY ▣ 🗩

Consider some of the following examples, and discuss the effect of the choice of definite or indefinite article:

> Let's seek the opinion of the man in the street.
>
> The long sandy beaches and the exciting night life are part of San Pedro's main attractions.
>
> He was always a good father to his children.
>
> The curfew tolls the knell of parting day,
> The lowing herd winds slowly o'er the lea.
>
> A cat may look at a king.

● ●

In coming before nouns or noun phrases and modifying them in some way, determiners function in a similar way to adjectives. While you may be fairly sure that you wouldn't confuse 'a' or 'the' with an adjective, it may be easier to confuse some of the other determiners which seem closer to adjectives. But the main difference is that where we can choose to modify a noun with an adjective (or not), many single nouns must be preceded by a determiner. Here is a list of words which can function as determiners:

the	a/an	this	that
these	those	all	some
any	no	every	each
either	neither	one	several
enough	such	many	much
more	most	few	fewer
fewest	little	less	least
what	which	whatsoever	whichever

These words are functioning as determiners if they are replacing 'a' or 'the'. You will notice that many of them denote quantity or number. All add information to the noun and can be more precise than the article – they sharpen the focus:

This man is my father. (i.e. the one next to me – or not that one)

Those tomatoes are mouldy. (not the ones in the window)

All dogs like bones. (every single one)

Several astronauts have reached the moon. (more than one but not too many)

The words in the list are not, however, always determiners. In the sentence 'Look at those lovely bluebells', 'those' is clearly functioning as a determiner, coming before the noun and giving us more information about it. But if we merely say 'Look at those!' the noun itself disappears, and 'those' stand in place of it. In this case it also stands in place of the adjective, replacing a whole noun phrase. It is being used as a PRONOUN.

PRONOUNS

Pronouns are words which stand in for, or replace, a noun or noun phrase. For example, in the sentence 'The girl kicked the cat', 'she' could replace 'The girl' and 'it' could replace 'the cat': 'She kicked it.'

We speak of pronouns as being in the first, second or third person, starting with self 'I' (first person) and moving through the direct addressee 'you' (second person) to the other 'she', 'he' or 'it' (third person). Pronouns may take different forms if they are plural, if they are the object rather than the subject of the verb, and if they are possessive.

	First Person	Second Person	Third Person
Subject			
Singular	I	you	he/she/it
Plural	we	you	they
Object			
Singular	me	you	him/her/it
Plural	us	you	them
Possessive			
Singular	my/mine	your/yours	his/her(s)/its
Plural	our/ours	your/yours	their/theirs

As with the definite article, we can see that use of pronouns depends on shared knowledge between speaker/writer and listener/reader. For pronouns to work for us, we need to have some idea of which nouns they are replacing. In this way they make obvious links to previous sentences or utterances and shared context. For instance, in the example 'John had kumquats for breakfast. He had never eaten them before', 'He' can replace 'John' and 'them' can replace 'kumquats' in the second sentence, because we know what these pronouns refer to. In writing, the pronoun usually replaces a previous noun; in speech it is usually obvious from the context what is meant, for example 'Give it to me!' or 'Look at her!'

According to the sociologist Basil Bernstein, dense pronoun use is one of the markers of the RESTRICTED VARIANT – as used in institutions where everyone knows everyone else (and their business). We would stress that this theory has proved very controversial.

Pronouns are very useful words, helping us to avoid repetition of nouns and noun phrases, and, because of their referential function (referring back), they provide a cohesion, a cementing together or linkage between sentences or utterances. However, although they function as nouns, or noun phrases, there are limitations as to what we can do with them. We can't add adjectives to modify or qualify pronouns. We can say 'the old man' but not 'the old he'.

In public life we often hear the first person plural pronoun being used to suggest a feeling of identity or inclusiveness. If we are being included (and we want to be) we share in this feeling; if the 'we' being used does not include us, we end up feeling excluded. We are all familiar with the expressions 'he is not one of us' or 'it ended up in a them and us situation', where the distance between first and third person pronouns is used to imply a division. Most of us at some time have probably said something like 'Well, we don't agree with you' when in fact it was only our own individual opinion we were really sure of, but we wanted the extra weight added by the inclusive 'we'.

Public speakers exploit this cosy feeling all the time. At the point in their speech where they hope to have won you over you suddenly realise that the 'we' being used so expansively includes you. Advertisers use 'we' a lot to give more concerned authority to their claims: 'We know you will love our chocolates' sounds more human than 'The manufacturing division of Arnold's confectioners are sure that you will enjoy their chocolates.' In fact large business concerns and government departments all call themselves 'we' in publicity and information material, even though it was probably written not by them but by a public relations company. Pronouns do sometimes allow us to get away with being rather vague and woolly. Who exactly is this 'we' or 'they'? Sometimes it's important that we know!

The second person pronoun can also be used in a general, non-specific way. I've been addressing 'you' throughout this chapter, for instance, although I have no exact personal knowledge of who you are. In expressions like 'you never know really, do you?' the 'you' takes on a wider reference than just the person(s) you might be addressing. It's rare these days to hear 'one never knows, does one?', which sounds formal and strained. Although accepted in speech, the generalised 'you' is still not accepted in formal written English of the type required by academic essays, but eliminating it can cause problems.

There is currently something problematic about the third person singular pronoun – he or she or it; him, her, his etc. – which leads to particular problems in the age of equal opportunities. Other pronouns which stand in for people's names – I, you, we, they, me, them, their – are not gender-specific – that is, we don't have to specify the sex of the person. For a long time in English it has been conventional, and acceptable, to use the male pronoun 'he' or 'him' to include reference to both sexes in certain situations, for example, in sentences such as 'The person appointed to this post will need many qualities. He will have a wide experience of marketing and promotion' or 'In this College each student will be given the opportunity to develop to his full potential.' The 'he' or 'his' would have been understood to include female applicants or students too, or so the grammarians tell us. Many women, however, have pointed out that such use assumes that the normal state of affairs is that the applicant or student will be male, and can create expectations that he will be. Two solutions have been proposed. One is that both male and female pronouns are included, in writing separated by a stroke: 's/he will have a wide experience', 'his/her full potential'. This is fair, if clumsy, particularly in speech. The other solution is that the third person plural pronoun – which is neutral – replaces the singular: 'The person appointed to this post will need many qualities. They will have a wide experience…'; 'In this College each student will be given the opportunity to develop their full potential.' This is easier to say – in fact is familiar and common usage in speech – although technically incorrect, as plural pronouns should not replace singular nouns if you take a prescriptive view of grammar. Controversy rages but this shows that even function words are not immune to change – this debate is related to social change despite earlier remarks.

'It', on the other hand, is utterly neutral and a very versatile pronoun. It is even something of an exception to the general rule that pronouns carry a reference back, because we can use 'it' to anticipate subjects, to introduce utterances when it isn't yet quite clear what we are referring to: 'It was a nice day yesterday' or 'It seems to me that…'. We don't need to know beforehand what 'it' refers to as we know we are going to be told when the full noun is used later in the sentence.

Of course it is possible to use personal pronouns this way, so that 'He had never been seen in the neighbourhood before, the man with the brown check cap' could be the opening of a story but would be a deliberate withholding of information to create suspense. Normally we would not use 'you', 'he', 'she', 'we', 'they' etc. without some sense of who was being referred to, although some dialects use this form more than others, as in 'He's a great darts player, that Frank Robinson.' In fact one of the most striking features of many dialects is that pronoun use differs from that of Standard English. Thus, in Devon one can hear 'I like he' and 'Her's been looking for thee.' In Black English 'mi' stands for 'I', 'me' and 'my'.

....

ACTIVITY ◖◗ ◖◗

How do the following differ from Standard English in terms of pronoun use, and where might you hear them?

> Give us it.
>
> Her's no better than she should be.
>
> I like them big cars.
>
> He gave hisself a nasty shock.
>
> Me like you.

....

We have already remarked that pronouns take different forms depending on the job they are doing in a sentence. Take for instance these simple sentences involving the third person singular pronoun (male):

Sid tickles Nancy	He tickles Nancy.
Nancy tickles Sid	Nancy tickles him.
Sid's tickle annoys Nancy	His tickle annoys Nancy
Sid tickles himself.	

'He', 'him' and 'himself' all stand in place of 'Sid'. 'His' stands in for 'Sid' plus apostrophe 's'. 'His' is a possessive pronoun and 'himself' is what is called a reflexive pronoun: it refers back to the subject of the verb.

A different sort of pronoun can be used to ask questions (INTERROGATIVE pronouns):

> *Who* was that?
>
> *Which* is your bicycle?
>
> *What* is the matter?

and these 'wh' pronouns which ask questions can also be used to link clauses in a neat way that avoids repetition of the noun. This use of pronouns relates one piece of information to another, and so when 'which', 'who', 'whose' and 'whom' are used in this way they are called RELATIVE pronouns. For example, 'The girls picked up the books' and 'The books were on the table' can be linked by replacing the second 'the books' by 'which': 'The girls picked up the books which were on the table.' Similarly, 'I know a man. The man trains weasels' becomes 'I know a man who trains weasels.' 'Who' replaces the second 'the man'. 'That' can be used in the same way: 'These are the shoes. I like the shoes' becomes 'These are the shoes that I like.'

If we want to sound rather formal or grand in our writing we are more likely to use long sentences in which ideas and information are linked by the use of relative pronouns. A sentence such as this one is clearly characteristic of written, not spoken English:

> Yesterday I was honoured to meet a woman who has discovered a cure for a common disease which has blighted our lives for centuries, and who turned out to be one of the most unassuming people that I have ever met.

This type of structure is more likely in writing than in speech as it requires quite a lot of forethought and planning to produce such complexity. Legal language, on the other hand, uses fewer pronouns so that there can be no ambiguity about who a particular 'he' is, or what 'it' refers to. Pronouns can be consciously used to achieve various purposes, but as with so many language choices we need to keep an open mind about the effect which use of a particular word – or pattern of words – may be creating.

So there are different sorts of pronouns, but all are replacing – standing in for – nouns and noun phrases. We don't stop to think about them much. We acquire them at a very young age, and know when to use them. When and where might we use them – or avoid using them – for special effect?

The use of personal pronouns suggests familiarity. Sometimes this is inappropriate, and we use pronouns instead of proper names deliberately to belittle – 'you know what she's like' – on occasions when familiarity implies disrespect. However, in story-writing the central character in a particular episode might well be referred to more frequently by pronouns when other characters are given full names or titles. Here the familiarity suggests intimacy and helps to establish point of view. After all, we rarely think of ourselves by name, but that is often the way we think of and refer to others. Here is a passage from an American novel by Anne Tyler called *Dinner at the Homesick Restaurant*. Different sections of the novel are seen from the point of view of different members of a family, although none are written in the first person. Whose point of view is this and what effect does the contrast between the repeated 'She' and the use of names for other characters have?

> Oh, she'd been an angry sort of mother. She'd been continually on edge; she'd felt too burdened, too much alone. And after Beck left, she'd been so preoccupied with paying the rent and juggling the budget and keeping those great, clod-footed children in new shoes. It was she who called the doctor at two a.m. when Jenny got appendicitis, it was she who marched downstairs with a baseball bat the night they heard that scary noise. She'd

kept the furnace stoked with coal, confronted the neighbourhood bully when Ezra got beaten up, hosed the roof during Mrs Simmon's chimney fire. And when Cody came home drunk from some girl's birthday party, who had to deal with that?

Anne Tyler: *Dinner at the Homesick Restaurant*

PREPOSITIONS

The easiest way to introduce PREPOSITIONS is to look at some in action:

> Flora walked *into* the lab. She put the batch *of* specimens *on* the bench and called *across* the room *to* her assistant, '*In* a moment I'll show you something to make your hair curl.'

Prepositions relate words to one another in terms of time:

> *In* a moment
>
> The explosion occurred *during* the race.

or place:

> She put the specimens *on* the bench.
>
> The queue waited *outside* the cinema.
>
> I leaned my bike *against* the wall.

or possession:

> A batch *of* specimens
>
> She was having the time *of* her life.

or direction:

> She called *across* the room.

These examples are relating one thing or action to another. The predominance of any one type in a text might well add to a particular effect. Descriptions of places normally contain many prepositions indicating place, or as indicators of direction across, among, between, or through, to achieve a sense of movement. Narratives, where sequence and time are important, will probably contain that type of preposition.

∙∙

ACTIVITY ◼ ▧

This is a passage from a novel by Graham Swift, describing the fenland landscape. List the pronouns of place and direction.

> We lived in a lock-keeper's cottage by the River Leem, which flows out of Norfolk into the Great Ouse. And no one needs telling that the land in that part of the world is flat. Flat, with an unrelieved and monotonous flatness, enough of itself, some might say, to drive a man to unquiet and sleep-

defeating thoughts. From the raised banks of the Leem, it stretched away to the horizon, its uniform colour, peat-black, varied only by the crops that grew upon it – grey-green potato leaves, blue-green beet leaves, yellow-green wheat; its uniform levelness broken only by the furrowed and dead-straight lines of ditches and drains, which, depending on the state of the sky and the angle of the sun, ran like silver, copper or golden wires across the fields and which, when you stood and looked at them, made you shut one eye and fall prey to fruitless meditations on the laws of perspective.

Graham Swift: *Waterland*

Prepositions are very frequently so closely linked with verbs – as in 'look at', 'care for', 'come in', 'think about' – that they seem to become part of the verb phrase and not a neutral linking device. Coming after verbs they often introduce adverbial phrases or clauses of time or place.

It is striking how many idiomatic and colloquial phrases seem to involve prepositions; we seem to be able to use them to create such phrases. Consider the verb 'break' and how many different prepositions can be added to it. We can

break out
break off
break up
break in
break through
break down

The last three have come to function as nouns in their own right. 'Lock-out' and 'sit-in' are other verb-plus-preposition phrases which have now become nouns by a process called CONVERSION. Combined with existing nouns we have another sort of colloquial phrase: 'by car', 'in hand', 'in action', 'for good'. It is noticeable how many current 'in' phrases coming into common use involve prepositions: 'come out' in its new meaning; 'live-in lover'; 'I'm not really into computers.' 'I feel comfortable around him.' Many such phrases are currently more acceptable in spoken rather than formal written English and it will be interesting to see how many enter the official lexicon and are still used in fifty years' time. The new use of the preposition 'into' as meaning 'interested in' does seem to be a relatively rare example of a function word broadening its use and meaning.

CONJUNCTIONS: INTRODUCING CO-ORDINATION AND SUBORDINATION!

Rather like prepositions, CONJUNCTIONS are linking words, but they often do more than link single words or groups of words: they can signify a particular relationship between them too. The easiest conjunction to start with is the most common and neutral, the word 'and'.

We can use 'and' to link single words – 'fish and chips', 'dance and sing', 'tall and thin', 'quickly and quietly' – or to link groups of words – 'I am coming to Manchester next week and I hope to see you then.' The word 'or' is a similar sort of conjunction: 'Do you want fish or chips?' 'I can't dance or sing.'

'And' and 'or' are CO-ORDINATING CONJUNCTIONS, linking words or phrases without discriminating between them in terms of importance. There are very few co-ordinating conjunctions, only 'and', 'but', 'either', 'or', 'neither' and 'nor'. If we say, for example, 'I like her but she annoys me', the two statements 'I like her' and 'she annoys me' both have equal importance and weight. Any extra significance we feel 'I like her' has, comes from its position in the sentence. We could change the two statements round and the meaning would not be substantially affected. Co-ordinating conjunctions therefore give equal weight to the two items they are linking.

We would use 'and' if we wanted to link the following three statements in a way which gave them the same emphasis:

Mary walked along the road

Mary was chewing gum

Mary was wearing a red dress

We would probably replace the second two 'Mary's with the pronoun 'she' to achieve the acceptable (though not very elegant) sentence 'Mary walked along the road and she was chewing gum and she was wearing a red dress.'

This probably reminds you of the writing you did as a child, and red pencil marks in the margin of your work saying 'too many ands!' There is a stage in language acquisition (usually around three years of age) when children discover 'and', which enables them to generate seemingly endless utterances.

There are other ways of linking the three statements which would sound (or more likely, read) much better, but would probably involve us in the decision that one of the facts about Mary was more important than the others. Let's try linking just two of them in a more comfortable way: 'Mary was chewing gum as she walked along the road.' This reads better, but it has involved us in deciding that 'Mary was chewing gum' is the main fact we wish to convey, and 'as she walked...' is providing us with extra information. This main statement has become the main clause of the sentence. Unlike the previous example with 'but' this is not just because the gum comes first, because it would remain true if the sentence were ordered 'As she walked along the road, Mary was chewing gum.'

Conjunctions such as 'as', then, imply a subordination of one piece of information to another. There are many SUBORDINATING CONJUNCTIONS. One broad group of them is related to time, and they link information by sequencing it in some way. Such conjunctions include 'after', 'before', 'until', 'as':

I will mow the lawn before I take the dog for a walk.

Until I see you again, I won't discuss this with anyone.

The clause which begins with the conjunction is the subordinate clause, wherever it comes in the order.

Another group of conjunctions is used in contexts where we wish to suggest cause and effect, and therefore they are common in discursive, persuasive writing and talk. 'Because', 'although', 'unless', 'in order that' are examples of such conjunctions and they suggest causal relationships between pieces of information:

> I can't play basketball tonight because I've sprained my ankle.

> Because the French army were unprepared, they lost the war in Russia.

> You will not be able to take part unless you have prepared.

> Until you have £1,000, you cannot join the Enterprise Scheme.

We see from the above examples that it is perfectly possible to begin a sentence with a subordinating conjunction and we often choose to do so if it conveys information we want to stress, although it is not the main clause in the sentence. We may have been told in primary school not to begin sentences with 'because', but it is in fact perfectly acceptable to do so if it is followed by the main clause. It would still probably be only for deliberate stylistic effect – to suggest an afterthought, or a sense of 'piling on the agony' – that we would begin a sentence with the co-ordinating conjunction 'and': 'And another thing you said is …'. This in fact sounds more like speech than writing. Written forms that aim to sound like speech often do start sentences with 'and'. Look out for this in advertisements and some popular journalistic styles:

> They're both fed on Pedigree Chum Puppy Food.
> And that's all they're fed, because that's all they need. A growing pup demands two to three times the nutrition of an adult dog. And when it's building new bone and muscle quite literally overnight, it's important that the food it eats is the food it needs to do the job properly.

Co-ordination is much more a feature of speech than is subordination. In order to 'subordinate' one piece of information in a sentence or utterance to another we have to plan ahead, to manipulate long stretches of language, for example using relative pronouns. In speech we would be much more likely to add one fact to another, or pause and start again. Writing is more formal, and can be planned and redrafted. We 'craft' our sentences into an appropriate form and we divide writing into sentences. However, we do not divide speech into sentences in the same way, and 'Are you coming tonight?' 'Unless I've too much work to do' would be a perfectly understandable spoken exchange. We wouldn't feel the need to say the full sentence 'I am coming tonight unless I've too much work to do' in reply to the question: the 'main' clause is understood from the previous utterance. We consider sentences and spoken English separately in the next two chapters.

PHRASES AND CLAUSES

In this chapter we have considered words which come into their own when we begin to join words together into larger units. We have referred to units, groups, clauses and phrases without attempting definitions. Before we go on to look at the sentence as a unit of written language we need to clarify 'phrase' and 'clause' and to see what is the difference between them.

A PHRASE is any group of words which does not contain a verb with a subject. It can be as short as two words, or as long as you can make it: the concepts of phrases, clauses and sentences have nothing to do with length. 'Run!' is a sentence, whereas 'the purple grapes on the drooping vines' is not. Phrases are groups of words, such as 'my best friend', 'down the high street', 'on a windy day', 'came running'. Put them together in an acceptable order, so that we know who came running, and we have a sentence: 'My best friend came running down the high street on a windy day.'

The clause, not the sentence, is in fact the basic unit of English. The clause is a group of words which contains a verb with a subject, and if it makes sense on its own we would probably re-christen it a sentence. If we return to Mary with the gum and the dress for instance, 'Mary was chewing gum' is a clause, and a sentence; 'who was wearing a red dress' and 'as she walked along the road' are clauses: they both have verbs – 'was wearing' and 'walked' – and subjects – 'who' (a pronoun) and 'she' – but they do not make sense on their own. Put them all together and we have a sentence of three clauses: 'Mary, who was wearing a red dress, was chewing gum as she walked along the road.'

If you want to analyse this sentence you have to begin with it as it stands and break it into smaller parts. We began with the word as our smallest unit of language (there is a smaller one, the MORPHEME) but as we began to discuss combining words we have had to look at them in different types of groups. There is a limit to what you can say about an individual word. If we are concentrating on meaning or association we usually start to bring in other, similar words to define the word more exactly. If we want to comment on its function in a group of words, we need to know where it comes in the string and what it's doing. There is no simple progression up the hierarchy word–phrase–clause–sentence, and in the next chapter we discuss the larger units in terms of the constituent parts of their overall function.

Chapter 3
The Sentence

What is a sentence anyway?

There are really two answers to this question – a 'common sense' one and a grammatical one. As a language student you need to be in possession of both.

The common sense view holds that any group of words which make sense on their own equals a sentence, and that the visual markers of a sentence are a capital letter at the beginning and a full stop at the end.

In spoken language we easily recognise a meaningful utterance. Thus an exclamation like 'Out!' or the reply 'Dad' to the question 'Who told you?', makes sense to English speakers. It is context which enables us to supply the missing elements. In this case, these are the understood subject of the verb – 'you' – and the verb which relates to 'Dad' – 'told'. Nevertheless, these utterances do not conform to the grammatical definition of a sentence. This is because the rules for speech and for standard written language are simply not the same.

Even in written language the rules are not totally inflexible. Poets, novelists, headline writers and advertisers use what are known as MINOR SENTENCES all the time. Minor sentences are useful in creating an atmosphere or image quickly. Inessentials are omitted and we are left with a minor sentence which lacks either the verb or the subject.

In grammatical terms, a complete sentence must have two things:

1   A SUBJECT – the person or thing that the sentence is about, be it Jemima, a tragedy or a triumph

2   A PREDICATE – what the subject is or is doing. In some sentences the predicate will consist of a verb only, for example 'Jemima thinks.' In others, there will be an additional element, the ADJUNCT. This might be an adverb – 'Jemima thinks profoundly' – or a noun phrase – 'Jemima thinks profound thoughts.'

All subjects will include a noun or pronoun. They can be as little as one word – the aforementioned 'Dad' or 'he' – or they can be lengthened with determiners ('a', 'the', 'that' etc.), adjectives and so on; for example, 'Her somewhat insecure, though charming, Dad'. We could add information ad infinitum but the group of words would still be the subject.

The important thing is to see the bare bones or structure of a sentence and not to fall into the error that long means hard or complex. No-one would argue that a long list of the animals you saw at the zoo makes a difficult sentence! A feat of memory it may be; a feat of grammar it is not. Grammatical complexity is a matter of how many *clauses* there are rather than how many *words*. Remember that as a general guide.

Look at these two sentences:

> I talked and he listened.

> All the cinemas in town and even the local fleapit are showing the latest film from Walt Disney.

The second is much the longer because it has a COMPOUND subject, that is two nouns and a lot of additional information. The predicate is also long since its verb has an adjunct. However, it is still a simple sentence because it has only one verb and therefore only one clause.

The first sentence, though much shorter, has two verbs joined by a co-ordinating conjunction and is thus a compound sentence. More of this later!

Don't be misled by the form of the word in front of you. In some sentences the subject at first sight appears to be a verb – the present continuous to be precise – as in 'Swimming is good for the health'. But here 'swimming' is an activity and thus a noun. The verb proper (or main verb) comes into the sentence with the predicate. We might have the predicate 'took his daughter out for supper' to follow the subject 'Her somewhat insecure, though charming, Dad', or we might have 'was a generous man'.

It may seem downright awkward to have two standards of behaviour, one for speaking and another for formal, written language, but such is the situation. The way sentences are formed is not random and if you want people to understand you and to judge you a competent language user it's as well to follow the rules. Most of these rules don't need to be learnt by native speakers. It becomes entirely natural to us to place the subject of a sentence before the verb, for example (unless we're giving a command). No five-year-old would write 'Chips I like' or 'Thirsty is my Mum.'

WORD ORDER IN SENTENCES

Subject–Verb sentences

As we have said, all sentences need a subject and a verb (predicate). The most straightforward sentence type in English may thus be called in short S–V. 'Birds fly', 'Teachers teach' and 'People grumble' are all examples of this type.

Subject–Verb–Object sentences

Slightly more complicated is the sentence where the subject is doing something to someone else. This someone or something else is then the OBJECT of the sentence. S–V–O is a very common word order in sentences: 'The lion ate the gnu', 'The sadist whipped the masochist' and 'The teacher bored me' are all examples of this type.

Notice that all the verbs in the above examples are active verbs and can therefore take a DIRECT OBJECT. Verbs which can take a direct object are called TRANSITIVE.

Subject–Verb–Complement sentences

Some verbs cannot take a direct object and are INTRANSITIVE. These verbs are stative, i.e. they describe how something is or seems. Instead of a direct object they are followed by what is called a complement. This can be either an adjective or a noun. For example, 'My friend is a hairdresser' (here the complement is a noun) or 'My friend is muscular' (here the complement is an adjective). Do remember that it is not only the verb 'to be' which is intransitive: so are verbs like 'to seem' and 'to appear'.

Subject–Verb–Indirect Object–Direct Object sentences

Another sentence type involves two kinds of object, the direct, which actually receives the action of the verb, and the INDIRECT, which has an understood 'to' or 'for' before it. An example will clarify. In the sentence 'I gave him an expensive present' it is the present which is actually given, so this is the direct object. The present is given to him, so he is the indirect object. In English it sounds ridiculous to say 'I gave to him a present' (though many other languages do it that way). Instead, we omit the 'to' (or 'for') but leave the indirect object before the direct object. Hence the pattern S–V–I/O–D/O.

BASIC ELEMENTS

Before we go any further it might be an idea to check that you're with it so far.

··

ACTIVITY

Try to write the patterns of the following sentences down using the symbols S for subject, V for verb, D/O for direct object, I/O for indirect object and C for complement.

> The cannibal ate his cousin.
>
> He is disgusting.
>
> I offered him a pork chop.
>
> He refused it.
>
> I feel sick.
>
> I'm fainting.

It's very easy, isn't it? Of course, these examples are easy because there are no distracting bits tacked on, so all the elements of the sentences show through clearly. Consider if the first sentence said 'The ravenously hungry cannibal ate his cousin, a fat and therefore tempting youth.' The pattern is the same but the sentence appears far more complicated.

··

We repeat that you must look for the bare bones of a sentence – its basic elements – however long and chock-full of adjectival phrases and adverbials it is.

All this may seem rather pointless, but if you can see the patterns within sentences and you're presented with an enormously long, difficult-looking sentence, it's reassuring to be able to see that it's only S-V, heavily disguised. Start by finding the main verb. This, in turn, will help you to find the subject and object.

If we consider the sentence above which seemed complicated, 'The cannibal' has had an adjectival phrase tacked on: 'ravenously hungry'. We call it adjectival because it is telling us more about the noun 'cannibal'; it is a phrase, not a clause, because it has no verb. 'The cannibal' remains the subject of the sentence; 'ate' is the main verb; 'his cousin' has had the noun phrase 'a fat and therefore tempting youth' added to it. Though there is more information about the cousin, he remains the direct object of the cannibal's appetite!

SENTENCES ARE MADE OF CLAUSES

Another way of analysing sentences is by dividing them into clauses. By this system there are three kinds of sentences:

1   SIMPLE sentences have one main clause, or, if you prefer, one subject whether simple or compound, and one verb; e.g. 'Grammar isn't difficult.'

2   COMPOUND sentences have two or more main clauses which are of equal importance – two subjects and verbs. These two clauses are linked by a co-ordinating conjunction. As you know, there are only six co-ordinating conjunctions so simply spot them if you find that easier: they are 'and', 'but', 'or', 'nor', 'either' and 'neither'.

3   COMPLEX sentences are the most complicated, and thus usually signal a relatively sophisticated style. Like compound sentences they have two or more clauses. The difference is that whereas compound sentences have two main, independent clauses, complex ones have an independent clause linked to a dependent one. The two are linked by a subordinating conjunction.

There are a lot more subordinating conjunctions than there are co-ordinating ones. They include such words as the relative pronouns 'who', 'which', 'whom' and 'what'; conjunctions relating to time, like 'after' and 'while', and purpose, such as 'because' and 'since'. The thing to remember is that these conjunctions introduce clauses which do not make sense on their own. That is why they are called dependent: they depend on another, independent clause to complete their sense.

Here are a few examples in case your mind is boggling:

I ate the soup and the chicken.

(One independent clause – because only one verb, 'ate' – therefore simple sentence)

I ate the soup and I ate the chicken.

(independent clause + independent clause = compound sentence linked by co-ordinating conjunction 'and')

After I ate the soup, I ate the chicken.

(dependent clause + independent clause = complex sentence using subordinating conjunction 'after')

ACTIVITY ▣ ⬀

Have a go at these yourself:

You're reading this book because you're studying English.

My students, who have been the guinea pigs, are helping me.

Writing books isn't easy!

Explaining things verbally is easier but people prefer to read books.

I hope that you understand the book.

Have you managed that?

Notice that in the above examples you could differentiate between the sentences in several ways. First, you could say what pattern they follow as far as S, V, D/O etc. goes. Secondly you could say whether they are simple, compound or complex. Thirdly and finally, you could say what job they're doing, i.e. their function.

WHAT PURPOSE DO SENTENCES SERVE?

By this I simply mean whether they are making a statement, asking a question, giving a command or uttering an exclamation. In other words what is their FUNCTION?

If they are statements, they will have a full stop at the end and their technical name is DECLARATIVES. By all means call them statements if you prefer.

If they are questions, then they must end with a question mark and you can call them questions or INTERROGATIVES.

Commands can – depending on how polite they are – end with a full stop or an exclamation mark. They can be called commands or IMPERATIVES.

Exclamations are often minor, i.e. incomplete, sentences. Remember that if they are telling someone what to do they are actually imperatives. Exclamations are emphatic statements like 'What enormous feet you've got!' or 'The nerve of him!' EXCLAMATORY sentences always end with an exclamation mark.

When you first glance at a piece of writing, you can often judge its general tone by noticing the punctuation marks. If it is awash with question and exclamation marks it is likely to be dramatic and, possibly, persuasive. If it is all statement – that is, all full stops – the tone is likely to be more matter-of-fact: you probably have a piece of informative writing in front of you. A second glance, considering tone, should differentiate between form and function. Sometimes a question mark signals an interrogative form but the function is rhetorical and so the question is really a statement!

SUMMARY

In this chapter, we have outlined three ways in which you can look at sentences:

1   You can see the basic structure of a sentence in terms of its subject, verb and object.

2   You can look at the type of sentence in terms of clauses — is it simple, compound or complex?

3   You can see what the sentence's function is — statement, question, command or exclamation.

When you analyse prose, it is vital to say something about sentences and it really isn't adequate to talk about 'long' sentences or 'hard' ones. You need instead to recognise why someone's prose style is less accessible — perhaps because there are a lot of subordinate clauses — or why the tone seems matter-of-fact — perhaps because all the sentences are declaratives. Or why the style seems dramatic — perhaps because the sentences are nearly all very short subject-verb structures.

Naturally, you won't always want to talk about all these possible aspects, but at least one of them will be relevant to a particular piece of writing that you're considering. Writers select their structures just as they do their words, so it makes little sense to dwell only on vocabulary in analysis.

Chapter 4
Writing about Talking —
Discourse Analysis

The first thing to accept when you are writing about talking is that it is not governed by the same rules as writing. People do not ignore word order and syntax when talking but it is pointless and inappropriate to say that an UTTERANCE is 'not a complete sentence'. We do not always speak in sentences, so when people attempt to do so the effect is very stilted indeed.

Nevertheless, speech is not entirely, or even remotely, anarchic: it does have its own rules and features. These have been recognised by DISCOURSE ANALYSTS. However, before you can discuss speech you sometimes have to catch it by transcribing some.

TRANSCRIPTIONS: THE WAY TO WRITE DOWN SPEECH

If you are going to study spoken language, listening to it is not enough: you will need to make a transcription. This effectively freezes the language so that you can have a good look at it.

Transcriptions are fairly time-consuming, though a little practice speeds you up. Never use speech marks and be careful about the use of question marks and full stops. Many transcribers prefer to use no punctuation marks at all. Rather than theorising, let me give you an example:

T   now today we're going to look at business letters

P   (quietly) oh no (.) not again

T   did someone speak

P1   no sir …

P2   no-one did, sir

T   erm, well, let's get on with it

In the above, teacher and pupil are shown as T and P. A pause is shown by a full stop between brackets, and running full stops … indicate an unfinished utterance. If two people speak at once this can be shown by bracketing their utterances together. If a pause is particularly long, you can write the number of seconds in the brackets. If a word is strongly stressed this can be conveyed by capitalisation, for example, 'Jenny DID NOT say that'. Sophisticated transcription also shows INTONATION (whether the voice goes up or down in pitch) by a line above the words going up or down. This is particularly useful to clarify whether something is a question or a statement, since questions rise intonationally and statements do not. In the example above, the teacher's comment 'did someone speak' is not a genuine question: it is a way of pointing out and objecting to the grumbling. Thus the *form* may look like a question but the *function* isn't. Getting quite clear in your mind the difference between these two is vital for good discourse analysis.

The importance of intonation can be fully grasped if you consider an utterance like 'I didn't tell him because you were there.' Does the speaker here mean she did tell him but not because you were there, or that she didn't tell him on account of your presence? The only way to be sure is by marking STRESS and intonation. For the first meaning you would have

> I didn't / TELL him because / YOU were there. `

and for the second meaning

> I DIDN'T tell him because you were / THERE. `

The simplest way to mark intonation is with the marks used above. You put / on the line before the word that starts a rising intonation. This is often also a word which is stressed, as in 'tell' in the first meaning above. You put ` above the line after the word which starts a falling intonation. A falling intonation often betrays embarrassment or hesitation.

If you want to show the contour of a whole utterance, you can put a horizontal line above it which has an arrow to the right, either level to show flat intonation (statement); pointing up to show rising intonation (question or surprise) or pointing down to show falling intonation (running out of steam or interest, feeling unsure):

> I didn't tell him. I er don't know why.

We all use stress and intonation all the time so the problem is not hearing them but putting them on paper correctly. It's a bit of a chore at first but it does make your transcription far more interpretable and it's a very useful skill to develop for project work.

....

ACTIVITY 🎱 💬

Try to mark the following conversation for stress and intonation:

> Are you coming tonight?

Not sure really.

Look, are you or aren't you? I need a decision.

Er well, I don't think so.

Terrific. Thank you very much!

Honestly. You are so unreasonable.

No, I'm not. I'm just utterly fed up with your indecisiveness.

I'm not being indecisive – just polite. Okay. I have absolutely no intention of coming: it'll be a bloody bore. Happy now?

When you've marked the conversation, act it out with a friend. Are their stresses the same as yours? Check if they'd have transcribed it in the same way.

Whether you have trapped or been given a stretch of discourse, you now need to analyse it systematically.

GENERAL FEATURES OF SPOKEN LANGUAGE

The most striking thing about the average person's speech is the presence of NON-FLUENCY FEATURES. Only a rare few can talk with never a 'sort of' or 'you know' to provide thinking time. These silence-fillers are called just that – FILLERS – and English has plenty of them. Some speakers fill the sentence with a meaningless noise, 'erm' being a popular choice. Such a noise is called a VOICED PAUSE and by extending its length a signal can be given that talk is about to begin. At other times the silence is left undisturbed and what you get is an UNVOICED PAUSE.

Even when speakers have started on a sentence they sometimes decide to re-phrase what they're saying: 'wouldn't you say...' or 'I mean, wouldn't you agree that...'. This phenomenon is called a FALSE START or REFORMULATION.

Confusion is also signalled by a speaker's trying to re-sequence his material. This can be recognised by a remark like 'I should have mentioned this before.' This too has a technical name: it is referred to as BACK-CHANNELLING.

One other feature of many people's speech is perhaps worth mentioning. This is REPETITION. Repeating the same word or phrase gives the speaker time to think. A phrase such as 'I don't know about that' is often said more than once.

We all use non-fluency features, though some of us have more recourse to them than others and all are affected by CONTEXT. They are an inevitable consequence of making up the script as we go along. When we write, we use complete sentences, make a conscious effort to vary our vocabulary and think about the sequence of events. If we don't get it right the first time we can always re-draft. This is not possible in speech which is spontaneous. Speech which is not spontaneous but planned in detail ahead, such as public speeches, sermons, lectures and commentaries, shares many more of the features of written language. It would be naïve to assume that everything spoken is spontaneous.

IDIOLECT

When we talk, favourite words and phrases will tend to be oft-used. This can be irritating and distracting but it is perfectly normal. It is just one of the ways in which speech is a less crafted and thus more spontaneous mode than writing. An individual's IDIOLECT – their own unique cluster of language features including the volume and pitch of their voice, their accent, lexical choice and so on – comes through far more strongly in speech than in writing. Though literary critics may well be able to tell Jane Austen from Charles Dickens, the vast majority of us would find it far easier to differentiate people by the way they talk than by the way they write. So, one approach to analysing and thus writing about speech is to look for the usual features of spoken language. They will be there.

INDIVIDUAL SPEECH FEATURES

Once you've considered general speech features and interactive ones, there only remains the markers of INDIVIDUALITY. The first of these of course is voice – high or low pitched; generally quiet or loud; monotonous or varied in tone. All these features are very difficult to include in transcription but they clearly have an effect on listeners.

Easier to see in a transcript are ACCENT and DIALECT features. It is not usually necessary or practicable to use phonetic symbols to convey precise accentual features. Spelling is often able to do the job. For example 'I'm goin' up the 'igh street wiv me bruvver' is clearly differentiated from 'I'm going to the city centre with my brother.' Not only does the Cockney speaker drop hs and say th as v, which are accent features, he also uses dialect forms such as 'up' for 'to'. Dialectal features include lexical items – do you make, mash or brew tea? Do you eat tea or dinner in the evening? Do you eat sandwiches or butties? – and grammatical ones – do you use Standard English 'I was' or Northern 'I were', Standard 'I am not' or Cockney 'I ain't'? Clearly one could give numerous examples. The point is that speakers tell us far more about themselves than writers (except for dialect poetry) habitually do.

Clues to personal identity

Regional

Look for letters omitted, like initial 'h' and final 's'. Black and East Anglian English have 'she like him'. Northerners use 'sat' for 'sitting' and 'stood' for 'standing'. They also often use adjectives adverbially, though this, like many non-standard dialect features, is common to many areas – we have all heard football managers insist that 'the lads played great'.

Again it is important to remember that non-standard does not equal wrong or inferior; it means different. As I said at the beginning of this chapter, the rules of written and spoken language are not the same. Written language is written in STANDARD ENGLISH so that it is comprehensible to all readers; spoken language can be differentiated for different audiences and purposes, and regional dialect is often perceived as more 'sincere' and 'friendly' by its users than Standard English. Many of us operate along a language continuum from Standard English in formal contexts to speech marked by regional dialect features in more informal situations. However, formal Standard English is perceived as more prestigious and is associated in many people's minds with educational levels. It's perfectly possible, in fact usual, to speak Standard English with a regional accent; some speakers do tend towards the more prestigious RECEIVED PRONUNCIATION.

Gender

Research tends to suggest that our sex affects the way we speak. Research as well as instinct tells us that men swear more than women. Women seem more anxious to speak 'correctly' by the standards of written language and use non-standard dialect less than men. Their accents are also less pronounced. Men are less polite when it comes to turn-taking than women and butt in far more often. Women more frequently use tags at the end of sentences like 'don't you agree?' to seek approval and they are more likely to say 'It seems to me that…' where men will go for the more assertive 'I think'. These are, of course, huge generalisations but they are supported by evidence and are food for thought. We have not space here to quote much research, but here are two examples. They are quoted from J. Coates's book *Women, Men and Language*, which we recommend to those interested in this topic.

The variable [ŋ] in Norwich

100 = RP pronunciation [ŋ] as opposed to non-standard [n]

In casual speech	Middle middle class	men	69
		women	100
	Upper working class	men	3
		women	12
In formal speech	Lower middle class	men	73
		women	97
	Middle working class	men	9
		women	19

Turntaking (Zimmerman and West 1975)

Overlaps	men	9	women	0
Interruptions	men	46	women	2

Incidence of swearing (Gomm 1981)

	single sex	mixed	total
men	21	4	25
women	7	2	9

Jennifer Coates: *Women, Men and Language*

Men swear twice as often as women in mixed company and three times as often 'with the lads'.

Age

One can often tell the age of a speaker by the sort of informal lexis they use, since many people adopt colloquialisms in their youth and never update them. (Someone older trying to use the current trendy words can sound very silly anyway, so I suppose you can't win!)

Some examples of informal lexis include:

War-time words: prang (crash car), sippers and gulpers (naval slang for small and large rum ration)

Words of the fifties: fridge, telly, DA (teddy boy's hairstyle)

Words of the sixties: pad (your place, flat etc.), chick, bird (young girl – not popular with feminists), swinging (trendy), pot (marijuana)

Words of the seventies: heavy, no way, iffy

Words of the eighties: fit, toy-boy, yuppies

Words of the nineties: spin doctor, surfing the net, eco warriors.

I'm assuming that you don't need the more recent ones translating!

Class

This category is one beset with problems, not least that of defining what is meant by working class and middle class. That said, there is a correlation between class and usage, as mentioned in the section on dialect. The difficulty lies in deciding whether a speaker uses a certain phrase or word because of their class or because of their birthplace. 'Mam', for example, could be regarded as a 'working-class' variant of Mum or as a Northern one.

The sociologist Basil Bernstein's theory that the working class used a RESTRICTED CODE which was topic-fixed, based on shared assumptions and highly predictable whereas the middle class used an ELABORATED CODE which was more flexible, generalised and context free has caused, and continues to cause, great controversy. It is perfectly possible to find examples of 'middle-class' speech which exemplify elaborated code; likewise 'working-class' speech that is highly anecdotal, but the problem with Bernstein's theory is that it subdivides people and speech variants on very broad bases. Even his reformed view that the middle class use both restricted and elaborated code while some working-class speakers have no option does seem to take into too little account the fact that any individual speaker is influenced by who they are with, what they are talking about and where they are, quite as much as by their 'roots'.

SPEECH STRATEGIES, OR THE VERBAL GAMES PEOPLE PLAY

Most speech is conversational – that is, people speak to one another. All the jokes about talking to oneself are based on the fact that it is deviant behaviour because talking is a social activity. Most conversations start with friendly, reassuring noises of the 'How's things? Nice day, isn't it?' variety. This is called PHATIC COMMUNION and is very socially significant. It is against the unwritten law to answer the polite noise 'How are you?' with a detailed explanation of all the problems in your life. This is mistaking the form or usage (a question) with the function or use (a greeting, expecting a reciprocal 'Fine, how are you?').

The skill of INTERACTION – talking to people – is not hearing what they say but knowing what they mean. If someone says 'Do you think I'm a fool?' they are not asking for your assessment of their IQ, they are pointing out that you are treating them as if you do think that they're a fool. The answer 'Actually, I do' would therefore be both rude and inappropriate.

Question forms can, in fact, function as greetings or statements, or as what are called rhetorical questions, expecting no reply.

Single moves

Every time we make a conversational MOVE (the term discourse analysts use) we are sending a message, and not only with words. The able analyst of the spoken word will be able to sort out what the message is.

The most common opening move is a greeting. Sometimes, however, we are not in the mood for niceties. Few ADDRESSERS would lead into 'Where the bloody hell have you put my cheque book?' with 'How are things going?' Likewise, few ADDRESSEES (people spoken to) would reply with a straightforward answer like 'It's in the top drawer'; they will tend to reply in kind – 'You're in a charming mood, aren't you?' – before answering.

Another possible starting point is the business-like, organising approach which Chairs of meetings and teachers specialise in. 'Now today we are going to…' and 'I've convened this meeting in order to…' function in two ways: they initiate a certain kind of discourse – the work one – and they make clear that the speaker is in charge.

Let us now take a more detailed look at some of the moves people can make.

INITIATING   In this move the speaker starts things off. By their choice of type of lexis (formal or informal) and type of opener (statement, demand, greeting) they effectively set the tone for the conversation. Thus the initiating remark is very important.

SOLICITING   This move may follow or replace the opening one. It occurs when a speaker makes a specific demand of their listeners. 'Would you just…', 'I would like you to…' and 'Who knows what…' are all solicitations.

RESPONSES These are the direct, relevant answers to soliciting questions or demands. The range of possible responses is wide but the running sense (COHESION) of conversation depends on responses being appropriate to solicitations. Thus the question 'Did you have a good time?' does not expect the response 'I'm wearing a new dress.' Totally inappropriate responses indicate something seriously wrong with the addressee, such as mental or physical illness or senility. We have all heard conversations where the people involved are following their own train of thought rather than responding to one another. This is more normal, but a sorry comment on their relationship and sensitivity. This kind of 'non-communication situation' is often re-created by dramatists like Harold Pinter for humorous and telling effect.

For the majority of the time most of us follow the rule of TURN-TAKING. That is, we follow what the other person has said and make an appropriate response in terms of content – what they say – and style – how they say it. If people refuse to play this civilised game it can be quite frightening and annoying.

Question and answer sequences are not of course the only kind of conversation people have (though they are firm favourites in the classroom). Statements can be supported or opposed by other speakers. An EVALUATION or ELUCIDATION may be offered. If an evaluation is given, a clear indication of power has been made, since we only feel able to judge at least our equals and more often our inferiors. Elucidations are really a kind of support since they are helping the previous speaker to get their point or information across. Thus they are often the act of a friend or well-wisher, who understands what the speaker wants to say. 'I think what Fred means is...' may sound a bit patronising but it is friendly in intent, whereas 'Look, just what are you trying to say?' is clearly hostile.

NOISES AND PARALINGUISTIC FEATURES

If it is at all possible it is far more instructive to watch people talking rather than simply to listen to them. This is because so many of the messages sent by the addresser and addressee are non-verbal, or PARALINGUISTIC. This large umbrella term covers gesture, facial expressions, body language in all its manifestations, and noises as opposed to words. These latter can certainly signal a good deal: writers refer to people 'tut-tutting' and we all know what that means; 'erm' and 'yeah' with a nodding head will always be read as support, and movements of the shoulders can completely change the meaning of an 'mm' from straightforward 'yes' to 'I'm not too sure about that.' Wagging the head from side to side changes its meaning again to 'perhaps, perhaps not'. All this is rather difficult on paper but I'm sure you take my point.

SUMMARY

What it seems, then, that we need to do is to consider any speaker from at least four viewpoints:

1   As a speaker, not a writer. Remark the speech features like fillers.
2   As an individual with a basic voice, regional accent, dialect and preferred code. See if you can assess region, sex, class and age.
3   As a conversationalist interacting with other people and reacting to feedback.

Recognise their motives for saying what they do.

4   As a member of society who is affected by external factors such as where he is, who she's with and what is being discussed. Decide what register(s) the speaker has adopted and why.

If you look at talking from all these points of view, you should have plenty to say about it! The last, register, is the most difficult. We feel the first three will give you sufficient ammunition for many analyses. However, comparative analysis or more profound discussion will benefit from exploring the fourth and final aspect of analysis. This considers the more all-embracing aspects of discourse. We might most usefully call these REGISTER. This notion is complex but is particularly useful if you are comparing a range of discourse examples – something NEAB candidates will need to do in the Investigation exam.

Discourse analysis – in the context of investigation exams

For the purposes of these exams you may need an even greater understanding of discourse than that needed to analyse a single stretch of discourse. Let us have a quick look at some linguistic concepts that might help you push analysis of discourse further.

FIELD, TENOR and MODE which add up to 'register'

Field is simply the topic being discussed. It's called 'domain' or 'province' by some linguists and tends to affect lexis most. Specialist, technical and jargonised language are all relevant here. Syntax can be affected too – consider legal talk. If you're told the jobs of speakers it's well worth looking for field markers.

Tenor is really all about how informal or formal your tone/style is. Who you are talking to, and where, will affect this; so will mood and individuality. Most language students pick up on formal or colloquial lexis but try to be a little more searching and subtle. As well as the different modes ('frozen' to 'intimate'), you might consider whether a speaker gives bald commands 'Get out this minute!', makes a statement 'I'd like you to leave' or asks a question 'Would you mind leaving now?' Most functions can be achieved in different ways. You could employ a continuum from 'direct' to 'polite'.

••

ACTIVITY ⬛ 📖

Try scaling these utterances

    Can't you say it again?

    Are you going to help me or not?

    You might try to help.

    Why don't you run it past me again.

    I wonder if you could explain that again?

••

Some good clues to tenor include

> Terms of address (Mum or Denise; 'mate' or 'madam')
>
> Polite noises ('please' and 'thank you')
>
> Modality ('could you', 'might you'; 'certainly', 'perhaps')
>
> Euphemism and vagueness
>
> Phatic communion, i.e. ritualised content-free remarks like 'How are you?' and 'Nice weather for the time of year.'

The tenor you take might well depend on your purpose/goal. SPEECH ACT THEORY puts forward options such as explaining, questioning, persuading, as well as more precise ones like accusing, reprimanding, sentencing. Some are very specific, indeed ritualistic, such as christening, thanking and sentencing, and use what are termed PERFORMATIVE VERBS ('baptise', 'pronounce', 'name' etc.)

Mode at its broadest is the difference between speech and writing; however, it's possible to be far more precise:

> Is someone's speech spontaneous (solo-monologue; interactive dialogue)?
>
> Or prepared (recitation, formal speech)?

The more prepared discourse stretches have fewer non-fluency features and a greater kinship with writing! You can't talk about all talk as though it's identical.

As a final bit of confusion, consider written language like playscripts and naturalistic dialogue in novels. These mimic speech and will often be informal, dialectal, taboo-laden and contain 'ums' and 'ers'!

· ·

FINAL ACTIVITY

Try to write a list of unspoken rules of discourse for someone unversed in its intricacies! Consider the use of silence, how you know when to speak, how much you're allowed to say. You might take this even further and do different sets depending on your status, gender or age since the goalposts definitely shift depending on these factors...

· ·

Finally... Want to know more?

If you'd like to pursue discourse analysis further, some books we've found useful are:

Wardhough: *How Conversation Works*

Austin: *How To Do Things With Words* (Oxford University Press 1962)

Searle: *Speech Acts* (Cambridge University Press 1969)

Coulthard: *An Introduction to Discourse Analysis*

Leech   *Principles of Pragmatics* (Longman 1983)

A MINIMUM VOCABULARY FOR DISCOURSE ANALYSIS

How speech works

INTERACTION   the whole conversation

TRANSACTION   the comments on one topic

EXCHANGE   one Q and A

one statement and dis/agreement

MOVE   one Q statement or command

A MOVE MAY NOT BE A COMPLETE UTTERANCE, FAR LESS A SENTENCE

What are we up to when we speak?

Every MOVE has a PURPOSE in terms of the conversation.

INITIATING   opening the topic/setting the scene

SOLICITING   seeking a response – often by Q

RESPONSE   A to Q, logical progression

REACTION   emotional reaction; illogical and often irrelevant

SUPPORTING   clarifying statement or agreeing with it. An 'erm' or 'yeah' will do.

FILLING IN   making polite noises, filling the silence

Clue words

Certain words and phrases often signal what sort of move you're making.

FILLERS   'you know', 'sort of', 'wait a minute'

NEW TOPIC   'right', 'well', 'so', 'well then'

SUPPORT   'true', 'that's right', 'I do so agree', 'ah-hu', 'erm' (+ head up and
down)

REACTION   swearing and emphatics like 'never!'

SOLICITING   tags like 'wouldn't you say?' 'didn't we' and 'isn't it fair to say?'

It's worth learning to recognise certain well-worn strategies and remembering:

INTERACTION IS TWO WAY.

FEEDBACK: the response we give should affect the speaker!

Chapter 5
Linking the Theory to the Practice

The previous four chapters have given you some terminology for describing language, but how will this help you when you're faced with a text to explain or to analyse? What does an analysis of a text consist of? Merely being able to identify features is a pointless exercise unless it's linked to a wider explanation of why the stretch of language in front of you is as it is. The first questions to be asked of any text are not 'How many proper nouns are there in this?' or 'What is the average sentence length?', but much more immediate (and simple) ones such as:

▶ Where might this be from? (Context)

▶ Who is it addressed to? (Audience)

▶ What is language being used for here? (Purpose)

Only after you have noted your initial responses to these questions should you start to look at the language in greater detail and to relate the features you see to the context, audience and purpose of the text.

As students of language, you will begin to develop a fascination with language for its own sake and an ability to note recurrent or unusual patterns of vocabulary and structure within anything you read or hear. However, such observations should *always* be related back to the overall context and purpose of the text. This is reassuring because as a social being, and a fluent member of the language community as speaker/writer or reader/listener, you will almost always know the answers to these straightforward questions, and they will be your starting points for any more detailed analysis. Your understanding of the nuts and bolts of language and its structures can then come into play to fill in the details and to enable you to describe more precisely what the language is doing. You might of course change or modify your initial reactions as a result of taking a closer look. A text that on first glance looked like one thing, might turn out to be another, but your initial reactions are always worth recording.

A SYSTEM FOR TEXT ANALYSIS

There are often predictable links between the context of a text, its audience and purpose (from now on referred to as CAP) and certain specific features of lexis and structure, but you need to look at all three in combination. There are a few examples of text or transcript where, for example, the context alone will explain all the features of a piece (for example the simple sign DANGER!). In most instances it is the answers to all three questions together which will give you the basis for an explanation of a text.

As an example of how to apply this in analysis we offer this piece of sports journalism from a tabloid newspaper. It is not a great work of literature, written (hopefully) to stand the test of time, but a piece of ephemera, as will be many of the texts you will be asked to analyse.

villa @ uefacup.win.uk

BRIAN LITTLE will spend Christmas Day in cyber-space plotting the downfall of UEFA Cup opponents Atletico Madrid.

Between bites of turkey and training his Aston Villa team, Little plans to log on to soccer's information super-highway.

In the constant search for success, Little has discovered how he can find Atletico's own website which will provide a full dossier on the Spanish giants. Little said 'Actually most of the credit should go to my 15-year-old son Andrew. He's the techno-wizard in the family, not me.'

'I'm not much good on computers, but thanks to Andy's help, we've managed to access the Atletico file.'

'Although we aren't due in the Spanish capital until March 3 for the first leg of our Euro quarter-final, that's less than 10 weeks away.'

'So the quicker I start to build up my thoughts about Atletico, the better. A few minutes spent in front of the computer now could prove invaluable,' said Little.

Little has plenty to learn about Atletico, who beat Coca-Cup holders Leicester 4–1 on aggregate in the opening round.

Brazilian star Juninho, who cost £12 million last summer, heads an impressive cast list of players bought for a total of well over £50 m.

Before Atletico, though, Little needs to halt Villa's slump with victory over fellow Premiership strugglers Tottenham on Boxing Day.

Villa's entire squad have been placed in quarantine following the outbreak of a flu virus which has so far hit Gareth Southgate, Steve Staunton, Ian Taylor and Michael Oakes.

If we ask the three questions and jot down our first impressions we come up with something like this:

Where is this from? A newspaper, it's typed in columns, and has a joking, eye-catching headline.

Who is this for? People who already know quite a bit about football and want to know more.

What is this for? To inform readers about Aston Villa's possibly unusual preparations for the UEFA cup and to get a certain amount of publicity for the team.

Now all this might seem blindingly obvious, but these answers will help you when you go on to comment on the text in more detail. We'll go on now to fill out these first impressions with more detailed reference to the text.

Where is this from?

The fact that this is from a newspaper means that you can expect the information to be broken into short, easily digestible chunks, hence the large number of paragraphs in such a short piece, and the fact that several consist of only one sentence. In order to catch the reader's attention the headline draws the eye, not in this case by the use of a pun but by being in the form of an e-mail address. There is an expectation, possibly surprising, that the reader will recognise this format. The headline is intriguing but relates directly to the subject of the story, which is Aston Villa's use of the Internet to obtain information on their rivals. The first sentence continues the mystery and requires that you read on in order to find out exactly how this is going to happen. The carefully constructed introduction is a feature of journalistic writing, as is the subsequent lapse into much more straightforward presentation (possibly of a press release?) when the journalist begins to quote Little. There is a certain amount of research which shows that newspaper readers often don't read complete articles, and newspaper pieces frequently show this 'tailing off' effect. Most of the ingenuity goes into the headline and the opening.

You could probably deduce from the layout and from the very short paragraphs that this is from a tabloid newspaper. If, however, this leads you to assume that we will also find shortish sentences and a lack of complex sentence structures, your closer analysis will show you that this is not the case. If we concentrate on the language outside the quotation marks the average sentence length is 21.8 words, with the shortest being 19, and the majority (paragraphs 3, 8, 9 and 10) contain dependent clauses, indicating complex sentences. All the sentences show a variety of ways of including as much information as possible around the main clause. I have a hunch that the language used in the sports pages of tabloid newspapers is more sophisticated, as measured by sentence length, vocabulary and complexity of structure, than that used in much of the rest of the paper. An A-level student's English language project did confirm that hunch in relation to the sample he looked at. It showed that the average length of sentences in the sports pages was 20% greater than in the rest of the tabloids he examined. The reason for this (if it is true) probably relates to the answer to the second question:

Who is it for?

This is written for specialists, people who already know about football and the current state of the various leagues and competitions, and who want to know more. It is full of what are known as 'insider references'. For example, this article never actually explains who Brian Little is. Those of you who read sports pages regularly will say that it's obvious, he's the manager of Aston Villa, but to those of you who don't, it may not be so clear. The writer is able to assume such knowledge exactly because of the context of this article. If you don't know who Brian Little is, why have you strayed into this corner of the paper? This piece assumes shared knowledge throughout. Other pages of tabloid newspapers assume in-depth knowledge of TV soap operas and are completely mystifying to those who don't watch them. Other examples from this piece would be the wider context that the paradox of Villa in the 1997–8 season was that their performance in European competition was much better than in the English premiership, but this is too obvious to be spelt out here and is only referred to in passing. Juninho is picked out for mention because he has played for an English team and readers would know who he was. Equally they would immediately know the significance of those named players being on the sickness list.

You don't have to have this detailed knowledge yourself to be able to see that this writer assumes a certain level of expertise because you will be aware as a reader that if your motivation for reading is high, because you are reading about a subject which interests you, you will probably make more effort to read the piece through, complex sentences and all. As a writer you will write differently for an audience who shares your understanding of a subject than you will for those who know nothing about it. You can go into detail in a way which would be baffling for the uninitiated and if you can assume motivation in your readers you can give them the information straight and spend less time trying to interest them and to draw them in. This piece shows some of these features once you begin to look closely. Which brings us to the answer to the third question:

What is this for?

The primary purpose of this article appears to be an informative one.

You could take a longer view and say that the main purpose of all newspaper articles is to fill newspapers, which in turn are sold to make money for all concerned, and this (the mere fact that they have to be filled) might be something to take into account, but we will start from the premise that people buy newspapers to be informed and entertained. This article (headline aside) appears to be at the informative end of the spectrum.

The article really falls into two parts. The first three paragraphs and the last four are the work of the journalist and have been structured to include a lot of information in relatively little space. The middle four paragraphs appear to be a quote from Brian Little and contain personal as well as footballing information. The quote will almost certainly have been edited and may have come to the journalist via a press conference, a press release or a telephone call following a press release. Certainly the style is different in these paragraphs, with the use of first person pronouns, and it is interesting to speculate whether the basis is spontaneous speech, even allowing for the editing.

Speculation is legitimate in analysis provided it is based on evidence. The style is less complex than in the journalist's paragraphs, which might indicate speech, but the ordering in the third of his four paragraphs, with the main clause delayed, and the formality of 'could prove invaluable' at the end, seem more like written constructions. It's safest to speculate that this is a version of speech edited to condense the information into a smallish space.

As an example of how to fit information into a sentence, we could analyse the final paragraph, which is just one complete sentence. The main clause,

Villa's entire squad have been placed in quarantine

is followed by an adverbial phrase which has a dual function. It technically tells us when and it also tells us why,

following the outbreak of a flu virus

This in turn is followed by an adjectival clause telling us more about the virus and who it has affected,

which has so far hit Gareth Southgate, Steve Staunton, Ian Taylor and Michael Oakes.

Those non-specialists among you might be wondering why, if space is at a premium, he doesn't just say 'four players'. But this would not give the fans the information they need. Now they know which positions they might be weak in and can take an informed guess at the substitutes. The sentence is not exceptionally complex, but taking it to pieces shows how three different, but related bits of information are packed into the one structure.

Of course we do expect that information about this kind of subject in newspapers will be presented in ways which are also entertaining. Here the journalist has achieved this by dramatising the situation to some extent in presenting a picture of Mr Little and son interrogating the Net on Christmas Day itself. Such phrases as 'spend Christmas Day in cyber-space', and 'between bites of turkey and training' (note the alliteration), liven up the piece as do such sporting clichés as 'plotting the downfall' and 'halt Villa's slump'.

As well as giving information to the reader, this piece gives information about the team and about Brian Little in particular and he comes across in a very positive light, not only conscientiously working for his team (on Christmas Day!) but also giving due credit to his son. This promotional aspect to the story is not a major one, but it is present and could be seen as a direct attempt by Aston Villa to get some positive publicity (after all, they're in a slump), or as an intention by the journalist to give the story some human, as well as footballing interest.

This look at one article has not provided an exhaustive analysis of the text, but has attempted to link the context/audience/purpose of the piece to a closer look at the language. In the next few pages we will give you some indication of features you might expect to see in a range of examples in relation to CAP.

You must be on your guard, however, as we do like to play all kinds of games with language, and things are not always what they seem. There are certain varieties such as pastiche and parody where people deliberately try to subvert our expectations by exaggeration or mimicry. This can happen for humorous or serious purpose, but the usual effect is to make the original rather ridiculous. If this seems a rather out-of-the-way example, consider a technique that most of us use or suffer from at some time, sarcasm, where both parties and any audience usually realise very quickly that what is meant is the opposite of what is being said. In these instances the context will probably transform the apparent purpose.

We will return to some of these tricky examples (sometimes favoured by examiners) later, but for the rest of this chapter we will concentrate on giving you some suggestions about what to look for in any example of language in relation to context, audience and purpose. After that, in the next three chapters, we will look at different texts grouped under these three headings separately. The focus of the 'Context' chapter will be to concentrate on examples where the context in which the language is used appears to be particularly significant, to be highlighted, but again we would want to stress that it is the interplay between the context, audience and purpose of any stretch of language which explains the way it is as it is.

The following diagram is an attempt to indicate how these three aspects of text inevitably overlap.

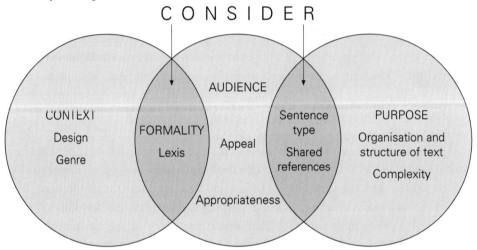

However, if you would prefer for the moment to focus more sharply on one or two aspects only, we suggest in the following few pages the sorts of texts and features it would be most useful to consider. For each aspect we have identified four texts. We shall consider some of them in detail in the appropriate sections that follow. A profitable activity for a group of language students to engage in would be to take a category of text, for example instructions, and each find their own example. These could then be swapped, analysed and made into a bank of materials for fellow and future students.

Such a bank of materials also provides models for your own writing. We have included suggestions for writing as well as analysis throughout the rest of the book because we believe that the two activities are linked. An A-level English Language course raises your level of understanding of different varieties of language and asks you to develop your skill as a language-user through your own writing, which in turn increases your consciousness of the choices you make every time you yourself put pen to paper. Or that's the theory.

We deal in more detail with the link between analysis and writing in Chapter 18 at the end of the book, but if you are currently more confident as a writer of text than as a decoder of it, maybe you would benefit from reading that chapter now.

CONTEXT

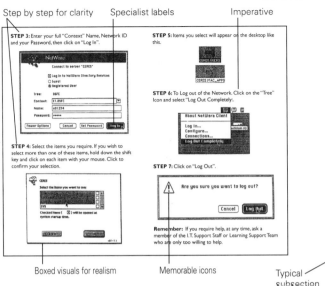

Step by step for clarity — **STEP 3:** Enter your full "Context" Name, Network ID and your Password, then click on "Log In".

Specialist labels

Imperative — **STEP 5:** Items you select will appear on the desktop like this.

STEP 6: To Log out of the Network. Click on the "Tree" Icon and select "Log Out Completely".

STEP 4: Select the items you require. If you wish to select more than one of these items, hold down the shift key and click on each item with your mouse. Click to confirm your selection.

STEP 7: Click on "Log Out".

Remember: If you require help, at any time, ask a member of the I.T. Support Staff or Learning Support Team who are only too willing to help.

Boxed visuals for realism

Memorable icons

Instruction leaflet

From THE SERENGETI to the VICTORIA FALLS

Visiting the Great Game Parks of Tanzania – the Serengeti, Lake Manyara, Ngorongoro Crater, the Tarangire & Victoria Falls

Euphemism for tourist

Numerous proper names

with an optional
7-night extension to Grand Comore
14 nights from £1695.00

This journey takes the traveller directly to Kilimanjaro and the great game parks of Tanzania without the need to make tedious road journeys from Kenya and back again. Here, over the course of a week, we shall visit the Serengeti, Lake Manyara, Ngorongoro Crater, Tarangire National Park and Arusha to witness the wildlife wonders which are available here in such profusion. Accommodation has been arranged at the 5-star Sopa lodges which command outstanding locations in the parks and offer a wide range of facilities for the traveller.

From Kilimanjaro fly directly to Victoria Falls for seven nights at the 5-star Elephant Hills Hotel. Over the course of the next week you can relax in the hotel's extensive grounds which includes an 18-hole golf course or participate in one of the many different excursion programmes: a Zambezi Sunset cruise, the Flight of Angles over the Falls or a visit to the Falls close up on both the Zimbabwe and Zambian sides. In addition you may visit the Hwange Game Reserve or Chobe National Park, just across the border into Botswana. Whatever your choice the stay at the Falls will be an experience to be remembered.

Itinerary

Day 1 Depart London Gatwick in the evening via Luxor to Kilimanjaro with Monarch Airways Boeing 757. Journey through the night.

Day 2 Arrive Kilimanjaro in the morning and transfer directly to Tarangire National Park and more particularly the 5-star Sopa Lodge with its fine facilities to spend the next two nights. After unwinding make a late afternoon game drive or a general orientation to our visit to the park.

Day 3 Tarangire gets its name from the river that threads its way through the length of the reserve and is famous for the dense wildlife population including wildebeest, zebra, eland, elephant, leopard, buffalo and the fringe-eared oryx which migrate from the Masai steppe to the Tarangire River with lions and other predators following the herds. Make both an early morning and late afternoon game drive.

Day 4 Depart after breakfast to Serengeti National Park, on the way visiting Olduvai Gorge the site of the Leakey family's famous excavations for the origins of man. Continue to the 5-star Serengeti Sopa Lodge and spend the next two nights.

Day 5 The Serengeti is undoubtedly one of the world's last great wildlife refuges which covers and area of some 5,700 square miles. It is here that once a year a million wildebeest and zebra gather to make their migrations. The area is home to some of the largest concentrations of wildlife anywhere set against the backdrop of stunning scenery. During our stay we shall visit various parts of the park and observe its many different aspects.

Day 6 After breakfast travel to the world famous Ngorongoro Crater and the 5-star Ngorongoro Sopa Lodge to spend the next two nights. The hotel has a fine restaurant, swimming pool, bar and magnificent views over the crater.

Day 7 Today make a visit to the crater's rim allowing awe-inspiring views, including savannah, lakes, rivers, swamps and, with aid of binoculars, it may just be possible to spot grazing wildlife. Then descend into the crater itself. This is the area where the Masai graze their cattle cheek by jowl with some 25,000 animal species including zebra, wildebeest and hyenas. Return to the hotel for the night.

Day 8 Today travel to Gibbs Farm, a beautiful family homestead set in a coffee plantation for a welcome rest, before proceeding to Lake Manyara with its teeming wildlife, especially birds. Later continue to the town of Arusha and, if time permits, visit the snake park at Meserani. Overnight at the Mt Meru Novotel.

Day 9 After breakfast transfer to Kilimanjaro airport for the flight to Victoria Falls (approx 2½ hours). On arrival transfer to the 5-star Elephant Hills for the next seven nights. See supplement for the Victoria Falls Hotel. Please refer to page 21 for details of optional excursions around Victoria Falls.

Day 16 Depart Victoria Falls in the morning and connect with the flight from Kilimanjaro to London Gatwick arriving in the evening of the same day. Since the flight operates via Grand Comore you may elect to extend with a 7-night sojourn at Le Galawa Beach Hotel.

Sopa Lodges
Probably the finest accommodations in the game parks the Sopa Lodges (the Masai word for welcome) are truly 5 star and come with all the modern facilities that you might expect at this category including full private facilities, extensive public areas and many with swimming pools - making them ideal bases from which to explore and relax.

The Elephant Hills Hotel
Three kilometres up from the roar of the Falls, Elephant Hills is unique in both style and location. This world-class resort provides a truly spectacular panorama combining the surrounds of the Zambezi River and its surroundings with the plush fairways of the famous golf course. Apart from golf, there is tennis, squash, swimming and a wide range of boating and game viewing activities. With its 276 luxury rooms, its expansive swimming area and its sophisticated casino, Elephant Hills provides a memorable blend of luxury and wilderness.

Typical subsection

List

Persuasive numbers

Positive lexis

Superlatives

Advert

Dialogue with speakers named

BIFF: Dad, you're never going to see what I am, so what's the use of arguing? If I strike oil I'll send you a cheque. Meantime forget I'm alive.

WILLY [TO LINDA]: Spite, see?

BIFF: Shake hands, Dad.

WILLY: Not my hand.

BIFF: I was hoping not to go this way.

WILLY: Well, this is the way you're going. Good-bye.

[BIFF *looks at him a moment, then turns sharply and goes to the stairs.*]

WILLY [*stops him with*]: May you rot in hell if you leave this house!

BIFF [*turning*]: Exactly what is it that you want from me?

WILLY: I want you to know, on the train, in the mountains, in the valleys, wherever you go, that you cut down your life for spite!

BIFF: No, no.

WILLY: Spite, spite, is the word of your undoing! And when you're down and out, remember what did it. When you're rotting somewhere beside the railroad tracks, remember, and don't you dare blame it on me!

BIFF: I'm not blaming it on you!

WILLY: I won't take the rap for this, you hear?

[HAPPY *comes down the stairs and stands on the bottom step, watching.*]

BIFF: That's just what I'm telling you!

WILLY [*sinking into a chair at the table, with full accusation*]: You're trying to put a knife in me – don't think I don't know what you're doing!

BIFF: All right, phony! Then let's lay it on the line. [*He whips the rubber tube out of his pocket and puts it on the table.*]

HAPPY: You crazy –

LINDA: Biff! [*She moves to grab the hose, but* BIFF *holds it down with his hand.*]

BIFF: Leave it there! Don't move it!

WILLY [*not looking at it*]: What is that?

BIFF: You know goddam well what that is.

WILLY [*caged, wanting to escape*]: I never saw that.

BIFF: You saw it. The mice didn't bring it into the cellar! What is this supposed to do, make a hero out of you? This is supposed to make me sorry for you?

WILLY: Never heard of it.

BIFF: There'll be no pity for you, you hear it? No pity!

WILLY [*to* LINDA]: You hear the spite!

BIFF: No, you're going to hear the truth – what you are and what I am!

LINDA: Stop it!

WILLY: Spite!

HAPPY [*coming down toward* BIFF]: You cut it now!

BIFF [*to* HAPPY]: The man don't know who we are! The man is gonna know! [*To* WILLY] We never told the truth for ten minutes in this house!

HAPPY: We always told the truth!

BIFF [*turning on him*]: You big blow, are you the assistant buyer? You're one of the two assistants to the assistant, aren't you?

HAPPY: Well, I'm practically ...

Stage directions

Imitation of natural speech

Drama

Compound words

I, JOHN SMITH, *of 99 Dronfield Road, Salford, in the Metropolitan County of Greater Manchester, company director,* HEREBY REVOKE *all wills and testamentary documents heretofore made by me and* DECLARE *this to be my* LAST WILL AND TESTAMENT.

1   I APPOINT *my wife Joan Smith, and my solicitor, Thomas Jones, to be jointly my executors of this my will.*

2   I DEVISE *my freehold cottage known as* THE LILACS, *at Coniston in the county of Cumbria, unto my son* ROBERT SMITH *in fee simple.*

3   I BEQUEATH *the following specific legacies:*
    (i)   *to my son, Robert Smith, any motor-car I may own at the date of my death.*
    (ii) *to my daughter Jane Smith, all my shares in the company known as Imperial Chemical Industries.*
    (iii) *to my said wife all my personal chattels not hereby bequeathed for her absolute use and benefit.*

4   I BEQUEATH *the following pecuniary legacies:*
    (i)   *To my daughter Jill Smith, the sum of £3000*
    (ii) *To my daughter Jenny Smith, the sum of £3000*

5   I DEVISE AND BEQUEATH *all the residue of my real and personal estate whatsoever and wheresoever not hereby or by any codicil hereto otherwise expressly disposed of as to my freeholds in fee simple and as to my personal estate absolutely unto my said wife, Joan Smith, for her own absolute use and benefit.*

6   I DIRECT *that any executor of this my Will being a solicitor or a person engaged in any profession or business, may be so employed and act and shall be entitled to make all proper professional charges for any work done by him or his firm in connection with my Estate including work done which an executor not being a solicitor or a person engaged as aforesaid could have done personally.*

IN WITNESS *whereof I, the said John Smith, the Testator have to this my* LAST WILL *set my hand this thirty-first day of December One Thousand Nine Hundred and Ninety Eight.*

SIGNED AND ACKNOWLEDGED *by the above-named John Smith, the Testator, as and for his* LAST WILL *in the presence of us both present at the same time who at this request in his presence and in the presence of each other hereunto subscribed our names as witnesses:*

John Smith _____
(signed)

Frank Ellis, (signed)   Jeremy Goodall, (signed)
6, The Crescent   2, High Street,
Salford,   Bolton,
Clerk   Chartered Accountant

Introductory formulaic statement

Numbered points

Archaic lexis

Latinate/ specialist lexis

Signed, dated and witnessed

Will

AUDIENCE

Simple language

Short sentences

WHAT'S THE MATTER?
or
**HOW TO DO NOTHING
AND LOSE EVERYTHING**

*Him and her. You can make your own
mind up which is 'him' and which is 'her'.*

What's the matter?
Nothing.
Something's the matter.
No, it isn't.
Then what are you sulking about?
I'm not sulking.
Well you're not exactly happy, are you?
I'm all right.
You don't look it.
I don't have to show it.
You used to.
So now I don't.
You're telling me.
Yes, I know I'm telling you.
Something's the matter then.
No, it isn't.
Yes, it is.
Well, if you know so much about me
  you don't need me to tell you.
No, I suppose not. I'll be off then. I'll see you
  when I see you.

Michael Rosen

Young

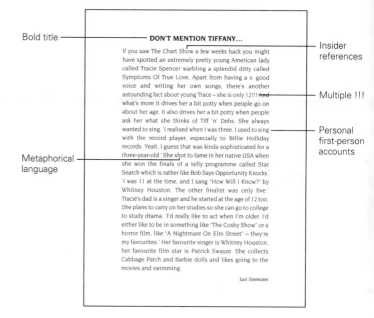

Bold title

Insider references

Multiple !!!

Personal first-person accounts

Metaphorical language

DON'T MENTION TIFFANY...

If you saw The Chart Show a few weeks back you might
have spotted an extremely pretty young American lady
called Tracie Spencer warbling a splendid ditty called
Symptoms Of True Love. Apart from having a v. good
voice and writing her own songs, there's another
astounding fact about young Trace – she is only 12!!! And
what's more it drives her a bit potty when people go on
about her age. It also drives her a bit potty when people
ask her what she thinks of Tiff 'n' Debs. She always
wanted to sing. 'I realised when I was three. I used to sing
with the record player, especially to Billie Holliday
records. Yeah, I guess that was kinda sophisticated for a
three-year-old.' She shot to fame in her native USA when
she won the finals of a telly programme called Star
Search which is rather like Bob Says Opportunity Knocks.
'I was 11 at the time, and I sang "How Will I Know?" by
Whitney Houston. The other finalist was only five.'
Tracie's dad is a singer and he started at the age of 12 too.
She plans to carry on her studies so she can go to college
to study drama. 'I'd really like to act when I'm older. I'd
either like to be in something like "The Cosby Show" or a
horror film, like "A Nightmare On Elm Street" – they're
my favourites.' Her favourite singer is Whitney Houston,
her favourite film star is Patrick Swayze. She collects
Cabbage Patch and Barbie dolls and likes going to the
movies and swimming.

Just Seventeen

Young/teenage

Uncertainty as well as facts

Long sentences

Uncommon words

WHAT WAS IT that departed during the first week of September?
Much of the country was not convulsed by grief, although we
do not know the proportion that stayed unmoved, or even
critical, and perceived the events as a Southern or heartland
spectacle. Yet it appears to be true that even among the more
detached, many found themselves touched by unsuspected
melancholy, strangely coupled to a sense of liberation and
change. An inescapable shift was occurring, displayed in
unheard of symptoms like the applause in Westminster Abbey,
as well as the mountains of flowers and poems.
     But what was the nature of the shift – and what exactly
shifted? For all that has now been written around the event,
the answer remains obscure. There are nevertheless a number
of possibilities, of which the strongest might look something
like this: a fairly long-lasting structure of English national
identity which, though already in serious trouble, required this
sudden blow from an unexpected angle to collapse. Much of
the evidence remains circumstantial, but that is often the case
when 'identity' is involved. What we are discussing is (or was)
a subcutaneous circuit of attitudes and feelings which
functioned best when it was unconscious, or taken for granted.
Except when called upon, the mechanism invisibly behaved
itself. While there and available, few paid it much heed. When
it broke down, on the other hand, everyone noticed, was
affected to some degree, and looked for an explanation. 'She
called out to the country,' Elton John sang at the funeral. But
may it not have been the English Rose's country which, in the
aftermath of loss, ceased being able to call out in a traditional
way? If so, a call long responded to – not really 'down the ages'
but for quite a long time, about a century and a half – would
not be made or heard again.

London Review of Books 30 October, 1987

Sophisticated

Untranslated French

Abbreviations

Costly, upmarket

Lexis used in specialist sense

Precise and lengthy pre-modification

Extreme adjectives

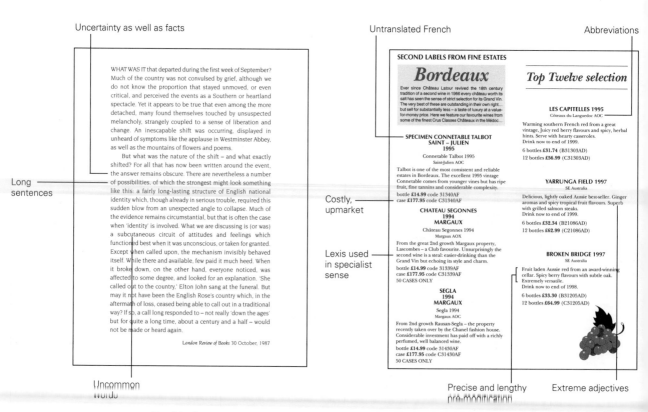

SECOND LABELS FROM FINE ESTATES

Bordeaux

Ever since Château Latour revived the 18th century
tradition of a second wine in 1966 every château worth its
salt has seen the sense of strict selection for its Grand Vin.
The very best of these are outstanding in their own right...
but sell for substantially less – a taste of luxury at a value-
for-money price. Here we feature our favourite wines from
some of the finest Crus Classes Châteaux in the Médoc.

**SPECIMEN CONNETABLE TALBOT
SAINT - JULIEN
1995**
Connetable Talbot 1995
Saint-Julien AOC

Talbot is one of the most consistent and reliable
estates in Bordeaux. The excellent 1995 vintage
Connetable comes from younger vines but has ripe
fruit, fine tannins and considerable complexity.
bottle **£14.99** code 31340AF
case **£177.95** code C31340AF

**CHATEAU SEGONNES
1994
MARGAUX**
Château Segonnes 1994
Margaux AOX

From the great 2nd growth Margaux property,
Lascombes – a Club favourite. Unsurprisingly the
second wine is a steal: easier-drinking than the
Grand Vin but echoing its style and charm.
bottle **£14.99** code 31339AF
case **£177.95** code C31339AF
50 CASES ONLY

**SEGLA
1994
MARGAUX**
Segla 1994
Margaux AOC

From 2nd growth Rausan-Segla – the property
recently taken over by the Chanel fashion house.
Considerable investment has paid off with a richly
perfumed, well balanced wine.
bottle **£14.99** code 31430AF
case **£177.95** code C31430AF
50 CASES ONLY

Top Twelve selection

LES CAPITELLES 1995
Côteaux du Languedoc AOC

Warming southern French red from a great
vintage. Juicy red berry flavours and spicy, herbal
hints. Serve with hearty casseroles.

6 bottles **£31.74** (B31303AD)
12 bottles **£56.99** (C31303AD)

YARRUNGA FIELD 1997
SE Australia

Delicious, lightly oaked Aussie best-seller. Ginger
aromas and spicy tropical fruit flavours. Superb
with grilled salmon steaks.
Drink now to end of 1999.

6 bottles **£32.34** (B21086AD)
12 bottles **£62.99** (C21086AD)

BROKEN BRIDGE 1997
SE Australia

Fruit laden Aussie red from an award-winning
cellar. Spicy berry flavours with subtle oak.
Extremely versatile.
Drink now to end of 1998.

6 bottles **£33.30** (B31205AD)
12 bottles **£64.99** (C31205AD)

Specialist

PURPOSE

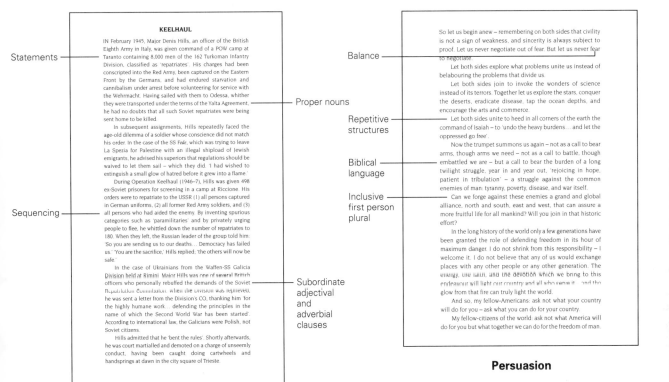

Statements

Proper nouns

Sequencing

Subordinate adjectival and adverbial clauses

KEELHAUL

IN February 1945, Major Denis Hills, an officer of the British Eighth Army in Italy, was given command of a POW camp at Taranto containing 8,000 men of the 162 Turkoman Infantry Division, classified as 'repatriates'. His charges had been conscripted into the Red Army, been captured on the Eastern Front by the Germans, and had endured starvation and cannibalism under arrest before volunteering for service with the Wehrmacht. Having sailed with them to Odessa, whither they were transported under the terms of the Yalta Agreement, he had no doubts that all such Soviet repatriates were being sent home to be killed.

In subsequent assignments, Hills repeatedly faced the age-old dilemma of a soldier whose conscience did not match his order. In the case of the SS *Fale*, which was trying to leave La Spezia for Palestine with an illegal shipload of Jewish emigrants, he advised his superiors that regulations should be waived to let them sail – which they did. 'I had wished to extinguish a small glow of hatred before it grew into a flame.'

During Operation Keelhaul (1946–7), Hills was given 498 ex-Soviet prisoners for screening in a camp at Riccione. His orders were to repatriate to the USSR (1) all persons captured in German uniforms, (2) all former Red Army soldiers, and (3) all persons who had aided the enemy. By inventing spurious categories such as 'paramilitaries' and by privately urging people to flee, he whittled down the number of repatriates to 180. When they left, the Russian leader of the group told him: 'So you are sending us to our deaths… Democracy has failed us.' 'You are the sacrifice,' Hills replied; 'the others will now be safe.'

In the case of Ukrainians from the Waffen-SS Galicia Division held at Rimini, Major Hills was one of several British officers who personally rebuffed the demands of the Soviet Repatriation Commission. When the Division was reprieved, he was sent a letter from the Division's CO, thanking him 'for the highly humane work… defending the principles in the name of which the Second World War has been started'. According to international law, the Galicians were Polish, not Soviet citizens.

Hills admitted that he 'bent the rules'. Shortly afterwards, he was court martialled and demoted on a charge of unseemly conduct, having been caught doing cartwheels and handsprings at dawn in the city square of Trieste.

Information

Balance

Repetitive structures

Biblical language

Inclusive first person plural

So let us begin anew – remembering on both sides that civility is not a sign of weakness, and sincerity is always subject to proof. Let us never negotiate out of fear. But let us never fear to negotiate.

Let both sides explore what problems unite us instead of belabouring the problems that divide us.

Let both sides join to invoke the wonders of science instead of its terrors. Together let us explore the stars, conquer the deserts, eradicate disease, tap the ocean depths, and encourage the arts and commerce.

Let both sides unite to heed in all corners of the earth the command of Isaiah – to 'undo the heavy burdens… and let the oppressed go free'.

Now the trumpet summons us again – not as a call to bear arms, though arms we need – not as a call to battle, though embattled we are – but as a call to bear the burden of a long twilight struggle, year in and year out, 'rejoicing in hope, patient in tribulation' – a struggle against the common enemies of man: tyranny, poverty, disease, and war itself.

Can we forge against these enemies a grand and global alliance, north and south, east and west, that can assure a more fruitful life for all mankind? Will you join in that historic effort?

In the long history of the world only a few generations have been granted the role of defending freedom in its hour of maximum danger. I do not shrink from this responsibility – I welcome it. I do not believe that any of us would exchange places with any other people or any other generation. The energy, the faith, and the devotion which we bring to this endeavour will light our country and all who serve it, and the glow from that fire can truly light the world.

And so, my fellow-Americans: ask not what your country will do for you – ask what you can do for your country.

My fellow-citizens of the world: ask not what America will do for you but what together we can do for the freedom of man.

Persuasion

Word play

One sentence paragraphs

Unattributed quotations

Going Apes! Chimp family have caused fury by moving into the £85,000 council house

EU CHIMP RULING MAKES US LOOK LIKE MONKEYS

TAXPAYERS went bananas last night after it was revealed that an £85,000 council house has been let to a family of CHIMPANZEES.

Protests about the 'monkeys from hell' have already been lodged by residents on the same tree-lined estate.

And they were even more irate when they learned that £8,000 has been spent adapting the three-bedroomed semi for its hairy occupants, whose rent bill is also being picked up by the public.

But a local authority spokesperson has defended the move, saying: 'The EU made us do it. Our hands are tied by red tape.'

'There are no suitable establishments in our catchment area to place them in but we have a duty under European law to see they are looked after. This house is all we had available.'

Starving

The crisis began when the chimps – an adult male and female and their two offspring – were found starving in a boarded-up pet shop by animal rights outreach workers.

They were unable to find a temporary place to keep them properly cared for despite a desperate ring round of safari parks, zoos and vets.

The spokesperson for the London authority, which cannot be named while legal proceedings are underway, added:

'We fully realise this is a ridiculous situation and that some people will think it's a waste of taxpayers' money. We are contesting the ruling through the courts.'

Meanwhile the chimps are running amok in their luxury home.

Entertainment

Questions   Direct address

Short sentences   Slogan   Attempts to sound like speech

Condom.

It's not that difficult to say is it!

Well if it's not, what's stopping you?

He might laugh at you for mentioning it. He might think you're easy.

Well here's something else to think about.

In Britain the number of people with AIDS is still on the increase.

And for every person with AIDS, we estimate there are thirty with HIV.

Human Immunodeficiency Virus is the virus which leads to AIDS.

Someone can have it for several years and still look and feel perfectly healthy.

But through unprotected sex, they can pass the virus on to you.

A condom can help protect you.

So think about using one, and talk about it with your boyfriend.

You never know, he might just be pleased you suggested it.

Think about not having sex at all if you're not certain, or you don't really know him well enough.

And more important, never feel shy about asking him to use a condom.

AIDS. YOU'RE AS SAFE AS YOU WANT TO BE.

Education

Section Two

LANGUAGE IN ACTION

In this section we will consider a range of literary and non-literary texts in detail. These will be explained using the key of context, audience and purpose.

Chapter 6: Context
Where is the writing from?

Chapter 7: Audience
Who is the reader?

Chapter 8: Purpose
What is the piece trying to do?

Chapter 9: Take Me Away From All This
Travel writing and genre fiction

Chapter 10: Literature with a Capital 'L'
Something more serious

Chapter 11: Establishing Voice and Point of View
Who's telling the story?

Chapter 12: Creating a Sense of Place
Setting the scene

Chapter 13: Sending a Message
Writing that persuades and makes a statement

Chapter 14: Make them Cry
Writing that moves you

Chapter 15: Make 'em Laugh – Humour
A little light relief

Chapter 6
Context

This chapter examines in more detail what we described as context (Where is this writing from?) in the previous chapter, and it looks at examples where the context is particularly important in determining the choice of words and structures in the texts we use.

It might seem that the answer to the question 'Where is this from?' is the easiest of the three questions to answer and sometimes too obvious to state. Here we are interested in the impact that the expectations dictated by the context have on an example of language, and the most important thing to say about context is that consideration of it focuses us on language use. It highlights the situation in which language is used, rather than the characteristics of the user or the addressee.

We can all vary the way we speak or write according to the situation we are in and what we deem to be appropriate. Sometimes this is because of our audience, but sometimes it is because of the occasion or surroundings. We would speak differently, for instance, during or immediately after a wedding or a funeral ceremony than we would a few hours later in the company of the same people at the reception because there is something about the occasion which imposes its own rules. The fact is that context reduces the user's flexibility and focuses on use.

Similarly there are certain varieties of language which impose their own conventions and rules; varieties such as the religious, scientific and legal. For example, a vicar uses the subjunctive 'Let'; a scientific writer will use a great deal of specialist lexis to achieve precision and a fair amount of the passive voice in describing experiments, where it's the process not the agent which is important; and a legal writer (see below) will go in for compounds such as 'hereunder'. Often of course, it is the lexis which gives the game away and tells us exactly where a text is from.

Equally often it's the physical layout on the page which gives us clues. Journalese is usually in columns; recipes usually start with lists. We form expectations when we see these signals, so much so that when we see an advertisement written in the format of the news piece (with 'advertisement feature' in minuscule type at the top), we feel cheated. It was this physical layout, or visual signals as we dubbed them, that we exemplified in Chapter 5. Most of the rest of this chapter concentrates on the verbal signals that different contexts demand.

So what language issues does context raise? Formality is one of the crucial ones. If you regarded swearing as a context of use, as well as part of the idiolect of the user, you'd soon identify likely settings – and they wouldn't include church or Sunday lunch with Gran. Settings for this mode of language are informal, often intimate. At the other end of the spectrum might be a sermon, which would be encoded in a far more formal way. In some languages, like German and Greek, there are actually high and low versions of the language available to speakers. In Britain, we don't go that far but we do vary our style enormously depending on – you guessed it – context.

Linguists refer to these different varieties as DIGLOSSIA. A linguist called Loos labelled words along a formality continuum as:

FROZEN	FORMAL	CONSULTATIVE	CASUAL	INTIMATE
Written	mostly written	polite, using 'you'	colloquial	earthy and taboo-laden

To exemplify: a *frozen* notice might inform you that 'Expectoration is prohibited'; the *consultative* version could be 'You are asked not to spit'; an *intimate*, 'Don't gob in 'ere you ****'. You can supply your own expletive and decide what the formal and casual versions might be. You'll notice that grammatical choices like whether or not to use the passive, and accental ones like whether or not to sound an initial /h/, also come into it.

You'll also have noticed that the spoken and written choices have reared their heads. It's important to consider use and register when you look at a text. The spoken mode is often less formal than the written because it's often used for face-to-face, personal interaction as opposed to long-distance (over space or time) impersonal discourse. However, there are exceptions. Speeches use the spoken voice for dramatic effect but they are often very rhetorical and formal in structure and word choice. Scripted drama mimics reality and uses colloquial lexis but has a good deal of high-level literary language too, as we shall see when we look at *Death of a Salesman* later on. E-mail is really chatting by computer much of the time and its outputs reflect this. Conversely, among older and non-business types the answering machine message is not naturalistic and colloquial but stilted and full of embarrassed pauses.

Some linguistic specialist lexis can help to sort out the element of register or context. As we said, its about *use* not *user*. Bernstein's codes and Trudgill's triangles of accent and dialect aren't the point here; they tend to relate to user. Instead, it's helpful to use Halliday's three concepts:

FIELD	MODE	and	TENOR or MANNER
(What it's about)	(spoken or written)		(formal/informal, user relation)

Specific *fields* are easy to identify; they're often called 'varieties' (some linguists use the term DOMAIN for the same thing). In this section we will focus on legal language but glance at a couple of others.

We do not intend to look at *mode* in detail, since we discuss spoken language in detail in both Chapter 4 and the Investigation section. However, we will take a look at jargon 'context'. This is because the jargon and/or specialist lexis used in a text is such an invaluable guide to what sort of animal it is.

The *manner* or *tenor* of the text is basically its formality level so we'll look at a number of texts with this mostly in mind. Swearing is an extreme and thus useful case. At the other end of the spectrum are uses like sermons, which are very high diglossia. You might usefully return to your varieties list and try to place them on a tenor continuum. Generalisations can be misleading but most linguists would regard scientific prose as more formal than advertising language and discourse as less formal than instruction. Broad, common-sense principles are valuable starting points in analysis.

ACTIVITY

Make a list of the varieties with which you are most familiar as a language student. Try for each of the easiest three to list their lexical and structural hallmarks.

FAMILIAR FIELDS

The formal and the legal field

Though the mode may vary, a use or variety of language will have some fixed hallmarks of the kind you listed. Let us begin (to use religious field language) with legal language.

There are times when the seriousness of an occasion demands a special form of words. We want to make a fully binding promise and we do so publicly and in a set manner. The fact that we do not make up our own form of words is important: certain ritualised forms have developed over the centuries and use of them stresses the social as well as individual nature of the promise. However, some small allowances can be made for personal preference: for example, many women of the late twentieth century, though willing to promise to love and even honour their husbands, are not prepared to add obey. However, it is important to keep most of the wording the same: the form of words derives its potency and conviction from being ritualised – it is almost like a charm.

When you think about it, most of the major watersheds in our lives are signalled and sealed by the use of these special, legal forms of language. Fairly soon after our entry into the world, we may be baptised, if we are in a Christian community, and some believe that a child cannot go to Heaven unless the words 'I baptise thee in the name of...' have been said. Others might not go that far, but they would certainly regard the ceremony as a statement of faith and intention on the part of the parents and godparents.

Later, the child has an opportunity to confirm or deny the promises made, at a confirmation ceremony. Such ceremonies are linked to the church, but this would not be the case in other cultures. The important thing to notice is that language is the tool people use to commit themselves, whether to a relationship – 'I'll be your best friend'; 'I will (take you as my husband/wife)' – or a duty – 'You have my word I'll do it'; 'I promise to pay the bearer on demand the sum of £50'. None of us takes these assurances lightly, and keeping your word is highly valued: 'he's a man of his word' is praise anywhere in the world and 'he speaks with forked tongue', however expressed, is blame.

Returning to the ceremonies we go through… an adult is likely to go through a wedding ceremony, whether in church or in a registry office. It would not do to say in the middle of the ceremony 'Go on then, I'll have him', and a practical joker who butted in with a witticism after 'Does anyone know of any just cause or impediment why these two may not be joined together in holy matrimony?' would wreck the whole affair.

Words matter because they can symbolically function as deeds. I suspect the much mentioned right a Muslim man has to say 'I divorce thee; I divorce thee; I divorce thee' and make it happen is very rarely, if ever, exercised. However, we are all familiar with the bottle-smashing and 'I name this ship the… May God bless her and all who sail in her.'

The last major occasion of our life – our funeral or cremation – again has very fixed formulae. We are not, of course, able to make a personal contribution, but by then we may have already made our feelings and wishes known in the very particular form of a Last Will and Testament (see page 74).

The first thing to say about wills is that they are all written to the same recipe. Only the names are changed to benefit the fortunate survivors.

The reason why there are so many givens in legal language is not because solicitors are idle, but because a form of words has been found over the centuries which is as unambiguous and unforgeable as possible. To be of any legal value, a will must be precise. Thus you don't have 'I, John' but the testator's full name, address and occupation. This is to ensure that he is not confused with any other John Smith. Adjectival phrases are scattered throughout the document. 'My wife/son/daughter' will not do: all sorts of people might start claiming that John had fathered or married them. So all benefactors are named in full. Places are similarly specified: 'my cottage in the lakes' might be meaningful to John and his family, but, to be watertight, its name and precise location are added. Legal language is an extreme example of elaborated variant: it may contain plenty of jargon but it eschews insider references.

The most vital element of any will is who gets what. The 'who', as already explained, is very exactly stated. The 'what' is divided into set categories in a set order, which helps to avoid forgery or misunderstanding. First, we have specific legacies – i.e. things – then the pecuniary ones – the cash – and finally, to cover all eventualities, we have the catch-all clause (clause 5) which gives anything else not mentioned to one person, in this case John's wife. Such a clause makes argument well-nigh impossible.

More blatant thieving by alterations is also discouraged. The date – vital in the case of a will – is written in words since numbers are relatively easy to 'rearrange'. The very fixity of the form, the fact that everyone knows what should come where, also helps. Tacking on a new paragraph or omitting one would be noticed immediately.

I, **JOHN SMITH**, *of 99 Dronfield Road, Salford, in the Metropolitan County of Greater Manchester, company director, HEREBY REVOKE all wills and testamentary documents heretofore made by me and DECLARE this to be my LAST WILL AND TESTAMENT.*

1   *I APPOINT my wife Joan Smith, and my solicitor, Thomas Jones, to be jointly my executors of this my will.*

2   *I DEVISE my freehold cottage known as THE LILACS, at Coniston in the county of Cumbria, unto my son ROBERT SMITH in fee simple.*

3   *I BEQUEATH the following specific legacies:*
     (i)   to my son, Robert Smith, any motor-car I may own at the date of my death.
     (ii)   to my daughter Jane Smith, all my shares in the company known as Imperial Chemical Industries.
     (iii) to my said wife all my personal chattels not hereby bequeathed for her absolute use and benefit.

4   *I BEQUEATH the following pecuniary legacies:*
     (i)   To my daughter Jill Smith, the sum of £3000
     (ii)   To my daughter Jenny Smith, the sum of £3000

5   *I DEVISE AND BEQUEATH all the residue of my real and personal estate whatsoever and wheresoever not hereby or by any codicil hereto otherwise expressly disposed of as to my freeholds in fee simple and as to my personal estate absolutely unto my said wife, Joan Smith, for her own absolute use and benefit.*

6   *I DIRECT that any executor of this my Will being a solicitor or a person engaged in any profession or business, may be so employed and act and shall be entitled to make all proper professional charges for any work done by him or his firm in connection with my Estate including work done which an executor not being a solicitor or a person engaged as aforesaid could have done personally.*

IN WITNESS whereof I, the said John Smith, the Testator have to this my LAST WILL set my hand this thirty-first day of December One Thousand Nine Hundred and Ninety Eight.

SIGNED AND ACKNOWLEDGED by the above-named John Smith, the Testator, as and for his LAST WILL in the presence of us both present at the same time who at this request in his presence and in the presence of each other hereunto subscribed our names as witnesses:

John Smith _____
(signed)

Frank Ellis, (signed) _____   *Jeremy Goodall, (signed)* _____
6, The Crescent   *2, High Street,*
Salford,   *Bolton,*
Clerk   *Chartered Accountant*

The standard running order is as follows: first, the testator states that he revokes all previous wills and that this is his last one. (You'll see now why the date matters.) Key words like 'hereby revoke' and 'last will and testament' are capitalised for emphasis.

Next, two executors are appointed. One is normally a solicitor. This makes a lot of sense since the form of wills is very much written for a specialist audience – of solicitors!

Before the specific and pecuniary legacies we have the 'devising' of a freehold cottage in fee simple. At this point you should all recognise that this document is indeed written for lawyers and not for the man in the street. We may just have coped with the archaic 'hereby revoke', but we will not be familiar with this usage of 'devise' and I doubt whether any of us could hazard a guess as to what 'fee simple' means. I certainly couldn't! I know that it is from French, like much of the jargon of the legal trade, and I also know that many other legal words have been culled from Latin ('declaration', 'habeas corpus', for example), but to some extent I have to take it on trust that lawyers know their job and have good reasons for the use of such words.

The next section of the will stretches our faith in solicitors to its limits. It is the clause which, with surprising vagueness, states how much money the 'solicitor or any person engaged in proper, professional business' will be entitled to. It doesn't give any maximum! Instead it promises to pay 'proper professional charges'. The person who decides what those proper charges might be will, presumably, be the solicitor!

At the end of the will we have another cluster of set features. The testator – now referred to as 'the said testator' – 'sets his hand to' (an archaic version of signs) this, his last will. Two others, both in the presence of the testator, also sign it. They, too, are specified with full names and addresses.

And there we have it: a document designed to be clear and incontrovertible. A document written with lawyers in mind – only they and vicars talk about 'chattels'. It is not very lively to read, of course, because it is precisely designed to lack colour, personality and individuality: these would get in the way. John's being a Northerner, a keen amateur photographer and a working class man do not shine through; legal language is not the place for dialect forms and colloquialisms.

....

ACTIVITY ● ▨

Imagine that you are a solicitor. Wilf Woffler has come to consult you, bearing his stab at a last will. Rewrite it so that it is legal, i.e. clear and watertight. Don't forget the solicitor's payment clause!

```
19/8/98

I haven't got much but I want the house and most of the
cash to go to Barry. Our Freda can have £500 so long as
she looks after the cats. If the car passes its MOT our Jim
can have it 'cos his Mam can't drive. He can have me
cufflinks, too, if he'd like 'em.
```

I'd like me best mate, John, and Mr Clark on the High Street to do the business. I've got all me chairs at home.

Wilf Woffler

· ·

ACTIVITY ◐ 🗩

Next for your consideration is some business legal language of the type textbook writers receive. Quickly identify its field markers.

ALCS

protecting and promoting authors' rights

Annual General Meeting

NOTICE is hereby given that the Nineteenth Annual General Meeting of the Company will be held at New Connaught Rooms, Great Queen Street, London WC2 on Thursday 27th November 1997, at 6.45 p.m.

1 To receive and adopt the Council's Report and Accounts for the period 1 April, 1996 to 31 March, 1997.

2 In accordance with the Articles of Association of the Company, the following elected members of the Council are retiring:
   Chris Barlas
   John Bowen
   and, being eligible, Chris Barlas offers himself for re-election.

   Nominations to fill both vacancies should be in the prescribed form and sent to ALCS by 13th November, 1997. (See note overleaf.)

3 To re-appoint Messrs Feltons, Chartered Accountants, of 12 Sheet Street, Windsor as Auditors of the Company and to authorise the Directors (i.e. the Council) to fix their remuneration.

4 To consider and, if thought fit, pass the following resolution as a Special Resolution:

   a) THAT the Articles of Association of the Company be and they hereby are amended by adding to Clause 1 the following sub-paragraph:

   (xxviv) 'Performing right' in relation to any literary, dramatic or musical work means the right to perform the work in public excluding the right in any work which has been previously assigned to any society in any country whose principal object is to administer the said right.

   b) THAT the Articles of Association of the Company be and they hereby are amended by adding to paragraph (o) of Article 7 the following sub-paragraph:

   (x) The performing right

5 To consider and, if thought fit, pass the following resolution as a Special Resolution:

b) THAT the Articles of Association of the Company be and they hereby are amended by inserting to sub-paragraph (iv) of paragraph (c) of Article 7 the following phrase (as emboldened):

(iv) the right to communicate the work to the public by any means of cable diffusion which expression includes diffusion over any path provided by a material substance or by retransmission or rebroadcasting of the work to the public by the technical means known as MMDS or any similar technical means of omnidirectional microwave or ultra high frequency transmission using terrestrial transmitters or other terrestrial equipment;

BY ORDER OF THE BOARD

Christopher Zielinski, Company Secretary

27th October 1997

Authors' Licensing & Collecting Society Ltd
Registered Office: Marlborough Court. 14–18 Holborn. London EC1N 2LE.
tel: 0171 395 0600 . fax 0171 395 0660

Other fields of use

ACTIVITIES

Here are four further identifiable worlds. In groups of four, take one each and list 10 markers of its field. Read your lists to one another, checking whether the markers make the fields obvious, i.e. whether you can match the markers to the text at a glance.

Jurassic mark

An important new chunk of fossil ichthyosaur – a dolphin like reptile – has been discovered in Jurassic rocks near Lyme Regis, *writes Michael Taylor*. Though the 200-million-year-old fossil comprises just the end of the body and tail, it does contain traces of petrified soft tissues, unlike most other specimens. Especially valuable is the outline of its tail fin, according to David Martill of the University of Portsmouth *(Palaeontology, vol. 38, pp897–903)*. This confirms that some ichthyosaurs had acquired a fish-like tail early in the Jurassic period, and should help palaeontologists understand how it evolved for more efficient swimming. The fossil is now on show at the Yorkshire Museum.

Pandora's début

Zoologists have discovered a new animal species which is so distinctive that they have placed it in a new phylum, the Cycliophora, *writes Stephen Young*. Animals are classified in 35 or so phyla according to their basic body plan – examples include molluscs, chordates and arthropods – and the discovery of a new phylum is of major importance. *Symbion pandora* is less than a millimetre long and lives on the mouthparts of Norway lobsters, according to Peter Funch and Reinhardt Kristensen of Copenhagen University *(Nature, vol. 378, pp711–4)*. Periodically, it produces internal buds that replace its entire feeding apparatus, and it can reproduce both asexually – via a mobile stage called the pandora larva – and sexually. The tiny male spends its life perched on the female.

① **The common tern** is the yardstick by which to judge the rest. Adults are pale grey, paler beneath, white around the tail. By early autumn they have a white forehead. The forked tail may lose its tapered streamers, the wings – in moult – can look a little ragged. Compared with arctics, they are longer-billed, longer-necked, shorter-tailed, with longer, broader inner wings, *darker streaks* on the top of the longest wing feathers (primaries) and broad, dusky tips to the outer six or so beneath; *translucent only behind the 'wrist'.*

② **Arctic terns** are more refined than commons, lighter, neater, the wingtip longer, *more tapered and more translucent*, the inner wing shorter. Since they do not moult here, the wingtip is smoother in autumn because no feathers are missing and the black cap remains almost complete. The bill is shorter and spikier, all red, the tail longer, legs shorter. Above, the wingtip looks *cleaner, smoother grey*; below the wing is purer white with a thinner, sharper dark line along the rear edge towards the tip which is *translucent*.

③ **The black tern** is often over freshwater but does fly over the sea: it is only a migrant in the UK (the others nest here) and appears over lakes and reservoirs far inland for a day or two, sometimes in big flocks scattered all over a lake. Autumn black terns are small, *mid-grey* above *(including the tail)*, with a white forehead, a black cap extending over the sides of the head like ear flaps and a black bill. The underside is white but the grey back spills over in front of the wing into a short, dark *smudge of grey* on the side of the chest.

Black terns feed by dipping to the surface (which commons and arctics often do over freshwater), not by diving.

④ **Sandwich terns** are bigger, paler; with *long, black bills*; longer, *black* (not red) legs and longer, angled wings. The outer wing looks uneven in autumn because of moult and has blackish streaks on top; the tail is short. The forehead is white from June or July, leaving a speckled crown and a spiky black crest at the back of the head. Sandwich terns look especially pale, call distinctive, grating, rhythmic sounds, like *kia-rink* or *kierik* and dive in for fish with particularly dramatic headlong dives. Young ones have dark tail tips and brownish speckling above.

⑤ **Little terns** are *small*, fast-flying, frenetic terns, always with white foreheads and *yellow bills and feet*, never red. They look very pale, except for a thin, solid black triangle on the outermost wing feathers. They are usually at the coast, diving for fish right at the water's edge in rolling surf.

From THE SERENGETI to the VICTORIA FALLS

Visiting the Great Game Parks of Tanzania – the Serengeti, Lake Manyara, Ngorongoro Crater, the Tarangire & Victoria Falls

This journey takes the traveller directly to Kilimanjaro and the great game parks of Tanzania without the need to make tedious road journeys from Kenya and back again. Here, over the course of a week, we shall visit the Serengeti, Lake Manyara, Ngorongoro Crater, Tarangire National Park and Arusha to witness the wildlife wonders which are available here in such profusion. Accommodation has been arranged at the 5-star Sopa lodges which command outstanding locations in the parks and offer a wide range of facilities for the traveller.

From Kilimanjaro fly directly to Victoria Falls for seven nights at the 5 star Elephant Hills Hotel. Over the course of the next week you can relax in the hotel's extensive grounds which includes an 18-hole golf course or participate in one of the many different excursion programmes: a Zambezi Sunset cruise, the Flight of Angles over the Falls or a visit to the Falls close up on both the Zimbabwe and Zambian sides. In addition you may visit the Hwange Game Reserve or Chobe National Park, just across the border into Botswana. Whatever your choice the stay at the Falls will be an experience to be remembered.

Itinerary

Day 1 Depart London Gatwick in the evening via Luxor to Kilimanjaro with Monarch Airways Boeing 757. Journey through the night.

Day 2 Arrive Kilimanjaro in the morning and transfer directly to Tarangire National Park and more particularly the 5-star Sopa Lodge with its fine facilities to spend the next two nights. After unwinding make a late afternoon game drive as a general orientation to our visit to the park.

Day 3 Tarangire gets its name from the river that threads its way through the length of the reserve and is famous for the dense wildlife population including wildebeest, zebra, eland, elephant, leopard, buffalo and the fringe-eared oryx which migrate from the Masai steppe to the Tarangire River with lions and other predators following the herds. Make both an early morning and late afternoon game drive.

Day 4 Depart after breakfast to Serengeti National Park, on the way visiting Olduvai Gorge the site of the Leakey family's famous excavations for the origins of man. Continue to the 5-star Serengeti Sopa Lodge and spend the next two nights.

Day 5 The Serengeti is undoubtedly one of the world's last great wildlife refuges which covers an area of some 5,700 square miles. It is here that once a year a million wildebeest and zebra gather to make their migrations. The area is home to some of the largest concentrations of wildlife anywhere set against the backdrop of stunning scenery. During our stay we shall visit various parts of the park and observe its many different aspects.

Day 6 After breakfast travel to the world famous Ngorongoro Crater and the 5-star Ngorongoro Sopa Lodge to spend the next two nights. The hotel has a fine restaurant, swimming pool, bar and magnificent views over the crater.

Day 7 Today make a visit to the crater's rim affording awe-inspiring views, including savannah, lakes, rivers, swamps and, with aid of binoculars, it may just be possible to spot grazing wildlife. Then descend into the crater itself. This is the area where the Masai graze their cattle cheek by jowl with some 25,000 animal species including zebra, wildebeest and hyenas. Return to the hotel for the night.

with an optional 7-night extension to Grand Comore
14 nights from £1695.00

Day 8 Today travel to Gibbs Farm, a beautiful family homestead set in a coffee plantation for a welcome rest, before proceeding to Lake Manyara with its teeming wildlife, especially birds. Later continue to the town of Arusha and, if time permits, visit the snake park at Meserani. Overnight at the Mt Meru Novotel.

Day 9 After breakfast transfer to Kilimanjaro airport for the flight to Victoria Falls (approx 2½ hours). On arrival transfer to the 5-star Elephant Hills for the next seven nights. See supplement for the Victoria Falls Hotel. Please refer to page 21 for details of optional excursions around Victoria Falls.

Day 16 Depart Victoria Falls in the morning and connect with the flight from Kilimanjaro to London Gatwick arriving in the evening of the same day. Since the flight operates via Grand Comore you may elect to extend with a 7-night sojourn at Le Galawa Beach Hotel.

Sopa Lodges

Probably the finest accommodations in the game parks the Sopa Lodges (the Masai word for welcome) are truly 5 star and come with all the modern facilities that you might expect at this category including full private facilities, extensive public areas and many with swimming pools – making them ideal bases from which to explore and relax.

The Elephant Hills Hotel

Three kilometres up from the roar of the Falls, Elephant Hills in unique in both style and location. This world-class resort provides a truly spectacular panorama combining the wilderness of the Zambezi River and its surroundings with the plush fairways of the famous golf course. Apart from golf, there is tennis, squash, swimming and a wide range of boating and game viewing activities. With its 276 luxury rooms, its expansive swimming area and its sophisticated casino, Elephant Hills provides a memorable blend of luxury and wilderness.

espite their efforts, the Malicounda women were reviled as revolutionaries and publicity seekers who had betrayed their Bambara race and sold out to the West. However, they still managed to take their message to neighbouring villages, using plays to catch the conscience of the chiefs and Imans.

Villagers in nearby Ngerin Bambara declared that they, too, should stop this practice. Oureye Sall, who is president of their women's association, should have succeeded her cutter mother. Oureye revealed that when her mother circumcised her granddaughter the girl nearly bled to death. When Oureye took her daughter to the doctor, she pretended that the girl had fallen out of a mango tree, but no one was fooled. This detail has been incorporated into Malicounda's touring play.

'We worried that our children might not get married if they weren't circumcised,' says Oureye, 'but I have seen too much blood. We must tell the truth.'

Since then the women's pledge to end the mutilation – the Oath of Malicounda – has gathered momentum. Earlier this year they were joined by 13 other villagers pledging the Declaration of Diabougou, and then by several villages in the Korda region. Now the word of the Malicounda women has spread throughout the Senegal. The country's President, Abdou Diouf, who declared FGM a human rights issue after the oath, has recommended that it be included in forthcoming legislation. And in April, the women received the ultimate blessing: the US president wife Hillary Clinton invited them to attend a Dakar human rights discussion as special guests.

As Molly drives into Malicounda she is welcomed with dancing, drumming, a special performance of the play and lengthy speeches. The village's Iman says that the taboo

ACTIVITIES

Scientific: Collect scientific prose examples and then rank order them as archetypal examples of the genre. You could calculate the ratio of specialist to non-specialist words; or the incidence of passive verb forms; or the use of Latin and Greek words as measures.

Technical: Compose a reader's guide to technical language, clearly differentiating it from scientific. The number of sophisticated as opposed to specialist terms might help here; so might a comparison of sentence types; so might a consideration of the nature of the graphics.

Adverts: Rather than getting embroiled in the persuasive features of these texts (of which many!) we want you to consider layout and tone. What sort of fonts do ad men use? Are there any conventions? Which mode do you consider most ads to be in? – i.e. are they truly 'written'?

Journalese: The best way to get a clear reminder of the techniques of journalism is to re-render some information as a news article. Compare it and the original. Not only will you (we hope) have added visual markers such as headlines, straplines and columns; you'll also have used buts and ands at the start of sentences, puns and alliteration. If you haven't, go back to the drawing board!

was not imposed by Islam but by husbands, 'like parents who tell their children there is a hyena on the road to scare them, but one day the children discover there is no hyena'.

Issa Tou Saan, who was a respected cutter in Diabougou, where the girls were circumcised at seven years old, tells me: 'I was very angry when I first saw the Malicounda women's play. We did it to protect the girls from getting pregnant before marriage. I cut very quickly and no girl ever haemorrhaged. They would stand up immediately afterwards, hold their breasts and declare they were real women.

'I did it to my own daughters and granddaughters, who never cried. Never. They felt they shared something special.'

Then Issa Tou Saan attended Tostan's education programme and learned about circumcision's often deadly consequences. 'Please don't condemn me,' she urges. 'I didn't know.'

In the tiny village of Tatin Bambara, the village elders, rather than the women, elect to respond to Molly's questions. Producing a leather-bound Koran, the Iman leafs through pages, then declares, 'Mohammed had been travelling from Mecca to Medina when he met two midwives about to cut a woman. He urged that she should be gentle.' The Tatin women look on miserably as he opines: 'Cutting honours women and makes them more beautiful.'

In the small town of M'bour, conversation grows sticky in the molten glow of the late afternoon sun. A young woman demands to know why the Malicounda women have ignored a Muslim woman's duty to be circumcised and caused Senegalese women to be insulted by Mrs Clinton. As the woman grows more indignant, Molly explains why FGM is such a health risk.

'Bring your Tostan programme here,' demands the woman, 'and let us decide.'

FGM – female genital mutilation

The Times Educational Supplement, 1998 Friday 11 September

THE FIELD OF BATTLE – SPECIALISM AND JARGON

I think we all know specialist lexis when we see it. It's a useful exercise to identify 20 of your own specialist language uses. Consider your job, and hobbies. This reminds you we all have specialist language.

However, also ask yourself when does necessarily specialist language which communicates effectively, become jargon – that is, unnecessarily bewildering terms designed to exclude non-specialists? We may as well begin with the million-dollar question!

The answer may lie in another question: has the language-user adopted agreed-by-all-interested-parties labels to simplify matters, or needlessly elaborated the simple to boost his ego and trample yours?

This question is usually relatively easy to answer. We are not offended if a mechanic refers to camshafts and tick-overs – such terms are clearly the shorthand of his trade. If I chose to, I could make the effort and learn the basic vocabulary needed to talk about car engines, but I prefer not to. It is a different matter, I suspect, if a doctor tells me to exercise my cardio-vascular system when he means get my heart beat going: it is less clear, it is liable to be misunderstood and it is unhelpful. He is using jargon, and his main purpose seems to be to remind me that he understands these things and I don't. He wishes to preserve the mystique of his profession. Clearly, this is not what we, as contributors to the National Health Service, are paying our doctors for: we'd prefer to be enlightened and reassured, not baffled and put down.

Doctors are an obvious example, but most professionals can, and on occasion do, play the same game. The average parent is bewildered by talk of objective assessment, unit accreditation and profiling. What is worse, the teacher who is glibly trotting out these formulae is well aware of the fact; and since teachers are paid to be good communicators, such linguistic tactlessness is even more unforgivable. So why does he do it?

The first and most charitable construction that we can place on his behaviour is that he does not know that he's doing it: the specialist terminology has become so familiar that he fails to notice that he's using it. He has the same problem, arguably, that any adult has when talking to a child: how do you recognise the hard bits when to you it's all easy? Predicting which parts of your everyday language will be bewildering or offensive to others can be genuinely problematic.

All of us belong to several speech communities (that is, groups of people who talk in the same way because they're all Mancunians or teenagers or lawyers). We switch styles in different company so as to fit in, just as surely as we change our dress. Certain specialists such as civil servants, lawyers and doctors seem to find the quick verbal change difficult. However, if specialists are to interact successfully with the rest of humanity, they need to recognise the common core of their language and keep their specialist vocabulary strictly separated from it.

The sad truth is that some specialists are not prepared to go to this trouble, in the first place because they are lazy and do not want to sieve what they say to check its appropriateness; in the second place because knowing fancy, specialist terms makes them feel good. They haven't studied their subject for donkey's years in order never to display their esoteric knowledge! Words are valuable social weapons and it is only human not to want to yield a hard-won advantage.

What jargon users need to recognise is that their stunning array of abstruse terms is not an advantage in the human game of communication: the little they gain on the 'cleverness' scale is more than outweighed by the loss on the 'sensitivity' one. Perhaps if they wanted to have their cake and eat it they could use the specialist term (subtext 'Look how clever I am') but then translate it for you (subtext 'Look how considerate I am'). However, having to express everything you say twice is rather time-consuming and, one suspects, would rapidly become very irritating.

Many of the readers of this book, consisting as they do of an educational elite, are the potential specialists – and jargon users – of the future. Perhaps you ought to reach a decision now, on both a practical and a human basis, that jargon, if used to the general public, is not 'worth what it does cost the keeping'. You can bully, but not persuade those whom you make to feel inadequate; you might inspire awe but not affection and co-operation. So ask yourself very seriously, is it worth it? Isn't language supposed to be a bridge builder, not destroyer?

In case anyone remains unclear what jargon looks and sounds like, we are going to look at some prime examples. But before we do, it might be an idea to isolate certain elements of jargon in a more systematic way.

Features of jargon

Words are often long and needlessly confusing. Additions to words are often Latin or Greek prefixes and suffixes.

Euphemisms abound! Governments don't bomb, they give 'air support'; you aren't promiscuous, you 'practise distributive sex', and you don't become pregnant you're 'in an interesting condition'.

Certain **vogue words** which are trendy are oft-used by jargonauts. Thus interfaces, facilities and situations co-exist; facilitators enable and share; people flag up their problems and get on board to address them.

Tricks for **stretching language** are used: nouns become noun phrases, so that a canteen is now a refreshment facility, a dustman is a refuse disposal operative and the blind are visually challenged.

Empty phrases and **fillers** are also used. Some favourites include 'at this point in time', 'from where I stand' and 'it seems to me'.

Needless verbs are added: for example, we now perform an investigation rather than investigating. This makes for a rather pompous, 're-stating the obvious' style.

This pomposity often comes out in **stock phrases**, which politicians seem especially fond of. They tell us 'it must be understood/noted/remembered' and 'cannot be stressed/emphasised too strongly'. Towards the end of their speeches (and far too often, towards the end of English essays) we find 'in conclusion/to sum up/ to summarise'.

Redundant features (i.e. extra words that add nothing to meaning) are merely an irritation; other features of jargon are more sinister. The **use of the passive** is a case in point. This is a well-known ploy for avoiding responsibility: jargonauts don't like to be quoted! Jargon can also be used to fudge and positively mislead.

....

ACTIVITY ▪ 💬

Our first example below splendidly fulfils two of the three aims of jargon: it is very much for insiders and it is certainly out to impress. Before you are told anything about the passage, see what you make of it. See whether the text has any of the hallmarks of jargon which are specified. Do try not to use our guide as a 'shopping list', though.

Try to decide two things:

1   What is there, and
2   Why it is there.

....

GUIDELINES FOR INITIAL DISTRICT CONSIDERATIONS

The enclosed (blue) documents are included to assist Districts in their deliberations regarding TVEI (E). The process can be seen in six stages.

1   <u>A Consideration and Definition of the District Consortium</u>. The large chart has been designed to illustrate to colleagues that districts

already provide a considerable service to young people. What is perhaps not readily available at present is an overview, both to individual providers and more importantly to young people. The initial task is therefore to take stock in the form of a

2   District Audit. This is not intended solely as a paper exercise but as an opportunity to bring together the various agencies at District level to more fully understand and appreciate the variety of provision available and the role of education, training, industry and the community in the lives of young people. It is anticipated that this process will form the basis for a cohesive approach to policy and planning between education, training, industry and the community, the first stage of which will be

3   Establishing Aims and Objectives for the District. This is an essential criterion in establishing TVEI (E) consortia at the District level and affords the opportunity for continuing, or establishing, working relationships on a sound footing. To achieve this degree of commonality of purpose it will be necessary to establish a

4   Consultation Programme. This may be seen in three stages
    i)   March/April 1987 – initial district response to meet the April 10th deadline
    ii) April–July 1987 – detailed district response
    iii) September 1987–August 1988 – the proposed consultation/TVEI (E) lead-in year

5   The District Management Structure is to be indicated on the pro forma. Particular attention may be drawn to the representative and cohesive nature of such a structure to reflect the multiplicity of interests in the proposal as outlined in Part A, Review.

6   Further Consultations between April 1987 and August 1988 will focus upon possible delivery mechanisms e.g. cluster arrangements; defining specific curriculum developments; determining support strategies and presenting individual institution curriculum responses.

You might end up with notes along the lines of the following:

Specific features of jargon

Latinate words: 'consortia', 'criterion', 'pro forma'

Euphemisms: 'young people', 'facilitators'

Vogue words: 'overview', 'providers'

Noun phrases: 'commonality of purpose', 'possible delivery mechanisms'

Needless repetition: 'aims and objectives', 'understand and appreciate', 'continuing' and 'establishing'

Fillers: 'on a sound footing'

Passives: the chart has been designed; the process can be seen; documents are included.

ACTIVITY ⬤ 🗗

Now you have your notes and ours, try to write an analysis of the piece. It comes, by the way, from an educational manager to his staff. It ought to fill your heart with pity for teachers!

••

This passage purports to inform – sorry! – pretends to tell you something. The six numbered points give a veneer of organisation, but try to summarise what it says. Difficult, isn't it? Let's look at why.

First of all, there is no honest statement of opinion. This would be appropriate if the document were totally objective yet in fact it is not. A point of view is implicit in 'overview' (someone has to provide it) and 'commonality of purpose' (someone has decided that this is desirable). The writer seems to have made decisions which he is unwilling to take responsibility for, hence the passive form of the verbs: 'the chart has been designed', 'the process can be seen' and 'documents are included'. Thus also the total absence of the first person pronouns, which are replaced by demonstratives: 'This is' and 'This is not'.

Next we are struck by the vagueness of so many of the words. Look at the title: 'Guidelines for Initial District Considerations'. Of these words, only 'district' is a concrete noun with precise meaning; the rest make no firm promises. These guidelines provide an 'opportunity' and 'may be seen': again no quotable commitment. This feeling we have of vagueness derives from all the abstract nouns. No-one can pin down what 'a cohesive approach' and 'possible delivery mechanisms' are. This last – 'possible delivery mechanisms' – is a high-faluting noun phrase replacing the more straightforward ways to deliver (noun + verb). There are very many long nominal phrases in this text. Two particularly extended ones are 'The basis for a cohesive approach to policy and planning between education, training, industry and the community' and 'The representative and cohesive nature of such a structure'.

The elaborate, formal nature of the language disguises the fact that there is little content. This writer prefers to employ formulae and avoid simple lexis, so we have 'commonality of purpose' and not same aim, and 'support strategies' rather than help. There are many more!

In this document, we never find a small word where a larger one will do. Thus 'institution' is used for centre, 'initial' for first and 'solely' for only. All these words are used to assure the reader that the writer knows his stuff. For good measure he throws in a few educational vogue words: teachers become 'providers', basis is 'criterion' and groups are 'consortia'. Jargon writers love Latinate words: they sound so much more impressive!

It is easy to mock, but in fact it's very easy to slip into jargon yourself in the misguided belief that it's the appropriate register. If people are really unaware of doing it, this is very worrying. It is even more disturbing when politicians, the armed forces and lawyers, amongst others, use jargon with a deliberate euphemistic purpose so that the unpalatable becomes acceptable: a leading politician keeps the president in the dark to provide a 'plausible deniability situation'; a bombing raid is re-christened a 'pre-emptive strike' and a jail is a 'total incarceration facility'.

As far as using language to fudge goes, estate agents probably take the gold medal. Having recently bought a house, I am now able to offer the world:

A receiver's guide to the language of estate agents

Terraced houses become 'cottages' or 'quasi-semis', which are not cramped but 'deceptively spacious', not falling apart but 'offering plenty of scope for flair and personalisation'. 'Ideal for first time buyer' means cheap and probably nasty; 'ideal for professional couple' indicates that it has one bedroom, a tiny kitchen and no garden. The 'low overheads' which sound so attractive turn out to mean that the house is cheap to heat because it is minuscule.

Translating can be fun but it's no joke for those innocent first-time buyers seeking out their dream home – they are shamefully misled and inevitably disappointed.

ACTIVITY ◼ 💬

Collect 5 different estate agent's sheets. Identify common features, then try to identify and group the different agents' house styles.

The jargon of estate agents is mainly a matter of imprecision and exaggeration. Very different is that of the academic. This sort of language, whether it intends to or not, tends to exclude and intimidate the outsider. Here is an example from a field we are all interested in – Linguistics:

> These quasi-physical aspects of technical organisation – time, physical shape, sound pattern – have all been regarded as less important in the novel (and in prose generally). Novels are generally less punctuated in space, the printed lines reach regularly to the margin, encouraging fast, unbroken reading. But it is clear that the conventions of spatio-temporal attention and reading speed, applied to two different genres, differ relatively not absolutely.

Well? What did you make of that? Let me translate it into plainer English:

> People normally notice the look of and sound of words in a novel less than in a poem. This is because the words aren't chopped up into lines and so you read them quickly. In fact, attention to detail and speed of reading are only less noticeable when reading prose, not unnecessary.

I think that is what the writer meant. I can't pretend to be certain what 'the conventions of spatio-temporal attention' are – and this despite the fact that linguistics is my discipline.

ACTIVITY ◼ ▧

Here are some more examples. Try to translate the first one into simpler English. Get rid of unnecessarily long or meaningless words. Avoid the passive where you can. Look at repetition of nouns and verbs. See if you can reduce sentence length.

It is precisely and only because it is in this and other ways possible to assess philosophical expertise independently of any judgement of the truth or falsity of some particular position that we are able to conduct university examinations which set questions in philosophy as opposed to questions asking what some philosopher as a matter of fact said.

Nevertheless, although generally distinctions can be seen as relevant or irrelevant and arguments to be valid or invalid independent of any categorical assessment of the truth or falsity of premises or conclusions in a particular case, a collection of premises may be known to be true, and then, given also suitable arguments we may claim to know the conclusions derived from those statements.

ACTIVITY ◼ ▧

Having flexed your muscles on that text, have a look at two more. These are from a Trade Union Booklet and a police training book respectively. For each, try to make sense of it, try to summarise it and analyse it.

LEGAL AND PROFESSIONAL SERVICES

The review of legal services was concluded with positive decisions in line with the development of a structure of regional delivery. The ready and prompt availability of efficient and effective legal services was reaffirmed as a crucial feature of union benefit. Problems in established practice were quickly identified by the review. There has been an enormous increase in the volume of law affecting teachers and the education service. This had the effect of narrowing the delivery of legal services to those members who are sensitive to the fact that they have problems which they need to have addressed. Many others have faced the fact that legal changes have been interpreted to their disadvantage.

Combined with this has been a massive escalation in legal costs expended through the established use of the Union's local Solicitor system – a figure for 1987 over two and a half times the 1983 figure. This represents an expenditure on casework problem-solving rather than problem prevention involving delivery to only a narrow section of the membership.

National Union of Teachers

PRINCIPAL DIFFERENCES BETWEEN FELONIES AND MISDEMEANOURS:

1   The distinction between principals and accessories is recognised in felonies.

2   To compound a felony is a criminal offence.

3   The powers of arrest without warrant are wider in felonies than in misdemeanours.

4   In felony the prisoner must be tried at the bar, he is given in charge to the jury and must be in the dock throughout the proceedings. The form of the oath taken by the jury varies therefore in felonies and misdemeanours.

5   A person convicted of felony may be ordered to pay compensation not exceeding £100 for loss of property caused by the felony.

6   Conviction of some felonies involves a disqualification for certain offices.

Harris: *Criminal Law*

You will, we hope, by now be aware that jargon does exist and can exist in many forms with several possible purposes.

WHAT MANNER OF WORDS? THE QUESTION OF TENOR

Tenor is mostly about formality levels. Certain contexts or situations require different degrees of informality.

When the pressure builds up to an intolerable level, people let off steam by swearing and stamping their feet. They don't even require an audience. My sister-in-law, an extremely polite, rather quiet person, can often be heard chunnering when a sponge cake has stayed as flat as a pancake or a piece of steak has refused to tenderise 'Oh, sod it all!' My brother, sensible man that he is, keeps well out of the way until the swearing is done before going in to make helpful and reassuring noises.

We have all done it. Our terms vary, of course, depending which particular taboos we recognise. Some of us will strew 'bloodies' and 'buggers' around pretty freely, but avoid 'the F word' (except for really violent outbursts); others of us will use any swear word but jib at blaspheming because we, or someone we care about, believes in God. Even in swearing, most of us have our standards!

Part of the socialising process in every culture is learning which words and phrases are totally unacceptable, and which can be used on special occasions. Swear words are an important part of the lexicon, which is why it seems a pity if they are used endlessly and gratuitously — not because it offends us but because, like any medicine, they lose their efficacy when overused. Everyone builds up a tolerance to them and they lose their impact. They cease to signal anything, except perhaps insensitivity. And what do constant swearers have recourse to when they really need to let go?

Like individuals, cultures build up a store bank of insults, depending on what matters in their social setting. Different groupings develop different ritual insults. In some cultures the way to wind someone up is by being suggestive or rude about their mother; in others by casting doubt about their gender or parentage; in yet others by comparing them to a camel or donkey. We all know, by a certain age, what really hurts – how best to get the verbal boot in. It may not be nice, but it's a fact of life and language.

ACTIVITIES

It's a useful exercise to identify how we manifest strong emotion and intimacy linguistically. Take a look at two examples: one is literary but we judge it to be realistic. See if you agree. For each text decide how an informal, emotive tenor is conveyed. Separate the realistic spoken examples from the literary and dramatic.

The first is taken from Arthur Miller's *Death of a Salesman*. In this scene, Biff, Willy's eldest son, is trying to convince his father that both of them are insignificant, failed men. Willy cannot accept this and the scene is full of strong and varied emotion.

BIFF: Dad, you're never going to see what I am, so what's the use of arguing? If I strike oil I'll send you a cheque. Meantime forget I'm alive.

WILLY [*to* LINDA]: Spite, see?

BIFF: Shake hands, Dad.

WILLY: Not my hand.

BIFF: I was hoping not to go this way.

WILLY: Well, this is the way you're going, Good-bye.

[BIFF *looks at him a moment, then turns sharply and goes to the stairs.*]

WILLY [*stops him with*]: May you rot in hell if you leave this house!

BIFF [*turning*]: Exactly what is it that you want from me?

WILLY: I want you to know, on the train, in the mountains, in the valleys, wherever you go, that you cut down your life for spite!

BIFF: No, no.

WILLY: Spite, spite, is the word of your undoing! And when you're down and out, remember what did it. When you're rotting somewhere beside the railroad tracks, remember, and don't you dare blame it on me!

BIFF: I'm not blaming it on you!

WILLY: I won't take the rap for this, you hear?

[HAPPY *comes down the stairs and stands on the bottom step, watching.*]

BIFF: That's just what I'm telling you!

WILLY: [*sinking into a chair at the table, with full accusation*]: You're trying to put a knife in me – don't think I don't know what you're doing!

BIFF: All right, phony! Then let's lay it on the line. [*He whips the rubber tube out of his pocket and puts it on the table.*]

HAPPY: You crazy –

LINDA: Biff! [*She moves to grab the hose, but* BIFF *holds it down with his hand.*]

BIFF: Leave it there! Don't move it!

WILLY [*not looking at it*]: What is that?

BIFF: You know goddam well what that is.

WILLY [*caged, wanting to escape*]: I never saw that.

BIFF: You saw it. The mice didn't bring it into the cellar! What is this supposed to do, make a hero out of you? This is supposed to make me sorry for you?

WILLY: Never heard of it.

BIFF: There'll be no pity for you, you hear it? No pity!

WILLY [*to* LINDA]: You hear the spite!

BIFF: No, you're going to hear the truth – what you are and what I am!

LINDA: Stop it!

WILLY: Spite!

HAPPY [*coming down toward* BIFF]: You cut it now!

BIFF [*to* HAPPY]: The man don't know who we are! The man is gonna know! [*To* WILLY] We never told the truth for ten minutes in this house!

HAPPY: We always told the truth!

BIFF [*turning on him*]: You big blow, are you the assistant buyer? You're one of the two assistants to the assistant, aren't you?

HAPPY: Well, I'm practically …

BIFF: You're practically full of it! We all are! And I'm through with it. [*To* WILLY] Now hear this, Willy, this is me.

WILLY: I know you!

BIFF: You know why I had no address for three months? I stole a suit in Kansas City and I was in jail. [*To* LINDA, *who is sobbing*] Stop crying, I'm through with it.

[LINDA *turns away from them, her hands covering her face.*]

WILLY: I suppose that's my fault!

BIFF: I stole myself out of every good job since high school!

WILLY: And whose fault is that?

BIFF: And I never got anywhere because you blew me so full of hot air I could never stand taking orders from anybody! That's whose fault it is!

WILLY: I hear that!

LINDA: Don't, Biff!

BIFF: It's goddam time you heard that! I had to be boss big shot in two weeks, and I'm through with it!

WILLY: Then hang yourself! For spite, hang yourself!

Arthur Miller: Death of a Salesman

ACTIVITY ◐ ▧

Next consider this slice of 'real life drama'. What can you deduce about the two speakers C and D, and what are the linguistic hallmarks of a real row?

C I've put up with your bullshit for years and I'm not f–ing well putting up with any more.

D Don't you eff in front of my wife. Gerrout before I kick you out.

C You and whose army? Anyway, I didn't know it was her turn.

D Oh, that's typical of you, bloody smart-arse. Not man enough to fight fair… no respect for your elders and betters. If I were…

C Spare me the impotent man's futile threats. I'll leave when I'm ready.

D You'll leave now. This bloody minute. Christ, you've got a nerve. You come in here; you swear like a trooper for all your fancy language and stuck-up accent. You think you're somebody but …

C I think I'm wasting valuable time arguing with an ignoramus like you. You'll be telling me what I 'turned round and said' next.

D Southern bloody jessie!

C Well, I think we've plumbed the last depths of your ingenuity now, so I'll say goodnight. Are you coming, Ann?

D Our Annie's stayin 'ere where she belongs.

I think it's clear that the two people in this extract are of a different educational level and wage verbal warfare in different ways. Analyse the language use of each of them and then the interaction between them.

■ If you were the unfortunate Ann, would you go or stay?

■ Do you sympathise more with C or D?

■ How does this transcription indicate accent? Does it matter?

Attempt an analysis yourself before looking at my comments.

This argument took place between a working-class, relatively uneducated man of 55 and his middle-class graduate son-in-law of 35. Was all that fairly obvious? If it wasn't, look back and see if you can tell, now that you know.

The older man uses assertion and imperatives in an attempt to be forceful. He tells the younger man to 'Gerrout' (notice the non-standard accent). His language, angry as he clearly is, is liberally sprinkled with taboo words like 'smart-arse', 'bloody' and 'Christ'. However, he does not use 'the F word', which, in his terms, is only acceptable when ladies aren't present.

His son-in-law's pun on 'in front of your wife' (he pretends his mother-in-law wanted to swear first) makes his contempt clear: he treats the older man's anger as a joke. He deliberately uses sophisticated words like 'ignoramus', 'impotent' and 'ingenuity' to wrong-foot his opponent. The opponent's only reply is abuse: 'Southern bloody jessie!'

There is little doubt that the younger man 'wins' the fight: he keeps cool enough to make sarcastic remarks, for example mocking the northern phrase 'turn round and say'; he interrupts the older man; he decides when to accelerate the row and when to stop it. Whether this is a good purpose to put a university education to is another question...

From the other end of the formality spectrum, consider these *written* General Arrest Conditions.

25. (1) Where a constable has reasonable grounds for suspecting that any offence which is not an arrestable offence has been committed or attempted, or is being committed or attempted, he may arrest the relevant person if it appears to him that service of a summons is impracticable or inappropriate because any of the general arrest conditions is satisfied.

(2) In this section, 'the relevant person' means any person whom the constable has reasonable grounds to suspect of having committed or having attempted to commit the offence or of being in the course of committing or attempting to commit it.

(3) The general arrest conditions are

  (a) that the name of the relevant person is unknown to, and cannot be readily ascertained by, the constable;

  (b) that the constable has reasonable grounds for doubting whether a name furnished by the relevant person as his name is his real name;

  (c) that
    (i) the relevant person has failed to furnish a satisfactory address for service; or
    (ii) the constable has reasonable grounds for doubting whether an address furnished by the relevant person is a satisfactory address for service;

  (d) that the constable has reasonable grounds for believing that arrest is necessary to prevent the relevant person –
    (i) causing physical harm to himself or any other person;
    (ii) suffering physical injury;
    (iii) causing loss of or damage to property;
    (iv) committing an offence against public decency; or
    (v) causing an unlawful obstruction of the highway;

  (e) that the constable has reasonable grounds for believing that arrest is necessary to protect a child or other vulnerable person from the relevant person.

(4) For the purposes of subsection (3) above an address is a satisfactory address for service if it appears to the constable –

  (a) that the relevant person will be at it for a sufficiently long period for it to be possible to serve him with a summons; or

  (b) that some other person specified by the relevant person will accept service of a summons for the relevant person at it.

Harris: *Criminal Law*

ACTIVITY

Which of the features of the 'Arrest Conditions' remind you of instructive and technical writing? Jot down the striking features of this text. You need not write a full analysis since it ought to be clear to you by now what you would include.

ACTIVITY

A more useful, and hopefully more interesting, exercise might be to re-render this information as spoken instruction, thus changing its manner, i.e. its formality level, and also its mode. You will see that hard and fast subdivisions are difficult to achieve in English language.

Imagine that you are an instructor at the police training academy. You are to give a short talk explicating for your probationers the general conditions of arrest. It is vital that you do not mislead them; at the same time you ought to try not to bore them to death. Write your script!

ACTIVITY

1 In pairs agree a topic/idea/story. It could be how an accident occurred; how to get from one of your homes to college; the digestion of a cheese sandwich...

Now identify two very different contexts for this language item. For the last an extract from an A-level Biology book, an extract from a diet plan and a presentation to classmates would be very unalike. Write a different one each and compare them, giving one another verbal feedback on your use of verbal and visual signals. Are they as unalike as they ought to be?

ACTIVITY

2 Now swap your two texts with another pair's. Can they tell what is in front of them? Remember here that your focus is on what, not for whom (audience), or for what reason (purpose).

ACTIVITY ◼ ▨

3   At home, take any piece of junk mail that comes through your door – a rich resource.

(a) What world does it belong to?

(b) How can you tell?

If you've written a broad category like 'adverts' decide how far along a continuum of formality for 'animals' of this type this particular specimen is. Also ask yourself what field of life it relates to and how this affects lexis and tone. Be as subtle and detailed as possible.

ACTIVITY ◼ 💬

4   Now find any three sets of instructions and award them gold, silver and bronze awards for:

use of jargon

use of specialist lexis

visual clarity

Chapter 7
Audience

Audience is the aspect of language which, arguably, we are most aware of when we begin to write or speak ourselves. Communication is most effective when we judge correctly the appropriate tone and content for the person we are speaking or writing to. It's a skill we need for A-level English Language too. Both the major exams in English Language focus on audience in their sylistics questions: the AEB Paper One in 1996 asked students to 'discuss how writers use language to fit their audience' in relation to magazine articles for girls and bikers. The NEAB Issues and Stylistics paper almost always has a comparative question where the same material has been written up for two very different audiences – for example bee-dancing, for a science journal and as a children's story about Honeybee.

Re-presenting material for different audiences as well as in different contexts is also a crucial exam skill. Section B of the AEB Paper Two and all tasks for Paper C (the case study paper) for NEAB require it. Clearly, original writing exams or coursework also depend upon an awareness of audience. We would like to start this section by looking at the skills you need as a writer to re-present material for different audiences, before going on to look at texts written for audiences of various ages, educational background and specialisms.

WRITING FOR CHILDREN

ACTIVITY

The following page (p. 96) is taken from the BBC's *Music Magazine* written for interested adults. Re-write this material as it might appear for Year 8 students 'doing' Music and needing two pages of their 'Famous Composers' handout on Prokofiev.

Remember that specialist lexis and insider references are out because the Year 8 students will be unfamiliar with most musical terms. Also avoid words and structures which are too sophisticated. How many twelve-year-olds do you know who discuss 'aesthetic treatises'?

'Writing down' activities of this kind are frequently required in exams as it would scarcely be fair to expect candidates to write as experts. In such 'write down' exercises children are a particularly likely audience.

LIFE & TIMES

Sergei Prokofiev's career in the context of cultural and political events of the time

Prokofiev is born in Sontsovka in the Ekaterinoslav district of the Ukraine on 11 (old-style calendar)/ 23 April, where his father is an agricultural engineer and his mother is a pianist, passionate about music	**1891**	
	1898	Leo Tolstoy publishes his aesthetic treatise, 'What is Art?', outlining his belief that good art should be simple enough to be understood by all. Prokofiev later sets his 'War and Peace' as an opera
Having shown musical precocity under his mother's tutelage (he had started composing aged five), he begins lessons with Glière	**1902**	
Aged only 13, Prokofiev enters the St Petersburg Conservatory where Rimsky-Korsakov is director	**1904**	
	1905	A peaceful protest against the autocratic rule of Tsar Nicholas II escalates into mutiny aboard the Battleship Potemkin
	1909	Russian cubist Kasimir Malevich (1878–1935) paints 'To the Harvest (Marfa and Vanka)'
Prokofiev graduates from the Conservatory, having won the Rubinstein Prize for piano with a performance of his own controversial and virtuosic First Piano Concerto	**1914**	
	1917	Tsar Nicholas II is forced to resign. In October the anti-communist White Army is defeated by the Red Army of Bolsheviks; Lenin seizes power and Russia becomes the world's first communist state
Travelling to the USA after the Russian Revolution, his opera 'The Love for Three Oranges' fails to make an impact at its first performance in Chicago	**1921**	
	1923	In September Prokofiev marries the Spanish-born singer Lina Llubera and they settle in Paris
Prokofiev's former tutor Glière composes his ballet 'The Red Poppy', which is considered one of the first works of socialist realism and earns him a place as the founder of Soviet ballet	**1927**	
	1932	Shostakovich completes his opera 'Lady Macbeth of Mtsensk'
After accepting a commission from Leningrad's Kirov Theatre for a 'Romeo and Juliet' ballet, Prokofiev returns to live in the USSR	**1936**	The Great Purge begins. Joseph Stalin rids the Soviet Union of real or imagined enemies. 'Pravda' savagely condemns Shostakovich and his music
	1937	Prokofiev plays violinist David Oistrakh at chess; the loser has to give a recital
Prokofiev's score for Eisenstein's film epic 'Alexander Nevsky' is a great success and a year later he reworks the music into a cantata. His marriage begins to break up following his friendship with a young student	**1938**	
The USSR joins World War II, the 'Great Patriotic War'	**1941**	
	1947	Prokofiev works on his operatic version of Tolstoy's masterpiece, 'War and Peace'. The Supreme Soviet issues a decree making marriage to foreign nationals illegal even in retrospect, nullifying Prokofiev's marriage; Lina is sent to a labour camp
Andrei Zhdanov introduces even more repressive measures in the arts. At the First All-Union Congress of Composers in 1948 many of Prokofiev's pieces are proscribed	**1948**	
	1953	Prokofiev dies of a brain haemorrhage on 5 March 1953, the same day as Stalin

ACTIVITY

In groups of four, gather information on any topic of interest to you which is educational. You might choose a historic event, a scientific process or different definitions of a sentence. Each of you should now write a two-side A4 digest and guide: one for 7-year-olds, one for 9-year-olds, one for 11-year-olds and one for 13-year-olds. When you've finished, swap your four with those of another group. First, see if you can tell which is which. Our guess is that you'll find it difficult.

Consider:

Words: average length, how sophisticated, how formal?

Structures: average length, type (look back at Chapter 4), order

Layout: visual appeal, clarity, grouping and sequencing

Choose the four you consider the best targeted and using them as exemplars, now write a guide for those writing for children. Include a section on the problems they might encounter; for example, writing without baffling or patronising children is a real skill.

Now we'll look at some professional attempts. Your experience of attempting to write for children should help you to comment on them.

ACTIVITY

Now look at some entertaining writing for children at Key Stage 3.

WHAT'S THE MATTER?
or
HOW TO DO NOTHING
AND LOSE EVERYTHING

*Him and her. You can make your own
mind up which is 'him' and which is 'her'.*

What's the matter?

Nothing.

Something's the matter.

No, it isn't.

Then what are you sulking about?

I'm not sulking.

Well you're not exactly happy, are you?

I'm all right.

You don't look it.

I don't have to show it.

You used to.

So now I don't.

You're telling me.
Yes, I know I'm telling you.
Something's the matter then.
No, it isn't.
Yes, it is.
Well, if you know so much about me
    you don't need me to tell you.
No, I suppose not. I'll be off then. I'll see you
    when I see you.

Michael Rosen

How has the poet tried to engage the audience in terms of content, layout and most crucially, style? Are there lessons to be learned from these?

....

ACTIVITY ⊞ ◪

In groups, collect twenty poems you think twelve-year-olds would enjoy. Structure them into an anthology with an introduction explaining your choice and how the poems form a group or a series of groups. You will need to link, and perhaps gloss, the poems. If you had the opportunity actually to use these with a group of school children you would also need to produce tasks for the children to do; some for individuals, some for groups; some written, some spoken. Anthologising material is another useful life and exam skill.

Before we finish considering children as a particular audience, we would like you to analyse a piece written for children by an A-level examination student. It was written for the NEAB A-level exam which requires candidates to write a commentary on the work they submit, explaining the various stylistic choices they have made.

Hello everyone! I'm Harriet the House-fly. I'm here to tell you all about me and my family.

I come from a very big family. I have about 90,000 cousins. Just to name a few there are Holly the Horse-fly, Minnie the Midge and Danny the Drone-fly.

I am one of the smallest of all my family. I measure only 15 mm. That's about as big as your finger tip.

You probably see more of me than any of my cousins. I'm the one that hangs around your house, especially in summer.

I began my life as a larva. A larva is a small maggot (like a worm) that lives in things that are rotting away.

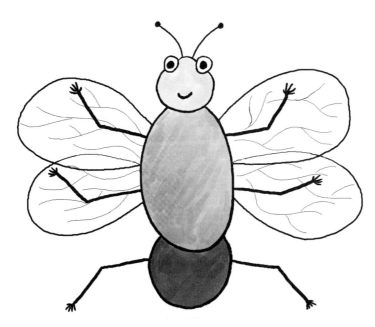

Now that I've grown up I have six legs, a pair of wings, antennae (said like "Anne-ten-eye"), a pair of eyes that stick out of my head, and a mouth that's perfect for sucking up your lemonade.

I don't think that I'm bad looking, but some of my cousins, like Billy the Blue-bottle and Gladys the Green-fly say that they are much better looking than me, because they are brightly coloured and I am plain black.

Shall I let you into a secret? Have you ever wondered how flies stand on the ceiling and don't fall off?

Well a fluid comes out of the hairs on our feet (Yes, we have hairy feet!) and this helps us to grip, so that we don't fall off. Clever, isn't it?

Not all my family are as nice as me. My cousin, Monty the Mosquito, is not very nice at all. He doesn't like humans very much. He prefers to bite them rather than talk to them!

It's time to go now. Thank you for letting me tell you all about myself and my family. I hope you enjoyed reading it. Next time you see my flying about give me a wave, and I'll try to wave back.

ACTIVITY ●📝

Write a commentary for this piece. Imagine that you wrote the piece and use the first person in your commentary.

ACTIVITY ◼ 💬

Now compare your remarks with those of the candidate.

COMMENTARY FOR 'THE NATURE SERIES:
ALL ABOUT FLIES'

Andrea Pickering

Our original idea was formed as a group. We decided to produce a series of books for children all about different wildlife. We were all assigned an aspect of wildlife to research, and produce a book on.

My primary aim was to inform the readers about flies, but I feel that by trying to make the book as appealing as possible to the audience, that a secondary product of this has been that the book is entertaining. I feel that this encourages the child to read on, as they are not just being bombarded with facts, but also entertained in the process.

The audience for my book would be within the 5–7 age range. The language that I have used is all simple enough to be understood by a child of this age, and the entertaining sections are all easily understandable. The audience do need to possess reasonable reading skills in order to understand this book alone, but I would recommend that the first time that this book was read, was with an adult for support. This would be useful as any words or concepts that the child does not understand could be explained therefore enabling the child to read the book alone later, and fully understand it. There are no class implications with this book, and it would be suitable for all children within this age group, as long as they were not significantly intelligently under or over developed.

In order to research for my book I collected books for adults and reformed the information so that it would be suitable for a child. In order to find out the popular form for children's books I visited the children's section of my local library and studied the format of the wildlife books for the age range that I have written for.

I find the presentation of the book very suitable to the age group. The small amount of writing per page does not 'overload' the child's mind, and the size of the writing makes the layout look much clearer. The cartoon-like illustrations are clear cut and eye catching. They illustrate important points raised in the writing, and in some cases clarify them.

On page one, the illustration used introduces the character that will be leading them through the story (Harriet the House-fly). I feel that this is very important, as the child now feels a certain attachment to the character, and has a persona of Harriet in their minds. The language used to introduce Harriet is clear, and direct. Harriet is portrayed as a friendly individual who has the purpose of informing the children about herself and her family.

On page two the illustrations of the different types of flies shows that there is more than one type, and that they all look slightly different. This is useful, as many children of this age will not realise that there are actually different types of fly, and that they vary in appearances. The further personification of the flies helps the child to identify with the creatures, as names have been found to be important to children of this age group.

I find that the picture on page three is particularly useful in clarifying a point. The way that the finger tip is clearly labelled helps the child to understand actually how big a fly is. I decided to illustrate it in this way, because a child of this age may not be clear about the actual size that 15mm represents. I have also shown who Harriet is by describing her as '...the one that hangs around your house...', rather than using complex descriptions of her habitat.

On page four I have briefly described how Harriet began her life. I have not gone into too much detail with this, as I feel that the early life of a fly is very complicated and this would only confuse the child unnecessarily. The illustration of the half eaten apple with maggots living in it on this page illustrates where the larvae grow, and is also easily recognisable to a small child.

On page five the description of Harriet as she is now provides the child with valuable information as to the anatomy of a fly, in a clear and direct way. The hint on how to pronounce 'antennae' (i.e. Said like 'Anne-ten eye') helps the child with the difficult and technical word if they are reading the book alone. In all other instances of technical terms I have been able to omit them and in their place put another (e.g. On page seven I have used '...comes out of ...' instead of 'Secretes').

In order to communicate to the audience that some species of flies are colourful I have used the description of the way that Harriet's cousins feel about her. This adds humour to the piece, and also again provides something that the child can relate to. The illustration that goes with this page also adds to the humour and helps to clarify the point.

I feel that the way that the child is made to feel as if he is being let into a secret encourages the child to read on, and makes the facts seem much more interesting. The illustration that goes with this page is quite comic, and provides (as many of the pictures do) 'light relief' from the facts.

Page eight describes part of Harriet's family that is not very pleasant. The Mosquito. This is done in a way so as not to frighten the child, but to inform them of the habits of other types of flies. The Mosquito is also personified, by giving him a name, and this helps the child to remember what he is called as it fits in well with Mosquito (i.e. Monty the Mosquito).

The final page takes a very similar format as the first. It portrays Harriet as a friendly and helpful character, and rounds the book off well. I feel that the last sentence, 'Next time you see me flying about give me a wave, and I'll try to wave back,' gives the child the impression that they are part of a secret group, and that they now have some sort of bond with flies!

Overall I am very happy with my piece. Although it does not contain a lot of detailed information I feel that what information is available through the book is presented in such a way that it will all be absorbed. It is much better to present information in this way to a child than to overload their brains, and cause them to be bored. The minimal amount of words that I have put on each page, and the illustrations all contribute to the understanding and humour created by this book.

WRITING FOR TEENAGERS

After children, the next distinct 'age group' in terms of audience, and one increasingly targeted by magazine journalists, is teenagers. Many A-level students are familiar with the styles deemed appropriate for this audience and enjoy writing for them. Magazine articles about anorexia, cautionary tales about wannabes and humorous guides to surviving GCSEs/parental separation are all suitable subjects.

ACTIVITY

Magazines are a particularly useful readers' guide to audience. All have to find their niche in the market. In pairs (preferably one male and one female), write down the names of all the magazines you and your friends regularly read. Next write down the names of those your parents and grandparents read and any specialist magazines that anyone you know reads. If you now pool your attempts you should have a guide to magazine reading by age, gender and interest.

Problem pages too represent an amusing but worthwhile topic of study.

....

ACTIVITY ▦ ◪

In threes collect different problem pages from teen magazines. Choose one good example each from the problems presented.

Now rewrite the answer as you feel it would appear in a magazine of your choice written for an older audience.

....

HOUSE-STYLE TO SELL LIFE-STYLE – WORDS USED TO FOSTER GROUP IDENTITY

Detailed analysis of magazine articles will raise your skills as readers and writers. Such publications cater for a wide range of ages, tastes and income brackets, from (at the time of writing) *Jackie* and *Smash Hits* through *Q* and *Vogue* to *My Weekly* and *Good Housekeeping*. Their success depends on identifying a 'target' readership and appealing successfully to it. Many are lavishly illustrated and several aspects of newspaper layout are employed. They make money for writers, publishers and the manufacturers whose products are featured, but they do not succeed unless they entertain their readers at the same time.

It is vital, therefore, that the language used by each magazine strikes the right note. It must create a sense of rapport with the readership. It would be no use at all to address the readers of *Kerrang!* (heavy metal fans) in the manner expected by readers of *Woman's Own* (women of twenty-five and upwards, usually with a family). Particularly at the youth end of the market, any inappropriate or old-fashioned terms would affect the magazine's credibility (unless used tongue-in-cheek). Some magazines clearly see themselves as style-setters who create taste, but they must also reflect style. How can language reflect 'style' in its wider sense? What is style anyway?

Style

Style is a difficult word to define. Most words are capable of carrying various interpretations, but style is a particularly slippery one. In its most 'neutral' sense it is impossible not to display style in the same way as it is impossible not to communicate. This is true of visual or audio style as well as style in speech or writing. Whenever we select clothes or words and put them together we will be exhibiting some sort of style, maybe unique to ourselves.

In another more widely accepted meaning of the word, style is 'a coherent, recurring set of expected features' which identify the style of an individual or a larger recognisable group. This could be punk, yuppie or hippy in clothes, or a 'legal' or 'formal' style in writing.

Yet another way the word style is used is to imply something desirable in itself: 'she has real style' or 'your essays so far lack a sense of style'. In this sense, whether applied to language or to appearance, it is a term of approbation.

A definition which holds good in all situations is impossible to achieve. What we are interested in looking at is how magazines which exist to inform us about styles in other areas of life try to create a language style (as in 'set of recurring features') which appeals to and suits their audience and is therefore 'appropriate'.

When any publication strives to achieve this appropriate style or specific voice for itself, it has to aim for consistency throughout. Many different writers may contribute to it, but somehow the style has to be recognisable as that of the particular publication. In order to do this it creates a 'house-style'. In order to accomplish this many newspapers, magazines and periodicals produce guidelines for their writers in the form of style sheets, which outline the features they hope will identify their particular house-style. Here are a couple of hints from the style sheet of *The Economist*, which is aimed at an educated audience interested in current affairs:

> Do not be stuffy or pompous. Use the language of everyday speech, not that of spokesmen, lawyers or bureaucrats. (So prefer **let** to **permit**, **people** to **persons**, **colleague** to **peer**, **way out** to **exit**, **present** to **gift**, **rich** to **wealthy**.) You can avoid offending women without using **chairperson**, **humankind** and **Ms**. Prefer **chairman** (for a man) or **in the chair**, **mankind**, so long as the context is not offensive, and the precision of **Mrs** and **Miss** whenever you can.
>
> Do not be too chatty. The sentence '**So far, so good**' neither informs nor amuses. It irritates. So do **Surprise, surprise, Ho, ho**, etc.
>
> *The Economist*

Perhaps on the basis of these guidelines alone you could make some further assumptions about the audience of *The Economist*. As language students you should be able to make some comments on the attitude to language shown.

A style to suit the audience

Many different sorts of magazines and periodicals produce style sheets. It would be particularly interesting to find those issued by publications in which a conscious effort appears to have been made to produce a house-style for a very specific audience in terms of age. Here is an example of such a style: it may be fairly dated by the time you read it but any example taken from this type of journalism will date pretty quickly. When you have read it you might try to re-create the guidelines it's based on!

DON'T MENTION TIFFANY...

If you saw The Chart Show a few weeks back you might have spotted an extremely pretty young American lady called Tracie Spencer warbling a splendid ditty called Symptoms Of True Love. Apart from having a v good voice and writing her own songs, there's another astounding fact about young Trace – she is only 12!!! And what's more it drives her a bit potty when people go on about her age. It also drives her a bit potty when people ask her what she thinks of Tiff 'n' Debs. She always wanted to sing. 'I realised when I was three. I used to sing with the record player, especially to Billie Holliday records. Yeah, I guess that was kinda sophisticated for a three-year-old.' She shot to fame in her native USA when she won the finals of a telly programme called Star Search which is rather like Bob Says Opportunity Knocks. 'I was 11 at the time, and I sang "How Will I Know?" by Whitney Houston. The other finalist was only five.' Tracie's dad is a singer and he started at the age of 12 too. She plans to carry on her studies so she can go to college to study drama. 'I'd really like to act when I'm older. I'd either like to be in something like "The Cosby Show" or a horror film, like "A Nightmare On Elm Street" – they're my favourites.' Her favourite singer is Whitney Houston, her favourite film star is Patrick Swayze. She collects Cabbage Patch and Barbie dolls and likes going to the movies and swimming.

Just Seventeen

At a glance it can be seen that this is aimed at a different audience from that of *The Economist*! The readership of this magazine is clearly young. Its title is *Just Seventeen*, although we suspect the average age of the readers is lower. This particular item is taken from a double-page spread which contained eight such 'news' pieces giving information about pop stars (sic), films and fashion. Much of this information probably arrived at the *Just Seventeen* offices in the form of press information handouts or other publicity material. The house-style of the magazine must be imposed upon it, and this is a fairly typical example.

So, what are the distinctive features of *Just Seventeen* house-style as revealed in this short extract? (By the time you are reading this you will probably need scholarly 'footnote' style information to inform you that Tiffany and Debbie Gibson were young American singers (songstresses?) who were high in the pop charts in summer 1988. They were part of a wave of mid-teenage female solo vocal artists and obviously Tracie Spencer aspires to join them.)

We'll submit this text to the basic questions:

Who is this written for?
    Audience: young people interested in pop music.

What is it written for?
    Purpose(s): to inform (about Tracie Spencer) – to publicise her might be more specific.
    To entertain – the subject of the piece is not so well known that you would read on regardless.

How does the writer sound?
    Tone: apparently direct and chatty, but also rather amused and detached (patronising?).

What we now have to show is how this tone is created. There is a direct, conversational approach achieved in several ways. The reader is directly addressed in the second person: 'Don't mention Tiffany', 'If you saw…'. There is an appeal to a shared frame of reference: the writer expects the reader to know who 'Tiff 'n' Debs' are. There is an attempt to establish the immediacy of a conversational tone through speech rhythms: 'And what's more', 'Tiff 'n' Debs'. There are colloquial expressions such as 'spotted' and 'telly' and abbreviations which appear in speech: 'Trace', 'Tiff' and 'Debs'. There is one other abbreviation though, which only appears in writing, and that is 'v. good', usually only to be found in school exercise books, which might strike a chord with the teenage readership and emphasise that 'Trace' herself is only a schoolgirl.

These points show some of the ways in which the familiar, chatty, direct tone is established. But there is something else going on here. There is a detachment in the style which shows that the writer of this piece is not exactly convinced of Tracie's talents, and is having a laugh (giggle might be more precise) at her expense.

How is this conveyed?

The answer to this seems to be that it is done mainly through the lexis (word choice). There are several words and phrases here which do not belong to a familiar, chatty, colloquial register. When did you last hear anyone say 'warbling a splendid ditty' (more typical of Edwardian music hall) or anyone under thirty say 'drives her potty', which is from altogether another generation's slang?

The clichés in this extract also come thick and fast: 'shot to fame', 'native USA', 'astounding fact'. There is liberal use of exclamation marks and of intensifiers and positive modifiers: 'extremely', 'splendid', 'astounding'. These are used so close together that a tone of sarcasm or irony is established. Irony operates by making the readers aware that the writer's real point of view is not the same as the apparent one.

Surely the effect of this self-conscious exaggeration is to alert the reader that the writer – and possibly *Just Seventeen* – does not take 'young Trace' very seriously. Certainly not as seriously as she takes herself – listening to Billie Holliday at the age of three!

You will probably have noticed that about half-way through this piece the features that mark the house-style seem to fade and what we have is a relatively unadorned directly informative series of statements:

'Tracie's dad is a singer', 'She plans to carry on', 'Her favourite singer is…', 'She collects…'. These sound much more like a straight 'lift' from a press handout, but there is so little attempt to disguise it that the effect is to add to the generally amused air the piece maintains towards its subject. It rather implies that 'young Trace' is being manufactured, packaged and then sold. *Just Seventeen* is part of this process, so it cannot afford to be too directly critical. The selection of items which are chosen to be included in this final section emphasises her youth and possibly a certain British detachment from the American scene: 'The other finalist was only five', 'She collects Cabbage Patch and Barbie dolls.'

Just how is this style, which uses a mixture of outdated phrases and old slang terms, features of teenage writing such as 'v. good' and '!!!' and obvious show-biz cliché, going to appeal to the readers of *Just Seventeen*? Some of it is hardly the language they themselves would use, but that is probably the point. Teenage current slang varies from group to group and region to region and is 'in' and 'out' of the vocabulary so quickly that to try to reproduce it accurately would be impossible and produce more discordant notes. Nothing is worse than trying to sound trendy and failing. Therefore the magazine creates a style which is lively and rather disconcerting in its switches of tone but which very quickly becomes recognisable to regular readers. It changes its 'in' words frequently but they are particular to the magazine, and in its self-conscious use of slang terms which are obviously out of date it avoids looking as if it is trying to keep up.

A glance at another issue of the same magazine produces these similarly 'fossilised' expressions: 'chinwag', 'slightly squiffy', 'give you a tinkle', 'girlies', 'chappie', 'easy-peasy', 'jammy young lass', 'silly old sausage' and 'ne'er do well kind of chap'. Mixed in with these dated terms are some coinings (made-up words): 'hunkster', 'songstrel' (in the phrase 'crinkly old songstrel' as applied to Barbara Streisand). There are also some conscious archaisms – 'simple, is it not?'   and abbreviations – 'list of celebs' – or even elongations – 'sperlendid' – again mirroring speech.

Sometimes this mix is funny, sometimes it seems formulaic, as it possibly is in the case of the item we looked at, where it may have been employed to 'customise' an information or press handout. If it appeals to you, you probably find the mix of styles lively and amusing; if it doesn't you probably find it irritating and mannered. That is part of style – you like it or you don't. At the time of writing, this is a very successful magazine. This is of course because of its photographs of and interviews with famous stars as well as its written style, but that is true of most magazines of this type.

···

ACTIVITY ◼ ▱ or ▦ ▭

Now look at the light-hearted Valentine's Day special from another magazine, one for which the audience is less easy to categorise. Look first at the choices of love songs. Just from this it is difficult to guess the age range of this magazine's readership. Is this aimed at the (very difficult to write for and possibly mythical) general public? Now read the first paragraph of the article. Are you any the wiser? The second, however, gives the game away. The piece is from *The Big Issue*, the paper sold by homeless people.

Discuss who you think buys this paper. Students? Kindly grannies? Social Workers? Who doesn't? Now read the rest of the article and discuss its style. What attitude does the writer have to accountants? And fashion victims? How would you describe the tone?

CUPID

**To celebrate Valentine's Day, we polled the nation
to find the Top 40 love songs of all time.**

By Simon Rogers

1 **Say A Little Prayer**
Aretha Franklin
1968

2 **Woman**
John Lennon
1980

3 **Sexual Healing**
Marvin Gaye
1982

4 **Nothing Compares 2 U**
Sinéad O'Connor
1990

5 **I Will Always Love You**
Whitney Houston
1992

6 **You Do Something To Me**
Paul Weller
1996

7 **Perfect Day**
Lou Reed
1972

8 **When A Man Loves A woman**
Percy Sledge
1966

9 **The Power Of Love**
Frankie Goes To Hollywood
1984

10 **Wonderful Tonight**
Eric Clapton
1978

PLAY IT AGAIN

So it's Valentine's Day, you're feeling romantic and you turn on the radio. But, oh no, it's All Saints. Mood over. Because – for a subject that forms the heart of almost every song ever written – love gets pretty bad coverage. Love might change your life, but for most songwriters it's just an excuse to find a word that rhymes with 'unrequited'. So, where do you go if you want the real thing? We decided to find out.

We polled Britain's best music journalists, staff at 'Big Issue' offices around Britain and anybody else we could get our hands on to come up with the most comprehensive and moving Top 40 records ever produced. And just for good measure, we also researched a complementary Top 10 of the sexiest songs on the planet.

Some things were predictable. Staff at Debenhams head office coming back with Whitney Houston as number-one favourite, for example (office staff at the BBC were into this big time, too). Or 'The Big Issue' accounts office's fascination with Glenn Medeiros. Then there's the staff at Air France who went for Nat King Cole's 'Let There Be Love' (unfortunately not enough to get it into the Top 40). Or there's the weird – The Prodigy's 'Firestarter' and 'Smack My Bitch Up' were chosen by an accountant.

But the more surprising truth is that romantic songs are the skeletons in the cupboard of even the trendiest of trend spotters. The name of the 'Dazed & Confused' journalist who chose Eric Clapton's 'Wonderful Tonight' will forever remain a secret, but they weren't alone. 'Lady In Red' surfaced in the most unlikely of places (a fashion victim of the first order), as did Billy Joel. According to 'Mojo' magazine contributing editor Paul Du Noyer, love songs are, well, different. 'The best romantic songs seem to be so moving because between the words and music they communicate this spark of divinity that love brings into your life,' he says. 'Romance is just the highest form of sex – and in that way it tells us that we're angels as much as apes.' A good love song, like our winner here, can change your life – remember that when you start to think that the list looks more like Heart FM's too-soppy-for-us playlist.

So, here is our Top 40. No room for Sam Cooke's 'Wonderful World' or Elvis's 'Love Me Tender', Van Morrison, Fleetwood Mac, Al Green or Stevie Wonder. They were all voted for, but not by enough people. Love is a battlefield.

Another, perhaps more typical article from *The Big Issue* reviews the Princess Diana tribute album.

Blowing in the wind

The release of a new all-star tribute album to
Diana, Princess of Wales leaves Gary Crossing mystified

MUSIC
Opinion

MICHAEL JACKSON, ONE OF THE ARTISTS ON 'DIANA, PRINCESS OF WALES – TRIBUTE'

When Elton John performed his tear-jerking new version of 'Candle In The Wind' at Princess Diana's funeral it signalled that this nation had reached a baffling all-time low as far as emotional manipulation was concerned.

As a tribute from one friend to another, it was valid enough. But it became the soundtrack to the over-the-top outpourings of grief which were a tad difficult to take. And now the slush factor is set to go through the roof with the release of the double album 'Diana, Princess of Wales – Tribute'; 36 tracks donated by George Michael, Paul McCartney, REM, Simply Red and Michael Jackson and others. All proceeds go to the Diana, Princess Of Wales Memorial Fund.

One day the nation was shaking its head at the latest front-page exploits of a privileged young lady, the next there was a gaping hole in the lives of millions. Launderettes, newsagents and ordinary people hastily cut out pictures of Diana and stuck them in their windows. TV chat shows were packed with self-promoting biographers and so-called royal experts, all talking as though they knew her intimately. The tabloids angrily accused of hounding this young mother to her death brought out special souvenir issues and citizens rushed to buy them in droves. London was almost submerged under a tidal wave of bouquets.

And a fading pop star goes straight to number one with a revamped tribute intended for a movie sex-goddess, which just happened to have a track from his new album on the other side. The sheer hypocrisy and gross commercialism which followed the untimely death of a vivacious young woman seemed to overshadow the genuine mourning. But in a world where Nelson Mandela reckons that the day he met the Spice Girls was the greatest of his life, anything can happen.

No doubt the people who bought their souvenir copies of The Sun, queued for hours to sign a book of remembrance and forked out for 'Candle In The Wind' will rush out to buy 'Diana, Princess of Wales – Tribute' as well.

Released on Richard Branson's V2 Records, it features elegiac tracks from many of pop's biggest names. Thirteen are new recordings, several are exclusive and many more you will have heard already. Most take death, womanhood or motherhood as their theme, so it's not exactly what you might call a family party album.

George Michael's 'You Have Been Loved' was penned in memory of his mother; Eric Clapton's 'Tears In Heaven' was written about the loss of his son, Connor; The Bee Gees' 'Wish You Were Here' is dedicated to their dead brother Andy… get the picture?

The cause is worthy, the reason for the cause quite tragic. The concept, however, is simply naff. If it was called 'Now That's What I Call Bereavement' and raised money for Bosnian orphans it wouldn't sell half as well.

The album is out on December 1 on V2 Records.

Are there any house-style similarities between this and the previous article?

ACTIVITY

Before we leave the subject of Diana, which was the media event of 1997, another interesting aspect of this last piece that you might consider is its political stance. The writer disapproves of the 'over the top' outpourings of grief. Which are the words and phrases which make the bias clear? Do you think the writer is trying to persuade readers, or reinforce existing opinions? We all like to read articles with which we can whole-heartedly agree at least as much as those which challenge our prejudices, something that all newspapers and magazines are aware of in attracting their audiences.

AGE – THE LAST CHAPTER

Before we leave completely the issue of age as a factor in writing for particular audiences, let's look at some texts clearly written for older readers. As the years roll by, readers become less interested in popular music and more aware of their mortality. Funeral plans aren't something most of us want to think about too much and so selling them is quite a challenge. Before we look at some, consider some of the problems.

GOLDEN CHARTER
Pre-Paid Funeral Plans

The most *thoughtful* decision you could make.

THERE COMES A TIME IN LIFE when it's natural to think about loved ones and what you'd like to leave them.

Not the burden of funeral costs, obviously.

Odd isn't it, that most of us plan for things that might happen, taking out all kinds of insurance policies, while forgetting to plan for the event that definitely will?. Yet a Golden Charter funeral plan will give you instant peace of mind. By deciding on the arrangements and paying in advance, you can be sure loved ones will be spared unnecessary distress at the time of need.

Your family or estate will *never* be asked for more.
Once you've paid for your *Golden Charter* plan, that's it – a guarantee that *defies* inflation. You can also be assured your money is secure. A legally separate trust administers the funds.

No loose ends, no hidden *extras*.
In recent years funeral expenses have outstripped inflation. This is mainly because of rising cemetery and crematorium costs, as well as an increase in fees charged by doctors and clergy.

Unlike many other funeral planning companies, *Golden Charter* allows you to fully cover these expenses. Your plan is complete.

Proven *value*
Many people see the sense of organising their funeral in advance, but wonder about paying now for it. *'Would it be better to put my money in the building society?'* is a common question.

On past evidence, the answer is a definite no. Building society accounts have failed to keep up with rising funeral costs. If, in 1991, you'd invested £640

(then the price of a simple funeral) in a building society, it would have grown to £830 over the next seven years.* Yet the same funeral would have cost £1050.

The shortfall would have been £220.

Complete *freedom* of choice
Golden Charter offers you a choice of four flexible funeral plans, which can be personalised in any way to suit you. You also have complete freedom of choice of funeral director. You may want the local firm that has served your family for generations. Unlike some funeral planning companies who are now ultimately American owned, we are proud to be British.

Our funeral planning network is the largest in the UK, with 1500 other independent family funeral directors. You may select any one.

Now your *thoughtfulness* can live on forever
When you purchase a plan a tree will be planted on your behalf by the Woodland Trust in a planting site near you. You'll receive a certificate to record the planting and a directory of the sites.

A beautiful way to be remembered.

For peace of mind, read our *free* brochure
It contains all our prices and explains why choosing a *Golden Charter* funeral plan is the most thoughtful decision you could make.

Send this coupon *today* – no stamp required.

Or call us – FREE ☎ 0800 833 800

Recommended by **SAIF** INDEPENDENT FUNERAL DIRECTORS

01 Mar 1991–01 Apr 1998 BLDG SCTY 2500 plus Index. Source: Micropal

A FOUNDING MEMBER OF THE FUNERAL PLANNING COUNCIL

Your funeral should be a celebration of your life.

We can arrange it for you.

A well-run funeral plan is a good idea for people who would like to make arrangements in advance in order to spare family members unnecessary trouble and expense.

The Dignity Plan, however, does rather more.

Your funeral can be tailor-made to the kind of person you are and the kind of life you've led. It can be as simple as you like – or as elaborate – depending on the kind of ceremony you want it to be. It's all planned between yourself and an experienced, understanding funeral consultant, right down to the last detail.

The Dignity Plan also guarantees that all the main items of the funeral you have specified will be provided at the price you have agreed – however much costs rise in the years ahead. And you have the reassurance of knowing that the payment you make is held by National Funeral Trust with Barclays Bank plc as Custodian Trustee.

Find out about the Dignity Plan. For more information without obligation, please telephone our free advice line on **** *** ***, or send off the Freepost coupon.

There is no-one quite like you.
There will be no funeral quite like yours.

THE DIGNITY PLAN

ACTIVITY ⊞ 🖪

What ingredients would you include if you were trying to 'sell' funerals (and they are pretty expensive) to people in advance of their deaths? These plans are not aimed at the recently bereaved but are persuading people to save and to plan for their own ceremonies. Which emotions would you appeal to? Guilt? Fear? Pride? Prudence?

What would you call such a plan? What images would you use? Presumably not coffins!

Brainstorm your ideas and come up with a sketch for an advert including the name, catch phrase and 'image' you will use.

Now look at two such advertising leaflets and answer the above questions in relation to them. Consider these questions:

■ What are the respective connotations of 'Golden Charter' and 'The Dignity Plan'?

■ Which do you prefer?

■ Does 'a celebration of your life' strike a different chord from 'the most thoughtful decision you could make'.

■ Do the images used in the two adverts appeal to different ages and genders in your opinion?

■ Which emotions are the two appealing to?

■ Does the greater detail and the discussion of precise sums of money in Golden Charter reassure or alienate?

■ How and why do the adverts use different fonts?

■ Is the brevity of the Dignity Plan a good thing?

■ Which of them is more romantic, which more practical?

■ Openers and closers are vitally important. Which seems stronger in this respect?

When you've answered all these questions you should compare notes with others. Is one ad a clear 'winner' or do they have differing appeals? We consider that the Dignity Plan is more male orientated, practical and egotistical. Perhaps this is why this advert was dropped several years ago. The Golden Charter is more romanticised yet reassuring and we suspect it would appeal more to women. Would you agree?

Lest you think death is the only reality for the older generation we'll end this 'age and house-style' section with an extract from a popular regional magazine for the older reader, *The Dalesman*.

YORKSHIRE WORDS

Once again, by the way of a New Year Resolution, I will try to catch up on my correspondence. My reference to the use of **thou/thee** still brings in comments. Howard Turner of the Yorkshire Itinerants, for example, writes to remind me of the phrase "**Na, dooan't thee thee-tha me. Tha thee-**

tha's them as thee-tha's thee!" M. Busfield of Staveley wrote of "asking a neighbour to **sholl on** (move up) along the village bench. (She thought I was greeting her in Hebrew.)" Vernon Pickles says that in Barnsley the word I gave as **Sither**! was pronounced with a short i as **Sithi**! He thinks that the original "See thee!" was a kind of vocative, as in a phrase like "**Ey, Thee ovver theeare!**"

Ken Griffin writes to thank me for the series and says, "**Ah allus 'ave a skeg at it afooare owt else**". He makes the interesting point that **Ey up!** is really the equivalent of the schoolboy Latin warning – "I say, Cave, you chaps", as used by Billy Bunter. He also adds to the list of phrases involving personal names one I remember well: "**Tha's wahr ner mi Aunt Kate!**" One I have never heard, used in his native Beeston, Leeds, was the non-committal reply on being asked where something was: "**Oh, it's at t'back o' Leathers's**". Some of these sayings involving names are very localised, others more general, such as the weather expression commonly heard in South Yorkshire: "**It's black ovver ahr Bill's mother's**" (or **Bill's wife's mother's**).

The mystery of who the original people were will in most cases for ever remain a mystery, including "Throp's wife". Sheila M. Cooper wrote to me from Oamaru, New Zealand, enclosing Professor F. W. Moorman's 1920 account of having tracked "Throp's wife" down to the Cowling area – but it is surely written tongue-in-cheek. On firmer ground are phrases like the one sent to me by Mrs D. Moore of Rastrick: "**It's ossin' ter slaht**". This means "It's trying to rain", **slaht** literally meaning "to splash". Both this word and **oss** appear in my own *Yorkshire Dictionary of Dialect Tradition and Folklore*, as well as in the six-volume *English Dialect Dictionary* (1905) by Joseph Wright. The value of letters to *Dalesman*, though, is that they sometimes come up with a bit of dialect that all the dictionaries have missed!

Arnold Kellett

JANUARY 1997 (49) *Dalesman*

As you'll know from your study of dialect use, older people use regional dialect far more than younger ones. Dr Arnold Kellett's feature would certainly not get a response in *Just Seventeen*, but we selected it as of more interest to language students than 'The Diary of a Yorkshire Farmer's Wife' or 'A Circular Journey through Time', which surrounded it. Notice the formal tone and scholarly asides in this article. How many of our readers are familiar with the 'vocative'? We suspect its use disappeared with Latin from most schools' curricula.

WRITING FOR A SPECIALIST AUDIENCE

A specialist audience which regularly features in NEAB case-study tasks are 'culture vultures'; visitors to museums and galleries, art cinema and theatre, who also watch BBC2 and Channel 4. To conclude this section on a slightly more intellectual note let's consider how writers appeal to this group.

ACTIVITY ◼ ▨

Programmes for events often include biographical blurbs about the writers/creators. Compare the Terence Rattigan biography with that of Christopher Bruce. Which is more complimentary? Can you guess why? List the insider references and specialist lexis that each contains.

CHRISTOPHER BRUCE

It was in 1969 that Bruce began to choreograph stimulated by his exposure to contemporary, classical and popular dance as well as an appreciation of theatricality. His talent was quickly recognised – he was awarded the first Evening Standard award for dance in 1974 for both his performances and his choreography – and prior to developing a career as a freelance choreographer he had created more than twenty works for Rambert. He is indeed recognised as the last choreographer to have been nurtured by the Company's founder Marie Rambert. In addition to performing and choreographing he was Associate Director of Ballet Rambert between 1975 and 1979 and in 1980 became the Company's Associate Choreographer.

During his career he has built up a special relationship with a number of companies including Nederlands Dans Theater, Royal Danish Ballet, Cullburg Ballet, English National Ballet (where he was Associate Choreographer 1986–1991), Le Ballet du Grand Théâtre de Genève and Houston Ballet (where he has been Resident Choreographer since 1989). He has also choreographed for musicals, plays (for the Royal National Theatre and Royal Shakespeare Company), operas, television and videos.

TERENCE RATTIGAN

During the forties and early fifties, the West End theatre was dominated by the 'well-made play', of which Rattigan was a supreme exponent. Foremost among the presenters of those glossy productions were H. M. Tennent Ltd, presided over by the powerful and legendary Hugh "Binkie" Beaumont. It was to Beaumont, in 1951, that Rattigan offered the script of *The Deep Blue Sea*, which he had been working on intermittently for more than two years and which he admitted had been 'the hardest of my plays to write because of the emotional angle'. He re-wrote the last act many times.

The Deep Blue Sea had a brief try-out at the Theatre Royal, Brighton, in February 1952, and opened at the Duchess Theatre, London, on 6 March. It was an immediate success, hailed by the critic Kenneth Tynan as 'the most absorbing new English play for many seasons'. This observation was especially welcome from Tynan, the scourge of what he saw as middle-class, pro-establishment theatre, who had often been scathing about Rattigan's work in the past. The same critic noted that, with the exception of Shaw in Saint Joan, Rattigan was the first dramatist since Pinero capable of writing a lengthy, strong, emotional part for an actress.

Another brief extract from the Rambert programme makes clear, we hope, that ballet fans can take much more literary and extreme style about ballet than they can about music. Each to her specialism...

> 'The choreography for *Airs*, while maintaining a formal, almost traditional structure and movement language, suggests the sweep, surge and buoyancy of water and air currents.
>
> 'Although the dance is expansive and filled with reflected light, it never loses a sense of power and gravity.'
>
> Susan McGuire

> The musical score for *Airs* comprises ten short pieces of Handel, picked and put into sequence by Paul Taylor. Five of them are movements from the six Concerti Grossi, Opus 3; the others are orchestral movements from the operas *Ariodante*, *Berenice* and *Alcina*, and the oratorio *Solomon* (The Arrival of the Queen of Sheba). While musical purists are reluctant to cull individual movements from different pieces and stick them together randomly, this is what Handel himself did when he had the chance to publish his Concerti Grossi, Opus 3 in the 1730s, drawing on material that he had written during the previous thirty years.

Educational level

Is not quite the same as specialism: try not to confuse them in analyses. Educational level refers to general knowledge and level of literacy. Reading age is clearly relevant here. Rather than looking at a *Sun* story (reading age – in all but the sports pages – about 8) let's consider two relatively sophisticated readerships who are nevertheless separate.

ACTIVITY

Read the following extracts from articles about Diana's death and the nation's response to it. One is from the *Daily Telegraph*; the other from *The London Review of Books*. Which would you expect to have a more educated audience? On the basis of these two pieces, you may feel more able to say.

> 'I FEEL so sorry for those poor boys.' We can all sign up to that. It is what Ian Jack's partner said when they woke up on August 31 to the news of a car crash in Paris in which the mother of those boys, and her lover, were killed. A great deal more was said in the phenomenal wave of emotion which broke over this country in the ensuing days.
>
> More than four months on, how is it looking? Books are being written. I know of two anthropologists who met prowling around outside Harrods, when people were signing the book of condolence for Dodie. Meanwhile Ian Jack, as editor of *Granta*, opens this issue with a collection of pieces by

and 'bizarı
paediatric
· · · · · · · · · · ·

Special

The two l
SPECIALl
Specialist
activities.
are a 'bird
grasp of sl
a ragout a
'twitch'; ı
'moderate
not jargon
euphemist
long as the
    Peopl
spend 18%
abound. A
Oz Clarke
the 'noses
descriptio
· · · · · · · · · · ·

ACTIVIT

CLA

1995
classi
north
each

Châ
Pess
Froı
fam
exhi
and
of F
Hac
bottl
case

'those who felt differently' – people baffled or disgusted by the national mood, who were made to feel heartless and excluded. 'I felt everybody else had gone mad. I felt angry,' writes Elizabeth Stern, a music student.

If not real grief, then what was this collective experience? It was 'recreational grieving', says Ian Jack. It was 'grief-lite', and it was enjoyable, as being part of a large, like-minded crowd is enjoyable: at a football match; at the last night of the Proms. I think we like to recapture that stage in our evolution when we were all 'of one mind', like the ants and the bees. So cosy to be part of it, so chilling to feel alienated. Several of the dissidents say they were reminded of fascism – 'floral facism', in Maggie Winkworth's phrase – by the hostility they encountered if they opened their mouths. The *Guardian*'s Isabel Hilton felt that 'if a powerful demagogue had arisen from the crowd, they would have stormed the palace gates'.

The dissidents are not heartless. They are sad and sympathetic. One of them – John Bradshaw – sent a message to the Prince of Wales: 'I quite like the bloke. He seems a reasonable egg.' All the dissidents – intellectuals and professionals – are reasonable eggs. But this is a story about unreason.

Daily Telegraph, January 10, 1998

WHAT WAS IT that departed during the first week of September? Much of the country was not convulsed by grief, although we do not know the proportion that stayed unmoved, or even critical, and perceived the events as a Southern or heartland spectacle. Yet it appears to be true that even among the more detached, many found themselves touched by unsuspected melancholy, strangely coupled to a sense of liberation and change. An inescapable shift was occurring, displayed in unheard of symptoms like the applause in Westminster Abbey, as well as the mountains of flowers and poems.

But what was the nature of the shift – and what exactly shifted? For all that has now been written around the event, the answer remains obscure. There are nevertheless a number of possibilities, of which the strongest might look something like this: a fairly long-lasting structure of English national identity which, though already in serious trouble, required this sudden blow from an unexpected angle to collapse. Much of the evidence remains circumstantial, but that is often the case when 'identity' is involved. What we are discussing is (or was) a subcutaneous circuit of attitudes and feelings which functioned best when it was unconscious, or taken for granted. Except when called upon, the mechanism invisibly behaved itself. While there and available, few paid it much heed. When it broke down, on the other hand, everyone noticed, was affected to some degree, and looked for an explanation. 'She called out to the country,' Elton John sang at the funeral. But may it not have been the English Rose's country which, in the aftermath of loss, ceased being able to call out in a traditional way? If so, a call long responded to – not really 'down the ages' but for quite a long time, about a century and a half – would not be made or heard again.

London Review of Books 30 October, 1997

informal and familiar – 'and you kept schtum…' – sometimes more formal and respectful – 'of your own home…'.

The other feature the two advertisements have in common is the use of positive lexis to refer to the product. The Parkfield Court advertisement is much less subtle here. It uses adjectives in the first paragraph, 'convenient', 'attractive'; nouns in the second, 'ambience', 'comfort', 'privacy' and 'independence' (isn't it by this last word we most clearly spot the audience?); and in the last paragraph that old superlative standby 'best' twice.

By contrast, the Saab advertisement seems to be giving us facts. But hidden away in this fluent, casual style are such words as 'stunning', 'exclusive', 'new', 'power', 'faster', 'legendary'. True, they are not all applied directly to the car, but they are there, and their associations 'rub off'.

Where the two differ is in tone. The Parkfield Court advertisement is formal, bordering on frozen, in the recognisable register of estate agents: 'convenient location', 'attractive development'. The tone of the car advertisement is a mixture of the occasionally formal – 'May we suggest', 'Allow us to make a suggestion' – with the clearly colloquial – 'kept schtum', 'brand new metal'. The effect of this mixture is to

IS THIS… UM, HOW YOU'D… WELL, FEEL ABOUT… ER,… ASKING YOUR BOYFRIEND… TO… UM… WELL… ER… USE A CONDOM?

create a familiar, 'jokey' tone appropriate to the apparent task in hand, that of conspiring to deceive the Financial Director.

The next text has a much more serious persuasive purpose. It too has a clear target audience, and also uses direct address, but it is not a commercial advertisement. It was published by the Health Education Authority as part of the campaign to raise awareness of the danger of AIDS among young people, and to persuade them to change their behaviour.

Like the Saab advertisement, this is designed to sound like direct address.

ACTIVITY

- Who is the apparent recipient of this advice?
- If you wanted to reach this audience, where would you place this advertisement?

In fact in this particular Health Education campaign, different advertisements were written to address different 'at risk' groups. This one is aimed at teenage girls, and appeared in a magazine many of them read, *Smash Hits*.

Condom.

It's not that difficult to say is it?

Well if it's not, what's stopping you?

He might laugh at you for mentioning it. He might think you're easy.

Well here's something else to think about.

In Britain the number of people with AIDS is still on the increase.

And for every person with AIDS, we estimate there are thirty with HIV.

Human Immunodeficiency Virus is the virus which leads to AIDS.

Someone can have it for several years and still look and feel perfectly healthy.

But through unprotected sex, they can pass the virus on to you.

A condom can help protect you.

So think about using one, and talk about it with your boyfriend.

You never know, he might just be pleased you suggested it.

Think about not having sex at all if you're not certain, or you don't really know him well enough.

And more important, never feel shy about asking him to use a condom.

AIDS. YOU'RE AS SAFE AS YOU WANT TO BE.

- What impression is the text on the left-hand side of the spread intending to make, and how is this conveyed?
- What has been identified (probably on the basis of some market research) as one of the problems girls might have in taking responsibility for 'safer sex'?

. . . .

The other difficulty this piece is concerned with is one of language. It is that of making the term 'condom' more acceptable and generally used. There are many colloquial expressions in general use for this particular item, but they don't have respectable connotations, vary in different parts of the country and in different age groups, and are more often heard from men. So the embarrassment to be overcome is not only a behavioural one, but a linguistic one, the possibility that the boyfriend might find the word funny, as much as the suggestion. The AIDS campaign had to find a more 'neutral' term which a wider range of people would feel comfortable with. 'Condom' was the solution, but it had to be launched into general use. Only time will tell if this campaign has succeeded.

. . . .

ACTIVITY ◐ ◑

Think about the different types of sentence used in this text:

- Why do you think it begins with questions and continues mainly with statements?
- What is achieved by asking the readers questions? After all, they can't answer – or can they?
- Why are three of the last sentences commands? Is this the most important part of the text?
- Why is the text broken up into so many short major and minor sentences?
- Why do three of them begin with co-ordinating conjunctions, usually to be found in the middle of sentences and not at the beginning?
- Can you find any attempts to make this writing sound like speech?
- What do you think about the vocabulary in this piece? Is it mainly formal or colloquial?

Now ask the same question of the style of the advertisement as a whole: formal or informal? Are the answers the same to both questions?

. . . .

If you have tried this sort of persuasive piece yourself, aiming like this one to reach a lot of people, have you found that the main problem is to get the tone right? If you try to be too chatty and colloquial you run the risk of sounding patronising, and detracting from the serious subject. On the other hand, if the tone is too formal or impersonal, it will not engage your target audience. Do you think this advertisement – and it could just as well have been a leaflet – is successful in striking a tone which will appeal to its audience, and thus have some hope of being effective in changing people's behaviour?

PUBLIC SPEAKING

Having progressed from commercial to public service advertisements, let's look now at a different form of public persuasion altogether, the public speech. We know that throughout history there have been great orators, people who have been able to sway multitudes by the power of their words. Of course, we know of most of them by report only, and can judge others merely by reading their words on the page, a pale shadow of the real thing. Contemporary examples are harder to find, as modern politicians know that they can reach far more people through the more intimate medium of television. We can, however, still catch a whiff of the excitement of stirring public speech-making at election times, at religious or political rallies, at party conferences, and even (occasionally) now that parliament is televised. But most commentators agree that it is a dying art. It's an art, however, that as language students we should consider, as it is an example of language at full tilt. These orators were the first of the public persuaders.

The example we are going to look at is a famous one. It is President Kennedy's inaugural address, delivered in Washington on 20 January 1961.

So let us begin anew – remembering on both sides that civility is not a sign of weakness, and sincerity is always subject to proof. Let us never negotiate out of fear. But let us never fear to negotiate.

Let both sides explore what problems unite us instead of belabouring the problems that divide us.

Let both sides join to invoke the wonders of science instead of its terrors. Together let us explore the stars, conquer the deserts, eradicate disease, tap the ocean depths, and encourage the arts and commerce.

Let both sides unite to heed in all corners of the earth the command of Isaiah – to 'undo the heavy burdens... and let the oppressed go free'.

Now the trumpet summons us again – not as a call to bear arms, though arms we need – not as a call to battle, though embattled we are – but a call to bear the burden of a long twilight struggle, year in and year out, 'rejoicing in hope, patient in tribulation' – a struggle against the common enemies of man: tyranny, poverty, disease, and war itself.

Can we forge against these enemies a grand and global alliance, north and south, east and west, that can assure a more fruitful life for all mankind? Will you join in that historic effort?

In the long history of the world only a few generations have been granted the role of defending freedom in its hour of maximum danger. I do not shrink from this responsibility – I welcome it. I do not believe that any of us would exchange places with any other people or any other generation. The energy, the faith, and the devotion which we bring to this endeavour will light our country and all who serve it – and the glow from that fire can truly light the world.

And so, my fellow-Americans: ask not what your country will do for you – ask what you can do for your country.

> My fellow-citizens of the world: ask not what America will do for you
> but what together we can do for the freedom of man.

President Kennedy was concerned in this speech not to target one section of the community, but rather to include as many members of it as possible. He had just won the election by the narrowest of margins, and his purpose was to unite his previous opponents by creating a sense of national purpose. He was also keen to make the transition from national politician to international statesman. This is the climax of the speech, which he concludes by addressing 'My fellow citizens of the world' (and you can't get much more inclusive than that!).

This oration has few features in common with spontaneous speech and many more in common with literature. Yet it was written to be spoken and clearly exploits sound and rhythm.

As you read it through we expect that one of the features which struck you immediately was the balanced structure of many of the sentences. Write down as many as you can find.

If a balanced, parallel structure is used to highlight contrasting or opposite notions, then the technical term for it is antithesis. An example of antithesis is the sentence 'Let both sides explore what problems unite us instead of belabouring the problems that divide us.' In this sentence 'unite us' is balanced by its opposite 'divide us', and although the rhythmic balance is not exact (as it would have been if he had used 'not' rather than 'instead of'), the effect of this is to draw attention to the contrast. The sentence is balanced on the pivot phrase 'instead of'.

Other pivot words or phrases are 'and', 'but' or 'not'; in other cases the pivot is a pause indicated by a punctuation feature such as a comma or a dash.

In two noticeable examples, the antithetical contrast is further emphasised by word inversion: 'Let us never negotiate out of fear. But let us never fear to negotiate.' Here 'fear' is used first as a noun, then as a verb. The other example is the famous 'ask not what your country can do for you – ask what you can do for your country'. In this case the two parts of the sentence contain almost identical vocabulary, but by reversing the words in subject and indirect object positions the meaning is dramatically altered.

These are instances of the most carefully structured word-play. The parallel structures, vocabulary and sounds ('not'/'what') combine to make the phrases easily memorable. Some of the earliest language we learn and retain, nursery rhymes and riddles, uses repetitive rhyme and rhythm. It may not be a very technical remark to make, but rhyme, rhythm and word-play give us pleasure and stay in our heads: this is something advertising copywriters are as much aware of as are American presidents. We admire verbal ingenuity.

There are other repetitive features in this speech. Certain key words are repeated frequently, 'both sides' for example. Lists are used to build to a crescendo. They have a sense of predictability with which we can join in. Sometimes the lists are positive ones, suggesting boundless opportunity (the lexis is catching): this is the case in the 'wonders of science' section. Other lists are negative, to suggest the size of the challenge, as in the 'common enemies of man' section.

The invocation 'Let' is used many times as a form of direct address. This is a deliberate echo of the Bible and the pulpit. In fact there is a lot of biblical lexis used, as well as direct quotation.

··

ACTIVITY ◨ ◪

Make a list of all the biblical words you can find here. Why do you think there are so many of them?

Compare the vocabulary with other famous examples of American rhetoric: Lincoln's Gettysburg Address and Martin Luther King's 'I have a dream...' speech.

··

Besides the biblical references, the speech is full of formal, elevated lexis, as of course you'd expect. Kennedy is declaring what he would like to see happen during his presidency, but it is not a practical plan of action. Look at the heavy preponderance of abstract nouns such as 'freedom', 'energy', 'faith' and 'devotion': these are all heavily-charged words which uplift us. However, it isn't going to be easy: we must also 'struggle' and 'fight' against 'tyranny', 'poverty' and 'disease'. An opponent might say that the president hasn't actually said very much, but inaugural speeches are meant to inspire, not to get bogged down in 'concrete' details.

'We' seems the most natural pronoun to use in the previous paragraph because it is used continually throughout the speech to achieve a sense of inclusive purpose, of common identity. Towards the end of the speech the first person singular 'I' begins to feature, and it is 'my', not 'our', which opens the final sentence. What is the effect of this?

This is a cleverly balanced speech overall. The picture of the future which is painted is not too rosy: it is going to be difficult, but it is a worthy enterprise, and the president makes us feel that we are worthy to join it. He appeals to our better selves, as do most persuaders: berating your audience is not a good selling tactic.

We have spent a long time on this one example because it contains so many language features which are 'foregrounded'. You probably found just as many that we failed to mention. But most persuasive language uses words in this obviously crafted way. After all, if someone is trying to change what you buy, what you think, what you feel or what you believe in, the odds are that they will put a lot of thought and a fair bit of craft into it. Like the president, they have to pay you the compliment of appearing to think you're worth it.

Kennedy's speech is undoubtedly effective: the President of the United States can command a team of top writers and then endorse it with his own personal status. The judgement of history may be that JFK was longer on charisma than on sincerity but his speech nevertheless inspired many. Other writers may be more sincere but lack the linguistic resources or status to affect their audience. Consider this flyer.

THE DEVIL IS A LIAR

Jesus said, The devil abode not in the truth, because there is no truth in him. When he speaketh a lie, he speaketh of his own: for he is a liar, and the father of it. John 8:44.

THE WAY TO HAPPINESS – THE BIG LIE – Many Television, and Video Programmes, and a lot of Magazines, and books give the impression that the way to happiness is the way of selfish indulgence. The Scarlet Sins of adultery, and of immoral living are glamorized as love. Drunkenness, nakedness, indecency, divorce, and revelling are shown as proper and legitimate. Tens of thousands of our people have swallowed this big lie, which is aimed at wrecking the homes of our nation. The sad results of this can be read every day in the Newspaper Reports of One Parent Families, Broken Homes, Broken Hearts, and Broken Children. The saddest wreck on earth is a wrecked home.

THE TRUTH – One of the greatest blessings God has given to mankind is Home and Family, with all its love and provision for those who could not care for themselves. The Bible says, 'God setteth the solitary in families.' When a man and a woman marry they become one flesh. Jesus said 'What God hath joined together, let not man put asunder.' The way to true happiness is the way of keeping God's commandments, 'Thou shalt not commit adultery,' and 'Keep yourself pure.' Father, Mother and Home should be three of the sweetest words in our language.

THE PRETTIEST PICTURE God ever made, or the world ever looked at, is a father and mother who love Jesus Christ, and they take hold of the hand of their oldest child, and the next child down to the youngest, and the whole family go happily along the road to Heaven. The darkest picture the world may see, is the breaking up of a home, and the parting of a father from his wife, and the children torn between the two. A man or a woman is a fool to swallow the devil's lie, and as a result to destroy their own happiness and also destroy the happiness of each person involved.

A POOLS WIN, SIN BIN SOCIETY – Recently the President of the National Union of Teachers declared that young people need the help of parents to reject the lies about life which are being fed to them. The Big Lie is leading many of them to believe that the way to happiness is to live in – A Pools Win, Sin Bin, Wimpey Bar, Two Car, First Name Loose Dame, Ansaphone, Loud Sound, Sleep-Around, Disco Scenes, Tight Jeans, Colour Tele, Sligawelly, Page 3s, Deep Freeze, Opt Out, Lout, Dull Void, Unemployed – type of society.

THE TRUTH – It is a thrill to realize that before each young person there lies the possibility of a life of happiness, usefulness, and honour. Jesus told us of a man who built his house upon a rock, and of another man who built his house upon the sand. When the storm came the house on the rock stood safely, but the other house fell in ruins. Jesus said that those who obey His words are building upon a Rock. The true way to happiness is to repent of sin and receive the Lord Jesus Christ as your personal Saviour, and to live in obedience to the teaching of the Bible.

ACTIVITY ⬤ ◩ OR ⬛ ◩

In two columns note quotes from the text which appeal to head and heart. Religious belief is highly personal and controversial.

■ How has the writer used assertions to transform opinion into fact? (Have you placed these assertions in your head or heart column?)

■ Why has s/he chosen to quote from the Bible so extensively? Is repetition effectively used?

■ What other techniques of persuasion do you recognise in this text?

Once again a profitable group exercise would be to make a 'From the Heart' collection of extreme and manifestly sincere texts.

THAT'S ENTERTAINMENT?

In this chapter we have concentrated mainly on the purposes of informing and persuading and looked at how these are combined in different contexts. In the next chapter we are going to look at some texts which come under the broad heading of entertainment, as does literature, which also occupies several later chapters.

We are going to conclude this chapter with two examples of entertaining news reporting, although you might question the word 'news' in relation to both pieces. The first is ostensibly informative although included in the paper (the *News of the World*) predominantly for its entertainment value. The second is entertaining but with a heavy persuasive element and leaves you wondering whether or not the joke is on the reader. The impact of the first piece is somewhat lessened because we cannot show you the picture of the lady magistrate 'mooning'.

When reporting relatively trivial events most journalists take the opportunity to exercise their sense of humour and verbal skills and many of the tabloid papers, particularly on a Sunday, contain lots of such jokey pieces, often of a rather 'saucy' variety as this first one is. Even the earnest writer of 'The Devil is a Liar' was attempting something of this style at times. Look again at that text and identify the attempts at tabloid catchiness. Are they effective?

Newspapers are particularly fond of puns and alliteration (readers of our first edition may recall the sizzling sir who gave lessons in sex). They also use graphics, headlines and subheads to pull the reader in. This edition's prime example of the tabloid at its most unsubtly entertaining is from the *News of the World*. This time the authority figure whose misdemeanours are publicised is a lady magistrate (why not just magistrate?) and her 'crime' was to bare her bottom.

ACTIVITY ⬤ 🗏

List all the puns upon posteriors. Some are quite ingenious.

Find all the references to the magistrate's class or gender. Why do you think these are stressed? Does this say something about the *News of the World*'s audience?

What else would you regard as amusing in this story?

THE LAW IS AN ASS

Angry lady magistrate moons at farmer in horse row

As upper-crust magistrate Josie Lewis takes her seat on the bench she appears every inch the strait-laced paragon of virtue.

In her role as a rock-solid pillar of the community she becomes the scourge of wrongdoers – fearlessly doling out punishment, proudly upholding our justice system and jealously guarding the moral well-being of the nation.

But faced with a personal out-of-court wrangle among the county's horsey set the cracks began to show in her bigwig image…

Finally the angry top-drawer JP delivered her bottom-line verdict on the row – by DROPPING her jodhpurs and MOONING at shocked stable boss Brian Woodfield!

'This is what I think of you!' she yelled, giving the outraged farmer a mouthful to go with his unexpected eyeful.

Then she calmly hitched up her undies and giggled at her stunned target.

But, determined not to be beaten, Brian replied quick as a flash:

'Your a*** isn't half as ugly as your face!'

Knickers

Trouble began when middle-aged divorcee Josie arrived at Brian's massive estate in the posh Wiltshire village of Wootton Bassett – home of Prince Charles' favourite Beaufort Hunt – to collect some showjumping equipment.

'When I asked her to sign a receipt saying she'd removed her stuff from my land she got very bitter,' revealed Brian, 46. 'And when she refused it got nasty. She

started shouting abuse at me. Then she began insulting my wife Rose so I called the police.

'As soon as the officer arrived Josie was quick to inform him that she was an upstanding Justice of the Peace.

'While she walked around looking smug and picking up her property I started to take some snaps as proof.

'Then she said to my teenage grooms, 'Shall I give him something to photograph, girls?'

'At that she pulled down her breeches and knickers and bent over.

'I took the picture because I thought nobody would believe me.

'I was very offended and upset. In fact I've been under the doctor since then.

'How someone in her position can do something like this is beyond belief.

'I was absolutely disgusted. She probably even passes sentence on people who expose themselves. It's sickening.'

Brian immediately made an official complaint to the police and gave them a statement.

'If I'd done that sort of thing to her I'd probably have been locked up straight away, and no butts,' added Brian.

Apart from sitting in judgement on society's felons Josie runs a news agency preparing press releases, reports and stories.

But on Thursday her rear end was back in its official role, sat on a bench in Swindon Magistrates' courtroom No 3.

Stern-faced she sifted case notes, listened to lawyers and remanded alleged troublemakers

It's a coveted job she earned only after passing vigorous vetting procedures leading up to a recommendation to the Lord Chancellor.

But had the town's villains been privy to our exclusive set of pictures they would have sworn she had a cheek.

Bursting

Later our reporter confronted Josie with the explicit photograph evidence at her home, less than a mile from the Woodfields' spread.

After scrutinising our Exhibit A she pleaded not guilty.

Amazingly Josie blamed the entire incident on a bursting bladder.

'I wasn't allowed to use the toilet so I just had to wee in the yard,' she claimed. 'I won't have to resign over something like that.

'I'm having a wee and he took a saucy picture of me.

'Have you never had a pee on the side of the road? When I've been out for a night with boyfriends they've stopped for one.

'If this case came up before me on the bench we'd throw it out – insufficient evidence.'

A spokesman for Wiltshire Police said 'We've investigated but this incident appears to have been on private property and the offence of indecent exposure has to be in public.

'Still, it gave us a chuckle. And I wouldn't mind a look at the pictures!'

On that bizarre legal note the News of the World rests its case.

From now on JP Josie will be known as Justice of the Pees…

And finally we offer you the front page story of the *Sunday Sport*

Going Ape: Chimp family have caused fury by moving into the £85,000 council house

EU CHIMP RULING MAKES US LOOK LIKE MONKEYS

TAXPAYERS went bananas last night after it was revealed that an £85,000 council house has been let to a family of CHIMPANZEES.

Protests about the 'monkeys from hell' have already been lodged by residents on the same tree-lined estate.

And they were even more irate when they learned that £8,000 has been spent adapting the three-bedroomed semi for its hairy occupants, whose rent bill is also being picked up by the public.

But a local authority spokesperson has defended the move, saying: 'The EU made us do it. Our hands are tied by red tape.

'There are no suitable establishments in our catchment area to place them in but we have a duty under European law to see they are looked after. This house is all we had available.'

Starving

The crisis began when the chimps – an adult male and female and their two offspring – were found starving in a boarded-up pet shop by animal rights outreach workers.

They were unable to find a temporary place to keep them properly cared for despite a desperate ring round of safari parks, zoos and vets.

The spokesperson for the London authority, which cannot be named while legal proceedings are underway, added:

'We fully realise this is a ridiculous situation and that some people will think it's a waste of taxpayers' money. We are contesting the ruling through the courts.'

Meanwhile the chimps are running amok in their luxury home.

....

ACTIVITY

Let's come straight to the point. Do you think there is any truth in this story at all?

■ Is there a single verifiable fact in it?

■ What is the purpose of this story?

■ What is the appeal of stories like this? What reaction is this one trying to evoke?

■ Is this in fact primarily entertaining, or is its purpose political, or even quite nasty?

■ Apart from the puns, what other forms of journalistic cliché are used here?

Although as language analysts we avoid making judgements, we think it is probably necessary to reassure you after this that we are now moving on to some rather more tasteful and subtle forms of entertaining writing.

Chapter 9

Take me away from all this

In this chapter we are going to continue our consideration of entertaining texts. Some varieties of writing, for example travel writing, are relatively hard to categorise but we shall consider questions of context, audience and purpose in relation to them as seems appropriate. The texts in this chapter are chosen around the theme of 'escapism' and represent the sort of books/articles we choose to read to try to transport us away from our everyday existences: many of them come under the rather baggy heading of 'entertainment'. With these escapist texts the readers' requirements are as significant as the writer's intentions and this fact is one of many that give these a kinship with literature.

The first section looks at travel writing of different sorts. Travel writing's aim is very open-ended – many of us like to read it even though we have no immediate plans to visit any of the places described.

The second section considers genre fiction such as detective stories, science fiction and romance, which rarely comes under the banner of 'literature', but is immensely popular. We have chosen these because we think they represent some interesting and subtle texts, because they seem to us to be in between non-literary and literary texts and also because they provide examples of the sorts of writing you might like to practise yourselves.

TRAVEL WRITING

Our first travel texts are from the start of the year *Independent Saturday Magazine*, which, like all papers at that time of year, has an extended holiday section. Therefore the context is the same (newspaper journalism) and so is the audience, but in style they are quite different and it's interesting to consider why. The feature they are from had twelve suggestions for holiday destinations, one for each month of the year (if only we could!). April's tip is Dubrovnik, December's New York.

Let's think first about the context of this feature. It is appearing in a broadsheet newspaper at a time of the year when people are planning holidays and looking for ideas about where to go. They want information, but they also want to be entertained and interested in what they're reading. The writer is (as is usual with journalistic travel writing) taking a positive view of the place he is describing, which is here presented as

April **Dubrovnik**

No cars, no bikes, no rip-offs, no pretension – Dubrovnik is the ideal location for a romantic European break, says **David Robson**

Put it down to inexperience – I am not a world traveller – but if anyone can tell me of a place that better repays a short visit than Dubrovnik, I should be very surprised.

There are towns in Italy stiff with the masterpieces of the Renaissance, cities in central Europe stuffed with cakes and romance. There is Paris and Barcelona and all that. Go there for the weekend and come back and tell the tale. But to walk through the gates of the old town of Dubrovnik is to enter a milieu of deeply moving perfection. The guide books will mention certain artefacts and buildings which are more important than others, and they will tell the history of the centuries-old capital of a maritime empire, its triumphs and its troubles. But this is not a place that depends on the thunder of portentous old facts or bruited masterworks to beguile you.

It is a small walled city on the Adriatic with marble streets and four-storey, flat-fronted, light grey buildings. It is old, and it feels old and almost unmolested by modern life. And yet, of course, few places have been so molested. The bombardment came from the sea and, much more painfully, from the hills that loom behind the town; it is only six years since the mortars rained down, wreaking damage that began to sound irreparable.

'I've just been to Dubrovnik,' you say to people in England.

'Oh really,' they said, 'Isn't it horribly destroyed?'

The answer to that question is no, not now. The restoration has been so fast and so meticulous that you have to take a hardish look to know this was recently a war zone. The locals are proud of what has been done, but there is a certain ambivalence. They are happy that you are there.

They are pleased that the place is alive and restored and working but, understandably, they would not like you to forget their ordeal.

You can stay in the old town and there are plenty of hotels within walking distance. Or you might stay, as we did, a few miles down the coast on a beach. You ride the Formica-seated local buses to the bus station outside the old town, you get off, pass through the ranks of motorcycles and through the gates into another world.

Ahead of you, running the length of the town, is a wide, white marble street. On either side, those big stone buildings, very Italian-looking to my untutored eye. The side streets to the left are unforgettable, and well-nigh unclimbable on a hot day. Very steep themselves, they transmute into steep steps leading up to the city wall. They are punctuated a third and two-thirds of the way up by narrow cross-streets thick with restaurants.

You could walk the walls, mosey round the harbour, explore every alley, and dutifully examine the places of special interest easily in one day. But that is not what I did. Dubrovnik is not a place to 'do'. It is a place to be. There are no cars, no bikes, no rip-offs, no pretension. Just serenity, beauty and elegance.

If Dubrovnik was not battered into the ground, the tourist industry certainly was. To my surprise, the flight I took last year was the first British charter since the war. We were greeted by television crews, plied with liqueurs and serenaded by a local band. And that is another part of the secret. The vast majority of the people taking an evening saunter down that wide white marble street are pleasant looking, pleasantly behaved local youth.

But once upon a time everyone went to Dubrovnik and they will again. I suggest you beat them to it.

How to get there

Reach Dubrovnik on Croatian Airlines (0181-563-0022) from Heathrow via Zagreb, for £287 in April. Croatia National Tourism Office, 2 The Lanchesters, 162–164 Fulham Palace Road, London W6 9ER (0181-563-7979).

a personal choice, so there is an element of persuasion in the piece. However, this is not an advertisement or a hard sell, although presumably the journalist had been subsidised to visit Dubrovnik in the hope he would write a favourable feature on it. Somehow the reader is not as surprised as Mr Robson is that this was a special flight celebrated by a reception party on its arrival. What is interesting about the article is the way different types of informative writing (descriptive and factual) are combined and the persuasive element is worked in. This sort of multi-functional writing is beloved of A-level English Language examiners.

There are three main points being made about Dubrovnik here:

Dubrovnik is peaceful, beautiful and unspoiled.

This is surprising in view of its recent history.

Partly because of this recent reputation there are relatively few tourists there and therefore you can beat the rush (lots of tourists like to go to places that others haven't discovered).

ACTIVITY

- How are the three central points structured into the article?
- What is the transitional sentence in paragraph 3 which introduces the section about the recent war damage?
- Where does the practical advice to the traveller make its first direct appearance?
- What type of reader is this aimed at, and how is this evident in the style of the piece?

This is typical of travel writing in that the writer is present in the first person, but not so typical in that he mentions a couple of times that he is not a seasoned traveller. Why do you think he wants us to know this and what effect does it have on the way we receive his advice?

ACTIVITY

You expect travel writing to evoke the atmosphere of the place both by physical description and by re-creating the ambience. Collect examples of the writer doing both these things. What sort of words predominate in each? Do you think that he is equally successful in both types of description?

For contrast, here are just a couple of paragraphs from December's choice, New York City.

In a cold winter, New York is an ice city. Snow is bulldozed into banks on the corners of streets, where it freezes and refreezes into gnarled glassy pyramids. Ice bulges over ornate lintels of Thirties skyscrapers, while creamy floes of it clunk down the Hudson and jostle in the slate-grey waters of the harbour around the toes of the Statue of Liberty.

Visitors used to the city in summer can find the change of landscape unsettling. Gone are the food-stalls and lolling crowds, the Latin music blaring from passing cars. In their place are monochrome streets, where steam leaks from manholes, and the crowds are focused and rapid.

But, really, the character of the place is just the same.

New York is a city with an unerring instinct for the very best ways of showing off. The same brash, edgy energy that's on display in the swimming pools and street corner basketball courts in summer transfers to the open-air ice-skating rinks. New Yorkers understand that the rinks are ideal places for posing. While the sensitive performers and groomed fashion victims twirl on the ice, the brassy capitalists capture their audience by donating and naming the rinks, or renovating them in high-profile campaigns.

ACTIVITY

Compare the physical description of Dubrovnik in the paragraph beginning 'Ahead of you', with these few paragraphs from the feature on New York. This is a very different sort of writing. Individually write responses to these questions.

- What is the writer's main aim here?
- Why doesn't he write in the first person?
- What are the main differences between this and the Dubrovnik piece and which do you prefer?
- Which might tempt you to consider visiting the place described?

ACTIVITY   OR

Think of a place you know well and write five paragraphs about it first in the 'Dubrovnik' and then in the 'New York' style. Alternatively work in a pair and each slip on whichever of the two styles you feel more comfortable with.

Even when the context, audience and complex purpose of the texts are the same, as in these examples, there is still a rich variety of styles available to a writer. Neither writing, nor the analysis of it should be completely mechanistic. You might like to compare these evocations of place with some of those in the literature section later in the book, for example the passage from *Tess of the D'Urbervilles* on page 188. How much do you feel they have in common?

The context of the next passage is not journalism. It is from a guide to Greece. The intended audience for this guide is people who have already made up their minds where they are going. So, it's a guide for people who want to know things, therefore the purpose has to be informative. Or does it?

Such guides are generally divided into sections for reference purposes and the early sections usually provide background information on the country. In this case the character of the Greek people is summed up in just over a page.

NATIONAL AND REGIONAL CHARACTERISTICS

While Greece is too small and compact a country to have major regional characteristics, the Greeks themselves tend to differentiate among three main groupings: mainland Greeks, island Greeks and 'overseas' Greeks. The last-named are not so much those still living in the communities abroad, who are flattered and supplied with the means of preserving their ethnic identity as if they were indeed a potential fifth column, as those who have repatriated either from choice or by force of circumstances.

Greece Today

Mainland Greeks

The mainlanders are the ordinary Greeks; those who have become modern in their pursuits and ambitions at the cost of their sense of comradeship, feel themselves oppressed, insult one another with vociferous abandon, and frequently give the impression of regarding any government, even one they voted for, as an occupying power. When you get to know them better, you may find they are not altogether unjustified. It naturally follows that the mainland is particularly disorganised.

Island Greeks

The islanders are reputedly calmer, shrewd rather than crafty, and closer to nature and the sea; their young menfolk are the mainstay of the Greek merchant navy. Until fairly recently, they were only too frequently ambitious to convert themselves into mainlanders; they have now been given less reason to feel isolated, through improved communications, better services, the expansion of the tourist movement and the levelling effect of television. For the most part, they still contrive to live at a more leisurely pace.

Within the islander context, those of the Ionian islands regard themselves as the more cultured – the readiness of considerable numbers of other Greeks to concede this suggests that there might be some truth in it – while inhabitants of the more numerous Aegean islands, from Thassos and Samothrace in the north to the most southerly of the Dodecanese, retort that they at least can keep their women in better order.

Everything is just a little larger than life on Crete, as if the megalonissos – the 'big island', and in fact the biggest – were to Greece what Texas is to the United States. The Cretans are a little prouder, a little more generous and hospitable, a little readier to take offence and a little more prepared to die for a cause (consider the novels of Cretan Nikos Kazantzakis and the 1941 Battle of Crete). They provided Greece's greatest modern statesman, Eleftherios Venizelos; the present leader of the opposition is a Cretan, and no prime minister could form a cabinet without at least one Cretan member. In the villages of Crete, national costume is still common and the vendetta is not yet dead; in Athens, any nightclub providing folk dances will include some from Crete. Cretans even tend to write with a larger hand. El Greco was a Cretan, and Zorba 'the Greek' could have come from nowhere else.

Overseas Greeks

Greeks from the communities abroad, for the obvious reasons of education and fluency in languages, are already disproportionately represented in Greece's managerial class; their share is likely to increase still further if governmental hopes of attracting high-technology industries and more international business and services bear fruit. As may be imagined, Greeks from the 'diaspora' are not particularly well-liked by those who see the plums go into their baskets in the multinationals, the travel industry, foreign and Greek banks and foreign diplomatic missions.

To some extent, they are only living up to their reputations: any Greek will tell you that the Greeks 'do better' abroad than in their own country, work and study harder, are more law-abiding and pay their taxes with greater willingness and honesty. The conclusion drawn is that there must be something wrong with Greece, as state and society; the reaction is a widespread ambition among Greek families of even modest means to send at least their sons abroad for advanced studies and character-building

Informative? Well, certain things are as we'd expect. The statement is the predominant sentence type in an informative piece and here we have nothing but. This extract could safely be described as 'opinionated' although there is no first person to signal this with an 'I think', or 'I have always found…'. In fact it's interesting to note who the writer does attribute these opinions on the Greek people to, where they are attributed, and also what constructions s/he uses where the opinions are not attributed.

ACTIVITY ⊞ 💬

- By these means, does the writer manage to escape the personal responsibility for stereotyping?
- In fact, is this piece primarily informative or is it entertaining?
- To what extent is it meant to be taken seriously? If it isn't, what evidence would you put forward to support your argument? (There might be some in paragraph 4.)
- Is it informative at all? What do we find out about the Greeks? Anything we could put into a geography or history essay? Could the reader learn anything here that might help them to meet and talk to Greek people?
- There is a skill in writing this sort of generalised piece without being offensive. Do you think this writer has succeeded?

Look at the next passage now, which has a similar theme, but this time a bit closer to home because it's about the British. It's from *Notes from a Small Island*, a humorous account of a journey around Britain by the American writer Bill Bryson, who in some of his other books writes about language.

NOTES FROM A SMALL ISLAND

One of the charms of the British is that they have so little idea of their own virtues, and nowhere is this more true than with their happiness. You will laugh to hear me say it, but they are the happiest people on earth. Honestly. Watch any two Britons in conversation and see how long it is before they smile or laugh over some joke or pleasantry. It won't be more than a few seconds. I once shared a railway compartment between Dunkirk and Brussels with two French-speaking businessmen who were obviously old friends or colleagues. They talked genially the whole journey, but not once in two hours did I see either of them raise a flicker of a smile. You could imagine the same thing with Germans or Swiss or Spaniards or even Italians, but with Britons – never.

And the British are so easy to please. It is the most extraordinary thing. They actually like their pleasures small. That is why, I suppose, so many of their treats – teacakes, scones, crumpets, rock cakes, rich tea biscuits, fruit Shrewsburys – are so cautiously flavourful. They are the only people in the world who think of jam and currants as thrilling constituents of a pudding or cake. Offer them something genuinely tempting – a slice of gâteau or a choice of chocolates from a box – and they will nearly always hesitate and begin to worry that it's unwarranted and excessive, as if any pleasure beyond a very modest threshold is vaguely unseemly.

'Oh, I shouldn't really,' they say.

'Oh, go on,' you prod encouragingly.

'Well, just a small one then,' they say and dartingly take a small one, and then get a look as if they have just done something *terribly* devilish. All this is completely alien to the American mind. To an American the whole purpose of living, the one constant confirmation of continued existence, is to cram as much sensual pleasure as possible into one's mouth more or less continuously. Gratification, instant and lavish, is a birthright. You might as well say 'Oh, I shouldn't really' if someone tells you to take a deep breath.

I used to be puzzled by the curious British attitude to pleasure, and that tireless, dogged optimism of theirs that allowed them to attach an upbeat turn of phrase to the direst inadequacies – 'well, it makes a change', 'mustn't grumble', 'you could do worse', 'it's not much, but it's cheap and cheerful', 'it was quite nice *really*' – but gradually I came round to their way of thinking and my life has never been happier. I remember finding myself sitting in damp clothes in a cold café on a dreary seaside promenade and being presented with a cup of tea and a teacake and going 'Ooh, lovely!', and I knew then that the process had started. Before long I came to regard all kinds of activities – asking for more toast in a hotel, buying wool-rich socks at Marks & Spencer, getting two pairs of trousers when I only really needed one – as something daring, very nearly illicit. My life became immensely richer.

Bill Bryson: *Notes from a Small Island*

This is a similarly opinionated piece of writing, but this time the author is present in the text. Earlier reading in the book will have informed us that Bryson has lived in England for some time and is completing this tour of the country before leaving to go back to live in America. He looks at the British with an outsider's eye, but that of a familiar outsider, and although he can be fairly scathing at times, his view is often affectionate. Whether or not his description of the British as 'the happiest people on earth' strikes any chords with you might depend on the sort of mood you are in and how much of your Britain you recognise in his 'teacakes, scones, crumpets...' picture.

ACTIVITY

Discuss whether, as with the previous piece, this one is to be taken entirely at face value. Does Bryson really want to join the ranks of 'the only people in the world who think of jam and currants as thrilling constituents of a pudding or cake'? Or is it that by contrast with them he feels that when his American self re-asserts itself by buying two pairs of trousers, not one, he suddenly seems 'daring, very nearly illicit' and thus his life is enriched? In fact, what is the main source of the humour in this piece? Does Bryson's tone convey personality here, and if so, how?

This is the sort of writing we have to give ourselves permission to write. We have so frequently to use a more discursive style, building up arguments gradually, taking account of the opposite point of view, that we find it hard to present opinions so decisively, as if there were no other way of looking at things, and with complete certainty. However, it's good fun and is positively expected in certain contexts.

ACTIVITY

With a friend, construct this type of tongue-in-cheek description of the inhabitants of your town/city/village, having decided how they could be stereotyped or what key idiosyncrasies sum them up.

The next piece is somewhat laconically titled 'A Ramble through Lebanon'. It was written by another American after a visit to the Lebanon in 1984, 'pretty much the last time an American could travel in that country with only a risk (rather than a certainty) of being kidnapped'. It is not describing somewhere any of us would choose to go for a holiday.

A RAMBLE THROUGH LEBANON

Beirut, at a glance, lacks charm. The garbage has not been picked up since 1975. The ocean is thick with raw sewage, and trash dots the surf. Do not drink the water. Leeches have been known to pop out of the tap. Electricity is intermittent.

It is a noisy town. Most shops have portable gasoline generators set out on the sidewalk. The racket from these combines with incessant horn-honking, scattered gunfire, loud Arab music from pushcart cassette vendors, much yelling among the natives and occasional car bombs. Israeli jets also come in from the sea most afternoons, breaking the sound barrier on their way to targets in the Bekaa Valley. A dense brown haze from dump fires and car exhaust covers the city. Air pollution probably approaches a million parts per million. This, however, dulls the sense of smell.

There are taxis always available outside the Commodore. I asked one of the drivers, Najib, to show me the sights. I wanted to see the National Museum, the Great Mosque, the Place des Martyrs, the Bois de Pins, the Corniche and Hotel Row. Perhaps Najib misunderstood or maybe had his own ideas about sight-seeing. He took me to the Green Line. The Green Line's four crossings were occupied by the Lebanese Army – the Muslim Sixth Brigade on one side, the Christian Fifth Brigade on the other. Though under unified command, their guns were pointed at each other. This probably augurs ill for political stability in the region.

The wise traveller will pack shirts or blouses with ample breast pockets. Reaching inside a jacket for your passport looks too much like going for the draw and puts armed men out of continence.

At the Port Crossing, on the street where all the best whore-houses were, the destruction is perfectly theatrical. Just enough remains of the old buildings to give an impression of erstwhile grandeur. Mortars, howitzers and rocket-propelled grenades have not left a superfluous brush stroke on the scrim. Turn the corner into the old market-place, the Souk, however, and the set is a Hollywood back lot. Small arms and sniper fire have left perfectly detailed havoc. Every square inch is painstakingly bullet nibbled. Rubble spills artfully out of doorways. Roofs and cornices have been deftly crenellated by explosions. Everything is ready for Ernest Borgnine, John Cassavetes and Lee Marvin in a remake of *The Dirty Dozen*, except the Lebanese can't figure out how to remove the land mines.

I met one young lady from Atlanta who worked on a CNN camera crew. She was twenty-six, cute, slightly plump and looked like she should have been head of the Georgia State pep squad. I sat next to her at the Commodore bar and watched her drink twenty-five gin and tonics in a row. She never got drunk, never slurred a word, but along about G&T number twenty-two out came the stories about dismembered babies and dead bodies flying all over the place and the Red Cross picking up hands and feet and heads from bomb blasts and putting them all in a trash dumpster. 'So I asked the Red Cross people,' she said, in the same sweet Dixie accent, 'like, what's this? Save 'em, collect 'em, trade 'em with your friends?'

Everyone in Beirut can hold his or her liquor. If you get queasy, Muhammad, the Commodore bartender, has a remedy rivalling Jeeves, in P. G. Wodehouse's novels. It will steady your stomach so you can drink more. You'll want to. No one in this part of the world is without a horror story, and, at the Commodore bar, you'll hear most of them.

Beirut night-life is not elaborate, but it is amusing. When danger waits the tables and death is the busboy, it adds zest to the simple pleasure of life. There's poignant satisfaction in every puff of a cigarette or sip of a martini. The jokes are funnier, the drinks are stronger, the bonds of affection more powerfully felt than they'll ever be at Club Med.

P. J. O'Rourke

This is not conventional travel writing, but it does use the genre. Several paragraphs start with short punchy statements commenting on aspects of life in Beirut, much as you would expect, 'Beirut, at a glance, lacks charm.' Usually there would be an expectation that the writer would go on to qualify this in some way ('but once you've penetrated the drab façade'), but no, it just gets worse. Charm and Beirut should not appear in the same sentence.

'Everyone in Beirut can hold his or her liquor.' A good place to party then, and said with the same sweeping certainty as in the guide to Greece above, but by this time we have a sense that this drinking is born of desperation.

'Beirut night-life is not elaborate, but it is amusing.' The rest of the paragraph goes on to say why. Danger intensifies all experiences and adds to the simple pleasures of life.

Another paragraph begins 'The wise traveller will pack shirts or blouses with ample breast pockets', in the brisk tone of a 'handy hints' column but yet again once the reason for this is given, the sinister overtones become apparent.

The rather grim humour of this piece comes in part from the contrast between the familiar travel writing style and the sordid content. But it does convey the atmosphere of the place from a particular point of view and this is partly done through the 'voice' the writer adopts. This is a hard-drinking tough guy who is unfazed when his taxi driver takes him to the front line rather than the tourist sights and who can compare this real city to a Hollywood lot. This, we feel, is the sort of approach to life you have to take in Beirut if you are to survive and enjoy life at all. It is entirely the outsider's view and there is little sense in these extracts of what life might be like for the inhabitants trying to go about their daily lives. That's fine because it suggests that there is something inpenetrable about this conflict for the outsider and no pretence that somehow you can really enter into the life of Beirut, in the way that articles which describe the joys of living in a French 'gite' for two weeks usually suggest you can become an honorary member of the community.

ACTIVITY

Imagine you are from Beirut and take exception to the tone and content of this article. Write a letter to its publisher giving a detailed critique of its approach to the subject. You might even suggest a few replacement paragraphs describing the real Beirut from an insider's perspective (we appreciate this would require a little research but this would give you an insight into the preparation required for genuinely informative writing).

In most of the examples so far you will have noticed the importance of detail. Sometimes lots of details are accumulated to build up a visual impression, as in the New York piece, or particular details are given significance and used somehow to sum up something about a people or place, as in the Bryson. The next brief example is from the notebooks of Bruce Chatwin, a writer known for his fiction and his travel writing. Here he is travelling in Mauritania, West Africa, and is jotting down details of his stay in Oualata 'the fabled scarlet town' and then in Nema. The notebooks were published after Chatwin's death and are not in finished form. They are the sort of details a writer jots down to use again later, in Chatwin's case either for travel writing or to re-surface in his novels. Many writers adopt this technique as do lots of people who have no thought of being published but who just want to use the jottings to remember people and events in their lives. It takes some discipline to do this systematically, but you would find it helpful for your own writing.

CHATWIN'S PHOTOGRAPHS AND NOTEBOOKS

2 March

Sipping sweet green tea in the Prefect's tent. It is woven of thin strips of white cotton about six inches wide, of double thickness. The poles have mushroom shaped ends to prevent them slipping in the sand.

I love to look at the blue patchwork of the tents. The use of patchwork for clothing is a sign of humility, but is often carried beyond that to another plane – that of worthiness – thus the Ottoman Sultans wore the most costly patchwork clothes as a symbol of their sanctity.

Bought hibiscus flowers in the market, cool delicious drink of incredible raspberry colour. Walked out along the road to Oualata. Smell of acacia-mimosa trees fresh and fragrant on the wind. Wind flapping through the hide of dead cattle, teeth protruding like sharks. A flat plain of hard gravel glinting stone and the ever present footprints of goats. The flat-topped cliffs' sides a luminous pale green smeared with scarlet. White tents through the mimosa scrub. Lemon coloured wasp offered its attention.

Nema

The Governor. Small moustache. Sad decadent eyes. Reclines instead of sits. White robes. Masseur. Pills. Decongestants. Chinese pills. French pills. Swiss pills. His assistant round-headed with cauliflower ears. The ex-Ambassador of Mali to Jiddah, elegant, decadent. Hand movements. With him an immensely tall bearded Negro in green satin and his permanent musician in cool pink, long fingers plucking at a guitar. Chauffeurs are invited to lunch comme nous sommes maintenant democratiques but are made to feel so uncomfortable that they leave. Then the perennial moan about the servant problem. Servants of the Governor claim that their wages are six months in arrears.

There is contrast within these two extracts between fully worked sentences and listings of noun phrases. Both reveal the importance of detail, the sort of details we easily forget, but which do lend a whiff of authenticity to the finished piece.

ACTIVITY

Use the information in these two extracts to write a finished piece. Before you do, decide what ratio of entertainment, information and persuasion you, as writer, are aiming at then ask a friend to read your piece and jot down their perception of the ratio of aims. If they differ do not assume you have 'failed'; as we said earlier, in this particular field, readers bring their own baggage.

THE BEST-SELLER

We move on now to a different form of entertaining writing, and one which is hugely popular, so it must satisfy many readers' needs and expectations. Barbara Taylor Bradford is one of the most successful novelists being published today. The cover of this novel hails a 'Multi million copy best seller—now a magnificent TV series' (it would be magnificent wouldn't it?). The cover of the particular copy I have mentions five million copies sold, which for a first novel isn't bad going. It is not exactly in the 'romance' category in the same way as Barbara Cartland or the rather more racy 'Black Lace' versions, but is referred to as a 'mighty saga', covering a large chunk of the heroine's life from rags to riches.

This is the opening:

A WOMAN OF SUBSTANCE

ONE

Emma Harte leaned forward and looked out of the window. The private Lear jet, property of the Sitex Oil Corporation of America, had been climbing steadily up through a vaporous haze of cumulus clouds and was now streaking through a sky so penetratingly blue its shimmering clarity hurt the eyes. Momentarily dazzled by this early-morning brightness, Emma turned away from the window, rested her head against the seat, and closed her eyes. For a brief instant the vivid blueness was trapped beneath her lids and, in that instant, such a strong and unexpected feeling of nostalgia was evoked within her that she caught her breath in surprise. It's the sky from the Turner painting above the upstairs parlour fireplace at Pennistone Royal, she thought, a Yorkshire sky on a spring day when the wind has driven the fog from the moors.

A faint smile played around her mouth, curving the line of the lips with unfamiliar softness, as she thought with some pleasure of Pennistone

Royal. That great house that grew up out of the stark and harsh landscape of the moors and which always appeared to her to be a force of nature engineered by some Almighty architect rather than a mere edifice erected by mortal man. The one place on this violent planet where she had found peace, limitless peace that soothed and refreshed her. Her home. She had been away far too long this time, almost six weeks, which was a prolonged absence indeed for her. But within the coming week she would be returning to London, and by the end of the month she would travel north to Pennistone. To peace, tranquillity, her gardens, and her grand-children.

This thought cheered her immeasurably and she relaxed in her seat, the tension that had built up over the last few days diminishing until it had evaporated. She was bone tired from the raging battles that had punctuated these last few days of board meetings at the Sitex corporate headquarters in Odessa; she was supremely relieved to be leaving Texas and returning to the relative calmness of her own corporate offices in New York.

Barbara Taylor Bradford: A *Woman of Substance*

It is interesting to consider this firstly as the opening of a novel. There are several other examples later in the literature chapters of this book.

In the opening paragraphs of any novel or story we expect as readers to gain some sense of what the story is to be about, often to meet the main character, to gather the point of view (literally) the story is being told from and the style in which the story is to be told. The writer will probably introduce some intriguing details to try to hook us and make us want to read on. As readers we then are in a position to make a decision about whether or not we want to, whether this is our sort of book. If we're browsing in a bookshop the decision may well be about whether to buy or not, a crucial decision from the writer's point of view too. For novels are not something we *have* to read. They aren't like business letters, a memo from the boss, a bill or a summons, instructions, or a signpost. Writing to entertain, like the other varieties in this chapter, is something we *choose* to read. And as we've already noted, millions of people have chosen to read this particular example.

So, what can we deduce about the rest of this novel from these opening paragraphs?

The central character is named and introduced. She moves in a world of wealth and power, but there is something troubled about her life: 'the one place on this violent planet where she had found peace, limitless peace that soothed and refreshed her'.

She travels far (literally) and is of an age to have grandchildren. The style is descriptive and consciously crafted in a way that we notice (the link between the blueness of the sky and her Yorkshire home).

ACTIVITY

There are quite a few proper nouns in this extract. Identify them and suggest the contribution each makes to the picture the reader begins to build up of what to expect from this novel.

Look at the first paragraph. How is the link made between the sky outside the plane and her home in Yorkshire? What does each step of the link contribute to your knowledge of the central character? What does it suggest about the style in which this novel is written? Does it appeal to you or not, and why?

Look at paragraph two. What impression of Pennistone Royal is conveyed, a positive or a negative one? Is the impression conveyed through physical detail or by other means?

What impression is given of Emma Harte? Jot down what you know of her life from this opening. Do you want to know more about her? If so, why?

....

The answers to some of these questions probably say something about your tastes as a reader. When it comes to 'genre' writing we usually know whether or not a certain type of fiction appeals to us as individuals or not. By 'genre fiction' in this context we mean distinct types of novels which follow certain conventions that both the reader and the writer accept. They deal with particular themes in particular ways and too radical a departure from the expected would result in disappointment. They contain similar ingredients in terms of plot, character and style, with just enough of originality or a twist to make it worth reading another example of the genre. Thus some people love detective fiction, 'who done its', where the plot is supreme and characterisation often of lesser importance. Some love romance, where the heroine always gets the right man, whom the reader has been able to identify from early on, with enough trials and tribulations and near misses along the way to keep the story going to the required length. It's easy to be sniffy about them, but there does seem to be something in most readers that responds to a little predictability and certainly many novels now considered 'literature' began life as genre novels.

A Woman of Substance falls into the family saga/romance category, if there is such a thing. Such novels have quite a sweep in terms of time-scale and social breadth. It would be the kiss of death for instance, in most romance fiction, to make your central character a grandmother, but in the 'saga' subset we know that this can be dealt with by an extended flashback technique. We have hints of the rags-to-riches element and the toll it has taken on Emma in this opening 'a faint smile played around her mouth, curving the line of the lips with unfamiliar softness'. This rags-to-riches element is another important ingredient. There is always some wealth and luxury as background to these sagas and perhaps the aspirations towards these are shared by the characters and by the readers and are an important part of their appeal?

....

ACTIVITY ▮ 🗩

Find two other novels by Barbara Taylor Bradford and compare their openings with this one, noting in particular, points of similarity.

....

From a very successful writer of family saga/romance fiction we turn to one who is described by the *Daily Mail* critic quoted on the cover of his books as 'probably the greatest storyteller of our age', Jeffrey Archer. Jeffrey Archer is the author of (at the time of writing) nine novels, which have all been world-wide best-sellers. They have various subjects, but are all thrillers, often with a political and/or international backdrop. This is an extract from *A Matter of Honour*. As you might expect from someone hailed as a 'great storyteller', the plot is fast and furious and the heroes and villains satisfyingly good and evil. The hero, Captain Adam Scott, has been left a letter (unopened) in his father's will. He opens it and is plunged into a world of betrayal and espionage and for the rest of the novel plays a major part in thwarting Russian attempts to claim a large chunk of America as Russian territory, and simultaneously clears his dead father's name of the slur of treachery. Adam is introduced in the first chapter as being very like his father,

> The same dark hair and deep brown eyes, the same honest open face, even the same gentle approach to everyone he came across. But most of all the same high standards of morality that had brought them to their (his family's) present sad state.

The novel, written in 1986, is set in sixties Britain in the period of the cold war and this passage occurs near the end as the plot is reaching its denouement. Mr Tomkins (the colonel) is working for a Russian spy called Romanov, Adam's principal adversary.

> He pushed open the swinging gate and made his way slowly up the path in a pitch darkness. Once he reached the corner of the house he searched for the third stone on the left. When he located the correct stone where he always left his spare key, he pulled it up with his fingers and felt around in the dirt. To his relief the key was still in place. Like a burglar he pushed it into the lock quietly.
>
> He crept into the hall and closed the door behind him, switched on the light and began to climb the stairs. Once he had reached the landing he switched off the hall light, turned the knob of his bedroom door and pushed.
>
> As he stepped in an arm circled his throat like a whiplash and he was thrown to the ground with tremendous force. He felt a knee pressed hard against his spine and his arm was jerked up behind his back into a half nelson. He lay on the floor, flat on his face, hardly able to move or even breathe. The light switch flashed on and the first thing Adam saw was the colonel.
>
> 'Don't kill me, Captain Scott sir, don't kill me,' he implored.
>
> 'I have no intention of doing so, Mr Tomkins,' said Adam calmly. 'But first, where is your esteemed employer at this moment?'
>
> Adam kept his knee firmly in the middle of the colonel's back and pressed his arm a few inches higher before the colonel bleated out, 'He went back to the Embassy once he realised the girl wasn't going to return to the flat.'

'Just as I planned,' said Adam, but he didn't lessen the pressure on the colonel's arm as he described in vivid detail everything that would now be expected of him.

The colonel's face showed disbelief. 'But that will be impossible,' he said 'I mean, he's bound to noti – Ahhh.'

The colonel felt his arm forced higher up his back. 'You could carry out the whole exercise in less than ten minutes, and he need never be any the wiser,' said Adam. 'However, I feel that it's only fair that you should be rewarded for your effort.'

'Thank you, sir,' said the fawning colonel.

'If you succeed in delivering the one item I require and carry out my instructions to the letter you will be given in exchange your passport, driving licence, papers, wallet and a guarantee of no prosecution for your past treachery. But if, on the other hand, you fail to turn up by nine thirty tomorrow morning with the object of my desire,' said Adam, 'all those documents will be placed thirty minutes later on the desk of Mr Lawrence Pemberton of the FO, along with my report on your other sources of income which you have failed to declare on your tax return.'

'You wouldn't do that to me, would you, Captain Scott?'

'As ten o'clock chimes,' said Adam.

'But think what would then happen to me, Captain Scott, sir, if you carried out such a threat,' moaned the colonel.

'I have already considered that,' said Adam, 'and I have come to two conclusions.'

'And what are they, Captain Scott?'

'Spies,' continued Adam, not loosening his grip, 'at the present time seem to be getting anything from eighteen to forty-two years at her Majesty's pleasure, so you might, with good behaviour, be out before the turn of the century, just in time to collect your telegram from the Queen.'

The colonel looked visibly impressed. 'And the other conclusion?' he blurted out.

'Oh, simply that you could inform Romanov of my nocturnal visit and he in return would arrange for you to spend the rest of your days in a very small dacha in a suitably undesirable suburb of Moscow. Because, you see, my dear Tomkins, you are a very small spy. I personally am not sure when left with such an alternative which I would view with more horror.'

'I'll get it for you, Captain Scott, you can rely on me.'

'I'm sure I can, Tomkins. Because if you were to let Romanov into our little secret, you would be arrested within minutes. So at best, you could try to escape on the Aeroflot plane to Moscow. And I've checked, there isn't one until the early evening.'

'I'll bring it to you by nine thirty on the dot, sir. You can be sure of that. But for God's sake have yours ready to exchange.'

'I will,' said Adam, 'as well as all your documents, Tomkins.'

Adam lifted the colonel slowly off the ground and then shoved him towards the landing. He switched on the light and then pushed the colonel on down the stairs until they reached the front door.

'The keys,' said Adam.

'But you've already got my keys, Captain Scott, sir.'

'The car keys, you fool.'

'But it's a hire car, sir,' said the colonel.

'And I'm about to hire it,' said Adam.

'But how will I get myself back to London in time, sir?'

'I have no idea, but you still have the rest of the night to come up with something. You could even walk it by then. The keys,' Adam repeated, jerking the colonel's arm to shoulder-blade level.

'In my left hand pocket,' said the colonel, almost an octave higher.

Adam put his hand into the colonel's new jacket and pulled out the car keys.

He opened the front door, shoved the colonel on to the path, and then escorted him to the pavement.

'You will go and stand on the far side of the road,' said Adam, 'and you will not return to the house until I have reached the end of the road. Do I make myself clear, Tomkins.'

'Abundantly clear, Captain Scott, sir.'

'Good', said Adam releasing him for the first time, 'and just one more thing, Tomkins. In case you think of double-crossing me, I have already instructed the Foreign Office to place Romanov under surveillance and put two extra lookouts near the Soviet Embassy with instructions to report the moment anyone suspicious turns up or leaves before nine tomorrow morning.' Adam hoped he sounded convincing.

'Thought of everything, haven't you, sir?' said the colonel mournfully.

'Yes, I think so,' said Adam. 'I even found time to disconnect your phone while I was waiting for you to return.' Adam pushed the colonel across the road before getting into the hire car. He wound the window down, 'See you at nine thirty tomorrow morning. Prompt,' he added, as he put the Ford into first gear.

The colonel stood shivering on the far pavement, nursing his right shoulder, as Adam drove to the end of the road. He was still standing there when Adam took a left turn back towards the centre of London.

For the first time since Heidi's death, Adam felt it was Romanov who was on the run.

Jeffrey Archer: A *Matter of Honour*

The first thing to comment on is the use of the pronoun 'he' as the subject of most of the verbs in the first three paragraphs. There is a real tension created here as we do not know exactly in context who this 'he' is. This is the start of a chapter and the reader would recognise that the subject could not be the same as the subject of the end of the previous one. The effect of this is rather similar to that achieved in films when we see the scene from the point of view of the camera, especially since it is night. We are unclear from whose perspective we are seeing these events and who is about to do what to whom. Since we are used to thrillers as a cinematic as well as a literary genre this comparison is apt, but whereas we recognise the convention immediately, in the last sentence of the third paragraph when the light comes on we see the scene from the hero's (Adam's) point of view.

ACTIVITY

- What does this switch of subject suggest about Adam's situation?
- How else is tension created in these opening paragraphs? Do you get the sense that something is about to happen? If this were a film, how might the tension be conveyed?
- Once the dialogue commences, how are the respective positions of the participants established and reinforced?
- Discuss the presentation of the violence in this episode? Is it under or overstated, and why?
- How is Adam's status as the hero made clear in this passage? What do his main character traits appear to be?

ACTIVITY

Re-write this scene as a film script, paying attention to what you could add (sound effects for example) and what you might edit (for example, would you need all this dialogue?).

The final extract of this chapter is from a novel which has been made into a well known film, *The Exorcist* by William Peter Blatty. The cover tells me that this is 'the electrifying international best seller of Satanism and possession'. Obviously horror is a very popular genre, both in book and film form, and it is interesting to consider why. We all like to be scared, to an extent: witness the enduring popularity of ghost stories, and we like to speculate as to whether 'there isn't something in it'. Some people, mainly those with strong religious convictions, have deep-rooted objections to Horror, feeling that the existence of evil, in the form of the devil, is too serious to be treated as entertainment. Most of us don't take it that seriously, but on the other hand it doesn't work unless the world created by the writer convinces us, at least while we enter it.

This is the novel's opening:

THE EXORCIST

CHAPTER ONE

LIKE the brief doomed flare of exploding suns that registers dimly on blind men's eyes, the beginning of the horror passed almost unnoticed; in the shriek of what followed, in fact, was forgotten and perhaps not connected to the horror at all. It was difficult to judge.

The house was a rental. Brooding. Tight. A brick colonial gripped by ivy in the Georgetown section of Washington, D.C. Across the street was a fringe of campus belonging to Georgetown University; to the rear, a sheer embankment plummeting steep to busy M Street and, beyond, the muddy Potomac. Early on the morning of 1st April, the house was quiet. Chris MacNeil was propped in bed, going over her lines for the next day's filming; Regan, her daughter, was sleeping down the hall; and asleep downstairs in a room off the pantry were the middle-aged housekeepers, Willie and Karl. At approximately 12.25 a.m., Chris glanced from her script with a frown of puzzlement. She heard rapping sounds. They were odd. Muffled. Profound. Rhythmically clustered. Alien code tapped out by a dead man.

Funny.

She listened for a moment; then dismissed it; but as the rappings persisted she could not concentrate. She slapped down the script on the bed.

Jesus, that bugs me!

She got up to investigate.

She went out to the hallway and looked around. It seemed to be coming from Regan's bedroom.

What is she doing?

She padded down the hall and the rapping grew suddenly louder, much faster, and as she pushed on the door and stepped into the room, they abruptly ceased.

What the heck's going on?

Her pretty eleven-year-old was asleep, cuddled tight to a large stuffed round-eyed panda. Pookey. Faded from years of smothering; years of smacking, warm, wet kisses.

Chris moved softly to her bedside and leaned over for a whisper. 'Rags? You awake?'

Regular breathing. Heavy. Deep.

Chris shifted her glance around the room. Dim light from the hall fell pale and splintered on Regan's paintings; on Regan's sculptures; on more stuffed animals.

Okay, Rags. Old mother's ass is draggin'. Say it. 'April Fool!'

And yet Chris knew it wasn't like her. The child had a shy and very diffident nature. Then who was the trickster? A somnolent mind imposing order on the rattlings of heating pipes or plumbing? Once, in the mountains of Bhutan, she had stared for hours at a Buddhist monk who was squatting on the ground in meditation. Finally, she thought she had seen him levitate. Perhaps. Recounting the story to someone, she invariably added 'perhaps'. And perhaps her mind, that untiring raconteur of illusion, had embellished the rappings.

Bullshit! I heard it!

Abruptly, she flicked a quick glance to the ceiling. There! Faint scratchings.

Rats in the attic, for Pete's sake! Rats!

She sighed. *That's it. Big tails. Thump, thump.* She felt oddly relieved. And then noticed the cold. The room. It was icy.

She padded to the window. Checked it. Closed. She touched the radiator. Hot.

Oh, really?

Puzzled, she moved to the bedside and touched her hand to Regan's cheek. It was smooth as thought and lightly perspiring.

I must be sick!

She looked at her daughter, at the turned-up nose and freckled face, and on a quick, warm impulse leaned over the bed and kissed her cheek. 'I sure do love you,' she whispered, then returned to her room and her bed and her script.

William Peter Blatty: *The Exorcist*

The opening paragraph makes it absolutely clear what the novel is to be about, 'the beginning of the horror passed almost unnoticed'. This is the way that most genre fiction works. We are not supposed to be surprised by what we read, although we may very well appreciate the skill and ingenuity with which the familiar formula is worked. But this is especially true of horror and ghost stories. We have to know its all going to turn horribly wrong even though there have to be passages of seeming normality to set against this terror, because as often as not the scariness is in the anticipation rather than the realisation of the awful events. Very few descriptions in prose, or manifestations on the screen, are actually as terrifying as what we anticipate.

ACTIVITY ⊞ 💬

- The opening paragraph contains a simile and a metaphor. What is the impact of this figurative language?
- By contrast, the first part of the next paragraph is full of nouns. It is written in minor sentences rather like a notebook. Why? How important is the physical setting?
- 'At approximately 12.25 a.m., Chris glanced from her script...'. The action begins. The action, the investigation of the sounds, is from then on interspersed with Chris's thoughts represented by italics. Why?
- Although Chris appears to be reassured when she thinks she's found a rational explanation, 'Rats in the attic for Pete's sake', her confidence, and ours, is immediately undermined. We know this isn't the explanation. How?

Horror works in this way, by contrasting strange details with normality, but ratcheting up each incident until the climax. It can't be scary all the time or we would want the whole narrative over too quickly, but because we know what we are reading we know the terror will return.

ACTIVITY ●

We have looked at only a few categories of genre fiction in this chapter. There are several other significant ones, straight romance, historical novels, fantasy and science fiction for example, that we haven't looked at. Choose one category, possibly one that interests you particularly, and pick three examples of it at random. You can usually do this easily enough in libraries or browsing in bookshops (borrow the books from somewhere else later). Compare the openings of the three, or if you are good at scanning or choose to read them all, pick later passages of about two pages in length. From this raw material, try to identify some of the distinguishing features of the particular genre you have chosen. Write these up as an essay, or as a presentation to your group.

Chapter 10
Literature with a Capital 'L'

Of all varieties of language the most difficult to analyse within the framework we have been suggesting is Literature. Literature with a capital 'L' that is. In fact defining exactly what Literature is in any watertight way is extremely problematic and has been the subject of very serious debate, even within university departments which exist to teach it, particularly over the last thirty years.

At one time it would have been accepted that Literature was somehow synonymous with quality, that it was the very highest form of writing and is represented by works that have stood the test of time. In recent years that view has been challenged, largely on the grounds of 'who says so?' There have been moves to widen the range of works deemed worthy of study beyond the accepted 'canon' of classic texts (from this point of view seen mainly as the work of DWMs, Dead White Males) to include more work by women and working-class writers, the sort of genre writing we glanced at in the last chapter, and contemporary popular culture including *EastEnders* and *Coronation Street*. This approach rejects the value-judgement approach of the old definition of English Literature, and in some cases English Literature Departments in universities have labelled themselves, or large chunks of their courses, as Cultural Studies.

However, whilst acknowledging the power and often positive influence of this iconoclastic approach, we *are* going to look at Literature as a distinct category in this section of the book, although we will from now on usually drop the upper case. This is because we are not wholly convinced that there isn't something in the 'quality' argument, both in terms of the ambition and the achievement of many works of literature and also because out there in the real world there is a recognition and general understanding that Literature exists. This is often accompanied by a pride and pleasure in the achievements of the greatest known writers in the language. There is also a much more pragmatic reason for us to accept that Literature exists, and that is that it is still on most school timetables as a separate curriculum subject and many readers of this book will be studying it as such, albeit that the range of texts now admitted to the body of 'set books' is much wider than it would once have been. From this purely common-sense point of view, it is obvious that Literature exists for several reasons:

- There is considerable agreement about what constitutes the pre-twentieth century canon.

- Makers of television serials and owners of buildings with literary connections know who the public regard as the big literary names and the interest these continue to exert for a large section of the population.
- Shakespeare is recognised around the world as as much of a British national institution as Manchester United (and as Tolstoy is for Russians or Molière for the French).
- When it comes to contemporary writing, broadsheet newspapers and literary magazines review certain writers (Ted Hughes, Iris Murdoch, Martin Amis among many) more consistently and seriously than, say, the latest work of Jeffrey Archer or even Barbara Taylor Bradford. Bookshops recognise the distinction between general fiction and genre writing in the way they shelve and display their books.
- Most literature discusses serious ideas, although not always seriously.

All these things contribute to the 'context' of literary texts, as do their structural conventions. Novels aren't written in acts and poems aren't written in chapters. Any literature student learns about the conventions which affect the shape and style of a literary text as well as its individuality. The long tradition of literary writing also contributes to the context in which literary texts are created, as does the fact that professional writers need to earn their living. 'Literature flourishes best when it is half a trade and half an art' observed W. R. Inge, writing mainly about the Victorian age, which certainly produced great novelists.

We are not going to attempt an all-encompassing definition of Literature here, but we would like to offer some characteristics which seem to us to identify features which contribute to distinguishing literary texts. Few of these are unique to literature, as we see from the first one, but taken together they suggest some of the ways in which literary texts are 'special' and difficult to pin down in terms of context and audience.

- Like genre fiction, as we discussed in the last chapter, literature is read for pleasure and not from necessity. It is not something we have to read, many people don't, and is not simply functional. This gives us some problems with saying what the purpose of Literature is, although we may be able to identify the purpose of particular texts or parts of texts, as indeed we try to do in the next few chapters. It also gives us problems in trying to identify the 'audience' for Literature.
- Readers often turn to literature to appreciate the freshness of the writer's ideas (originality) or the recognition of familiar ideas and feelings which are better or more memorably expressed in plays, novels and verses than elsewhere. In different moods we seek out texts which do either of these things.
- Within its umbrella literature contains a huge range of texts with different appeals – the avant-garde, the shocking, the reassuringly familiar.
- Literature from previous generations which is still published, read and performed usually displays complexity, ambiguity and resonance which make it capable of different interpretations at different times. We would suggest that this is something which does distinguish it from genre fiction or verses in greetings cards. This is probably what most serious contemporary writers are aiming for too. Literary writers are usually aware of the tradition they are working in.

- And lastly, but importantly for language students, language is the medium for literature. Writers take language very seriously, practise it as a craft and often do amazing things with it because they work with it all the time. Literature 'foregrounds' language, sometimes in ways which draw attention to it, sometimes in ways which don't. In fact we tend to agree with Flaubert, that in writing, 'simplicity' is the hardest thing to achieve.

Having made a long-winded attempt to describe Literature ourselves, we now offer some rather more succinct definitions, most of which are from writers:

What oft was thought but ne'er so well expressed

Organised violence done on language

The best words in the best order

Language at full stretch

The promotion of human awareness; awareness of the possibilities of life

Clearly the medium of literature is language, so it can be analysed using the approach and terminology we are suggesting. However, it seems to be something more and different; at once ordinary and extraordinary. It is because of this that descriptions above as various as 'organised violence done on language' and 'what oft was thought but ne'er so well expressed' can both be seen as valid. Which description best fits the following examples?

> As Gregor Samsa awoke one morning from uneasy dreams, he found himself transformed in his bed into a gigantic insect.
>
> Franz Kafka

> If they be so, they are two so
> As stiff twin compasses are two,
> Thy soul the fixed foot makes no show
> To move, but doth it th'other do.
>
> John Donne

> Her husband's tastes rubbed off on her soft, moist moral surface and the couple lived in an atmosphere of novelty in which, occasionally, the accommodating wife encountered the fresh sensation of being in want of her dinner.
>
> Henry James

> Darkling I listen; and for many a time
> I have been half in love with easeful Death,
> Called him soft names in many a mused rhyme,
> To take into the air my quiet breath.
>
> John Keats

WATCHWORDS

watch the words
watch words the
watchword is
watch words are
sly as boots
ifyoutakeyoureyesoffthemforaminute

                          up
and   they're   and
      away
          the   allover
                          place

                                Roger McGough

That's my last Duchess painted on the wall,
Looking as if she were alive. I call
That piece a wonder, now, Fra Pondolf's hands
Worked busily a day, and there she stands
Will't please you sit and look at her? I said.

                                Robert Browning

Know then thyself, presume not God to scan,
The proper study of mankind is man.
Placed on this isthmus of a middle state,
A being darkly wise and rudely great.

                                Alexander Pope

Looking at these we might well wonder how they can all come under the same umbrella title of literature.

All literary works do not have the same easily identifiable purpose. They are not reporting news or informing experts or selling baked beans. They do not relate the world in those functional sorts of ways, because they create their own world. The characters, themes and ideas of literary works only exist because of words. In the same way that a painter uses paint to create a new image a writer uses words to create a text which becomes a unique entity. A painting may well relate to reality (the model/landscape/situation) but it is a new thing. We might say that the purpose of creating these new things is 'to entertain', but when you read the poem 'Death of a Son' in Chapter 14 we think you'll find this broad category inadequate.

The analogy with painting is a useful one. Most of us when looking at a work of art are conscious of the craft and skill which has gone into its creation. Most of us would cheerfully acknowledge that we could not hope to achieve such a work, certainly not without years of practice and dedication. But somehow, probably because we all use language most of the time, we do not always acknowledge the similar amount of craft and skill which goes into the production of a literary text. We are often more likely to see it as 'the spontaneous outpouring of powerful feeling', to quote another famous definition, the product of inspiration as much as hard work. But most literary works have been crafted just as carefully and conscientiously as a painting but with words rather than paint as the raw material.

Some writers are overtly experimental: others less obviously so, but all are selecting and shaping language. Some write within a familiar traditional form, such as the sonnet or the rhyming couplet in poetry, or the epistolary form of the novel (one which is mainly composed of letters between the characters). Others aim for a more naturalistic style closer to 'a selection of language really used by men'. For example, a playwright or novelist may write a dialogue which is naturalistic in that it employs colloquialisms, dialect words and so on, but this dialogue will still be different from spontaneous speech. It will contain no non-fluency features and will probably be less repetitious, more focused and dramatic than ordinary speech. The art in this case is in making the unnatural appear natural.

Look at this example from a modern novel. In what ways is it like and unlike spontaneous speech?

'Red cabbage?' asked Shirley.

'Red cabbage? Red cabbage? I thought it was sprouts. We always have sprouts.' An angry interjection from the oldest Mrs Harper.

'It's sprouts as well,' said Shirley. 'I thought I'd do some red cabbage too. As a change.'

'He won't like it. He won't want any. He likes his red cabbage pickled.' So pursued the oldest Mrs Harper. Her husband smiled and nodded.

'Yes' mused Uncle Fred, 'families aren't what they were. It's all this moving around the country. Thank you, Shirley, that's grand. By the way, Brian asked me to London again, but I thought I'd wait till the weather's better.'

'All what moving about the country?' asked Cliff, largely to avert further discussion of sprouts and red cabbage, which he could see was imminent from the suspicious manner in which his mother was turning over the vegetables on her heaped plate.

'Oh, all this moving around for work.'

'Go on,' said Steve. 'No one moves round here. They stick fast, round here. Never been south of Nottingham, half the folks round here.'

'I think it's nice for the young folks to get out,' said Fred. 'I always encouraged my Brian. I didn't want to stand in his way.'

Margaret Drabble: *The Radiant Way*

Other forms of literature make no attempt to appear natural – in fact they deliberately surprise the readers' expectations. They might use familiar words in unfamiliar ways as e. e. cummings does, or they might coin new words as Gerard Manley Hopkins does. Perhaps we expect poets to use deviant language, but prose writers like James Joyce do it too.

This is the sort of literature which foregrounds language use, so there are lots of unusual features for the analyst to talk about. Nevertheless, other styles of literature whose use of language features is less immediately striking, are no less considered. A similar process of word choice and structuring will have been gone through. Jane

Austen redrafted her novels every bit as scrupulously as William Blake did the poems we shall look at in Chapter 13. These, like all writers, selected the form of words most appropriate to their purposes.

So, what is the purpose of a literary text?

Having mentioned earlier in the chapter that to establish context, audience and purpose in relation to literary texts is problematic, we are going to home in on the one we think is most helpful in approaching them, purpose. Not the overarching purpose of Literature as a whole, but the purpose of individual texts or stretches of writing. It is helpful to begin an analysis by asking the same question you will be answering when you write commentaries on your own writing: 'What is the writer trying to achieve here?'

Every analysis of a literary text needs to try to identify how it affects the reader. Start with your immediate response and ask yourself whether this particular text

- seems to be affecting your emotions. Which ones?
- seems to be telling you what to think
- seems to be making you laugh
- seems to be drawing a picture, evoking an atmosphere.

These are just some possibilities. Whatever your impression, jot it down.

Now ask yourself, as you look again at the text, how the writer has made you feel/think/laugh/see. It will be doing the writer less than justice if you assume that the effect is merely a happy accident. A literary writer's skill in finding the right words with the right connotations, the right sounds in the right combinations, is what enables the writer, when s/he is successful, to fuse form and meaning. Try very hard to regard literary forms and language use not as something in your way but rather as the writer's tools for making you, the reader, respond.

Since it is not feasible to analyse a complete novel or play in all its complexity in this book or in your exams, you are only likely to be given a representative passage to work on. Similarly, you are more likely to be given a short poem to look at than an epic. What you need to do, whatever text you are presented with, is as always to see what is there and to deduce something about why it is there. Your response will be the best clue to the 'why'.

We have decided, for the sake of clarity, that it might be best to look one by one at some of the major effects which literature provokes. Our list is a long way from being all-inclusive but some simplification is necessary for the sake of making sense of literary texts. We will look at the following:

Establishing a voice/point of view

Evoking an atmosphere

Sending a message

Affecting the emotions. Making people laugh or cry.

In the next few chapters we attempt some analysis ourselves to show you what a language analysis, rather than a literary one, might look like, and offer you some texts to examine yourselves.

Chapter 11
Establishing Voice and Point of View

It is impossible to tell any story, or describe any scene without deciding what is to be told and who is to tell it. This is a crucial first move for any writer: a first person narrator who is 'present' in the text, or a third person, an 'invisible' author who may or may not comment on characters and events? If first person, who is the 'I'? Only in autobiography is it the author. How does the character's situation and personality affect the way that the story is told? A third person narrator may seem neutral and objective, but rarely is. Establishing point of view is crucial to an analysis of any text.

A good place to look for the establishment of voice is at the beginning of a novel. Look at the opening of *Midnight's Children* by Salman Rushdie, which we referred to in Section One:

I was born in the city of Bombay... once upon a time. No, that won't do, there's no getting away from the date: I was born in Doctor Narlikar's Nursing Home on August 15th 1947. And the time? The time matters, too. Well then: at night. No, it's important to be more... On the stroke of midnight, as a matter of fact. Clock-hands joined palms in respectful greeting as I came. Oh, spell it out, spell it out: at the precise instant of India's arrival at independence, I tumbled forth into the world. There were gasps. And, outside the window, fireworks and crowds. A few seconds later, my father broke his big toe; but his accident was a mere trifle when set beside what had befallen me in that benighted moment, because thanks to the occult tyrannies of those blandly saluting clocks I had been mysteriously handcuffed to history, my destinies indissolubly chained to those of my country. For the next three decades, there was to be no escape. Soothsayers had prophesied me, newspapers celebrated my arrival, politicos ratified my authenticity. I was left entirely without a say in the matter. I, Saleem Sinai, later variously called Snotnose, Stainface, Baldy, Sniffer, Buddha and even Piece-of-the-Moon, had become heavily embroiled in Fate – at the best of times a dangerous sort of involvement. And I couldn't even wipe my own nose at the time.

Salman Rushdie: *Midnight's Children*

ACTIVITY 🔡 💬

- Who is telling the story?
- What are you able to deduce about the narrator so far? For example, would you regard him as a reliable informant? Does he strike you as modest or conceited?
- Is his tone consistent throughout? If not, where do the shifts occur?
- Is the passage amusing?
- Is it metaphorical?

Having considered the passage yourself, look at our analysis:

The writer of this opening clearly wishes to establish his central character, who is also the narrator, very strongly from the outset. He also wishes to stress the coincidence of the character's birth with the birth of a new nation: the moment of India's independence. This coincidence profoundly affected the rest of his life. The interplay of the personal and the historical perspectives is evident in the language of the whole paragraph.

There is an obvious attempt, almost literally, to establish the character's voice. Of the first few sentences, three are minor or incomplete, which in this context suggests speech. They read like utterances in one half of a conversation, two beginning with 'no' and one with 'well then'. One, a question, appears to be an answer to a question. There are other expressions which sound as if he's talking to himself, 'spell it out, spell it out'. Gradually the 'I' becomes more specific as if the information is reluctantly given – so the evasive story-telling technique 'once upon a time' in sentence one finally becomes 'at the precise instant' in sentence nine. The birth is referred to four times: 'I was born' (twice), 'I came', and 'I tumbled forth'. Details of time and place are added, although the metaphorical 'clock hands joined palms...' seems like further prevarication and the final announcement is delayed by a long adverbial phrase 'at the precise instant'.

Having established a rather colloquial tone in the opening sentences, the tenth builds on the note hinted at in the 'clock hands... respectful greeting'. The first part of the sentence is the incongruous and rather ridiculous information that his father broke his toe, but the second, much longer section after the semi-colon includes the unusual collocations of 'occult tyrannies', and 'blandly saluting clocks', alongside the more familiar, hyperbolic idiom of 'benighted moment' and the mixed metaphor 'destinies indissolubly chained'. The magical and political significance of the stroke of midnight is suggested by 'soothsayers had prophesied me', and 'politicos ratified'. The moment was important, as further emphasised by words such as 'decades', 'destinies', and 'embroiled in Fate' – but perhaps rather consciously important. Alongside this, the pathetic individual who 'couldn't even wipe [his] own nose', also came into existence. The contrast between the two is exploited for humour, and also for irony. The writer has established a central character (and narrator) who is humorous, self-conscious, articulate and reflective.

Here is another first person opening, from Doris Lessing's *The Diaries of Jane Somers*:

> The first part is a summing-up of about four years. I was not keeping a diary. I wish I had. All I know is that I see everything differently now from how I did while I was living through it.
>
> My life until Freddie started to die was one thing, afterwards another. Until then I thought of myself as a nice person. Like everyone, just about, that I know. The people I work with, mainly. I know now that I did not ask myself what I was really like, but thought only about how other people judged me.
>
> When Freddie began to be so ill my first idea was: this is unfair. Unfair to me, I thought secretly. I partly knew he was dying, but went on as if he wasn't. That was not kind. He must have been lonely. I was proud of myself because I went on working through it all, 'kept the money coming in' – well, I had to do that, with him not working. But I was thankful I was working because I had an excuse not to be with him in that *awfulness*. We did not have the sort of marriage where we talked about real things. I see that now. We were not really married. It was the marriage most people have these days, both sides trying for advantage. I always saw Freddie as one up.
>
> The word cancer was mentioned once. The doctors said to me, cancer, and *now* I see my reaction meant they would not go on to talk about whether to tell him or not. I don't know if they told him. Whether he knew. I think he did. When they took him into hospital I went every day, but I sat there with a smile, how are you feeling? He looked dreadful. Yellow. Sharp bones under yellow skin. Like a boiling fowl. He was protecting me. *Now*, I can see it. Because I could not take it. Child-wife.
>
> Doris Lessing: *The Diaries of Jane Somers*

ACTIVITY

Individually jot down answers to these questions.

- What can you tell about this person from the words she uses?
- What reason do you think the character had for writing her story?
- From what perspective is she telling her story? (Looking at the verbs might be helpful here.)
- What have you learnt so far about the character, her attitudes and life?
- This is written in the form of a diary entry. Is it convincing as diary style? What, if any, elements in it remind you of a diary?
- Of course, the fact is that this is the opening to a novel – what advantages does the diary form have?

By the time you have answered all these questions you should feel able to write a full analysis of the text. Go ahead and write this. Swap your analysis with a friend's. Check whether you have used the same evidence (quotes) and if you have used linguistic terminology where appropriate. Between you, you should now be able to construct a stronger analysis.

••

A DIFFERENT PERSON

The most straightforward way to establish a voice and point of view is to use the first person. However, narratives written in the third person can also stress one viewpoint or focus our attention upon one character. Omniscient narrators are not always objective. Consider the opening from the novel *The Life and Times of Michael K*:

> The first thing the midwife noticed about Michael K. when she helped him out of his mother into the world, was that he had a hare lip. The lip curled like a snail's foot, the nostril gaped. Obscuring the child for a moment from its mother, she prodded open the tiny bud of the mouth and was thankful to find the palate whole.
>
> To his mother she said, 'You should be happy, they bring good luck to the household.' But from the first Anna K. did not like the mouth that would not close and the living, pink flesh it bared to her. She shivered to think of what had been growing inside her all these months. The child could not suck from the breast and cried with hunger. She tried a bottle; when it could not suck from the bottle, she fed it with a tea-spoon, fretting with impatience when it coughed and spluttered and cried.
>
> 'It will close up as he gets older,' the midwife promised. However, the lip did not close, or did not close enough, nor did the nose come straight.
>
> J. M. Coetzee: *The Life and Times of Michael K*

••

ACTIVITY ○ ▧

1   List the references to the child.
2   What is their cumulative impact?
3   List the verbs for the mother's actions and reactions.
4   What is their effect?

••

Now look at another passage about a mother and child:

> Daylight began to seep through the faded curtains. In the corner of the room a baby was crying. It made a thin, continuous bleating noise. A shape on the bed moved and a girl heaved herself up on one elbow. She remained still for a time, listening. At last she disentangled herself from the bed and crossed the room to the cot. She shook it viciously. The crying stopped. The girl stood still, staring down into the shadows in the cot. The room was cold, the light a matching harsh, watery grey. The backs of her skinny legs and arms glinted fish-belly white.

The crying began again. She lifted the baby, holding it over her shoulder and began to pace the room. The noise stopped but she continued to pace mechanically, patting the baby's back rhythmically as she walked. She was very young, her body still thin and gawky as an adolescent's but with something pinched about it. She had not been allowed to flesh out into maturity. In the relentless dawn light her head was more of a skull than a face, the dark hollowness of eye sockets intensified by the dull glaze of her eyes and the smeared black mascara around them. Thin white skin was stretched taut over cheek and jawbone. She walked with face raised, like someone blind.

Jane Rogers: *Separate Tracks*

- How is the child presented? Compare this passage with the previous one.
- Consider the mother. Is she presented sympathetically? Look at adjectives and adverbs. The voice of verbs might also help.
- What effect does the description of the surroundings have? How does it relate to the characters? Look at the articles at the start of the text. Also, it might be helpful to notice the subjects of the verb: are they objects, people or sounds?
- How is the relationship between mother and child portrayed?

VIEWPOINT IN POETRY

Presenting a viewpoint is not only achieved in prose. Many poems present the view/story and attitudes of a central character or persona. Some of them obviously establish a voice which is not the poet's own. Such a poem is the following:

AN IRISH AIRMAN FORESEES HIS DEATH

I know that I shall meet my fate
Somewhere among the clouds above;
Those that I fight I do not hate,
Those that I guard I do not love;
My country is Kiltartan Cross,
My countrymen Kiltartan's poor,
No likely end could bring them loss
Or leave them happier than before.
Nor law, nor duty bade me fight,
Nor public men, nor cheering crowds,
A lonely impulse of delight
Drove to this tumult in the clouds;
I balanced all, brought all to mind,
The years to come seemed waste of breath,
A waste of breath the years behind
In balance with this life, this death.

William Butler Yeats

ACTIVITY ● ▨

Before you read our analysis jot down the three most striking things about this poem.

Given that this is the voice of a man in wartime facing inevitable death, the tone of this poem is remarkably detached and matter-of-fact. How is this achieved?

There are a lot of statements which are brief and appear factual rather than subjective. The opening line 'I know that I shall meet my fate' is very different in emphasis from 'I expect that I...', let alone 'I fear'. There then follows a series of one-line statements offering no pause for argument, qualification or explanation. This voice knows his own mind!

He states that he has 'balanced all' and no hint is given in the poem that this balance is lost — surprisingly in view of his situation. The title and topic would lead us to anticipate an emotional, perhaps patriotic, perhaps heroic voice but, as is often the case with poetry, our expectations are confounded. With the striking exception of the lines in which he speaks of the 'impulse' which 'drove' him, the lexis is as neutral as possible. A more emotive voice could have employed 'protect' rather than 'guard'; 'home' rather than 'country', and both friends and enemies are reduced to the pronoun 'those'. Words such as 'hate', 'love' and 'duty', which in other contexts might seem highly charged, are here all preceded by negatives which bring them down to earth. The prospect of victory or defeat is coolly referred to as the 'likely end'.

He is equally unconcerned about his own end: his past and future are both dismissed as 'a waste of breath' and thus his death or survival is a matter of indifference to him. This indifference makes it difficult to pity or admire the airman — two emotions which most war poetry evokes in its readers.

One of the reasons why we do not engage with the airman is that his voice is not individualised. There are no colloquialisms, indications of accent or speech rhythms. Instead the voice is regular, formal — clipped even. A surprising number of the words are monosyllables and metre and rhyme are very regular. This creates an unemphatic, almost monotonous effect which is only disrupted by the stress on the first syllable of a line — 'Drove' — rather than the usual second. The repetitions of phrases like 'Those that I' and 'waste of breath' and words like 'Kiltartan' and 'country' also contribute to the unremarkable sameness of the way he sees his life.

In sharp contrast to these impersonal descriptions are the more precise and emotive lines

> A lonely impulse of delight
> Drove to this tumult in the clouds;

'impulse' is not something we would associate with the man who 'balanced all', and although the impulse is a 'lonely' one the word 'lonely' also attaches itself to the airman himself. It is one of the very few adjectives in the poem, and certainly the only emotive one. Similarly, the abstract noun 'delight' is the only noun with unequivocally positive connotations. The word 'tumult' is unexpected, and unexpectedly precise. It is almost the exact opposite of 'balance', and yet this tumult was what attracted him.

We are intrigued by this individual, but he remains something of a mystery. In seeking for reasons to explain his lack of involvement with the conflict in which he is taking part we look again at the title of the poem. Perhaps the significant clue is the word 'Irish'. The reference to place is taken up again, this time more specifically, in line five, and reinforced by repetition in line six. In these lines his country and people are explicitly dissociated from any interest in the outcome of the war, and the connotations of words such as 'poor' and 'loss' imply that their lives are bleak and hopeless. This was his life too, until offered the chance of this one moment of 'delight', which is almost certain to be his last. There is irony in this, but also a deep sense of hopelessness.

Before we leave voice and viewpoint, we'd like you to look at two more poems. The first of these, 'Porphyria's Lover' by Robert Browning, dramatically presents one viewpoint; the other, 'Not Waving But Drowning' by Stevie Smith, switches from one voice to another for effect.

PORPHYRIA'S LOVER

The rain set early in to-night,
The sullen wind was soon awake,
It tore the elm-tops down for spite,
And did its worst to vex the lake;
I listened with heart fit to break.
When glided in Porphyria; straight
She shut the cold out and the storm,
And kneeled and made the cheerless grate
Blaze up, and all the cottage warm;
Which done, she rose, and from her form
Withdrew the dripping cloak and shawl,
And laid her soiled gloves by, untied
Her hat and let the damp hair fall,
And, last, she sat down by my side
And called me. When no voice replied,
She put my arm about her waist,
And made her smooth white shoulder bare,
And all her yellow hair displaced,
And, stooping, made my cheek lie there,
And spread, o'er all, her yellow hair,
Murmuring how she loved me – she
Too weak, for all her heart's endeavour,
To set its struggling passion free
From pride, and vainer ties dissever,
And give herself to me forever.
But passion sometimes would prevail
Nor could to-night's gay feast restrain

A sudden thought of one so pale
For love of her, and all in vain:
So, she was come through wind and rain.
Be sure I looked up at her eyes
Happy and proud; at last I knew
Porphyria worshipped me; surprise
Made my heart swell, and still it grew
While I debated what to do.
That moment she was mine, mine, fair,
Perfectly pure and good: I found
A thing to do, and all her hair
In one long yellow string I wound
Three times her little throat around,
And strangled her. No pain felt she;
I am quite sure she felt no pain.
As a shut bud that holds a bee,
I warily oped her lids: again
Laughed the blue eyes without a stain.
And I untightened next the tress
About her neck; her cheeks once more
Blushed bright beneath my burning kiss:
I propped her head up as before,
Only, this time my shoulder bore
Her head, which droops upon it still:
The smiling rosy little head
So glad it has its utmost will,
That all it scorned at once is fled,
And I, its love, am gained instead!
Porphyria's love: she guessed not how
Her darling one wish would be heard.
And thus we sit together now,
And all night long we have not stirred,
And yet God has not said a word!

Robert Browning

- Who is telling the story, and can you follow the narrative?
- Is the narrator a sympathetic character?
- Is the narrator interesting or unusual in any way?
- How does the narrator's use of language (e.g. word choice and order) help establish the character?
- Consider sound in the poem. Is it striking in any way?
- Is there anything to be said about the collocations of nouns and verbs in the first four lines?
- How effective do you consider the poem as a story, and as a presentation of world view?

Now consider 'Not Waving But Drowning':

NOT WAVING BUT DROWNING

Nobody heard him, the dead man,
But still he lay moaning:
I was much further out than you thought
And not waving but drowning.

Poor chap, he always loved larking
And now he's dead.
It must have been too cold for him his heart gave way,
They said.

Oh, no no no, it was too cold always
(Still the dead one lay moaning)
I was much too far out all my life
And not waving but drowning.

Stevie Smith

The narrative and message of this poem are perhaps easier to decode. They deal with an individual who has never been able to connect with other people, who has spent a lifetime being ignored or ill-understood. His final, desperate flounderings as he drowns are misinterpreted as a cheery wave!

ACTIVITY ▨ ▢ AND ◼ ▨

In groups of four, prepare this poem for performance. Listen to one another's versions, noting how many voices each group has used. Are there differences in the way you've chosen to perform this? Why?

Now individually write answers to these questions.

- How does the poet enable us to 'know' this man – to connect with him in fact?

- Separate out his lines. What does he communicate to you?

- Now decide who else speaks and what impression you get of them.

- Does the switching from voice to voice add to the poem's effect or merely confuse?

In this section we have been concerned with the writer's voice, the human voice. But characters don't exist in a vacuum; they exist in relation to place and time. The place and time may be an approximation of reality, or may be wholly fantastic. In either case the place needs establishing, and that is what we are going to look at in the next chapter.

Chapter 12
Creating a Sense of Place

A sense of place or atmosphere is obviously important to many different types of writing, from travel writing to ghost stories, from ballads to landscape poetry. We are going to look at two main approaches writers may adopt when seeking to evoke place. They can either use clusters of words within semantic fields to create atmosphere – in the way that an impressionist picture suggests poppies rather than delineating them – or they can give a lot of detailed information which enables the reader to see the scene in the mind's eye. This is a more realist, photographic approach. Each approach has its advantages, and in the hands of a talented writer each can be successful. Which particular approach you prefer is mainly a matter of individual taste; which approach a writer uses may well be influenced by the sort of text he is writing. Details of exactly what is where are useful knowledge in a whodunnit, but useless clutter in a novel about relationships, where the *mood* of a place may match the personality of the central protagonist.

ACTIVITY ● ✦

One of the most famous creators of mood through place is Thomas Hardy, so we will begin with a passage from *Tess of the D'Urbervilles*. When you have read it, jot down what impressions you receive of the places described.

■ What mood do you think is being evoked?

■ Which of the words are carrying the emotional load – the modifiers, the verbs or the nouns?

There had not been such a winter for years. It came on in stealthy and measured glides, like the moves of a chess-player. One morning the few lonely trees and the thorns of the hedgerows appeared as if they had put off a vegetable for an animal integument. Every twig was covered with a white nap as of fur grown from the rind during the night, giving it four times its usual stoutness; the whole bush or tree forming a staring sketch in white lines on the mournful grey of the sky and horizon. Cobwebs revealed their presence on sheds and walls where none had ever been observed till brought out into visibility by the crystallizing atmosphere, hanging like loops of white worsted from salient points of the out-houses, posts, and gates.

After this season of congealed dampness came a spell of dry frost, when strange birds from behind the North Pole began to arrive silently on the upland of Flintcomb-Ash; gaunt spectral creatures with tragical eyes – eyes which had witnessed scenes of cataclysmal horror in inaccessible polar regions of a magnitude such as no human being had ever conceived, in curdling temperatures that no man could endure; which had beheld the crash of icebergs and the slide of snow-hills by the shooting light of the Aurora; been half blinded by the whirl of colossal storms and terraqueous distortions; and retained the expression of feature that such scenes had engendered. These nameless birds came quite near to Tess and Marian, but of all they had seen which humanity would never see, they brought no account.

The traveller's ambition to tell was not theirs, and, with dumb impassivity, they dismissed experiences which they did not value for the immediate incidents of this homely upland – the trivial movements of the two girls in disturbing the clods with their hackers so as to uncover something or other that these visitants relished as food.

Then one day a peculiar quality invaded the air of this open country. There came a moisture which was not of rain, and a cold which was not of frost. It chilled the eye-balls of the twain, made their brows ache, penetrated to their skeletons, affecting the surface of the body less than its core. They knew that it meant snow, and in the night the snow came.

Thomas Hardy: *Tess of the D'Urbervilles*

So, what adjectives have you written down to describe this place at this time? 'Cold' would be an obvious one, since winter and snow are mentioned. Are there any subtler indications of cold? Is it a 'happy cold' or have you jotted down something like 'dreary' or 'bleak'? If your feelings about the place are being directed there is every chance that adjectives are the culprits. Have a look for some which add to the dismal nature of the scene.

But even 'cold and bleak' doesn't explain the unpleasant, fearful emotions this passage awakens. Many of you will also have felt that there is a threatening, sinister quality to this place, these 'silent' birds, this winter which 'comes on' (relentlessly?) Read the passage through again and seek to discover where the disquiet comes from. It might well be worth looking at verbs and their modifiers. You should now have a clear enough sense of the passage to read our analysis actively rather than passively.

In the opening paragraph, a sense of sinister purpose is attributed to the natural world. Somewhat paradoxically, the winter is bringing the world to life. This is explicitly stated in 'put off a vegetable for an animal integument' but is also implicit in the verbs 'came on', 'appeared', 'fur grown from the rind' and 'cobwebs revealed'. All these verbs would normally have animate subjects. In other words we have deviant collocation or personification. The simile 'like the moves of a chess-player' reinforces this sense of a person — and a subtle one! The twigs have 'four times [their] usual stoutness', which makes them sound powerful, and the bushes form a 'staring sketch'. Like 'crystallizing' later in the passage, 'staring', since it is formed from a verb, sounds active and purposeful. Nor does the purpose sound friendly: staring is usually regarded as an act of hostility — and being 'crystallized' — frozen solid — scarcely sounds a good experience.

All this sinister action is taking place in an appropriate setting. The trees are 'lonely', there are spiky 'thorns' and the sky is 'mournful grey'.

Things don't improve in the second paragraph. The 'dampness', bad enough in itself, is made worse by the verbal adjective 'congealed'. The birds arrive 'silently'. (Like the 'stealthy and measured glide' of the winter in the previous paragraph, the modifier suggests sinister intentions.) They are more than mere birds; they are a dark presence, 'dumb' and 'nameless'. They are connected to death, being 'gaunt and spectral', and have 'tragical eyes' which have seen unspecified (and therefore more frightening) horrors. These horrors are 'cataclysmal' and unimaginable, 'such as no human being had ever conceived'.

At this point the language becomes hyperbolic, and this hyperbole is associated with the almost surreal landscape which is the birds' natural home. In contrast with the winter landscape, the 'polar regions' are described in dramatic, but generalised terms. We have 'curdling temperatures', the 'crash of icebergs and the slide of snow-hills'. There is also the 'whirl of colossal storms'. This seems a far noisier world. This supernatural-seeming world seems to taint the natural one so that in the third paragraph the 'moisture' is 'not of rain' and the 'cold' 'not of frost'. Again, the cold and damp seem purposeful and malevolent: they 'penetrate' to the 'skeletons', the 'core'. The reader is bound to pity the hapless Tess and Marian caught in such a place and season.

The next place we would like you to look at is very far removed from the world of Tess. Here we are in the industrial North and with a modern writer, Alan Sillitoe. We want you to consider two short extracts; the first shows the 'hero' Arthur at play, the second at work. Read the two passages.

> He stood in the parlour while she fastened the locks and bolts, smelling faint odours of rubber and oil coming from Jack's bicycle leaning against a big dresser that took up nearly one whole side of the room. It was a small dark area of isolation, long familiar with another man's collection of worldly goods: old-fashioned chairs and a settee, fireplace, clock ticking on the mantelpiece, a smell of brown paper, soil from a plant-pot, ordinary aged dust, soot in the chimney left over from last winter's fires, and mustiness of rugs laid down under the table and by the fireplace. Brenda had known this room for seven married years, yet could not have become more intimate with it than did Arthur in the ten seconds while she fumbled with the key.
>
> He knocked his leg on the bicycle pedal, swearing at the pain, complaining at Jack's barminess for leaving it in such an exposed position.

'How does he think I'm going to get in with that thing stuck there?' he joked. 'Tell him I said to leave it in the back-yard next week, out of 'arm's way.'

Brenda hissed and told him to be quiet, and they crept like two thieves into the living-room, where the electric light showed the supper things – teacups, plates, jam-pot, bread – still on the table. A howl of cats came from a nearby yard, and a dustbin lid clattered on to cobblestones.

'Oh well,' he said in a normal voice, standing up tall and straight, 'it's no use whisperin' when all that racket's going on.'

They stood between the table and firegrate, and Brenda put her arms around him. While kissing her he turned his head so that his own face stared back at him from an oval mirror above the shelf. His eyes grew large in looking at himself from such an angle, noticing his short disordered hair sticking out like the bristles of a blond porcupine, and the mark of an old pimple healing on his cheek.

'Don't let's stay down here long, Arthur,' she said softly.

He released her and, knowing every corner of the house and acting as if it belonged to him, stripped off his coat and shirt and went into the scullery to wash the tiredness from his eyes. Once in bed, they would not go to sleep at once: he wanted to be fresh for an hour before floating endlessly down into the warm bed beside Brenda's soft body.

Arthur walked into a huge corridor, searching an inside pocket for his clocking-in card and noticing, as on every morning since he was fifteen – except for a two-year break in the army – the factory smell of oil-suds, machinery, and shaved steel that surrounded you with an air in which pimples grew and prospered on your face and shoulders, that would have turned you into one big pimple if you did not spend half an hour over the scullery sink every night getting rid of the biggest bastards. What a life, he thought. Hard work and good wages, and a smell all day that turns your guts.

The bright Monday-morning ring of the clocking-in machines made a jarring note, different from the tune that played inside Arthur. It was dead on half-past seven. Once in the shop he allowed himself to be swallowed by its diverse noises, walked along lanes of capstan lathes and millers, drills and polishers and hand-presses, worked by a multiplicity of belts and pulleys turning and twisting and slapping on heavy well-oiled wheels overhead, dependent for power on a motor stooping at the far end of the hall like the black shining bulk of a stranded whale. Machines with their own small motors started with a jerk and a whine under the shadows of their operators, increasing a noise that made the brain reel and ache because the weekend had been too tranquil by contrast, a weekend that had terminated for Arthur in fishing for trout in the cool shade of a willow-sleeved canal near the Balloon Houses, miles away from the city. Motor-trolleys moved up and down the main gangways carrying boxes of work – pedals, hubs, nuts and bolts – from one part of the shop to another. Robboe the foreman bent over a stack of new time-sheets behind his glass partition; women and girls wearing turbans and hair-nets and men and boys in clean blue overalls settled down to their work, eager to get a good start on their day's stint; while sweepers and cleaners at everybody's beck and call already patrolled the gangways and looked busy.

Arthur reached his capstan lathe and took off his jacket, hanging it on a nearby nail so that he could keep an eye on his belongings. He pressed the starter button, and his motor came to life with a gentle thump. Looking around, it did not seem, despite the infernal noise of hurrying machinery, that anyone was working with particular speed. He smiled to himself and picked up a glittering steel cylinder from the top box of a pile beside him, and fixed it into the spindle. He jettisoned his cigarette into the sud-pan, drew back the capstan, and swung the turret on to its broadest drill. Two minutes passed while he contemplated the precise position of tools and cylinder; finally he spat on to both hands and rubbed them together, then switched on the sud-tap from the movable brass pipe, pressed a button that set the spindle running, and ran in the drill to a neat chamfer. Monday morning had lost its terror.

Alan Sillitoe: *Saturday Night and Sunday Morning*

ACTIVITY

- Which style of description, the impressionistic or the photographic, would you say predominates here?
- There is a lot of detail in Sillitoe's descriptions. How, and using which particular parts of speech, is this precision achieved?
- Descriptions of place make appeals to different senses. Which senses are appealed to here, and through whom are we experiencing them?
- What class and region are these characters from, and how can you tell? Find some examples of significant word choice. How formal or informal is the tone?
- Is the tone consistent throughout each passage?
- Are we made aware of how Arthur feels about the two places described? If so, how?

ACTIVITY

Now write a comparative assessment of these passages with the extract from *Tess of the D'Urbervilles*.

POETIC PLACES

Though we've considered prose so far, many people, if asked to think of memorable descriptions of place, would think of a poem such as Wordsworth's 'Daffodils' or Gray's

'Elegy'. Whereas in prose, place is often a background or context for events and characters, in poetry it may conventionally be the subject of a whole poem.

Here are two brief examples by the same poet, Douglas Dunn, of word-picture poems. Read them both carefully.

ON ROOFS OF TERRY STREET

Television aerials, Chinese characters
In the lower sky, wave gently in the smoke.
Nest-building sparrows peck at moss,
Urban flora and fauna, soft, unscrupulous.

Rain drying on the slates shines sometimes.
A builder is repairing someone's leaking roof.

He kneels upright to rest his back.
His trowel catches the light and becomes precious.

A REMOVAL FROM TERRY STREET

On a squeaking cart, they push the usual stuff,
A mattress, bed ends, cups, carpets, chairs,
Four paperback westerns. Two whistling youths
In surplus U.S. Army battle-jackets
Remove their sister's goods. Her husband
Follows, carrying on his shoulders the son
Whose mischief we are glad to see removed,
And pushing, of all things, a lawnmower.
There is no grass in Terry Street. The worms
Come up cracks in concrete yards in moonlight.
That man, I wish him well. I wish him grass.

Douglas Dunn

The first of the poems, 'On Roofs of Terry Street', could hardly appear simpler. Only the second couplet presents any difficulty. What are these 'urban flora and fauna' and in what way are they 'unscrupulous'? Once this problem has been resolved, the poem appears to be a sequence of snapshots.

ACTIVITY

- How many separate pictures can you see?
- What is the effect of the total absence of linking words? In order to test this you could re-write the poem as three sentences. How is the impact altered?
- One way in which the impact will be different will be visually. Why do you think the poet chose to write in two-line stanzas?
- Do you see any connection between the poem's subject and its form?

ACTIVITY ◖● ▨

Compare this poem with the extract from Bruce Chatwin's notebooks in Chapter 9 (page 158). Re-write a passage from the notebooks as a poem in the style of 'On Roofs of Terry Street'.

The form of 'A Removal from Terry Street' is different. Compare the placing of full stops in these two poems. What effect does the run on of lines in 'A Removal' have? Unlike the snapshots of the other poem, we now seem to have a procession passing through the frame.

- Which words are most significant in terms of adding to the movement of the poem?
- How is it suggested in the first part of the poem that this is a familiar scene and at what point in the poem does the frame freeze – the general become particular?
- Consider the way in which people are referred to. As the poem progresses, how do we get a clearer sense of them and their relations to each other – and to the poet?
- At what point do we become aware of the presence of the poet?
- In the last three lines we move away from pure description. What is the effect of this?

  We have looked at a couple of poems where place is very much dominant. Next we are going to look at a poem which sets a person in their context. In this respect it is more akin to the passage from *Tess of the D'Urbervilles*. This is an extract from a long poem called *The Borough* written by George Crabbe in 1810, in which he describes an East Anglian fishing town and its inhabitants. One section of the poem tells the story of Peter Grimes, a fisherman ostracised by the community for ill-treating his apprentices. Here Peter, compelled to live alone, is placed in appropriately dismal surroundings.

Thus by himself compell'd to live each day,
To wait for certain hours the tide's delay;
At the same time the same dull views to see,
The bounding marsh-bank and the blighted tree;
The water only, when the tides were high,
When low, the mud half-cover'd and half-dry;
The sun-burnt tar that blisters on the planks,
And bank-side stakes in their uneven ranks;
Heaps of entangled weeds that slowly float,
As the tide rolls by the impeded boat.

When tides were neap, and, in the sultry day,
Through the tall bounding mud-banks made their way,
Which on each side rose swelling, and below

The dark warm flood ran silently and slow;
There anchoring, Peter chose from man to hide,
There hang his head, and view the lazy tide
In its hot slimy channel slowly glide;
Where the small eels that left the deeper way
From the warm shore, within the shallows play;
Where gaping mussels, left upon the mud,
Slope their slow passage to the fallen flood;
Here dull and hopeless he'd lie down and trace
How sidelong crabs had scrawl'd their crooked race;
Or sadly listen to the tuneless cry
Of fishing gull or clanging golden-eye;
What time the sea-birds to the marsh would come,
And the loud bittern, from the bull-rush home,
Gave from the salt-ditch side the bellowing boom:
He nursed the feelings these dull scenes produce,
And loved to stop beside the opening sluice;
Where the small stream, confined in narrow bound,
Ran with a dull, unvaried, sadd'ning sound;
Where all, presented to the eye or ear,
Oppress'd the soul with misery, grief, and fear.

George Crabbe

ACTIVITY ▨ ▧

Read the poem aloud.

- Does anything strike you about the sounds in the poem?
- What pace did you choose to read at? We'd be surprised if you read this poem rapidly. Why?

First of all, look at the length of the vowel sounds. Pick out a couple of lines which contain striking clusters of long vowels. Are there in fact examples of assonance (the recurrence, systematic or not, of a vowel sound throughout a passage)?

Now consider consonants. Which consonants seem to be repeated most often? The recurrence of a consonant throughout a passage is called consonance; if the consonant is repeated at the beginning of words it is called alliteration. Which of these sound effects can you find examples of?

The sense of slowness in this passage is not affected only by choosing sounds which take some time to say. The length and ordering of words within sentences is also important. There are several examples of sentences in which the subject is on one line, the main verb on another. One example would be the 'gaping mussels' which only 'slope' a line later. Can you find a couple more examples?

Although the rhythm and rhyme scheme of this poem are very regular, the regular units are broken down and the sense carried over by such methods as separating subjects from their verbs. Another way in which the sense of length and slowness is achieved is the use of numerous conjunctions, both co-ordinating ('and', 'or') and subordinating ('which', 'where'). Although the rhyme is at the end of lines, the sense is often carried over and the sentence extended by use of subordinate clauses:

> Through the tall bounding mud-banks made their way,
> Which on each side rose swelling.

Prepositions, which place one thing in relation to another, are similarly placed at the beginning of lines, and mean that the sense unit is carried over from one to the other and the line runs on:

> There hang his head, and view the lazy tide
> In its hot slimy channel slowly glide

It might be expected that the avoidance of commas and full stops at line ends would increase the pace of the verse; however, the effect is to create a longer unit of sense, and thus a slower pace. The use of frequent full stops to make shorter sentences results in a rapid, staccato rhythm which increases the speed, and this is true of verse as well as prose. We have dealt at some length with features of sound in this poem because they are a prominent aspect of the verse.

....

ACTIVITY ◼ ▨

Summarise the main points we have made about sound effects in this poem, illustrating them with your own examples. Then go on to describe other techniques Crabbe uses to achieve his effects.

....

The next poem we'd like you to take a look at is from a similar period to the one by Crabbe. It is 'This Lime-Tree Bower My Prison' by Samuel Taylor Coleridge. Although the poem is not rhymed, it is, in several ways, more overtly 'literary' than the Crabbe.

THIS LIME-TREE BOWER MY PRISON

> Well they are gone, and here must I remain,
> This lime-tree bower my prison! I have lost
> Beauties and feelings, such as would have been
> Most sweet to my remembrance even when age
> Had dimm'd mine eyes to blindness! They, meanwhile,
> Friends, whom I never more may meet again,
> On springy heath, along the hill-top edge,
> Wander in gladness, and wind down, perchance,
> To that still roaring dell, of which I told;

The roaring dell, o'erwooded, narrow, deep,
And only speckled by the mid-day sun;
Where its slim trunk the ash from rock to rock
Flings arching like a bridge; – that branchless ash,
Unsunn'd and damp, whose few poor yellow leaves
Ne'er tremble in the gale, yet tremble still,
Fann'd by the waterfall! and there my friends
Behold the dark green file of long lank weeds,
That all at once (a most fantastic sight!)
Still nod and drip beneath the dripping edge
Of the blue clay-stone. Now, my friends emerge
Beneath the wide wide Heaven – and view again
The many-steepled tract magnificent
Of hilly fields and meadows, and the sea,
With some fair bark, perhaps, whose sails light up
The slip of smooth clear blue betwixt two Isles
Of purple shadow! Yes! they wander on
In gladness all; but thou, methinks, most glad,
My gentle-hearted Charles! For thou hast pined
And hunger'd after Nature, many a year,
In the great City pent, winning thy way
With sad yet patient soul, through evil and pain
And strange calamity! Ah! slowly sink
Behind the western ridge, thou glorious Sun!
Shine in the slant beams of the sinking orb,
Ye purple heath-flowers! richlier burn, ye clouds!

Samuel Taylor Coleridge

ACTIVITY

Look at the lexis. Would you say that there were examples of literary and archaic lexis? If you would (and, to be frank you should!), find as many examples as you can.

Literariness is not only a matter of individual words, however. Word order is also significant. If you look at the first line, the inversion of 'here must I remain' is immediately striking. Can you find other examples of this technique?

Ask yourself if the style is formal/literary throughout or whether there is not also a less formal, spoken element. (Looking at punctuation marks may help you here.)

Given that elements of this poem are very literary (some commentators would call it 'poetic diction'), there is also a voice in the poem which is personal, emotional and spontaneous. Check which person this is written in and which references seem personal and emotional.

Once you have established that there is a person, a voice in this poem, ask yourself what the voice is up to. Is he merely describing a place he knows well or is there more to it than that? Why, for example, if he is describing a place he has seen, is he using the present tense? Write down what you would say the poet is doing in this extract.

We would argue that he is imagining (and the Romantic poets were very keen on the faculty of imagination) making this journey with his friends by recalling every tiny detail of their pathway and thus reliving it with and through them. The reader certainly gets a clear notion of their movements.

Take a look at the verbs of motion in this poem and list them. Now consider Coleridge's use of prepositions, which enable us to know not only how they are travelling but in what direction.

The poet takes the reader from scene to scene. Identify the different stages of the journey. How is each scene conveyed?

Are the modifiers important here?

Is only a visual scene being described or are any other senses engaged?

As this poem continues you will notice that the poet's tone becomes more philosophical; he is comparing the city and the country not merely in terms of appearance but in a moral sense. What is the poet's attitude to the city and how are we made aware of it?

At the end of this section of the poem there are three imperative forms. Find them and then ask yourself why they are there. What is their effect?

AWAY FROM ENGLAND

Finally, we would like you to look at one more prose piece and one more poem. Since so far in this section we have dealt only with England we felt it was high time other countries were represented. The poem is relatively close to home – Wales; the prose a little further away in all senses – Persia. Attempt a full analysis of each without any help from us. By now you ought to be asking yourselves the appropriate questions.

It is winter. A narrow, muddy street, flanked by low mud-brick walls beneath a cloudless steely sky. The ground rutted deep by cartwheels, pock-marked with mule and donkey hooves, covered with a thin layer of ice that crunches underfoot. Dirty patches of snow linger here and there at the base of walls. At the end of the street the embrasure of a door in front of which hangs an indigo-blue patched curtain, like a single spot of colour on a fawn canvas. From behind it comes a regular, monotonous muffled thud, like a distant hammer, followed by a whining screech.

This is my first memory – I must have been two or three years old. An inquisitive child, I stop and lift a corner of the curtain apprehensively: a pungent, spicy smell wafts across the street; inside is a small, dark room filled with clouds of yellow dust; in the middle a huge circular stone with a mast at its centre is being dragged round and round by a large, emaciated horse on bending spindly legs. His eyes are blindfolded with a black cloth and, as he rotates the stone, a mustardy-yellow flour pours from under it into the surrounding gutter. The scene is lit by a single glass eye in the domed ceiling far above, which shoots a diagonal shaft of light and illuminates a column of dust whose yellow specks dance as if to the rhythm of the horse's hooves on the stony floor.

'Come along, child, we must hurry.' My mother. She takes me by the hand and pulls me away. I cling to the door, mesmerised, as the blindfold horse pulls round and round, its yoke screeching, its hooves thudding, its nostrils puffing jets of steam into the icy yellow air – turning, turning.

'Why are his eyes covered, Mother?'

'So that he doesn't see where he is, otherwise he would get dizzy going round in a circle all day, and he would balk. Blindfold, he can imagine he is walking in a straight line, in a field. But don't worry, at the end of the day they take off the cloth from his eyes and give him some lovely oats to eat. He is quite happy, really…'

Shusha Guppy: *The Blindfold Horse*

HAY-MAKING

You know the hay's in
when gates hang slack
in the lanes. These hot nights
the fallen fields lie open
under the moon's clean sheets.

The homebound road is
sweet with the liquors
of the grasses, air
green with the pastels
of stirred hayfields.

Down at Fron Felen
in the loaded barn
new bales displace
stale darknesses. Breathe.
Remember finding
first kittens, first love
in the scratch of the hay,
our sandals filled with seeds.

Gillian Clarke

Chapter 13
Sending a Message

One of the purposes of much literature is to change people's attitudes. It is most unlikely that any writer would publish a test only to display his iambic pentameters or his metaphorical use of language. He is far more likely to have a statement or world view embedded in his text. Most readers approach a text wondering what it will have to say rather than how it's said, although we find the style of some writers more to our taste than others. We read for sense not form, though, we would argue, the latter contributes to the former.

Wilfred Owen, who wrote poems from and about the trenches in the First World War, obviously had a message to send to his readers. The way he put it was that 'the poetry is in the pity'. In other words the feelings evoked by the words were more important than the words themselves. Without the effect, the poetry would be pointless.

Let us start our look at didactic writing by considering Owen's poem 'Anthem for Doomed Youth'. To focus your attention upon the precision of his language use, consider alongside it an earlier draft 'Anthem for Dead Youth'.

ANTHEM FOR DEAD YOUTH

What passing bells for you who die in herds?
– Only the monstrous anger of the guns!
– Only the stuttering rifles' rattled words
Can patter out your hasty orisons.
No chants for you, nor balms, nor wreaths, nor bells,
Nor any voice of mourning, save the choirs,
And long-drawn sighs of wailing shells;
And bugles calling for you from sad shires.
What candles may we hold to speed you all?
Not in the hands of boys, but in their eyes
Shall shine the holy lights of our goodbyes.
The pallor of girls' brows must be your pall.
Your flowers, the tenderness of comrades' minds,
And each slow dusk, a drawing-room of blinds.

Wilfred Owen

ANTHEM FOR DOOMED YOUTH

What passing bells for these who die as cattle?
– Only the monstrous anger of the guns.
– Only the stuttering rifles' rapid rattle
Can patter out their hasty orisons.
No mockeries now for them, no prayers nor bells,
Nor any voice of mourning, save the choirs,
The shrill, demented choirs of wailing shells;
And bugles calling for them from sad shires.
What candles may be held to speed them all?
Not in the hands of boys, but in their eyes
Shall shine the holy glimmers of goodbyes.
The pallor of girls' brows shall be their pall;
Their flowers the tenderness of patient minds,
And each slow dusk a drawing-down of blinds.

Wilfred Owen

Read both versions in their entirety – you cannot look at the trees before the wood; remember that poems are an entity, not a jumble of lines. Which, if either, do you prefer? find clearer? find more moving or amusing?

Presumably the writer preferred the final draft and made quite conscious decisions about the effect he wished to achieve. You may not agree with him, but at least try to see what his intentions were.

ACTIVITY

Identify the changes that have been made. A systematic differentiation of types of change, e.g. lexical, phonological, syntactic may well help you later. Colour coding might be useful – or straight and wiggly lines!

Try to group the changes: it is dull and pointless to start at the beginning and wade through till you reach the end. You are likely to be repetitive and unclear. Possible groupings might include for these two versions:

(a) writing for a different audience

(b) altering to a more emotive lexical style

(c) gaining impact through sound, e.g. alliteration.

Next, prioritise your groups. Which clutch of changes seems to you most significant? You should deal with these first. Then go on to another group which is similar in effect. Then do the rest. If this sounds very mechanical we can only insist that people's personalities and talents do enable the same system to come up with very different results.

You should be in a position by now to see not only what Owen's message is in the poem but also how he is going about conveying it. Attempt a detailed comparison and evaluation of the two versions.

Now look at our students' answers. Which seems to you more thorough? Convincing? Linguistic? Give them a grade.

Response 1

The changes that have been made to the early draft, significantly alter the intentions and impact of the final draft in a variety of ways. The changes can be divided into three main elements. Firstly the changes made to the early draft result in the final draft being aimed at a different audience, consequently resulting in an alteration of the aims which the poem conveys. The changes result in an 'emotional shift', i.e. the final draft conveys much more emotion than the early draft. The third main element of change is evident in the manipulation of sounds which occurs to give the final draft much more drama and emphasis.

Upon reading the early draft, it is evident that the poem is slow and emotive and slower in pace. The presence of a much more emotional impact in the final draft is brought about mainly through a variety of lexical changes to the earlier draft. The first noticeable word change is apparent in the titles of the poems: the title of the early draft being 'Anthem for Dead Youth' and the title of the final draft 'Anthem for Doomed Youth'. The word 'dead' is an extremely final word, whereas 'doomed' is connotatively associated with something which has not yet happened, but which is ultimately inevitable, and conveys a sense of expectation. (Dead = it's over, final, nothing more can happen whereas doomed = what can happen before the inevitable; expectations.) 'Doomed' is much more dramatic and emotive than 'dead'. 'In herds' (early draft) is amended to 'as cattle' in the final draft, thus giving the poem a greater emotional impact to its audience. 'In herds' conveys numbers, but it is not very precise or descriptive as to how the soldiers died; 'as cattle' portrays not only numbers, but places much more emphasis on the way in which the soldiers died. 'As cattle' conjures up negative connotations to the audience. It is a simile, likening the death of soldiers to the death of cattle, i.e. cattle are slaughtered thus dying without dignity — inferring that humans were to be slaughtered. 'As cattle' is much more precise and clarifies the poet's intention of describing the terrible inhuman way the soldiers met their deaths.

'Mockeries' replaced 'chants' in the final draft as mockeries is a much stronger and more emotive word than chants. Chants could have positive connotations, i.e.: chants of encouragement for example, whereas mockeries has definite negative connotations, i.e.: to mock someone is jeering at and making fun of them. This lexical change, again helps the poet to clarify his point to the audience. 'We hold' in the early draft conveys a sense of 'here and now', i.e.: the present tense, whereas 'be held' is much more generalised and portrays the idea of forever, and expands into the future. Thus by this lexical change the poem can be for an audience of any era and is not just directed at an audience of the era when the poem was written, i.e.: World War 1; 1914–1918.

The use of 'comrades' in the early draft conveys the idea that other people care, whereas 'patient' in the final draft conveys the idea of those at home waiting for their loved one to return. Again this is much more emotive.

The final draft is directed at a different audience than that of the early draft. By amending the pronouns 'you', 'your' to 'these', 'their', 'them' in the final draft the poem is not only directed at a different audience, but a much broader audience also. The early draft is directed at those fighting in the war, i.e. the soldiers, yet the final draft is directed at a general audience and conveys the idea that war is the responsibility of everyone, NOT just the soldiers. In the final draft the poet is perhaps trying to change/influence public opinion at home whereas in the early draft he is conveying the obvious to the audience, i.e.: the soldiers.

By manipulating the sounds of the early draft, the final draft is far more dramatic, emotive and emphatic. 'Rapid rattle' is rhythmic, portraying the sound of a gun shooting. The alliteration of the 'r's and the assonance of the 'a's are effective in impact to the reader of the final draft. However, in the early draft 'rattled words', which is not as phonological, or as descriptive in expressing the rhythm of a gun shooting, was used instead. By using 'rapid rattle', Owen helps the audience to gain a greater feel of the mood of the poem. 'Rapid rattle' has far more impact than 'rattled words'.

Although the early draft has a slow pace, the final draft contains a far slower pace. In the early draft 'Nor balms, nor wreaths, nor bells' was changed to: 'no prayers nor bells' in the final draft, as the previous line read like a list, thus losing some of its emotional impact. By reducing the words in the line of the final draft, the emotional impact is retained. The semi-colon before, 'no prayers nor bells' gives a much longer pause and is much more rhetorical in effect. 'Shrill demented choirs' in the final draft is quicker in pace and is more emotive than 'long drawn sighs'. It infers the screams of dying people in phonology and connotations, having a greater, more frightening impact on the audience. 'Shrill demented choirs' has far shorter vowels than 'long drawn sighs', whose vowels are long and drawn out.

'Glimmer' is similar to an onomatopoeia (i.e.: glimmer is a faint hope, a flickering light) in its word effect. It is much more rhythmic in sound than 'light'. Light connotates a great hope, burning brightly, which is wrong for the context of the poem, as the poem is about the 'doomed', i.e. those awaiting death, and here 'glimmer' is much more suitable in connotation. By replacing 'drawing-room' with 'drawing-down' Owen includes alliteration of the 'd's, which are extremely final in sound — tying in with the theme of the poem. It is an action word and symbolises literally the death of a person (curtains drawn when in mourning). 'Drawing-down' is very final. It conveys the idea that now all will be dark and that the aforementioned 'glimmer' has now died.

The changes made to the early draft result in a much more meaningful, emotive and dramatic final version of Owen's poem, 'Anthem for Doomed Youth'.

Response 2

The first obvious difference that we notice between the first and final drafts of the poem, is that the first is directed at one soldier in particular and that the final draft is directed at all the soldiers.

The poet has a pessimistic view of the soldiers.

The final version is not as pessimistic as the first one.

The first version contains words such as: 'mourning', 'wreaths', 'long-drawn'. These words would normally be associated with sad occasions e.g. a funeral. They have been omitted from the final version.

The title of the first draft has a more angry tone to it than the final draft.

It is changed from 'Anthem for Dead Youth' to 'Anthem for Doomed Youth'. The first gives the impression that the soldiers have already been killed and that it is all over, whereas the second gives the impression that the soldiers are still in the process of being killed. That it is happening at present.

In the final draft the word 'cattle' is used instead of 'herds'. The poet is being more specific by stressing exactly what he means but the word 'cattle' also has a callous meaning to it. Because cattle are used as meat the reader would associate this with cattle being carted off to the slaughterhouse to be killed. It is as if the poet is implying that the soldiers don't have a chance, that they are walking into death.

Alliteration is used in the poem, e.g. 'rifles' rapid rattle'. There is repetition of the letter 'r'. If the words are said they sound like the rifle being fired. This is also an example of onomatopoeia.

The line that read
'No chants for you, nor balms, nor wreaths, nor bells'
has been changed to
'No mocking now for them, no prayers nor bells'.

The new line is quicker to say and has a much smoother rhythm. It has a sarcastic tone to it whereas the first draft has a bumpy rhythm and is drawn out.

Personification is used throughout the poem, e.g. 'And bugles calling for you...'. Here it is as if the bugles are people calling after the soldiers as they go to war.

'Wailing shells' is as if the bullets from the rifles are screaming as they are fired.

There is a sequence in how the lines rhyme.

The last line of the poem has a very emotional and morbid tone:
'A drawing down of blinds.'

The drawing of a blind/curtains is used as a mark of respect when somebody dies. It is a symbol of death. This ties in with the theme of the poem – which is the death of the soldiers.

Out of interest, we gave these answers a B+ and a D+. If you strongly disagreed with us, perhaps you would like to look again.

....

ACTIVITY ◉ ▨

If you feel you need to do more work on double drafts – and they are excellent practice – take a look at these two versions of 'London' by William Blake. Try an analysis of them using our suggested method. When you have completed yours, turn to the end of the chapter and look at ours.

....

LONDON (EARLY DRAFT)

I wander thro' each dirty street,
Near where the dirty Thames does flow,
And mark in every face I meet
Marks of weakness, marks of woe.

In every cry of every man
In every voice of every child
In every voice, in every ban
The german mind forg'd links I hear.

Jim tell him fi let goh a him
far him noh dhu not'n',
an him naw t'ief,
nat even a but'n.
Jim start to wriggle.
Di police start to giggle.

Mama,
Mek Ah tell y'u whey dem dhu to Jim;
Mama,
mek Ah tell y'u whey dem dhu to him:

dem t'ump him in him belly
an' it turn to jelly
dem lick him pan him back
an' him rib get pap
dem lick him pan him he'd
but it tuff like le'd
dem kick him in him seed
an' it started to bleed

Mama,
Ah jus' could'n' stan-up deh
an' noh dhu not'n':
soh mi jook one in him eye
an' him started to cry;
mi t'ump one in him mout'
an' him started to shout
mi kick one pan him shin
an' him started to spin
mi t'ump him pan him chin
an' him drap pan a pin.

an' crash
an de'd.

Mama,
more policeman come dung
an' beat mi to di grung;
dem charge Jim fi sus;
dem charge mi fi murdah.

Mama,
doan fret,
doan get depres'
an' doun-hearted
Be af good courage
till I hear fram you.

I remain,
your son

Sonny

Linton Kwesi Johnson

ACTIVITY ⬛ 🗐

- Make notes about this poem under these subheadings: consider effect and find quotes from the text.
  1 storytelling devices
  2 creation of Sonny's voice
  3 social protest
  4 emotional impact upon the reader
- The context is a letter. How can we tell?
- Does this context contribute to the poem's effect?
- In the course of the poem there are several changes in tone and emotional content. Could you divide the poem up into sections?
- Which section do you consider the most effective?

You now have enough material to write an analysis of the poem, as a poem and as persuasion.

DIDACTIC PROSE

Of course it is not only poetry writers who use literature didactically. Prose writers, too, are committed and usually have more space in which to persuade you. Some authors are renowned for their strong feelings and clear expression of them: try reading Charles Dickens or George Eliot! For a rather easier start than their prose style represents, take a look at this passage from D. H. Lawrence's book *Nottingham and the Mining Countryside*.

> The great city means beauty, dignity and a certain splendour, but England is a mean and petty scrabble of paltry dwellings called homes.
>
> The promoter of industry, a hundred years ago, dared to perpetrate the ugliness of my native village. And still more monstrous, promoters of industry today are scrabbling over the face of England with miles and square miles of red-brick 'homes' like horrible scabs. And the men inside these little red rat-traps get more and more helpless, being more and more humiliated, more and more dissatisfied, like trapped rats.
>
> Do away with it all then. At no matter what costs, start in to alter it. Never mind about wages and industrial squabbling. Turn the attention elsewhere. Pull down my native village to the last brick. Plan a nucleus. Fix the focus. Make a handsome gesture of radiation from the focus. And then put up big buildings, handsome, that sweep to a civic centre. And furnish them with beauty. And make an absolute clean start. Do it place by place. Make a new England. Away with little homes! Away with scrabbling

pettiness and paltriness. Look at the contours of the land, and build up from these, with a sufficient nobility. The English may be mentally or spiritually developed. But as citizens of splendid cities they are more ignominious than rabbits. And they nag, nag, nag all the time about politics and wages and all that, like mean narrow housewives.

D. H. Lawrence: *Nottingham and the Mining Countryside*

One read of this passage ought to be enough to tell you that it is a rhetorical piece of writing.

ACTIVITY

In pairs write answers to these questions.

- Why is this text split into three paragraphs?
- What is the content of each?
- Does anything strike you about verb forms in the final paragraph?
- Look at the nouns. Are they abstract or concrete?
- What difference does it make?
- What sort of connotations – positive or negative – do you have?
- Look at modifiers. Is the writer directing us or informing us? Which are the key words?
- Does this literary writer employ imagistic, metaphorical language? Does it work?
- Are there any sound effects in this passage?

Here is our analysis:

Lawrence's aim here is to point out a state of affairs as emphatically as possible and then provide the cure. He uses extreme, pejorative modifiers to describe our cities and homes, like 'mean', 'petty' and 'paltry' ('petty' and 'paltry' are further emphasised by an alliterative effect). The city is essentially 'great': it is what men have 'dared to perpetrate' upon it which is so dreadful. Their conduct is described as 'monstrous', a very extreme term. They have taken something with great abstract qualities – 'dignity', 'beauty' and 'splendour' – and reduced it to a cluster of 'rat-traps'. This is clearly not literally true. The passage uses language metaphorically to gain maximum emotional impact. The red-brick homes are seen as 'scabs' – the outward sign of damage to the body surface. The village is seen as damaged and broken as well as ugly.

The writer seems to feel the more strongly because what he is describing is not any old village but his own: 'my', the possessive pronoun, adds emphasis and personalises the issue. In turn, the place's ugliness affects those who live in it; they become 'humiliated' and 'dissatisfied'. They are the rats in the rat-traps.

Having identified how damaging the ugliness and soullessness of the village is, Lawrence uses a string of imperatives in the final paragraph to insist on what can be done. Adopting a more spoken, colloquial tone, he tells the reader 'Do away with it all, then.' The verbs are no longer stative, but dynamic. People must 'start in to alter', 'pull down', 'plan' and 'fix'. In short, do something! More positive evaluative adjectives are now used. Gestures and buildings alike will be 'handsome'. It will be a 'clean' — with all its connotations of purity — start. A new beginning is to be made, leading to 'a new England'. The vision is thus widened from the one village; it is seen as representative. The readers are told not only what to build but what to destroy: 'Away with little homes!' Lawrence exclaims. He has no patience with the thrice repeated nagging or the squabbling over pay. He insists that they must address themselves instead to creation — and creation of something of beauty. Not for them the timidity of rabbits, or the little-mindedness of housewives (not a phrase likely to endear Lawrence to feminists, I feel!). They must build the new Jerusalem.

Having cut your teeth on that, perhaps you could now have a look at the Victorian novelists in their full intensity. Here are two extracts, one from Charlotte Brontë's *Jane Eyre* and one from George Eliot's *Middlemarch*. Both seem to us to be fairly blatant in their message-sending.

Look at each and ask yourself the following question:

● What point, broadly, is each trying to make? Purpose is crucial here.

Answer the following questions as specifically as you can. They will give you the basis of a solidly linguistic analysis.

● What are the main structural devices employed by each of the writers?

● Which word-classes carry the major emotional meaning?

● Are any of the features you might expect in poetry such as deviant syntax, unusual collocations and densely figurative language used?

● Which of the two do you consider the more effective?

Jane Eyre

This passage from *Jane Eyre* has something in common with the Tony Harrison poem we have looked at. A young person is belittled by an authority figure.

'Her size is small; what is her age?'

'Ten years.'

'So much?' was the doubtful answer; and he prolonged his scrutiny for some minutes. Presently he addressed me –

'Your name, little girl?'

'Jane Eyre, sir.'

In uttering these words I looked up: he seemed to me a tall gentleman, but then I was very little; his features were large, and they and all the lines of his frame were equally harsh and prim.

'Well, Jane Eyre, and are you a good child?'

Impossible to reply to this in the affirmative: my little world held a contrary opinion: I was silent. Mrs Reed answered for me by an expressive shake of the head, adding soon, 'Perhaps the less said on that subject the better, Mr Brocklehurst.'

'Sorry indeed to hear it! She and I must have some talk'; and bending from the perpendicular, he installed his person in the arm-chair, opposite Mrs Reed's. 'Come here,' he said.

I stepped across the rug: he placed me square and straight before him. What a face he had, now that it was almost on a level with mine! what a great nose! and what a mouth! and what large, prominent teeth! 'No sight so sad as that of a naughty child,' he began, 'especially a naughty little girl. Do you know where the wicked go after death?'

'They go to hell,' was my ready and orthodox answer.

'And what is hell? Can you tell me that?'

'A pit full of fire.'

'And should you like to fall into that pit, and to be burning there for ever?'

'No, sir.'

'What must you do to avoid it?'

I deliberated a moment: my answer, when it did come was objectionable: 'I must keep in good health, and not die.'

'How can you keep in good health? Children younger than you die daily. I buried a little child of five years old only a day or two since – a good little child, whose soul is now in heaven. It is to be feared the same could not be said of you, were you to be called thence.'

Not being in a condition to remove his doubt, I only cast my eyes down on the two large feet planted on the rug, and sighed, wishing myself far enough away.

'I hope that sigh is from the heart, and that you repent of ever having been the occasion of discomfort to your excellent benefactress.'

'Benefactress! benefactress!' said I inwardly: 'they all call Mrs Reed my benefactress; if so, a benefactress is a disagreeable thing.'

'Do you say your prayers night and morning?' continued my interrogator.

'Yes, sir.'

'Do you read your Bible?'

'Sometimes.'

'With pleasure? Are you fond of it?'

'I like Revelations, and the Book of Daniel, and Genesis, and Samuel, and a little bit of Exodus, and some parts of Kings and Chronicles, and Job and Jonah.'

'And the Psalms? I hope you like them?'

'No, sir.'

'No? Oh shocking! I have a little boy, younger than you, who knows six Psalms by heart: and when you ask him which he would rather have, a ginger-bread-nut to eat, or a verse of a Psalm to learn, he says: 'Oh! the verse of the Psalm! angels sings Psalms,' says he; 'I wish to be a little angel here below.' He then gets two nuts in recompense for his infant piety.'

'Psalms are not interesting,' I remarked.

'That proves you to have a wicked heart; and you must pray to God to change it: to give you a new and clean one; to take away your heart of stone and give you a heart of flesh.'

Charlotte Brontë: *Jane Eyre*

Middlemarch

As you read this passage keep track of your opinion of Dorothea and Casaubon.

One morning, some weeks after her arrival at Lowick, Dorothea – but why always Dorothea? Was her point of view the only possible one with regard to this marriage? I protest against all our interest, all our effort at understanding being given to the young skins that look blooming in spite of trouble; for these too will get faded, and will know the older and more eating griefs which we are helping to neglect. In spite of the blinking eyes and white moles objectionable to Celia, and the want of muscular curve which was morally painful to Sir James, Mr Casaubon had an intense consciousness within him, and was spiritually a-hungered like the rest of us. He had done nothing exceptional in marrying – nothing but what society sanctions, and considers an occasion for wreaths and bouquets. It had occurred to him that he must not any longer defer his intention of matrimony, and he had reflected that in taking a wife, a man of good position should expect and carefully choose a blooming young lady – the younger the better, because more educable and submissive – of a rank equal to his own, of religious principles, virtuous disposition, and good understanding. On such a young lady he would make handsome settlements, and he would neglect no arrangement for her happiness; in return, he should receive family pleasures and leave behind him that copy of himself which seemed so urgently required of a man – to the sonneteers of the sixteenth century. Times had altered since then, and no sonneteer had insisted on Mr Casaubon's leaving a copy of himself; moreover, he had not yet succeeded in issuing copies of his mythological key; but he had always intended to acquit himself by marriage, and the sense that he was fast leaving the years behind him, that the world was getting dimmer and that he felt lonely, was a reason to him for losing no more time in overtaking domestic delights before they too were left behind by the years.

And when he had seen Dorothea he believed that he had found even more than he demanded: she might really be such a help-mate to him as would enable him to dispense with a hired secretary, an aid which Mr Casaubon had never yet employed and had a suspicious dread of. (Mr Casaubon was nervously conscious that he was expected to manifest a powerful mind.) Providence, in its kindness, had supplied him with the wife he needed. A wife, a modest young lady, with the purely appreciative, unambitious abilities of her sex, is sure to think her husband's mind powerful. [Does the writer believe this?] Whether Providence had taken equal care of Miss Brooke in presenting her with Mr Casaubon was an idea which could hardly occur to him. Society never made the preposterous demand that a man should think as much about his own qualifications for making a charming girl happy as he thinks of hers for making himself happy. As if a man could choose not only his wife but his wife's husband! Or as if he were bound to provide charms for his posterity in his own person! – When Dorothea accepted him with effusion, that was only natural; and Mr Casaubon believed that his happiness was going to begin.

ACTIVITY

- Look back over the passage so far and discuss with a partner your view of the couple.
- Label the next section for your partner. Try to pick out interesting and striking elements which indicate Eliot's intention or tone.

He had not had much foretaste of happiness in his previous life. To know intense joy without a strong bodily frame, one must have an enthusiastic soul. Mr Casaubon had never had a strong bodily frame, and his soul was sensitive without being enthusiastic: it was too languid to thrill out of self-consciousness into passionate delight; it went on fluttering in the swampy ground where it was hatched, thinking of its wings and never flying. His experience was of that pitiable kind which shrinks from pity, and fears most of all that it should be known: it was that proud, narrow sensitiveness which has not mass enough to spare for transformation into sympathy, and quivers thread-like in small currents of self-preoccupation or at best of an egoistic scrupulosity. And Mr Casaubon had many scruples: he was capable of a severe self-restraint; he was resolute in being a man of honour according to the code; he would be unimpeachable by any recognized opinion. In conduct these ends had been attained; but the difficulty of making his Key to all Mythologies unimpeachable weighed like lead upon his mind; and the pamphlets – or 'Parerga' as he called them – by which he tested his public and deposited small monumental records of his march, were far from having been seen in all their significance. He suspected the Archdeacon of not having read them; he was in painful doubt as to what was really thought of them by the leading minds of Brasenose, and bitterly convinced that his old acquaintance Carp had been the writer of that depreciatory recension which was kept locked in a small drawer of Mr Casaubon's desk, and also in a dark closet of his verbal memory. These were heavy impressions to struggle against, and brought that melancholy embitterment which is the consequence of all excessive claim: even his religious faith wavered with his wavering trust in his own authorship, and the consolations of the Christian hope in immortality seemed to lean on the immortality of the still unwritten Key to all Mythologies. For my part I am very sorry for him. It is an uneasy lot at best, to be what we call highly taught and yet not to enjoy: to be present at this great spectacle of life and never to be liberated from a small hungry shivering self – never to be fully possessed by the glory we behold, never to have our consciousness rapturously transformed into the vividness of a thought, the ardour of a passion, the energy of an action, but always to be scholarly and uninspired, ambitious and timid, scrupulous and dim-sighted. Becoming a dean or even a bishop would make little difference, I fear, to Mr Casaubon's uneasiness. Doubtless some ancient Greek has observed that behind the big mask and the speaking-trumpet, there must always be our poor little eyes peeping as usual and our timorous lips more or less under anxious control.

George Eliot: *Middlemarch*

FINAL ACTIVITY

Before you leave the area of literature that aims to persuade, perhaps a group of you could put together an anthology of pieces of writing which made you think or feel differently. This will also give you an opportunity to 'sell' your favourite writers.

OUR ANALYSIS OF BLAKE'S 'LONDON'

The alterations which immediately strike one are lexical. In the first two lines of the poem 'dirty' has been replaced by 'charter'd'; in terms of sound effect these are very similar, both being bi-syllabic and containing the fluid, alliterative r. However, their emotional impact is very different: 'dirty' is a word collocated with disapproval (its value is pejorative), whereas 'charter'd', whose signification is 'mapped out', is far more factual in tone. The lexical change in the third line is even more significant. Not only does the elision of the word 'mark' avoid an unnecessary and ineffective repetition but 'see', which replaces it, has two values: to see physically and to understand. 'Mark' has only the value 'notice', and thus is implying less sympathy. The choice of 'infant' in line six has a similar effect. Unlike 'child' it is collocated with the infant Jesus and thus has connotations of innocence and purity. 'Cry' is clearly more emotive than the factually descriptive 'voice'. The same emotional shift is evident in the change in the second line of the last stanza from 'midnight' with its overtones of darkness, loneliness and sinister activities to 'youthful' with overtones of innocence and freshness. 'Youthful' is a far more shocking, oxymoronic adjective with which to modify 'harlot' since one would expect a prostitute to be corrupt.

Sometimes, not wishing to lose the impact of an individual word, Blake has transposed it rather than omitting it. Thus he retains 'midnight' but places it in the first line, modifying 'streets', instead of the second. He also moves 'But most' to the opening of the final stanza rather than the third one. This clearly makes more sense since 'But most' would normally introduce a climax. Putting the climax at the end creates the usual build-up.

The final lexical alteration is in the final line of the poem, and has a dual purpose. 'Blights' not only achieves an alliterative and thus emphatic effect with 'blasts' but is also inherently more dramatic. 'Blights' could never be collocated with happy endings!

Often in the poem the need to alter one word has necessitated the entire re-wording of a line. For example, in the eighth line Blake has excluded 'german'. When Blake decided to drop it he had a problem. The omission of 'german' affects the rhythm of the line, leaving it two syllables short. The change from 'links' to 'manacles' rectifies this, and at the same time it creates an alliterative effect in combination with 'mind-forg'd' and collocates more closely in the reader's mind with imprisonment.

Not every alteration in the poem is purely lexical. If we consider the second stanza we can see that whereas in the first draft a parallel structure (preposition, adjective, noun) has been used to divide up units of meaning and to have repetitive force, in the later draft the parallel structure is abandoned and thus the commas are needed to separate the units. The structure has been altered to allow the inclusion of the more emotive lexical items 'cry of fear' and 'infant'.

Another line which has been altered radically is the second one of the third stanza. The tense change from 'blackens' (present simple) to 'black'ning' (present continuous) suggests that the process is on-going – is happening continually and cannot be stopped. The use of 'black'ning' as an adjectival modifier links it more closely to the church. 'Every... church' is far more emphatic than 'churches'; it denotes churches without exception rather than simply 'more than one church'. 'Church' (singular) also has the value of the institution, and thus the entire institution of the church is seen as being undermined, not just individual buildings. The use of 'appalls' is also interesting. An emotive verb usually collocated with animate objects, it is here used to emphasise that the church has feelings, is almost human. This is akin to personification.

To summarise, we can see that by altering lexical items, introducing more emotion, by changing phonological items to gain alliterative, emphatic effects and by careful use of punctuation and verb forms, Blake has achieved a more persuasive, dramatic whole.

Chapter 14
Make them Cry

We will now move on to that other aim of literature closely linked to message-sending; its ability to move us. No-one is suggesting that we all weep buckets when we read; many would consider this self-indulgent and superficial. However, one of the legitimate functions of literature is catharsis – the releasing of negative emotions.

POETRY

We will start with poetry, since it is easier to see the effect of the whole of a short poem than of a prose extract.

We have chosen the first poem because, despite the fact that it is about an incredibly emotional subject – the death of an infant son who, judging by the subheading, was brain-damaged – is not melodramatic or sentimental. Read it now and see if you agree with us. All readers respond personally, and for some of you it may be more upsetting or offensive than it is to us. If that is the case, adopt every reader's right and skip this bit of text. If, on the other hand, you agree with us that it is a moving, effective, interesting poem, think about it a little or discuss it with a partner before you read our analysis.

DEATH OF A SON
(who died in a mental hospital, aged one)

Something has ceased to come along with me.
Something like a person: something very like one.
And there was no nobility in it
Or anything like that.

Something was there like a one-year-
Old house, dumb as stone. While the near buildings
Sang like birds and laughed
Understanding the pact

They were to have with silence. But he
Neither sang nor laughed. He did not bless silence
Like bread, with words.
He did not forsake silence.

But rather, like a house in mourning
Kept the eye turned in to watch the silence while
The other houses like birds
Sand around him.

And the breathing silence neither
Moved nor was still.

I have seen stones: I have seen brick
But this house was made up of neither brick nor stone
But a house of flesh and blood
With flesh of stone

And bricks for blood. A house
Of stones and blood in breathing silence with the other
Birds singing crazy on its chimneys.
But this was silence,

This was something else, this was
Hearing and speaking though he was a house drawn
Into silence, this was
Something religious in his silence,

Something shining in his quiet,
This was different: this was altogether something else:
Though he never spoke, this
Was something to do with death.

And then slowly the eye stopped looking
Inward. The silence rose and became still.

The look turned to the outer place and stopped,
With birds still shrilling around him.
And as if he could speak

He turned over on his side with this one year
Red as a wound
He turned over as if he could be sorry for this
And out of his eyes two great tears rolled, like stones, and he died.

Jon Silkin

- List descriptors of the child.
- What emotions does the description of the child evoke?
- How are the other children in the home described?
- How is sentimentality avoided in this poem? Consider word choice and tone.
- Does the poem seem at all self-indulgent or mawkish?
- Are any lexical items hyperbolic?
- Finally, is the poem restricted to this one death or does it seem to have a wider relevance?

What we were struck by most on a first reading of this poem was the almost shocking apparent detachment of the writer. The very title 'Death of a Son' sounds so matter-of-fact. Why the indefinite article 'a' rather than the possessive pronoun 'my'? (That might be worth seriously considering.) The description of the child as 'some*thing*' which is very '*like* a person' is distressing, and the bald statement 'there was no nobility in *it*' (notice the neuter pronoun) is candid and clear. The last line of the stanza, the more colloquial, imprecise 'Or anything like that' is striking. The writer seems vague – indeed much of the poem conveys a seeking after understanding of the child and what he represented. His father compares him to things: 'Like a one-year-Old house'. He emphasises and re-emphasises the child's silence. At first this is seen negatively – 'dumb as stone' suggests lack of feeling and lack of intellect. In contradistinction the other children are animated: sing, laugh, are normal. The attitude of the writer to his son seems negative: he stresses what he did not do, that he 'Neither sang nor laughed', that 'he did not forsake silence' and 'did not bless silence... with words'.

At this stage an alert reader notices a lexical shift and a different emphasis. The choice of words suggests a religious context, almost a Christ-like peace. Later on, this is made more blatant in the phrase 'Something religious in his silence'. His silence begins to seem less and less passive and uninterested; it is 'breathing' – alive and yet dead-seeming. The child is described as a 'house of flesh and blood'. The 'flesh' here may well connote with God made flesh; again the link with Christ.

As the poem progresses, the words describing the child become more and more positive. There is 'Something shining in his quiet'. Nor is he selfish or callous: he stops 'looking inward'. He has made a choice, it seems, not to speak (not to complain?). It is as if he could speak (the modal auxiliary is vital here) and could be sorry for himself and mankind, but he will not utter a word. However, his pain and humanity are conveyed by the 'two great tears' which roll from his eyes. 'Great' would seem to have the meaning 'noble' as well as 'large' here. They are his final, human statement.

Just as the attitude to this child shifts, so does that towards the other children. At first, they are seen positively: they 'sang... and laughed'. At the next mention, they 'sang' only. Then, interestingly, they are described as 'singing crazy'. (Is this a reminder that they, too, are mentally handicapped but they take refuge in sound rather than silence?) Their noise is not normal or joyful. This is most clearly conveyed in the final reference to them – 'the birds still shrilling' – which sounds most unattractive.

Indeed, sound is an important element in the poem's impact. The line division of 'one-year-' from 'Old house' enables us to hear 'one-year-/Old house' as describing the infant's age as well as the house's. The collocation of 'one-year' and 'Old' is a strikingly strange one and neatly conveys the extreme youth yet the ancient wisdom of the child. 'Old' is stressed by its initial position so that he seems more old than young.

Rhyme also has a part to play. The rhyme linking 'laughed' and 'pact' accelerates the pace of the stanza and makes the other 'buildings' sound brighter and more active and jolly. The caesura before 'But he' gives it full emphasis and slows the pace down, conveying a more serious tone. The short, bald statement utilises long, slow vowels because the tone is contemplative – the poet is trying to puzzle out why. This explains the 'But rather', which has the flavour of a spoken voice explicating or re-expressing and searching for the right words. Part of this search necessitates similes. He is 'like a house in mourning' metaphorically as well as literally. He is also a 'breathing silence' and 'a house of flesh'.

Many vital words are placed initially after a run-on line. One example would be

> And then slowly the eye stopped looking
> Inward

Line length and layout also emphasise important parts of the text. Thus

> And the breathing silence neither
> Moved nor was still

is a two-line stanza standing out from the other four-line ones. The line 'Red as a wound' with its four monosyllables is noticeably short. The last line is the longest and mirrors a slow, painful yielding up of the child's life.

The next poem we'd like you to look at is also about loss, but this time the separation is between a man and wife, and voluntary — at least on the wife's part.

SONG FOR LAST YEAR'S WIFE

> Alice, this is my first winter
> of waking without you, of knowing
> that you, dressed in familiar clothes
> are elsewhere, perhaps not even
> conscious of our anniversary. Have
> you noticed? The earth's still as hard,
> the same empty gardens exist; it is
> as if nothing special had changed.
> I wake with another mouth feeding
> from me, yet still feel as if
> Love had not the right
> to walk out of me. A year now. So
> what? you say. I send out my spies
> to discover what you are doing. They smile,
> return, tell me your body's as firm,
> you are as alive, as warm and inviting
> as when I knew you first… Perhaps it is
> the winter, its isolation from other seasons,
> that sends me your ghost to witness
> when I wake. Somebody came here today, asked
> how you were keeping, what
> you were doing. I imagine you
> waking in another city, touched
> by this same hour. So ordinary
> a thing as loss comes now and touches me.

Brian Patten

- Look at the title and the first word of the first line. What is their effect?
- Who is the audience of the poem?
- Look at the layout of the poem. Is it a poem?
- Is the poem metaphorical or figurative at all?
- What sort of tone does it have?
- How would you describe the attitude of the writer (or his persona) to his wife?
- How effective do you consider the last sentence of the poem to be?
- Do you find the totality moving or not?
- Finally, select three lines or images which you feel work well and try to explain their effect.

The final poem we would like you to consider in this chapter returns to the theme of loss by death. It is a very well known poem by a writer far more literary and overtly 'poetical' than Patten – Dylan Thomas. The poem is directly addressed to another person.

ACTIVITY

- Decide to whom the poem is addressed.
- Look carefully at repetition in the poem. Is it emphatic and effective or merely tedious?
- Some have regarded Thomas's verse as 'sound and fury signifying nothing'. Can you see any justice in such a view?
- Write a full analysis of the poem which includes a judgement on its manner as well as its matter.

DO NOT GO GENTLE INTO THAT GOOD NIGHT

Do not go gentle into that good night,
Old age should burn and rave at close of day;
Rage, rage against the dying of the light.

Though wise men at their end know dark is right,
Because their words have forked no lightning they
Do not go gentle into that good night.

Good men, the last wave by, crying how bright
Their frail deeds might have danced in a green bay,
Rage, rage against he dying of the light.

Wild men who caught and sang the sun in flight,
And learn, too late, they grieved it on its way,
Do not go gentle into that good night.

Grave men, near death, who see with blinding sight
Blind eyes could blaze like meteors and be gay,
Rage, rage against the dying of the light.

And you, my father, there on the sad height,
Curse, bless me now with your fierce tears, I pray.
Do not go gentle into that good night,
Rage, rage against the dying of the light.

Dylan Thomas

PROSE

It is rather more difficult to find prose passages which have an immediate impact upon the reader because prose is so much more context-dependent. What we will do is to provide an introductory statement about each of the passages so as to put you in a better position to judge the passage's effect. The first extract is from Paul Scott's novel *Staying On*. The novel concerns an elderly, superficially unattractive couple who decide to 'stay on' in India after their retirement. Tusker, the husband, is irascible, seemingly selfish and by no means a model husband. The extract is a letter from Tusker to his wife Lucy, explaining what her position will be in the event of his death. In the context of the novel, it is in many ways a shock, because it allows us to see a very different side to Tusker's character. At the same time it contains many elements which are typical of him. At the end of the chapter, the letter is described as 'the only love letter she had had in all the years she had lived'.

ACTIVITY

Read the extract and do the following:

1 Decide whether *you* would describe it as a love letter. What evidence is there to support such a claim?

2 Attempt a character sketch of Tusker on the basis of the letter. How much do you learn about him and his idiolect?

3 Make notes about the thematic content of this novel. Do you think the Indian element is important? Or the fact of the central characters being old?

There was more night-illuminations in Pankot than there had been in the old days, and this made the stars look farther away. The outline of the hills was no longer so distinct against the sky, perhaps just an indication of how poorer her sight was now than then. The air was coming quite coldly from the mountains and she shivered, went in to make another cup of coffee and longed for the telephone to ring. While the kettle was boiling she read Tusker's note again:

'You asked for a clear statement of yr posn if widowed. Far as I can see you'd get from IMWOF about £900 pa plus a RW supplt of maybe £600. Say £1500 in all, adjustable from time to time to cost of living index. The Smalley Estate income dries up on my death but y've always known that, Luce, and for the past ten years quite apart from the fall in value of the capital investment it's also yielded less interest because some bloody fool at Coyne Coyne persuaded the trustee to reinvest some of it in so-called Blue Chip equities (young Coyne, I reckon). Been getting less than £200 a year out of it since about 1964. Always tried to keep some of that money back in London but gradually had to have it all transferred as it came in to the Bank in Bombay. Present bank balance here approx £500, maybe £200 in London. Life insurance only £2000 but the policy's with profits and been going long enough maybe to double that value at maturity.

What it all comes to Luce is you've enough to take you home if that's what you want though in yr posn I'd prefer to stay here, considering the sort of income you'll have. At home you can't starve really, what with supplementary benefits, and things like Distressed Gentlefolk (Ha!). Also they've got the Nat Health and Old People's Homes. Perhaps for a white person being poor in England's better than being poor in India, though by average Indian standards we're rich if not by the standards of the Indians we mix with. I'm sorry, Luce, if I seem to have made a mess of things. You'll be wondering where some of the money we've occasionally managed to get our hands on went and I don't really know. It was never much anyway. About £3000 compensation when my army career petered out with Independence and I was too old to transfer to British service. We spent a lot of that on that trip home for Smith Brown & McKintosh (because they only paid my expenses) but I'm not making that an excuse. I know I was a fool, Luce. The profit I made on the car we brought back from the UK and sold to old Grabbitwallah as I used to call him, in the days when that sort of gimmick was still legal was really no profit because it was paid for in black money, in one hundred rupee notes which I couldn't very well bank, and nothing goes quicker than hundred rupee notes. Some of them quick on the Bombay racetrack, as you know. In those days nearly everybody was bringing cars out from home free of UK tax because they were being exported and then selling them to Indians who couldn't get cars any other way except by waiting years. But I was playing out of my league because I thought of money like that as fairy gold whereas to people with a real instinct for turning a fast buck it was plain solid cash. Some of my separation pay from Smith Brown & McKintosh went on paying up arrears on my contributions to IMWOF, I'd got a bit behind, but I never mucked about with that, Luce, because I knew it would be your mainstay. Most of the rest went on that round-India trip before settling here. I know for years you've thought I was a damn' fool to have stayed on, but I was forty-six when Independence came, which is bloody early in life for a man to retire but too old to start afresh somewhere you don't know. I didn't fancy my chances back home, at that age, and I knew the pension would go further in India than in England. I still think we were right to stay on, though I don't think of it any longer as staying on, but just as hanging on, which people of our age and upbringing and limited talents, people who have never been really poor but never had any real money, never inherited real money, never made real money, have to do, wherever they happen to be, when they can't work any more. I'm happier hanging on in India, not for India as India but because I can't just merely think of it as a place where I drew my pay for the first 25 years of my working life, which is a hell of a long time anyway, though by rights it should have been longer. But there you are. Suddenly the powers that be say, Right, Smalley, we're not wanted here any more, we've all got to bugger off, too bad you're not ten years younger or ten years older. I thought about this a lot at the time and it seemed to me I'd invested in India, not money which I've never had, not talent (Ha!) which I've only had a limited amount of, nothing India needed or needs or has been one jot the better for, but was all I had to invest in anything.

Me. Where I went wrong was in thinking of it that way and expecting a return on the investment in the end, and anticipating the profits. When they didn't turn up I know I acted like an idiot, Luce, for years and years. The longest male menopause on record. One long Holi. Can't talk about these things face to face, you know. Difficult to write them. Brought up that way. No need ever to answer. Don't want you to. Prefer not. You've been a good woman to me, Luce. Sorry I've not made it clear I think so. I'm not going to read all this rigmarole through when I've finished – if I did I'd tear it up. So I'll just stick it in the envelope and forget it. Don't want to discuss it. If you do I'll only say something that will hurt you. No doubt will anyway. It's my nature. Love, Tusker.'

Paul Scott: Staying On

It probably required quite an imaginative leap for you to empathise with a couple of retired Anglo-Indians. If you did, so much more credit to Scott. One of the things many would claim for literature is that it widens our sympathies.

The following extract will probably make yet greater demands upon your abilities to empathise. It comes from a novel called *Walter*. Like the poem we looked at earlier it deals with the potentially mawkish subject of a brain-damaged person. What is interesting and daring about the novel is that it gives Walter a voice; an opportunity to express his point of view. The narrative often switches from his point of view to his mother's. The first extract we shall look at is from the mother's viewpoint. See if you find her situation and character pitiful.

Sleeping. He always slept well. She stood, watching him sleep, had risen earlier from her own bed than was necessary, in order to stand over him while he slept. Sleeping, she could bear him. If he slept for ever, she would be content.

Yet the face on the pillow never ceased to make her angry. She herself had been pretty, and had been told so, more than once. His father had looked – not handsome, not even passably good-looking, since his neck had been long and thin like a bird's neck, but at least alright; Eric had looked alright. But Walter, sleeping, Witless Walter, was a mistake made by nature, and God had chosen not to correct it. The heavy hooded eyelids, closed now over bulging eyes. The hooked nose, which resembled a joke nose one might buy at the seaside, with an elastic band to hang it over one's real nose. The large pointed jaw, and protruding teeth, yellow and green where they stuck out sharply from the gums. The oily, sallow skin and tiny, white-headed pimples.

Leaning over him, close to his sleeping face, she whispered, 'You must be the ugliest person in this town, and you spent nine months inside me.' His breath was foul. 'Constipated. Must be. Never thinks to tell me these things.'

She moved away, and sat against the wall on a straight-backed chair to watch him. There was plenty of time. She spoke to God, as she had spoken many times before. 'Why has my life been so ill arranged, Lord? Why allow me only one child, and that an ill-put-together, foul-smelling, dribbling lump of ugliness?' God might have replied that she had never tried to make another, that although matrimony was a holy state and sanctified for the procreation of children, she had denied her husband access to her womb after it had once been filled, so that He, God, could hardly be held responsible for any subsequent barrenness. But God was old and wise and knew well the futility of argument with a complaining woman. He permitted her to continue.

'I won't mince words with you, Lord. Not now; I'm too old.' She never had minced words, God sighed, and wondered whether a sparrow somewhere might be falling, to distract His attention. 'I've visited Your chapel twice every Sunday, since I was taken there, at five years old, to Sunday School. Almost sixty years, multiplied by fifty-two, then doubled. I can't begin to count the hours I've sat on hard benches or knelt on a prayer-stool to Your greater glory, and tried to cast everything from my mind but Your face.' It would be the face of Christ she meant; the other two persons of the Trinity didn't have a face. The Face composed itself in patience, and continued to listen. 'I never believed those pictures with the halo. Not like that. Not You. You had to be more beautiful in my mind, more masculine than any of those. Man was made in Your likeness.' She looked across at the sleeping figure. 'Is this what You look life? Is Walter made in your likeness? Is that Your likeness, a physically grotesque man of twenty-seven, with the brain of an infant? Why?'

Why the years of soiled blankets and sheets, the crying, shouting, screaming? Why the hope that he would improve, would learn, that with age he would change, would become at least less of an embarrassment? God had made that hope, had allowed it to persist, kept Sarah at it. Had His intention been to punish? If so, for what? 'Everybody has thoughts. Thoughts they shouldn't have. Unnatural.' Everybody must have those thoughts sometimes, the shameful, unnatural thoughts, which slipped into her mind and clung, like spiders clinging to the side of the bath. You might wish to wash them away down the dark plug-hole, and clean yourself, but there would be no hole in your mind down which to wash them, so they would persist.

But everyone would have such thoughts: it was unfair to punish her. God was unfair and heartless. She had complained to Him so often, and He never took any notice. Walter's mother wiped the tears from her face with a small lace handkerchief which smelt of lavender.

She returned the handkerchief to the pocket of her apron, and went over to the bed. It was time to wake her son.

David Cook: *Walter*

A very striking aspect of this passage is the mother's attitude to her son. She is distressingly negative about her child: 'Sleeping, she could bear him. If he slept for ever, she would be content.' Not only is the surface statement here upsetting, the fact is that she did literally bear him, so her callousness seems unnatural and frightening in its intensity. The wish that he might sleep forever is tantamount to wishing him dead.

The mother is not merely indifferent; she is positively repelled. The words used to describe Walter make this clear. He has 'heavy, hooded eyelids', 'bulging eyes', a 'hooked nose' and a 'large pointed jaw' with 'protruding teeth', both 'yellow and green'. 'Oily, sallow skin' dotted with 'tiny, white-headed pimples' completes the dreadful picture. She seems utterly relentless – cruel to the point of spitefulness – yet she has 'risen earlier than was necessary, in order to stand over him while he slept.' Was it only to indulge in a two-minute hate?

Look at the passage again. How does it make you feel about the mother, the son and their relationship? Try to pick out the key words.

Now look at Walter's description of his mother and his reference to himself in the following extract, considering as you read whether his or his mother's is the more credible, better conveyed viewpoint.

The first thing he saw every morning was her face.

Sleeping was like being dead. She would shake him out of sleep at half past seven every morning. He didn't like it. He was drowned, and she would pull him to the surface with a long rope. He would struggle, but the rope would only become tighter. The water round him would bubble, pulling him down, water up his nostrils and inside his head, hair flattened over his eyes.

He would come up slowly, gulping at the air when he reached the top.

'Come on, Walter. You can't lie there forever.'

That's what she always said, every morning. The water was warm. He liked it above his head. Not having to think. You can't ever go backwards. Even when you remember last week, you can't go there. The clock keeps ticking, moving you on. When you're in a pleasant bit of time, why can't you just stop there?

She shook him. He nodded. Alive, there was time to pass, things to remember, other people asking questions. Rules.

She watched him all the time. All the time, his mother watching. She said they were tied together by a rope he couldn't see. He always did as he was told now, yet she got no pleasure, not even when he was good. She used to like him to remember things. Now she liked nothing. Smile, he had seen her smile. But he could no longer remember her smile.

The first thing he saw every morning was her face. It was not like his own. Her face was small, round and shiny. She did not wear make-up like the Counter Girls. It was dirty stuff; she did not hold with it. 'Come on! Out you get!' He closed his eyes, remembering the warmth of the water, and she shook him.

Her eyes were not hooded like his. 'Move, will you?' He sat up, blinking. His mother's eyes did not stick out, but fitted with the rest of her face. They were red this morning, because she cried for him.

She took his ankles, and swung them round so that his feet were off the bed and touching the cold linoleum.

Her nose was not like the top half of a parrot's beak. He did not go to school any more; he was too old now to go to school. They had called him names 'Parrot Face' and 'Witless Walter'.

Her teeth did not stick out. They were false now, because she was old: he had seen them out of her mouth.

She stood back from the bed, and watched him. She would remain to make sure that he stood up, his body entirely leaving the bed. She would not leave the room until he had taken his pyjamas off. He could tell her he was alright now, but she would stand there; she would not go. He would whine, but she would wait. He took off his pyjama jacket. She should know now that he had grown out of messing himself, it was a subject no longer mentioned. He dropped his pyjama trousers to the floor, and turned round on the spot. No need for words now. Looks were enough.

She left him, and went into the bathroom. He heard the sound of water running, wrapped a towel around his waist, and sat on the bed until she called for him.

He sat on the toilet, while she waited outside the door, listening. He made water, but nothing else.

'I'll give you something this morning to make your bowels move. And if you have to go while you're at work, remember to clean yourself properly. And wash your hands.'

The sound of the toilet being flushed brought her into the bathroom. He sat in the lukewarm water, while she slid the lavender-scented soap all over his body. He didn't shout now, or scream, or make any noises to stop her. He didn't struggle. He just sat there.

She slid her soapy hands all over his chest, back and legs. She never touched his willy. She would point to that, and give him the soap. 'Do it some more. Come on. More soap. Between your legs.'

She was standing now, and she had a towel ready. As he stepped out of the bath, she turned her head away. 'You must be rotten inside, the way your breath smells.'

He stood there while she dried his back, legs and buttocks, rubbing them hard. 'If you can't do Number Twos in the morning, you must tell me. Alright?' He nodded. 'No sense in leaving it until you've got to smelling like a parrot's cage. What will they think at work?' He didn't know what they would think.

'Don't know was made to know. If people complain about you, you'll be out of a job. Woolworth's customers don't want you breathing down their necks, not with that breath.'

She finished drying his face, neck, ears and feet. He did the rest. He had clean underwear every other day. She would watch to make sure he wore it.

As I get into my clothes, I tell myself aloud what I have to remember. 'Don't dawdle!' 'You're slouching, Walter. Stand up straight.' 'Pay attention.' 'You are a cross for my back, Walter, you really are.' All my socks are darned. She does them well. I won't wear nylon socks. I'd rather break things up than wear socks that squeak and crackle. She knows now not to buy them. I taught her. 'It's not worth the screaming fits, even though wool is more expensive.' I wear a navy-blue suit to go to work in. At work I wear an overall. Seventy-four bus, that's what I got. 'Not the Forty-seven, Walter. Silly blockhead! Seventy-four, not the Forty-seven. Mill Hill, Chorlton, Flixstead. The number Six goes to Flixstead too. You don't want that.' I sit on my bed, rocking, taking time to dress. She watches. 'Number Two is a Special. Only bring it out at holiday times. Always clean, Number Two.' I laugh because she has to wait for me. No, Forty-Seven's not my bus, not for going home on. Seventy-four. 'There you are, you see. You're alright, Walter. Walter's alright. Only eleven pence to the shilling, but he knows what it's about.'

'Are you ready?'

I look at her and laugh, rocking backwards and forwards as I sit on the bed. She shakes her head, and looks at the linoleum on my bedroom floor. I stop laughing, and try to see what she is looking at. But there's nothing there, only the pattern. 'Li No Lee Um. Not lino, Walter, Linoleum.'

Breakfast was on the table. She would lay it out the night before, and come down before she woke him, to cook the rest. She couldn't sleep.

She sat beside him, not facing him. She had the view of the window to look at, and did not have to look at him. He swung his legs backwards and forwards as he ate. Whenever she heard them bang against the chair, she shouted at him to stop.

She wouldn't eat until after he had left the house.

She stared out of the window. She only looked at him to see whether he had finished.

She could feel him looking at her with those bulging eyes. The hooded lids blinked as he grinned and chortled to himself. How could she know what he was thinking?

If anyone looks at me, I point my finger at them, and start to laugh. I throw my head back, and laugh until they turn away. She taught me. At school, they would do that to me, and when I told her she said, 'Do it to them back, then,' but if I waited for them to do it first, I felt sad inside, and couldn't laugh. So I started to laugh at them before they had time to laugh at me. I put my hand over my mouth, and pointed, and laughed. It made them angry, and they called me names. Then they stopped laughing at me. They would pretend I was not there. Then I would laugh to myself. I started laughing a lot then. I keep myself ready in case somebody who doesn't know me should point at me and laugh. I'm laughing to myself now. It annoys her.

She woke me up.

David Cook: *Walter*

- How realistic is Walter about himself?
- How does he feel about his mother?
- How does he describe her and her actions?
- With whom do we sympathise in these passages?
- What emotions do they evoke?
- Are they in 'good taste'?

You will have noticed that when discussing the second passage we talked a lot about voice – which is where we began. It isn't really possible to divide up the aims or effects of literature into watertight compartments.

Chapter 15
Make 'em laugh — Humour

In the final part of this literature section we are going to end on a cheerful note by looking at some of the ways writers attempt to make us laugh.

Writing to make a reader laugh can of course be an end in itself, but frequently humour is harnessed to other purposes as well. It is rarely possible to say that a stretch of writing, still less a whole work, is written simply to make us laugh, or just to entertain, to teach, to illuminate the human condition, or any other of the clichés pressed into service to explain what a piece of literature is 'for'. We have already touched on the virtual impossibility of answering this question, so let's just accept that a lot of stories, poems or plays make us laugh, and look at how writers use words to amuse.

Sometimes the humour is closely involved with something we've just been looking at, the establishment of a 'voice'. The tone adopted by the writer is itself amusing, full of witty asides and comments, or it can be amusing by virtue of its inappropriateness, in which case we laugh at, rather than with, the narrator.

Sometimes the events and characters described are themselves fantastic or ridiculous, the literary equivalent of slapstick humour. By exaggerating characters and situations which are similar to those of 'real life' (if there is such a thing) humour can be used to comment on injustice, cruelty or evil. One of the most 'literary' forms of humorous writing is when one writer imitates, but exaggerates, the style of another, usually in relation to totally inappropriate subject matter. This is parody. Lastly, words themselves become the source of humour, as in puns, riddles, rhyme and word-play.

This is far from being an exhaustive list, but it includes some of the techniques used by the writers we are going to look at. The range of styles in humorous writing, and the uses it can be put to, are many and varied. Let's look at our first example.

HUMOROUS PROSE

This is an extract from a book called *Lake Wobegon Days* by an American, Garrison Keillor, who is usually described as a 'humorous writer'. The book is not a novel: it has no continuous narrative. Instead, Keillor creates a fictional small town in the middle of America and describes the characters who live there, its history and the main events of the year. He appears to be drawing on memories of his own childhood, and some of the humour comes from the fact that Lake Wobegon resembles real small towns in mid-America. This extract is fairly representative.

What's special about here isn't special enough to draw a major crowd, though Flag Day – you could drive a long way on June 14 to find another like it.

Flag Day, as we know it, was the idea of Herman Hochstetter, Rollie's dad, who ran the dry goods store and ran Armistice Day, the Fourth of July, and Flag Day. For the Fourth, he organized a double-loop parade around the block which allowed people to take turns marching and watching. On Armistice Day, everyone stepped outside at 11 A.M. and stood in silence for two minutes as Our Lady's bell tolled eleven times.

Flag Day was his favorite. For a modest price, he would install a bracket on your house to hold a pole to hang your flag on, or he would drill a hole in the sidewalk in front of your store with his drill gun powered by a .22 shell. Bam! And in went the flag. On patriotic days, flags flew all over; there were flags on the tall poles, flags on the short, flags in the brackets on the pillars and the porches, and if you were flagless you could expect to hear from Herman. His hairy arm around your shoulder, his poochlike face close to yours, he would say how proud he was that so many people were proud of their country, leaving you to see the obvious, that you were a gap in the ranks.

In June 1944, the day after D-Day, a salesman from Fisher Hat called on Herman and offered a good deal on red and blue baseball caps. 'Do you have white also?' Herman asked. The salesman thought that white caps could be had for the same wonderful price. Herman ordered two hundred red, two hundred white, and one hundred blue. By the end of the year, he still had four hundred and eighty-six caps. The inspiration of the Living Flag was born from that overstock.

On June 14, 1945, a month after V-E Day, a good crowd assembled in front of the Central Building in response to Herman's ad in the paper:

> Honor 'AMERICA' June 14 AT 4 p.m. Be
> proud of 'Our Land & People'. Be part of
> the 'LIVING FLAG'. Don't let it be said
> that Lake Wobegon was 'Too Busy'. Be on
> time. 4 p.m. 'Sharp'.

His wife Louise handed out the caps, and Herman stood on a stepladder and told people where to stand. He lined up the reds and whites into stripes, then got the blues into their square. Mr. Hanson climbed up on the roof of the Central Building and took a photograph, they sang the national anthem, and then the Living Flag dispersed. The photograph appeared in the paper the next week. Herman kept the caps.

In the flush of victory, people were happy to do as told and stand in place, but in 1946 and 1947, dissension cropped up in the ranks: people complained about the heat and about Herman – what gave *him* the idea he could order *them* around? 'People! Please! I need your attention! You blue people, keep your hats on! Please! Stripe No. 4, you're sagging! You reds, you're up here! We got too many white people, we need more red ones! Let's do this without talking, people! I can't get you straight if you keep moving around! Some of you are not paying attention! Everybody shut up! Please!'

One cause of resentment was the fact that none of them got to see the Flag they were in; the picture in the paper was black and white. Only Herman and Mr. Hanson got to see the real Flag, and some boys too short to be needed down below. People wanted a chance to go up to the roof and witness the spectacle for themselves.

'How can you go up there if you're supposed to be down here?' Herman said. 'You go up there to look, you got nothing to look at. Isn't it enough to know that you're doing your part?'

On Flag Day, 1949, just as Herman said, 'That's it! Hold it now!' one of the reds made a break for it – dashed up four flights of stairs to the roof and leaned over and had a long look. Even with the hole he left behind, it was a magnificent sight. The Living Flag filled the street below. A perfect Flag! The reds so brilliant! He couldn't take his eyes off it. 'Get down here! We need a picture!' Herman yelled up to him. 'How does it look?' people yelled up to him. 'Unbelievable! I can't describe it!' he said.

So then everyone had to have a look. 'No!' Herman said, but they took a vote and it was unanimous. One by one, members of the Living Flag went up to the roof and admired it. It *was* marvelous! It brought tears to the eyes, it made one reflect on this great country and on Lake Wobegon's place in it. One wanted to stand up there all afternoon and just drink it in. So, as our first hour passed, and only forty of the five hundred had been to the top, the others got more and more restless. 'Hurry up! Quit dawdling! *You've* seen it! Get down here and give someone else a chance!' Herman sent people up in groups of four, and then ten, but after two hours, the Living Flag became the Sitting Flag and then began to erode, as the members who had had a look thought about heading home to supper, which infuriated the ones who hadn't. 'Ten more minutes!' Herman cried, but ten minutes became twenty and thirty, and people snuck off and the Flag that remained for the last viewer was a Flag shot through by cannon fire.

In 1950, the Sons of Knute took over Flag Day. Herman gave them the boxes of caps. Since then, the Knutes have achieved several good Flags, though most years the attendance was poor. You need at least four hundred to make a good one. Some years the Knutes made a 'no-look' rule, other years they held a lottery. One year they experimented with a large mirror held by two men over the edge of the roof, but when people leaned back and looked up, the Flag disappeared, of course.

Garrison Keillor: *Lake Wobegon Days*

The comic effect of this passage relies on the interplay between the ridiculous, yet just plausible nature of the situation which is described, and the 'deadpan' tone in which the events are recounted. The narrator doesn't explicitly point to, or comment on, the humour of what is happening until the 'of course' in the final sentence.

It is important for the plausibility that the reader accepts the 'reality' of this place and these people, the authenticity of these events. How is this achieved?

Although the author does not represent himself as an actual participant in the 'living flag', which enables him to keep his detached, distant perspective on the scene, he does establish himself as a member of the community through such expressions as 'as we know it' (the inclusive first person plural), 'What's special about here' (not 'there'), and the description of Herman as 'Rollie's Dad', which carries no explanation of who Rollie might be. 'If you were flagless, you could expect to hear from Herman' he says conversationally, as if he'd seen it happen. He's clearly in the know: 'You need at least four hundred to make a good one.'

By such means the reader accepts the reality of the event and is drawn into it. Events become progressively more ridiculous and the final punch-line is built up to in a gradual and believable fashion. Did you see it coming? Something else which contributes to the impression that the writer is not describing this because it's funny, but because it's 'real' is the unadorned and factual nature of the prose. The narrative itself, as opposed to the direct speech, consists mainly of statements. There are relatively few adjectives, though Herman's 'hairy arm' and 'poochlike face' are obvious exceptions. The paragraph which begins 'His wife Louise handed out the caps' contains eleven statements, all with the same, simple subject-verb structure. The sentences are often linked by the co-ordinating conjunction 'and'. The final short sentence of the paragraph, 'Herman kept the caps', is just the sort of straightforward detail that confirms the authenticity. The effect of this apparent 'artlessness' is to make the reader feel she is not being led or manipulated by a lot of literary trickery, but is being told real events by a real voice. This final sentence is funny because by this time we feel we know Herman and we know what he would do. His patriotic fervour and his entrepreneurial talents have formed a happy combination. Herman's character is important to the humour. He is a serious organiser, a bit of a 'wheeler-dealer' who, despite his earnest attempts, is defeated by human nature.

Herman's defeat is best shown in the verbs used in the passage. In the early part, Herman is the subject of most of the verbs: he 'ran', 'organised', 'would drill', 'would say', 'asked', 'ordered' and so on. He is still there at the end: he 'cried', he 'gave them the box of caps' (as opposed to selling them!); but in the latter part of the piece, the Flag (note the capital) is taking over. As you would expect, either the Flag collectively or its constituent parts become the subject of many of the verbs: 'The Living Flag filled the street'; 'The Living Flag became the Sitting Flag'; 'everyone had to have a look'. The Flag has won. Herman is no longer in charge.

There are other humorous touches in the piece, such as the way the participants are referred to by their function in the flag: 'Stripe No. 4, you're sagging', 'one of the reds made a break for it'. Capitalisation of the Living Flag gives it an importance which is comic, as do the recurring military references: 'dissension cropped up in the ranks', 'a Flag shot through by cannon fire'. The event is apparently treated very seriously by the people involved, by the narrator at first and above all by Herman; but by the end it has become ridiculous.

The next extract is from Charles Dickens's novel *Bleak House*, and in it he describes tea-time with the Smallweed family. This follows a passage in which he has introduced old Grandfather and Grandmother Smallweed, a particularly dry and joyless couple, like most other members of the family. Dickens conveys the most representative family trait, lack of imagination, in an extended metaphor:

> Everything that Mr. Smallweed's grandfather ever put away in his mind was a grub at first, and is a grub at last. In all his life he has never bred a single butterfly.

All the Smallweeds are 'lean and anxious-minded', and never seem to have displayed or enjoyed the fun, irresponsibilities and imaginative pleasures of childhood. They all appear to have been born 'complete little men and women' until 'Mr. Smallweed's grandmother, now living, became weak in her intellect and fell (for the first time) into a childish state.' Having thus had the family characterised fairly explicitly for us, we join the Smallweed grandparents waiting for their tea:

> At the present time, in the dark little parlour certain feet below the level of the street – a grim, hard, uncouth parlour, only ornamented with the coarsest of baize table-covers, and the hardest of sheet-iron tea-trays, and offering in its decorative character no bad allegorical representation of Grandfather Smallweed's mind – seated in two black horse-hair porter's chairs, one on each side of the fire-place, the superannuated Mr. and Mrs. Smallweed while away the rosy hours. On the stove are a couple of trivets for the pots and kettles which it is Grandfather Smallweed's usual occupation to watch, and projecting from the chimney-piece between them is a sort of brass gallows for roasting, which he also superintends when it is in action. Under the venerable Mr Smallweed's seat and guarded by his spindle legs is a drawer in his chair, reported to contain property to a fabulous amount. Beside him is a spare cushion with which he is always provided in order that he may have something to throw at the venerable partner of his respected age whenever she makes an allusion to money – a subject on which he is particularly sensitive.
>
> 'And where's Bart?' Grandfather Smallweed inquires of Judy, Bart's Twin sister.
>
> 'He an't come in yet,' says Judy.
>
> 'It's his tea-time, isn't it?'
>
> 'No.'
>
> 'How much do you mean to say it wants then?'
>
> 'Ten minutes.'
>
> 'Hey?'
>
> 'Ten minutes.' (Loud on the part of Judy.)
>
> 'Ho!' says Grandfather Smallweed. 'Ten minutes.'
>
> Grandmother Smallweed, who has been mumbling and shaking her head at the trivets, hearing figures mentioned, connects them with money

and screeches like a horrible old parrot without any plumage, 'Ten ten-pound notes!'

Grandfather Smallweed immediately throws the cushion at her.

'Drat you, be quiet!' says the good old man.

The effect of this act of jaculation is twofold. It not only doubles up Mrs. Smallweed's head against the side of her porter's chair and causes her to present, when extricated by her granddaughter, a highly unbecoming state of cap, but the necessary exertion recoils on Mr. Smallweed himself, whom it throws back into his porter's chair like a broken puppet. The excellent old gentleman being at these times a mere clothes-bag with a black skull-cap on the top of it, does not present a very animated appearance until he has undergone the two operations at the hands of his granddaughter of being shaken up like a great bottle and poked and punched like a great bolster. Some indication of a neck being developed in him by these means, he and the sharer of his life's evening again fronting one another in their two porter's chairs, like a couple of sentinels long forgotten on their post by the Black Serjeant, Death.

Judy the twin is worthy company for these associates. She is so undubitably sister to Mr. Smallweed the younger that the two kneaded into one would hardly make a young person of average proportions, while she so happily exemplifies the before-mentioned family likeness to the monkey tribe that attired in a spangled robe and cap she might walk about the table-land on the top of a barrel-organ without exciting much remark as an unusual specimen. Under existing circumstances, however, she is dressed in a plain, spare gown of brown stuff.

Judy never owned a doll, never heard of Cinderella, never played at any game. She once or twice fell into children's company when she was about ten years old, but the children couldn't get on with Judy, and Judy couldn't get on with them. She seemed like an animal of another species, and there was instinctive repugnance on both sides. It is very doubtful whether Judy knows how to laugh. She has so rarely seen the thing done that the probabilities are strong the other way. Of anything like a youthful laugh, she certainly can have no conception. If she were to try one, she would find her teeth in her way, modelling that action of her face, as she has unconsciously modelled all its other expressions, on her pattern of sordid age. Such is Judy.

Charles Dickens: *Bleak House*

This could hardly present a greater contrast to the *Lake Wobegon Days* piece. In that, we noticed a lack of adjectives and little figurative language. Here, there is a lot of pre-modification, mainly in the form of adjectives, and post-modification in the form of similes. The reader's responses are quite clearly being directed by Dickens. It would be an obtuse reader who identified or sympathised with the Smallweeds. The humour depends on our being aware of the writer's perspective and laughing at these characters with him.

Yet on the face of it, Dickens uses some complimentary phrases to describe the family.

ACTIVITY ○ ▣

List all the words and phrases with positive associations used to describe the three Smallweeds. There are a fair number, aren't there? – Words such as 'venerable', 'good old'. If we include other expressions associated with them such as 'while away the rosy hours', this list would imply that this is a sentimental description of lovable Darby and Joan in contented retirement. But of course it isn't.

Now list all the words and phrases with negative connotations used to describe the Smallweeds. There are just as many of those words, such as 'spindle', 'horrible old parrot'. You might notice that the word 'old' had positive connotations when collocated with 'good', but negative ones when linked to 'horrible' and 'parrot', an example of how words are coloured by those surrounding them.

Yet there really aren't any problems for the reader in this mix of positive and negative descriptions of the same characters. Nor do we feel ambivalent towards the Smallweeds. This is because we recognise that the 'positive' description is not to be taken at face value. In other words we recognise irony, the gap between what the writer is apparently saying and what we know he means. Irony is a frequent feature of humorous writing. In this passage it is easy to spot because Dickens has already made his opinions of the characters he has created quite clear.

Now let's consider the way Dickens presents the events, which are themselves the source of much of the humour, concentrating on the paragraph which begins 'The effect of this jaculation…'.

ACTIVITY ○ 💬

Look first at that word 'jaculation', which actually means 'the action of darting, hurling or throwing'. Its main interest lies in the fact that it is rather obscure. If you look it up in the *Shorter Oxford English Dictionary*, it actually says that it is 'rare'. It is a word of Latin derivation, not in common use.

Can you find other examples in this paragraph, of Dickens choosing to use rather elevated words and phrases instead of more common or direct expressions? Words of Latin derivation are often associated with higher levels of formality, so you could note any of those too.

ACTIVITY ⊞ 💬

There are several examples both of elevated formal lexis, and of using a group of words where one might have done (technically this is called periphrasis), such as 'does not present a very animated appearance' instead of 'lifeless', or 'necessary exertion' instead of 'effort'.

What is the effect of this, and does it add anything to the humour of the passage? The contrast between the sordid, undignified events and the formal elaborate way that they are described certainly needs commenting on. The mismatch of tone and subject matter is seen throughout the passage, but is most noticeable in this paragraph.

ACTIVITY ◾ 💬

Easier to comment on, possibly, is the contribution made to the comedy of the piece by the use of figurative language.

Pick out four examples of this, two similes and two instances of metaphorical usage.

If one of the examples you have chosen is 'shaken up like a bottle and poked and punched like a great bolster', perhaps we should stop and consider why anyone might find it funny to imagine an old person being treated in this way. But this isn't the place for a lengthy disquisition on taste. If it is funny, the humour is in the ingenuity of the comparison, in creating incongruous, exaggerated pictures in words. After all, Grandfather Smallweed isn't real, although in depicting the life-denying constrictions of the Smallweed personality Dickens is clearly making serious comment. The humour of this piece is a mixture of the slapstick and the grotesque, but harnessed to a serious moral purpose. The 'pattern of sordid age' which has moulded Judy is not really anything to laugh at. No irony here, but maybe we take the point more seriously because of the previous laughter.

The next passage, which we'd like you to do the work on, is the opening of a short story by the contemporary writer Fay Weldon. Like Dickens, Weldon is using humour to make a serious point, and as with *Bleak House*, we are in little doubt about the author's perspective on her characters. However, she uses rather different methods. Here is the opening of Fay Weldon's story *Weekend*:

> By seven-thirty they were ready to go. Martha had everything packed into the car and the three children appropriately dressed and in the back seat, complete with educational games and wholewheat biscuits. When everything was ready in the car Martin would switch off the television, come downstairs, lock up the house, front and back, and take the wheel.
>
> Weekend! Only two hours' drive down to the cottage on Friday evenings: three hours' drive back on Sunday nights. The pleasures of greenery and guests in between. They reckoned themselves fortunate, how fortunate!
>
> On Fridays Martha would get home on the bus at six-twelve and prepare tea and sandwiches for the family: then she would strip four beds and put the sheets and quilt covers in the washing machine for Monday: take the country bedding from the airing basket, plus the books and the games, plus the weekend food – acquired at intervals throughout the week,

to lessen the load – plus her own folder of work from the office, plus Martin's drawing materials (she was a market researcher in an advertising agency, he a freelance designer) plus hairbrushes, jeans, spare T-shirts, Jolyon's antibiotics (he suffered from sore throats), Jenny's recorder, Jasper's cassette player and so on – ah, the so on! – and would pack them all, skilfully and quickly, into the boot. Very little could be left in the cottage during the week. ('An open invitation to burglars': Martin.) Then Martha would run round the house tidying and wiping, doing this and that, finding the cat at one neighbour's and delivering it to another, while the others ate their tea; and would usually, proudly, have everything finished by the time they had eaten their fill. Martin would just catch the BBC2 news, while Martha cleared away the tea table, and the children tossed up for the best positions in the car. 'Martha,' said Martin, tonight 'you ought to get Mrs Hodder to do more. She takes advantage of you.'

Mrs Hodder came in twice a week to clean. She was over seventy. She charged two pounds an hour. Martha paid her out of her own wages: well, the running of the house was Martha's concern. If Martha chose to go out to work – as was her perfect right, Martin allowed, even though it wasn't the best thing for the children, but that must be Martha's moral responsibility – Martha must surely pay her domestic stand-in. An evident truth, heard loud and clear and frequent in Martin's mouth and Martha's heart.

'I expect you're right,' said Martha. She did not want to argue. Martin had had a long hard week, and now had to drive. Martha couldn't. Martha's licence had been suspended four months back for drunken driving. Everyone agreed that the suspension was unfair: Martha seldom drank to excess: she was for one thing usually too busy pouring drinks for other people or washing other people's glasses to get much inside herself. But Martin had taken her out to dinner on her birthday, as was his custom, and exhaustion and excitement mixed had made her imprudent, and before she knew where she was, why there she was, in the dock, with a distorted lamp-post to pay for and a new bonnet for the car and six months' suspension.

So now Martin had to drive her car down to the cottage, and he was always tired on Fridays, and hot and sleepy on Sundays, and every rattle and clank and bump in the engine she felt to be somehow her fault.

Martin had a little sports car for London and work: it could nip in and out of the traffic nicely: Martha's was an old estate car, with room for the children, picnic baskets, bedding, food, games, plants, drink, portable television and all the things required by the middle classes for weekends in the country. It lumbered rather than zipped and made Martin angry. He seldom spoke a harsh word, but Martha, after the fashion of wives, could detect his mood from what he did not say rather than what he did, and from the tilt of his head, and the way his crinkly, merry eyes seemed crinklier and merrier still and of course from the way he addressed Martha's car.

'Come along, you old banger you! Can't you do better than that? You're too old, that's your trouble. Stop complaining. Always complaining, it's only a hill. You're too wide about the hips. You'll never get through there.'

Fay Weldon: *Weekend*

ACTIVITY

Look first at the opening three paragraphs. They end with Martin saying 'She takes advantage of you.' What was your reaction when you read that? If it was the same as ours, a hollow laugh and a 'she's not the only one', then Fay Weldon has made her point without any explicit statement. How? To answer this we suggest you look for a few specific things:

- Verbs: who are the subjects of them? Count them, and compare.
- What sort of verbs are they?
- Lists
- Repetition of structures
- Punctuation
- Frequency and placing of names (as opposed to pronouns)

Of course, seeing how point of view is created need have nothing to do with humour, but in this case it does. The predictable nature of this family's behaviour is important to the comedy. We 'see it coming' and the unrelenting pattern which is set up, like knowing which clown at the circus is going to get the bucket of water in his face, is part of what makes us smile. It's a form of exaggeration, but the exaggerated picture is in the selection and accumulation of detail, rather than the details themselves.

The relationship between Martha and Martin is not the only comic subject here. There is also social satire on the customs and lives of a particular class. How and where is this best conveyed? As the passage continues, a different sort of vocabulary enters for the first time. What sort of words are 'right', 'responsibility' and 'truth'? Does the introduction of this judgemental attitude affect our reaction to the situation?

Interestingly, the one person who does not have critical terms applied to him is Martin. Even when he gets angry he is described in positive terms: 'merrier still'. How do we receive his final remarks to the car?

Our final prose passage, for you to analyse, is another satire on (almost) contemporary life. It is from a novel by Tom Sharpe called *Wilt*. In it, the 'hero' Wilt, a teacher in a further education college, is 'teaching' a class of apprentice butchers with little enthusiasm. Describe how language is used to produce comic effects in this extract.

At five to two, none the wiser, he went down to Room 752 to extend the sensibilities of fifteen apprentice butchers, designated on the timetable as Meat One. As usual they were late and drunk.

'We've been drinking Bill's health,' they told him when they drifted in at ten past two.

'Really?' said Wilt, handing out copies of *The Lord of the Flies*. 'And how is he?'

'Bloody awful,' said a large youth with 'Stuff Off' painted across the back of his leather jacket. 'He's puking his guts out. It's his birthday and he had four Vodkas and a Babycham…'

'We'd got to the part where Piggy is in the forest,' said Wilt, heading them off a discussion of what Bill had drunk for his birthday. He reached for a board duster and rubbed a drawing of a Dutch Cap off the blackboard.

'That's Mr Sedgwick's trademark,' said one of the butchers. 'He's always going on about contraceptives and things. He's got a thing about them.'

'A thing about them?' said Wilt loyally.

'You know, birth control. Well, he used to be a Catholic, didn't he? And now he's not, he's making up for lost time,' said a small pale-faced youth unwrapping a Mars Bar.

'Someone should tell him about the pill,' said another youth lifting his head somnolently from the desk. 'You can't feel a thing with a Frenchie. You get more thrill with the pill.'

'I suppose you do,' said Wilt, 'but I understood there were side-effects.'

'Depends which side you want it,' said a lad with sideburns.

Wilt turned back to *The Lord of the Flies* reluctantly. He had read the thing two hundred times already.

'Now Piggy goes into the forest…' he began, only to be stopped by another butcher, who evidently shared his distaste for the misfortunes of Piggy.

'You only get bad effects with the pill if you use ones that are high in oestrogen.'

'That's very interesting,' said Wilt. 'Oestrogen? You seem to know a lot about it.'

'Old girl down our street got a bloodclot in her leg…'

'Silly old clot,' said the Mars Bar.

'Listen,' said Wilt. 'Either we hear what Peter has to tell us about the effects of the pill or we get on and read about Piggy.'

'Fuck Piggy,' said the sideburns.

'Right,' said Wilt heartily, 'then keep quiet.'

'Well,' said Peter, 'this old girl, well she wasn't all that old, maybe thirty, she was on the pill and she got this bloodclot and the doctor told my auntie it was the oestrogen and she'd better take a different sort of pill just in case and the old girl down the street, her old man had to go and have a vasectomy so's she wouldn't have another bloodclot.'

'Buggered if anyone's going to get me to have a vasectomy,' said the Mars Bar, 'I want to know I'm all there.'

'We all have ambitions,' said Wilt.

'Nobody's going to hack away at my knackers with a bloody great knife,' said the sideburns.

'Nobody'd want to,' said someone else.

'What about the bloke whose missus you banged,' said the Mars Bar. 'I bet he wouldn't mind having a go.'

Wilt applied the sanction of Piggy again and got them back on to vasectomy.

'Anyway, it's not irreversible any more,' said Peter. 'They can put a tiny little gold tap in and you can turn it on when you want a nipper.'

'Go on! That's not true.'

'Well, not on the National Heath you can't, but if you pay they can. I read about it in a magazine. They've been doing experiments in America.'

'What happens if the washer goes wrong?' asked the Mars Bar.

'I suppose they call a plumber in.'

Tom Sharpe: *Wilt*

Much of the humour of Wilt's rather desultory conversation with Meat One is the humour of speech. It does somewhat dignify the exchange:

'Old girl down our street got a bloodclot in her leg...'
'Silly old clot,' said the Mars Bar.

to call it wordplay, but it is wordplay of a crude and obvious kind. This passage is full of attempted jokes and asides at other people's expense, of bawdy and insulting comment, and of the sort of random connections between one subject and another which crop up in everyday talk.

HUMOROUS VERSE

These and other qualities of spoken language are often exploited in humorous verse, which delights in puns, rhymes, alliteration and the melody and stress patterns of speech. Some instances of such verse just have to be recited out loud for full effect. They are written to be performed, often in a particular accent and/or dialect, in which pronunciation adds to the humour. Examples of these would be 'Albert and the Lion' (Lancashire), 'Ilkla Moor Baht 'at' (Yorkshire) or many of the poems of John Betjeman (Southern RP).

There is a distinct satisfaction in verse with a regular rhyme and rhythm which lends itself to humour. Think of limericks you know, where the amusement is in spotting the final rhyme; or the familiar patterns of traditional pantomime, in which either the predictability or the ingenuity of the rhymes contributes a lot to the fun.

Here is a poem by the Jamaican poet Valerie Bloom. The basic joke is the puzzlement a newcomer to England experiences when she hears the variety of words which English people use for meals. As language students you will probably have discussed this question yourselves. Why is the same meal 'tea' for some people, but 'dinner' for others? To the native speaker, this can be a clear marker of class or region; to the stranger, it's just confusion.

WHA FE CALL I'

Miss Ivy, tell mi supmn,
An mi wan' yuh ansa good.
When yuh eat roun 12 o'clock,
Wassit yuh call yuh food?

For fram mi come yah mi confuse,
An mi noh know which is right,
Weddah dinnah a de food yuh eat midday,
Or de one yuh eat a night.

Mi know sey breakfus a de mawnin one
But cyan tell ef suppa a six or t'ree,
An one ting mi wi nebba undastan,
Is when yuh hab yuh tea.

Miss A dung a London ha lunch 12 o'clock,
An dinnah she hab bout t'ree,
Suppa she hab bout six o'clock,
But she noh hab noh tea.

Den mi go a Cambridge todda day,
Wi hab dinnah roun' bout two,
T'ree hour later mi frien she sey,
Mi hungry, how bout yuh?

Joe sey im tink a suppa time,
An mi sey yes, mi agree,
She halla, Suppa? a five o'clock,
Missis yuh mussa mean tea!

Den Sunday mi employer get up late,
Soh she noh hab breakfus nor lunch,
But mi hear she a talk about 'Elevenses',
An one sinting dem call 'Brunch'.

Breakfus, elevenses, an brunch,
lunch, dinnah, suppa, tea,
Mi brain cyan wuk out which is which,
An when a de time fe hab i'.

For jus' when mi mek headway,
Sinting dreadful set mi back,
An dis when mi tink mi know dem all,
Mi hear bout one name snack.

Mi noh tink mi a badda wid no name,
Mi dis a nyam when time mi hungry,
For doah mi 'tomach wi glad fe de food,
I' couldn care less whey mi call i'.

Valerie Bloom

In this poem the rhythm is not absolutely regular. Lines vary between three and five stresses, although the majority are three; but what is consistent is that the final line of each verse always has three stresses, and rhymes more or less exactly with the second line, rounding off each verse neatly and making the poem a series of minor jokes within the framework of the one which runs throughout.

By the end of the second verse we know what this basic joke is, and what we are waiting for, especially in performance, is to see what the next permutation is going to be. The structure tells us when the punchline is coming, and we know there's a limit to the number of terms the poet has to play with, so we try to anticipate what she will come up with this time. Because she is more ingenious than us, and because, although it works best in performance, this is written and cleverly crafted, Valerie Bloom delivers better lines than the ones we had anticipated.

The dialect contributes to the humour in other ways. It helps establish the character's perspective. It is often funny to look at something very familiar through a stranger's eyes. The poet Craig Raine does the same thing in his 'Martian' poems, in which ordinary objects and events are described by a visitor from outer space. In this case, the difficulty experienced by a visitor from another country in understanding our language customs has the effect of making us wonder why they are so curious and inconsistent. There is an explicit reference to the speaker's visitor status: 'For fram mi come yah...', but it is reinforced throughout mainly by the dialect.

Something of the speaker's character is conveyed through the 'voice'. There is a genuine sense of puzzlement throughout verse three, for instance: 'An one ting mi wi nebba undastan'; and finally we recognise that this is an outsider with a lot of common sense:

> For doah mi 'tomach wi glad fe de food,
> I' couldn care less whey mi call i'.

We can do little but agree that we are a rather odd lot to have constructed so many social hurdles around the simple subject of food. The joke is on us.

But it is a fairly gentle joke. Humour can be used in verse, as in prose, for more serious purposes. Alexander Pope, in the eighteenth century, wrote a long poem called *The Rape of the Lock*, in which he ridicules the 'high society' of his day by mocking the importance attached to fashion and social etiquette to the neglect of virtue and true morality. Much of the humour of this poem comes from his descriptions of minor social events such as card games, in the style traditionally associated in classical poetry with epic events like battles. In this short extract the sylphs, whose job it is to preserve the appearance of fashionable young women as they go about their social round, explain the difficulties of their task:

> 'Our humbler province is to tend the fair,
> Not a less pleasing, though less glorious care;
> To save the powder from too rude a gale,
> Nor let the imprison'd essences exhale;

To draw fresh colours from the vernal flowers;
To steal from rainbows, ere they drop in showers,
A brighter wash; to curl their waving hairs,
Assist their blushes and inspire their airs;
Nay, oft, in dreams, invention we bestow,
To change a flounce, or add a furbelow.

'This day, black omens threat the brightest fair
That e'er deserved a watchful spirit's care;
Some dire disaster, or by force, or flight;
But what, or where, the Fates have wrapp'd in night.
Whether the nymph shall break Diana's law,
Or some frail china-jar receive a flaw;
Or stain her honour or her new brocade;
Forget her prayers, or miss a masquerade;
Or lose her heart, or necklace, at a ball;
Or whether Heaven has doom'd that Shock must fall.

Alexander Pope

Here the rhyme scheme, and the rhythm, are absolutely regular. The lexis is elevated: 'humbler province', 'imprison'd essences exhale', 'invention we bestow'; but the task is mundane: 'save the powder', 'curl their waving hairs' or 'change a flounce'. The contrast between the language and the events is the source of the fun. At first it seems harmless: vanity might be a sin, but as manifested in these pretty young women, it hardly seems a deadly one.

The sting, however, is in the second part. The spirits are troubled by a sense of foreboding; something dreadful is about to happen. As they speculate on what this might be, they consider, in lines fifteen to nineteen of the extract, the worst things that could happen to a young woman.

The rhythm and rhyme scheme here balance the alternatives: she may lose her virginity ('break Diana's law') or crack a favourite ornament. The two things are equated in the verse, just as they are in the mind of the young women. This disturbs us: it's funny, but it's shocking. Pope goes on to list other 'calamities' whose juxtaposition has the same effect as the first. Is a vanity which equates the loss of a necklace with the loss of a heart really so harmless? Pope's humour is harnessed to serious purpose here, as in the poem as a whole.

The next poem for you to look at, by the contemporary poet Adrian Mitchell, does not use its humour for any purpose other than to call attention to itself in the exuberance of its language.

WATCH YOUR STEP – I'M DRENCHED

In Manchester there are a thousand puddles.
Bus-queue puddles poised on slanting paving stones,
Railway puddles slouching outside stations,
Cinema puddles in ambush at the exits,

Zebra-crossing puddles in dips of the dark stripes –
They lurk in the murk
Of the north-western evening
For the sake of their notorious joke,
Their only joke – to soak
The tights or trousers of the citizens.
Each splash and consequent curse is echoed by
One thousand dark Mancunian puddle chuckles.

In Manchester there lives the King of Puddles,
Master of Miniature Muck Lakes,
The Shah of Slosh, Splendifero of Splash,
Prince, Pasha and Pope of Puddledom.
Where? Somewhere. The rain-headed ruler
Lies doggo, incognito,
Disguised as an average, accidental mini-pool.
He is as scared as any other emperor,
For one night, all his soiled and soggy victims
Might storm his streets, assassination in their minds,
A thousand rolls of blotting paper in their hands,
And drink his shadowed, one-joke life away.

Adrian Mitchell

What is the 'one joke' on which this poem is based? If any of you come from Manchester you may consider this just another addition to the tired old jokes which stereotype your city as somewhere it's always raining, but there's a lot of variety in their wetness, isn't there?

ACTIVITY

- List the different ways the puddles are characterised.

- How has Adrian Mitchell employed the language to imply that they have a sense of purpose? Look at the titles he gives to the King of Puddles. What language devices are being used here? Can you invent some more titles of your own in the same vein?

- Where else in the poem does playing with the sounds of words add to the humour?

- How are the tables turned in the last five lines? Is there anything about these lines which makes you wonder for a moment whether Mitchell might have a serious purpose after all?

- There is no regular rhythm or rhyme scheme, but both rhyme and rhythm are exploited for comic effect. Where and how?

PARODY

Finally, we are going to ask you to look at an example of one of the most literary forms of humour – parody.

To write a parody, you must have a model. In your parody, you imitate the style of the model, but introduce inappropriate subject matter, or words from a different register. In a sense, Alexander Pope was writing a parody of the epic style in the example we looked at from *The Rape of the Lock*. He used the grand style for inappropriate subject matter, and we laugh at both the style and the society whose pretensions he was ridiculing.

Sometimes the purpose of parody is to ridicule, but just as often it's primarily to amuse. To show what we mean, here is an example of parody at its simplest, in an example you may well be familiar with:

> Hark! the jelly babies sing,
> Beecham's pills are just the thing,
> They are gentle, meek and mild,
> Two for a man and one for a child.
> If you want to go to heaven
> You must take a does of seven,
> If you want to go to hell
> Take the blinking box as well.

Obviously, this is a children's parody of the carol 'Hark! the Herald Angels Sing', in which the usual words have been replaced by mildly irreverent ones. Literary parodies, in which one writer mimics the style of another, are usually a bit more sophisticated, but the principle is the same. We leave you to make a detailed comparison of the following two poems.

HAWK ROOSTING

> I sit in the top of the wood, my eyes closed.
> Inaction, no falsifying dream
> Between my hooked head and hooked feet:
> Or in sleep rehearse perfect kills and eat.
>
> The convenience of the high trees!
> The air's buoyancy and the sun's ray
> Are of advantage to me;
> And the earth's face upward for my inspection.
>
> My feet are locked upon the rough bark.
> It took the whole of Creation
> To produce my foot, my each feather:
> Now I hold Creation in my foot

Or fly up, and revolve it all slowly –
I kill where I please because it is all mine.
There is no sophistry in my body:
My manners are tearing off heads –

The allotment of death.
For the one path of my flight is direct
Through the bones of the living.
No arguments assert my right:

The sun is behind me.
Nothing has changed since I began.
My eye has permitted no change.
I am going to keep things like this.

Ted Hughes

CROW RESTING

I sit at the top of the tree,
My mouth closed. I have been sitting here
Since the beginning of Time.
I am going to carry on sitting here
And if anybody tries to stop me sitting here
I will remove his head;
A single-mind-sized bite will do it.
I will eat his head and with a stab, a jerk
A bounce I'll have his bowels, balls,
Big toes, his colon and his semi-colon.
I will drink his blood from the goblet
Of his skull, his thin giblets
From the platter of his pelvic bone. And
I will spread his shit with generosity.
In other words forget it.
I was here first, I was here long ago.
I was here before you. And I will be here
Long after you have gone. What superbard says
Goes. I am going to keep things like this.

Edward Pygge

Section Three

YOUR OWN WORDS

This section provides advice on your own language work, both investigative and creative.

Chapter 16
Language Projects — Coursework

WHAT CAN I LOOK AT? – THE COLLECTION AND RECORDING OF DATA

So far in this book you have been looking at varieties of English which have been provided for you. The third section of *Your Own Words* aims to help you choose your own examples of language, spoken or written, to investigate yourself – a personal investigation.

As your curiosity and knowledge about language have been increasing alongside your skill in describing it, you will have become more sensitive to interesting features in language use you come into contact with every day, such as intriguing differences between one speaker and another, or the way a single speaker's language varies from one situation to another. You may have noticed significant distinctive features in the style of a newspaper or magazine you read, or a type of novel you enjoy. You might wonder why particular occupation or interest groups develop their own vocabulary and style, or notice the way particular 'slang' expressions come into and out of English and mark off one group from another. You might be fortunate enough to be in regular contact with a young child who is just learning to speak, or to read or to write, and be able to investigate their progress. In fact, the possibilities are endless, and any of these topics and many, many more could provide you with material for project work.

A language project is a personal investigation into a variety of English, spoken or written. It might be quite a small-scale one to begin with – just noting and recording the forms of address used by or to you in one day, for example, and suggesting what these might reveal about your social relationships. It could be a contribution to a larger group investigation into swearing, or telephone manners. If you choose to write a project as part of your course you will then have to undertake a thorough, well-defined investigation which is presented clearly in a formal fashion.

However large or small your project the same systematic and objective approach is necessary. Your project should not be a collection of random observations, it needs to be well planned and researched. Investigating language for project purposes enables you to apply your knowledge and understanding of it in greater depth to a relatively small area. You will be discovering things for yourself. In the process you will become quite an expert on your particular topic and sharpen the skills which develop your confidence in discussing language generally.

Although there is an enormous range of subjects which are suitable for investigation, all good language projects have a few basic features in common:

> They all have as their basis/starting point good and 'honest' raw material – data.

> They all have a focus for the investigation – a question, a theory or a hypothesis to 'test' in relation to the data.

> The findings are clearly presented in readable fashion.

This chapter explores project work in relation to these features. It answers the questions

What can I look at? – which gives some ideas for project work and suggestions about how to obtain useful data, spoken and written.

What should I look for? – which examines ways in which you can focus your investigation, and how to test your hypothesis.

How should I present my findings? – which gives advice on how to write a project in its final form, in itself quite a challenging exercise.

As a summary, this section gives hints on what makes a good and a bad project, and considers some examples.

There is one other feature which all good investigations must have in common and, although it is not treated separately, it underlies all the hints and advice in this chapter. It is most important of all that any findings which emerge as a result of your hard look at the evidence arise from the data itself and are not imposed by you. In other words, although you should have a hunch about what your investigation might come up with, you must see what is there, and not only what you expect to see. Your intuition might be the starting point, but, like a good detective, you must assume nothing, and take nothing on trust. You may miss the vital clue if you start with too many preconceived notions. You must be prepared to discover that the language of the *Daily Star* newspaper is more complex and sophisticated than the language of the *Guardian*, even if your instincts tell you it isn't. You must start with an open mind. A project which discovers the opposite of what it expected is just as valid as one which finds what was anticipated, provided that in both cases the findings emerge from an objective and systematic look at the evidence. And it would be no disgrace for a project conducted along these lines to come up with no hard or fast conclusions. The *process* of investigation is the most important factor.

What can I look at?

The answer to this is anything – any use of language you hear or see around you. Provided that the focus of your investigation is a question concerning language, the world (or in this case, word) is your oyster:

In practice, of course, although some language investigations do look at a new area in a totally original way, most fall into certain categories, and similar questions get asked in relation to different data. For instance, an investigation of the language development of a two-year-old child will be unique because that child's language will be unique, but it will also probably discover that it shows many of the features you would expect of other two-year-olds. In the same way, an examination of the way the same news story is presented by different newspapers with different readerships or political standpoints will be original because the news stories are new, but it will probably discover similar stylistic features to those of other such investigations. But these projects might also discover something new – something particular. Whether they do or not, however, is not crucial.

Take a good look at yourself

It is essential that you choose your own area of investigation and formulate your own project title. You are much more likely to feel committed to and involved in an investigation in which you have found the evidence and posed the questions, rather than one which has been given to you by a (despairing?) teacher! By all means seek advice, from teachers and from books, but choose your general area yourself. Draw on areas of interest, use your strengths and avoid drawing attention to any areas of weakness. This is possible if you are finding the material and narrowing down the focus. You are in control. This is possibly more important when deciding what to look for (in the next section) but should influence your choice of topic too.

Strengths

Familiarity

Let's be positive first: is there any area of language of which you have a particularly close knowledge or experience? This might be related to your life outside school or college or to your other subject areas. Do you know a lot about computer language? Do you spend a lot of time surfing the net, or e-mailing friends? Do you read a lot of science fiction, romance, or fantasy novels? Perhaps your other subjects bring you into contact with specialist magazines or forms of specialist language – legal, business or scientific. Do you speak a particular form of colloquial English or possibly patois, or are you bilingual? Do you watch a lot of soap operas, have a part-time job which uses occupational jargon, listen to a lot of local radio? Are you involved in a pressure group or interested in politics? The list is endless. A familiarity with a particular variety of English means you probably already know quite a lot about it and have an ear for its subtleties. You can build on and exploit this in an investigation, provided that you can step back and view it objectively.

Interest

You will probably be choosing your topic for investigation about halfway through the course. Which areas of study have interested you most so far? You are going to spend a long time looking very hard at a fairly small amount of data, so choose something you find interesting, or you could end up merely going through the motions. Perhaps you have become particularly engaged with certain topics – whether men and women use the same language, or recent changes in language use you have discussed, or the differences between spoken and written forms, or what you have learned about interaction and discourse analysis. Choose an area which intrigues and stimulates you, rather than something which seems straightforward (or even easy).

Access

Something else which might influence your choice is whether or not you have easy and natural access to any varieties of language which would provide you with good project material. Do you look after or live with a small child whose language is developing fast? Do you have a relative, friend or neighbour who speaks with a pronounced accent or dialect? At college, home or work is there anyone whose use of language interests you and can you observe them easily in particular or different situations? Perhaps your family speak a language other than English at home, or a mixture of English and mother tongue. Do you have letters from a foreign penfriend; all your school exercise books, old diaries or letters; an exhaustive collection of Stoke City football programmes or copies of the *Beano*? Again, the list is endless.

Of course, you can set out to search and find data by research and use of libraries, archives or by writing letters requesting access to observe and visit primary schools, old people's homes, magistrates' courts – anywhere you like – and we discuss these later. But look at your immediate environment first to exploit all possibilities. After all, why make problems for yourself?

Skills

What are you particularly good at? Do you have any special skills that you could draw on for your project? Do you have a particularly good ear for the sounds of language? If so, a project on spoken English which looked at accent, pitch and stress features might be a good idea. Are you developing skills related to other subjects which would be useful – for instance: Sociology (drawing up questionnaires, sampling techniques); Computing (handling and analysing a lot of data); Literature (this gives you a head start on stylistic analysis), another language (an insight into translation problems and comparing languages); Psychology (group interaction)?

All projects demand that you analyse language, but you might know that you are better at some aspects of this than others. For example, are you particularly sensitive to the meanings and associations of words? You might consider looking at news reporting or some project which concentrates on point of view. Draw on your particular strength, and avoid...

Weaknesses

Be honest. If you have strengths then you probably have some areas of weakness too. If phonetics remain a bit of a mystery, avoid projects on accent. If syntax is still something of a blind spot, then don't choose a topic which exposes this, such as most areas of close stylistic analysis. Fortunately, with almost any stretch of data, you can formulate different questions to focus on, so perhaps it is in the 'what to look for' section that we need to consider this more fully. It's important to set yourself a challenge with your project, but there's no need to be foolhardy. In choosing your topic, then, you need to balance interest, knowledge, realistic access to data, and strengths and weaknesses. None of these should dictate your topic area, but a balanced and honest look at yourself is a good place to start when you are deciding what to do.

Next you must decide on your approach.

Scientist or detective?

It cannot be too strongly stressed that the vital pre-requisite for a good project is an open-minded investigator. Good projects must reveal what is there – present in the language – not what you, the investigator, would like to see. You start with your 'specimen' of language – your data – and work outwards rather than looking at the evidence in the light of preconceived ideas. Like a good scientist or detective, you don't impose your conclusions, you come to them only after close and sceptical scrutiny. So whether you prefer to see yourself as a scientist or as a detective, you must question and look closely. But before any of this objective research can take place you need something to work with, so that's where we will start. Scientific principles are as important in the collection of data as they are in the actual investigation.

First catch your specimen

Just as in the laboratory, unless the raw material you are working with is pure and uncontaminated, you are never going to reach accurate conclusions. The data must be as genuine, as honest as possible. What does this mean?

First of all, what does 'data' mean? It's an awkward word. Is it singular or plural? Is the first 'a' pronounced as in 'date' or as in 'dart'? Turning to that useful research tool for any language investigator, an etymological dictionary, does provide us with some answers: 'data' is the plural form of 'datum' and is pronounced 'dayta'. The most useful meaning which is given for our purposes is 'something known or assumed as fact and made the basis of reasoning or calculation'.

Well… yes, but this doesn't accurately reflect common usage. Most people use the singular verb with this plural form, as in 'my data was hard to collect', and would extend the meaning in this case to include not only facts, but things – in our case words or sounds in combination. So the working definition of 'data' for our purposes is the stretch of language in recorded, transcribed or written form that we are looking at.

Finding such data may on the face of it seem easy: after all, we have said you can look at anything. However, there can be pitfalls in the collection and assemblage of data. As well as suggesting what you might look at, this chapter aims to help you to avoid these problems. Before you start collecting your specimen, you need to be aware of certain basic principles.

Be fair to your data

The only way to know what you're working with is to collect the data yourself. Perhaps this is best illustrated by examples. If, for instance, you wish to look at a particular form of regional accent or dialect as it is currently spoken, you must try to record speakers in as natural a situation as possible. Don't rely on actors' versions of the same dialect and don't ask the speakers to say particular words directly. This will make them self-conscious and distort the results. Don't use secondary sources, such as glossaries of how to talk 'proper Lancashire'. You would probably be looking at an outdated version of the dialect. If your project is on graffiti or slang, don't work with examples from books on the topic. You don't know where they are from. The authors might even have made them up, in which case they're not graffiti at all.

This is not to say that you could not do a project on actors' attempts to reproduce regional dialects in television dramas, provided that it was very clear that you knew you were not looking at the real thing; or that you could not write a project on dialect verse, again provided that you showed all the way through that you were looking at a particular literary version of dialect, not spontaneous speech. Know what you want to look at and what to call it.

Compare like with like

There are particular aspects to bear in mind in different project areas to ensure that you are fair to your data. If you are making any kind of detailed comparison between or within varieties for instance, you must try to ensure that you are comparing like with like and reducing the number of irrelevant variables. Is there any point in comparing the lyrics of a song by Cole Porter with those from one by Led Zeppelin? Just possibly, if they're on the same theme, or use a similar structure, but it seems unlikely. There must be some kind of framework for comparison. Comparing lager advertisements on television, the radio and in the press might similarly present too many variables in the media themselves – linked only by subject – unless you can think of a tight focus.

Investigation – not essay

And one last general principle before we go on to consider specific topics. If you are in the fortunate position of having too much data, or if the variety of language you wish to look at is readily available, don't select the actual material you eventually look at because it supports your thesis best, and don't select from within your data only those examples which suit you. You must not ignore evidence which you find inconvenient. If, for example, your hunch is that a particular newspaper presents images of women in a certain way, don't only choose those articles which prove your point and discard any which don't. If you did, you would not have undertaken an investigation, but written an essay putting forward a particular point of view with illustrations to support your argument.

So, before you even begin to collect material and certainly as you collect it, you must bear these points in mind in order to be fair to your data:

Have a fairly clear idea of what you want to look at. Don't select examples which are already beginning to prove your point and ignore those which are inconvenient.

Suggestions

On the following pages you will see examples of possible project areas. They are presented to give you some ideas and they do not aim to be exhaustive: that would be impossible and undesirable. You will choose your own area of language to investigate, which may or may not be prompted by the ideas presented here. It is important that you do choose your own topic and don't have one 'given' to you. Follow your own interests and observations. You're going to become very familiar with your own particular subject as your investigation proceeds and it is much better to be working with material you find intrinsically fascinating – even entertaining!

The suggestions which follow have been divided into three broad sections:

1   those where the data involved is primarily spoken English,
2   those where the data could be either speech or writing, or both,
3   those where the data is primarily written English.

We have deliberately not tried to match the focus of the investigation to the possible topics because there is a variety of questions to be asked of any stretch of language. We'll discuss what to look for in the next part of this chapter. The remainder of this one is concerned with particular aspects of data collection in relation to particular areas.

Working with spoken data

If data collecting had tariff ratings like highboard dives at the Olympics, the gathering and transcribing of spoken data would carry a very high one. Some forms, such as working from recordings of radio or television chat shows, phone-ins or sports commentaries, aren't too problematic. However, recording a discussion, conversation or argument in real life is very difficult, and achieving a good, accurate transcription of what was said is no mean feat in itself, even before you go on to analysis.

Some points to bear in mind before embarking on an investigation into forms of spoken English are:

Yourself You need a fair degree of patience and perseverance to collect data in this area. You must be prepared to make several attempts at achieving a good, clear recording. When you have obtained a taping which is good enough it will take you a long time to transcribe it into written form before you can start work on describing and analysing it. Just transposing the sounds into words in written form with no pronunciation or stress features marked can take a long time on its own. A good detailed phonetic transcription of ten minutes of tape could take you up to four hours to transcribe. Producing an accurate transcription is a challenging but rewarding task, and in the process of it you will learn a lot more about spoken language – but it will take time.

Good equipment Different types of tape recorder are available and you should try to obtain the use of one which best suits your purposes. But whether it is a large, visible piece of equipment or one small enough to conceal in your pocket, it will have to be a good one – especially if you are taping a subject against a fair amount of background noise. It must have a good microphone, whether separate or inbuilt. If you want to make your equipment less noticeable, the small pocket dictaphones designed for the dictation of business messages are ideal. If it is less important that your subject is unaware of being taped, then the larger, more conventional tape recorders are fine.

Test the machine out in advance of any taping session. Don't set up that crucial encounter or interview and then realise that the equipment is unequal to the task. Familiarise yourself with it too. Don't have to fuss and fiddle with it too visibly. It will make your subject(s) even more self-conscious. Will electricity sockets be readily available (with attendant trailing wires)? Or would a battery-operated machine be better? If so, make sure the batteries won't run out.

Situation Try to choose a place for the taping session which is as free of background noise as possible, but still maintains the level of formality or informality which is consistent with obtaining authentic data. This, of course, is easier said than done. If you want to record an informal discussion in the cafeteria or a pub, then you might think it impossible, but even within these areas there are quieter times and places. Recording conversations in clubs would surely defeat all but the most intrepid!

It's worth doing a bit of fieldwork in advance of any session. It might produce a technically better recording to interview a couple of four-year-olds in the nursery teacher's office, but will they relax and talk as freely there as in the reading corner of the nursery itself? You must weigh up the pros and cons of the situation, taking into account how well they know you and each other, the inhibiting aspect of having their friends around, and what you want the data for. If it's pronunciation rather than interactive features it may not matter very much. Consider whether you need a framework for your taping session. Is it important that your subjects discuss certain pictures perhaps, or toys for children? Or a script – something to read in which the particular pronunciation features you're looking for are bound to come up – or a 'plant' to steer the discussion along certain lines: someone who is your accomplice, who knows what you are doing but who is not personally crucial to your investigation. You shouldn't leave such matters purely to chance or the vital elements may be entirely missing from your data.

All or nothing – what to tell your subjects (victims?)

We are all self-conscious when we know someone is recording what we are saying, and this will affect the way we are speaking. It may make us more concerned to get things 'correct'. Accents may be modified to become closer to RP (there's a certain amount of evidence that this might be more true of women than men) and we may use less colloquial vocabulary. On the other hand we could become so nervous that there are many more false starts and long pauses than in our speech generally. The more accustomed we become to being recorded – if the session goes on a long time or happens frequently – the more we may forget the presence of the tape, but it is something anyone doing a project on spoken English needs to be aware of.

If you have decided that for your purposes it will make little difference whether your subjects know they are being taped, or if it is impossible for you to disguise the fact that you are recording, then you may decide to 'come clean'. You may need to ignore the early part of your recording when your subjects are most self-conscious, so it is a good idea not to start straight into the subjects and features you are most interested in. It may take several sessions before the subjects are relaxed enough to provide good data, but it is clearly possible. Think of all the 'fly on the wall' documentaries that you have seen on television, where people do seem to become oblivious to the cameras after a time. When examining your data or drawing conclusions from it you should, however, take into account that data may be distorted to a greater or lesser degree by the recording process.

If you want to tape people who are unaware of the fact they are being recorded you will have to choose unobtrusive equipment and set the situation up in advance. You may well need an accomplice, who knows what is happening but whom you will ignore when you are drawing conclusions.

Recording people without their knowledge may seem rather sneaky or unethical, but it is the only way to obtain some types of conversation 'in the raw'. However, using the material afterwards without the subjects' consent is, we think, unacceptable. Most people do not object after the event, but sometimes they consider it to have been an invasion of their privacy. They might think that the material discussed or the way they spoke is not for 'outsiders' to hear. This has happened to students of ours whose families have objected to what they considered private subjects and intimate forms of expression being 'published'. If this does happen you should respect your subjects' wishes. It is something to be borne in mind before attempting such investigations. Sometimes offering anonymity overcomes the objections.

There is a middle way which might help with your project. With this method the subjects are aware that they are being taped, but think it is for a purpose different from the real one (i.e. looking at language features). If you tell someone that you're interested in their childhood memories, whereas really what interests you is dialect features, at least your subject will not be self-conscious about the very feature you're interested in. If you tell students that you are interested in their views on the state of the student common room when really you're interested in how they pronounce 'smoking', they won't be distorting their pronunciation of the word. This may seem rather devious but it's a well-worn research technique.

Recording children

> 'Never work with children or animals.'
>
> W. C. Fields

This might be sound advice for the acting profession, but children are frequently the targets of attention for linguists and students of language. Investigating stages of development, comparing children of the same or different ages, comparing 'normal children' with those with a language delay, and charting the development of one child (takes long-term planning, this one) – all these and many more are productive topics for project work.

You are luckiest of all if you have a child of your own whose language you can record, or a younger brother or sister. If you have a young neighbour, or you babysit regularly for a child, you are fortunate too. In these situations you already have an established relationship to build on, and with frequent access can introduce the tape recorder naturally at a convenient time as part of play. Another advantage is that the child will be relaxed with you and likely to use language in a natural way. Depending on the focus of your project you may well have to structure the situation carefully and lead the conversation or exchange into areas you think will be productive. This may take some patience, but if you know the child you have a head-start.

If you're interested in this area, but don't know any young children well, don't despair. Playgroups, nurseries and infant classes are usually quite receptive to pleas for help, and are willing to co-operate. If you're interested in older children, try primary schools, Brownie and Cub packs, Sunday schools, even Youth Clubs.

Having established contact you need to decide what sort of role you are going to adopt when you meet the children. Are you going to be the outside expert with only one task in view (this may be appropriate if you are interested in language use in a fairly formal situation)? Or is it important to establish a more informal relationship, in which case you will probably have to make several visits and become involved in some other role – helper, story reader. Don't become too familiar – you won't be there for very long. Accept the advice and help of teachers and parents, who will almost certainly want to be present when you are recording. The presence of a familiar adult is usually a help.

Again, you will probably need a pretext for talking to the child, so consider what would be appropriate – books, toys, games or pictures. If your project is going to look at the way children interact with each other, or with teachers or parents, you will have to blend into the background and become as unobtrusive as possible. The co-operation and consent of the adult involved is vital. This is not an appropriate area for saying nothing. It is very important to give the impression that you know what you are doing and are prepared to explain it to people in as much detail as they require.

The accomplice

There are a few situations which might produce better data if you ask someone else to do your recordings for you. This is not suggested as the coward's way out, but only in situations where it might be more appropriate for someone in a role other than researcher to do the taping.

An obvious example of this would be the classroom discussion, in which it would be more natural for the teacher to be taping the proceedings. S/he might even enter into the spirit of things and announce a reason for doing this which is nothing to do with your language research, but we do not suggest that you expect this co-operation, which is above and beyond the call of duty.

There may be other places or situations in which your presence would be obtrusive and automatically alter or affect the way people spoke. Social clubs might be somewhere where it would be better for a parent or friend who was already part of the scene to do your taping for you. We do not especially recommend this, as control of the recording process is out of your hands and it may be imposing on the goodwill of others, but there are a few situations where it might be appropriate and desirable.

Other practicalities

Tact, sensitivity and ingenuity (at least!) are needed to obtain good recordings, but in the euphoria of having finally achieved them, you must also remember to record

the date, the time, the place

> the names of the participants (although you may use pseudonyms in the transcript if you or they wish)
>
> their ages – very precisely in the case of children; approximations may be preferred by adults
>
> their gender – even if this is not apparently of central concern
>
> other relevant information (e.g. places of birth and domicile in accent or dialect projects)

And of course, you must keep your tapes and submit them with the finished project. They are proof of your hard work, and that your data was not faked!

Taping from radio and television

Radio and television can provide examples of spontaneous and scripted speech to translate into data, and with none of the problems of live recording. The additional factor to consider in this is the element of 'performance'. Even the most apparently relaxed and casual interview or talk-show programme, even members of the public being interviewed for news and documentary programmes, know that they are on television, and this affects their speech. Some of the most apparently natural television and radio performers are of course just that – performers – exhibiting a great deal of skill which in turn is probably based on much experience (if not rehearsal). Of course this does not invalidate transcripts of talk on radio and television shows as 'honest' data for projects, just as long as you know what you are looking at and bear in mind this element. You could choose to make it the focus of your investigation, if you wished, and examine how the constraints of the media affect talk. The requirement about recording dates, times, participants, is exactly the same as for live recording.

How much should you transcribe?

Having obtained your recordings you now have to turn them into written data, which might seem a bit perverse. You have to make transcripts. Advice has been given about this in the first section of this book. Your first decision is how much of the tapes to transcribe. Listen carefully to your tape and decide which sections might be most useful to you. You do not need to transcribe every minute of every tape. You may well have an hour or more's recording, only a portion of which is relevant to the subject of your project.

In notes accompanying your transcript you should indicate the total length of the recording and give a brief description of the whole. If your project is focusing on interactive features there might, for example, be three extended exchanges which you wish to examine in detail. These should be transcribed and some indication given as to where they occurred in the exchange as a whole, but you do not need to transcribe sections to which you are not going to refer in detail. You could refer to the frequency of a specific feature in the entire conversation without transcribing everything. You have, after all, submitted the tape as evidence, so your claims can be checked.

If you are looking at a child's language development and have a lot of taped material you must choose substantial representative passages (or a single longer passage) to transcribe, and work from those, although again these could be supported by references to the frequency of these features in the rest of the recorded evidence.

It's a good idea to look at the problem of 'how much' from the reader's point of view. It should be possible to find parts of the transcript referred to in the body of your project easily. This will be harder to do if you have submitted pages and pages of transcript, not all of which is relevant. We talk about presentation in a later chapter, but it is always a good rule of thumb to consider your project from the point of view of those who might read it. Ease of reference is extremely important, more important than attempting to impress by sheer weight of material.

So, in answer to the question 'how much?' it seems that hard and fast rules are difficult to draw up. You must provide a substantial transcript of continuous discourse as the basis of a project on spoken English, and there may be more specific guidelines for different courses. You must consider the whole of your taped material, whether it's all transcribed or not. If your project consisted of a general commentary on the language of a two-year-old, for example, with only isolated examples transcribed to prove points, you would be writing an illustrated essay, not an investigation. You must not pick your examples and ignore inconvenient evidence which does not support your general thesis.

Which features should be marked?

Pronunciation It is not necessary or desirable to attempt a full phonetic (or even phonemic) transcription of all your data with every feature of stress, intonation and pitch marked. It would only be a slight exaggeration to say that could prove to be a lifetime's work! Obviously if you are going to refer to pronunciation features you should represent those phonemically.

You cannot refer to accent features without doing this. You may not, however, need to transcribe whole utterances phonemically if what you are interested in is the pronunciation of single words or specific sounds. A phonemic transcription is usually adequate for describing broad differences in accent (RP and Wigan), but to compare more similar accents (Wigan and Bury) you would need an excellent ear and the ability to make a phonetic transcription. The scope of most A-level courses would not prepare you for this, and unless you are exceptionally skilled in this area it should not be attempted. However, when you are referring to pronunciation features you must represent them phonemically – a more personal, ad hoc approach (e.g. 'he pronounced the oo in 'book' like the oo in 'you') is not acceptable, and could be meaningless or wrong in some areas of the country.

Stress and pitch If you are concentrating on interactive features it is more likely that you will want to mark pitch, stress and tone. Ways of doing this have been suggested in

Chapter 4. There are many different systems for indicating these features, and it does not matter which you choose as long as it is consistent and is adequate for your purposes, and you include a key. Use the one you feel most familiar with. Again, it is not essential to mark all features in every stretch of transcript, but only those utterances you are referring to in detail, or where stress, pitch and/or tone are features you are going to comment on.

The Golden Rule

Consider your reader – you must make your points clear and readily understandable. If you have been unable to indicate through your transcript what the language actually sounded like, and sound is what you are commenting on, you will have failed. However, if the actual sounds of speech are not important to the points you are making, then it is not necessary, and might even be distracting, to mark them all.

Projects on spoken language which do not involve taping

It is possible to conduct an investigation into a specific area of speech which will not involve your making tape recordings, although it will necessitate recording your findings quickly and simply in another way.

One student, for example, who had a part-time job in a shoe shop, was interested in the different ways in which customers addressed him. He designed a simple form which would allow him quickly to record after each transaction the sex and approximate age of each customer and the manner in which he was addressed. He was only interested in one feature, so it was possible to do this.

The American language researcher Labov did something similar as part of his famous survey of accent and class in New York. Choosing different department stores which were known to cater for broadly different income groups (an English equivalent might be Harrods and Woolworths), he devised a question for his researchers to ask which in each case would require the response 'fourth floor'. He was interested in whether the 'r' was sounded, and whether there were differences between stores. There was no need to tape responses, just to record on a form if the 'r' was or was not sounded.

If you are interested in such a straightforward, isolated feature you may not need to tape. What you must do, though, is to keep meticulous records of the dates and places where your research was undertaken; first to make sense of your findings, but also to authenticate your data.

Projects which involve collection and transcription of spoken language are likely to gain credit for the time, care and skill you have put into assembling your data and making it clear and comprehensible to the reader. Obviously you have to put more effort into the initial stages of your project than a colleague who has chosen three versions of a newspaper story to compare. There is more challenge in the initial stage of a project in spoken language, but you know that the data (if it's good) is original, and many of the most interesting investigations are undertaken in this area.

Working with written data

If you decide to investigate a variety of written language you will obviously have fewer problems about collecting your data. However, if this area attracts you primarily for this reason, a word of warning: a policy of least effort is bound to show elsewhere in your project. Although you may have fewer difficulties with the initial assembling of data than your intrepid colleague, you must be equally scrupulous in your choice, research and presentation. Sloppiness shows. A remark such as 'I decided to make a random choice of story/contract/newspaper to make sure it was representative' is nonsense, and will readily be spotted as an attempt to excuse laziness.

We are surrounded by print – books, newspapers, magazines, circulars, forms, advertisement hoardings, greetings cards. We write a lot ourselves, either by hand or on a word processor – letters, notes, memos, essays, diaries. All this material, unlike speech, has to be consciously destroyed if it is to cease to exist, and forms a mountain of printed and written words all waiting to be investigated and analysed.

Where to look

As always, the starting point should be your own interests and observations. It may be helpful to consult lists of suitable topics or investigations already undertaken, or to listen to suggestions from teachers and fellow students. These could provide initial stimulation to get you thinking, but in the end the decision is yours. Here are a few suggestions which may help you to accumulate suitable data for your investigation.

Be a hoarder

Save letters, circulars, interesting newspaper articles, diaries, exercise books, college prospectuses and official handouts. When people in the street are handing out leaflets for political causes, religious tracts, advertisements for new take-away restaurants or supermarket bargains, don't quicken your pace to avoid them, but accept them all. Some or all of this material might be just what you need. If you have your old files or exercise books from school (or a brother or sister does) these could provide the basis for an examination of developing style, or spelling difficulties. A collection of letters from a foreign penfriend could be the starting point for an investigation of the problems second-language learners have with English. When you are filling in an application form for a passport or a driving licence, keep a copy. If Jehovah's Witnesses come to the door, accept – even purchase – a copy of *The Watchtower*. Researching your next holiday? The glossy brochures in the travel agent's are free, and are there to be taken. The same is true of estate agents' handouts. There are endless free examples of written words around us, but it can be frustrating to have missed an opportunity to collect what you need through lack of foresight, so

Look ahead

You will know at which point in your course you will begin working on your project. Let's imagine for a moment it's June. If it occurs to you at that point that the language of political pamphlets and leaflets is worth looking at, and you've thrown away all the stuff that came free through the door in May, you are going to have to go to a lot of trouble to find it now. On Valentine's Day every year, the newspapers have taken to printing hundreds of messages and verses in their personal columns, which would make a fascinating topic for language investigation. Acquiring back copies of newspapers takes much more time and trouble than remembering to save them in the first place.

Be alert

At certain points in the year advertisers launch major new campaigns. Perhaps they are trying to change a product's image or to introduce a new product. The Government periodically makes vigorous attempts to stop us drinking and driving, or smoking, or to get us to adopt a healthier diet and to exercise. Are they using language in a particularly interesting way to do this? However, these moments may not be as predictable as election time or Valentine's Day, so you need to be alert and save the evidence.

If you know that you are interested in newspaper style or house-style of magazines, you need to familiarise yourself in some depth with the field before finding the best examples to look at in detail. Major news stories covered at length by a variety of newspapers are few and far between, as popular and 'quality' papers have very different interests and readerships, so it's as well to be on the lookout for them if that is what interests you.

It's impossible to indicate the whole range of possibilities in the area of written language, and in some ways the most satisfying thing of all is to come up with an original idea, although this is difficult (increasingly so) to do. We are not suggesting that you hang on to any piece of paper with writing on it which passes through your hands: all those cardboard boxes full of canvassing material, *Reader's Digest* free offers, back copies of *Pigbreeder's Monthly*, would constitute a fire hazard. But it does pay to be receptive, to be alert and to plan ahead if you are thinking of writing about some of the printed ephemera surrounding us.

If, however, you are interested in more 'permanent' printed material, here are a few more suggestions. You are not confined to Literature if you wish to work with the (permanently) printed word. Libraries and bookshops can be the source of all sorts and varieties of written language.

Letters, diaries, notebooks

The letters, diaries and notebooks of the famous are often printed in book format. Writers, painters, politicians, civil servants, spies, criminals, royalty, anyone who achieves fame or notoriety, is likely to have their written output collected, anthologised or quoted extensively in biographies. These can provide a rich source of material for investigation. Of course, many of the great and good wrote diaries and letters during their lifetime with half an eye to the publisher, but equally, much of the material here was not written in the belief that it would be collected and 'frozen' into print, and is more informal, more colloquial and unpredictable. If you are interested in language change, these collections can provide examples of styles from different periods, or you may be interested in the way individuals use language to express themselves in the more private examples of their writing, freed – if we ever are – from the constraints of audience.

It is more difficult to find examples of non-celebrity documents. Most of us do not have our correspondence and private writing preserved and made publicly available. However, it is not impossible to find the writing of 'ordinary' people in print in the Social History and Sociology sections of libraries. Compilations of first-hand accounts of the nineteenth-century factory system or the Great Fire of London can be found in abundance, if you know where to look. There is an obvious danger here in becoming more interested in what is being said than in the way it is being said – which should always be the focus of a language investigation – but provided you guard against this, projects in this area can be very worthwhile. More contemporary examples can be found in the material compiled by Mass-Observation, or the American writer and anthologist Studs Terkl, who compiles first-hand accounts and interviews with an enormous variety of people. The Oral History sections of some universities and polytechnics can even provide you with ready-made transcripts.

Textbooks

Textbooks written for different age groups or levels of expertise can provide interesting data. Of course, you will only have a few in your possession, but there are probably some fairly ancient ones mouldering away in your college or school stockroom, or to be picked up cheaply in secondhand bookshops. These could provide the basis for comparison of different styles from different periods, or an investigation of the 'textbook' style itself in the light of what textbooks are written for. Dare we suggest that grammar books from different periods might be interesting?

Children's books

The language of books written for children of different ages, sexes or periods is worth looking at – and most of us do keep our own favourites. Classic children's stories remain in print for a long time and provide accessible examples of how styles might have changed. Children's annuals – compilations of stories, articles and comic strips – from the past and present provide a range of writing within one volume, and comparisons of then and now in this area can be particularly illuminating. Ask friends or relatives if they have kept *Girl* or *Eagle* annuals intended for a previous generation.

If you are fortunate enough to know (or to be!) a genuine hoarder with a collection of, for example, comics, football programmes or Angela Brazil stories which stretches back for decades, you could really be lucky.

Popular fiction

The distinctive styles of popular genres, such as romance, crime, horror or science fiction, can provide good material for language projects. However, since you will need to narrow the scope of your investigation – four thousand words on 'The language of popular romantic fiction' could hardly fail to be a survey or an essay, not a project – it is important to pose a particular question or limit the focus of your project. We will discuss this in the next part of this chapter. A knowledge of the genre beyond the text(s) you are looking at closely will help, so again the advice is to follow your interests. If you would find it tedious to read half a dozen novels by Stephen King in order to write a project on how the tension is created in Chapter 7 of one of them, don't undertake the project in the first place. Acquiring examples of popular fiction from fifty to a hundred years ago might be difficult – possible, but difficult. On the whole, much of this sort of writing does not remain in print as long as the classics. So don't set yourself a comparison of past and present unless you are sure you can obtain the evidence you want.

Literature with a capital 'L' – an area for the enthusiast

There are few problems finding the data here. Your problem is more likely to be narrowing the focus or formulating a question related primarily to the language rather than writing a lit. crit. essay. However, there are some particularly suitable areas for language study in relation to literary texts, the most obvious being drafts of the same poem or passage, or changes between editions, and these can be difficult to come by. Here you would be looking hard at stylistic features. Comprehensive biographies are usually quite a good source of different drafts; libraries and secondhand bookshops, of different editions. This is definitely an area for the enthusiast. You will have to have some knowledge of what you're looking for, some knowledge that these different versions exist and are interesting, before embarking on any wild goose chase.

Translations

Different translations into English of the same foreign work provide good material for language projects too, but here you must have a liking for very close language study, and preferably some understanding of the language the work was written in. If you are bilingual, or are studying another language, however, translations – not only of 'great' works but of guides and tourist books, or instructions which seem to be rather literal renditions of some text clearly first written in the mother tongue – provide subjects which allow you to draw on your knowledge of language rather than English, and to compare different systems.

Grey areas: written or spoken? (Or even sung!)

Are speeches, play and film scripts and scripted commentaries, not to mention song lyrics, examples of spoken or written language? Written originally, they were scripted to be spoken and, sometimes, to sound like naturalistic speech. In varying degrees they exhibit the features of written language, combined with the delivery of spoken. For these very reasons, they make interesting subjects for investigation, although they may not always be as easy to find in printed form as other species of written English. Significant political 'set' speeches are often printed at length in the 'quality' papers; political speeches are available in full in *Hansard*.

Most plays written to be performed in the theatre exist in published text form, unless they are brand new. Television and film scripts have not often been published, and to make transcripts would take a much longer time than you have at your disposal. You can make life easier for yourself by working only with scripts which have been published, or you can transcribe from video or audio cassette the sections of the script which you want to look at in detail, along with a description of the programme, which puts them into context. It is not always readily obvious whether some shows are scripted or spontaneous. Watch out for this. As language students you should be particularly alert.

Song lyrics are usually published somewhere – most accessibly on LP covers and CD booklets. Famous and popular songwriters usually have their oeuvres collected and printed in book form, as do those whose lyrics are most frequently referred to as 'poetry' (Bob Dylan, for example). Rock and teenage magazines often publish the lyrics of current hits. It is surprisingly difficult to transcribe lyrics from listening to songs, as you may have discovered. (What 'saving his life for the pork sausages' has to do with the rest of Bohemian Rhapsody has long puzzled Queen fans. Turn to page 267 to solve the mystery, if you haven't already.)

A warning: your investigation should concentrate firmly on language features, but at the same time should be informed by an understanding of the immediate context of the language. You should steer a fine line between being distracted and side-tracked by the accompanying visual images (film/television drama) or music (song lyrics) and on the other hand ignoring these other elements completely and treating your material merely as words on a page.

Comparisons between written and spoken language

There are many possibilities for project work which involves a comparison between written and spoken language, and one of its advantages is that it provides you with an instant focus for your investigation – the differences between the two in terms of word choice and syntax. It is necessary to make sure that you are comparing two examples of language which are worth comparing. If, for example, you are looking at speech which is scripted to sound like spontaneous speech – whether in a Pinter play or *Emmerdale* – and comparing it with an example of conversation you have recorded and transcribed, try to ensure that the participants in the two have something in common. There would be little point in comparing the scripted speech of female pensioners in *EastEnders* with a conversation in a club in Widnes between two eighteen-year-old youths (unless you make the case very clearly!). The ground for comparison could be subject matter – a spoken commentary and written report on the same sporting event for instance; purpose – a political or promotional talk or speech compared with its written equivalent; participant(s) – a vicar's sermon compared with his parish newsletter. There are many possibilities, but the ground for comparison should be made clear.

General points

Secondary sources

What are these, and why is reliance on them to be avoided at all costs? First, this project is a personal investigation into an aspect of language. It is imperative that you find and select your own material. There may be a wonderful example of a conversation in patois in one of your textbooks, but you must not extract it and use it as your own data even if you credit it (and if you didn't, of course, it would be unfair practice). That transcript is someone else's data, and you would be using it secondhand – as a secondary source.

You may refer to this transcript and the way in which it is described or analysed, perhaps to acknowledge where you found some of your ideas and methods; in fact this would be the correct way to proceed. Obviously we are stimulated by books we read, and there is no requirement that your project topic and method of procedure be totally original. However, the material you work with must be what you have found for yourself.

It is easy to see how this is the case with spoken data. You must record and transcribe your own. But perhaps you want to look at literature, for example the creation of a new 'language' in Russell Hoban's *Ridley Walker*. You know this may have been done before and you may (should) have researched other work on the subject. How then can your data be fresh and original? Well, it can't be in the same way as a unique stretch of conversation is, but if you know that your selection of passages to analyse closely is entirely your own, and you think you have a new perspective on the material or you are going to approach it in a rigorous and systematic way, then that is perfectly acceptable. What you must not do is analyse the same passages in the same way as any other study you are aware of.

References

You must add a list of any books you have consulted at the end of your project, and if you quote from them within your investigation this must be clear and credited: that is accepted and expected academic practice. If you observe this there will be no suspicion that you are passing someone else's work off as your own.

Finally we come to a question which always worries students at the beginning of their work on projects: how much data is needed? The almost universal tendency is to take on too much. In fact the amount you will need varies from topic to topic. If you are working primarily with written language, there is a danger of merely providing a running commentary, or coming close to writing an illustrated essay. It is much more of a temptation, if you are working in an area where evidence is plentiful, to 'dip in' and use your examples to illustrate your argument rather than to allow your findings to emerge from a hard look at the evidence. If you do this you will have written an essay, not a project. So although you must start with a question, or a hunch about your material, you should not limit yourself to discussing only 'convenient' examples, but choose a large enough sample which will allow you to be fair to your data.

How much?

You may be interested in looking at a specific type of written language – for example the style of the language of pamphlets issued by the Benefits Agency for the information of benefit claimants. You might have a theory about it: perhaps it's impenetrable and you wish to look more closely at how and why. Or maybe you've discerned a welcome trend to simplify or to make plain. This would make an interesting area of project work, provided that it appeals to you.

Your first step would be to collect as much material as possible and to familiarise yourself with it. It would not be a good idea to pick up the first pamphlet you see and to analyse the language of that. Equally it would be inappropriate, not to say impossible, to try to do the same for every leaflet you pick off the rack in the local office… but you do need to be familiar with a range of material in order to select from within it an example you consider typical, or particularly interesting.

Don't take on too much: your project probably has to be of a certain length, it isn't a life's work. You will be aware of the particular constraints within which you're working. The immediate reaction of most of us when faced with a word limit is not 'How will I keep within it?' but 'How on earth will I write that much?'

[The solution to the Bohemian Rhapsody mystery is 'Spare him his life from this monstrosity'.]

WHAT CAN I LOOK FOR? – HOW TO ASK QUESTIONS OF YOUR DATA

It may seem strange to consider this question separately from 'What can I look at?' but in our experience students usually have an idea of the variety of English they wish to study before they have sharpened the focus into what, within that large area, they are going to look for. It's true that some work the other way round and start with a question – 'Why is the language of contracts so impenetrable? Does it have to be?' – before finding examples to concentrate on, but this is relatively rare. More frequently a student will say 'I've noticed that the way…' or 'I'd like a closer look at…'. then after reading or listening closely within a chosen area and beginning to pick out features of language, will decide what to concentrate on.

There is usually a lot of accurate description within a good project – of identifying and collecting patterns of sounds, vocabulary and structures. Why then do you also need to ask a question in relation to your data? Wouldn't a good, thorough description be adequate on its own? The answer to this is that it is virtually impossible to write a good description without asking questions. The questions, which may start as pretty obvious and basic, provide a framework for your description. You have to begin making sense of a stretch of language somehow, and applying the fundamental questions to it is a good technique to adopt.

Questions to ask

Since in the end your finished project will be of limited length and scope, you will almost certainly choose to restrict yourself to one or two aspects of the text or transcript, and you will have refined your questions and answers accordingly. However, to start this process going, here are some of the obvious questions to ask:

What is language being used for here? (functional focus)

Where is this language occurring? (Situation; register)

When is/was this language occurring? (language change/development)

How is language being used here? (stylistic focus)

Who is using language here? (register)

To whom? (audience; interactional features)

These questions are too blunt on their own to make an effective project topic, but a combination of the 'how' with one or two of the others in relation to your specific area will probably help you to come up with a hypothesis. For example, let's suppose you are interested in the style of theatre reviews. You have conscientiously collected the reviews from five different publications – local, evening, 'popular' and 'quality' papers, and an 'alternative' listings magazine – of the same five productions, a total of twenty-five reviews in all. How are you going to shape your writing about them into a project? If you apply the basic questions you see that you could end up with a different focus for your project:

What is language being used for? Purpose (The functional approach)	To inform To entertain To express an opinion To persuade	How do different reviewers combine these functions in their reviews?
Where is this language being used? Context (Register)	In journalistic publications, in expected position on the review pages	What are the features of this particular specialised example of journalism? (Look for similarities then differences.)
Who is using language here? (Establishment of point of view)	Anonymous reviewer Established reviewer	How are objective/subjective views combined in these reviews?
To whom? (Audience)	Readership of newspaper (Research this!)	How do considerations of readership affect the style of this particular species of journalism? (This might focus on differences, then on similarities.)
When is/was this language occurring?	Contemporary usage (This would only become an issue if you decided to introduce new material and compare your reviews with others from a previous era.)	
How is language being used? (Style)	Lexis Structures Layout Tone	What seem to be the major factors contributing to style – audience; lexical and structural choice – house-style: compare other articles from the same paper.

It will be obvious that the questions overlap. You cannot consider any of them in isolation from the others. It's just that you have to decide where to put the emphasis of your investigation. If you look at all twenty-five reviews in relation to each question you won't really get to grips with any of them. You will never look closely at language – which is the point of the exercise – but will skate over the surface illustrating general points with examples taken from here, there and everywhere. But once you have decided which focus interests you most, you can then make some decisions about the shape and scope of your project and how to use your data.

In the process of considering what your focus will be you may well decide not to use all the material. If you focus on how readership may be related to style, you may decide that 'popular'/'quality' and 'alternative' may well be enough, and that only a couple of examples of each will do for close analysis.

If you are interested in individual style and how reviewers develop their own, you may wish to concentrate on only two named writers, but look at all five of their reviews.

If you are interested in the functional features first and foremost, you will probably select the reviews which provide most contrast in emphasis – informative/entertaining or informative/critical.

Whichever tack you take you will almost certainly not want to devote the same amount of close analysis to all twenty-five reviews, although you may wish to refer to most or all of them for some purposes – a count of the frequency of proper nouns, or sentence types and lengths if relevant. You should probably include them in your appendix to show that you have surveyed a range before making your final selection. Why waste work after all?

Let's look at another possible stretch of data, this time a transcript of spoken language.

You are interested in the language used in group discussion and have made a longish (twelve sides) transcript of a tape recording of your drama group – seven students (four female, three male) and your teacher (female) – discussing two projects for the end of year assessment. Each possible production has its supporters and at times the discussion becomes heated. At one point the teacher is called away and is absent for a few minutes. It is a good, clear transcript, full of interesting and varied language use, but you are uncertain about how to start analysing it. Look at it first in the light of the broad questions what?, where?, who?, when? and how?

Again we see that there is overlap in all these areas – the 'where' and 'who' sections for example – and any investigation involves part of the 'how' answers, the features of the language. But if you tried to answer all these questions in the same amount of detail in relation to the whole transcript you would either have to write at least twenty thousand words, or you would end up treating them all so superficially that you would not have space to look hard at the language. If you wished to look at interactive features – what, rather than who, helped the decision along or obstructed the decision-making process – you might choose to look in detail at certain passages you identify as key points in the discussion.

Question	Overall purpose	Focus of investigation
What is language being used for here?	To attempt to reach a decision At different times during the transcript: to persuade, to inform, to insult	Interactive features of language Which utterances were constructive? Which prevented development of discussion and decision-making process? Use discourse analysis features
Where?	In a fairly structured classroom situation, although teacher absent for part of the time	If you wanted to see how this affected the language, you'd need to record some of same individuals in a more informal situation to compare, or, if there was enough, compare the discussion when the teacher was absent with when she was present.
Who?/To whom?	Participants: 5 females, 3 males Issues of dominance/gender	Again, you could focus on interactive features but with different emphasis, concentrating on roles of individuals, number and length of utterances etc. If you think the age of the participants is important, this could be a possible area. What roles did individuals appear to adopt? Any significant differences between male and female speakers?
When?	Contemporary	This question has little relevance to this material, unless you wish to focus on contemporary colloquial usage (but there probably won't be enough material). It's difficult to think of any way of getting similar language use from another time.
How is language being used?	Look at form and features of language	Look at the features of the spoken language itself. Does it change as participants become more involved? Incidence of fillers, false starts, minor sentences etc.

If you want to consider the part that gender might or might not play in the language of this mixed group, you would probably want to look at the transcript as a whole and to examine length of utterance, interruptions, use of supportive/destructive comments and questions, tentativeness etc. (a 'who' question).

If you are interested in the effect of the presence of the authority figure on the discussion you would want to concentrate on what happened when she left the room. If the answer to this is that there was very little change, then it's a non-starter unless you are prepared to record the same individuals in a less structured situation.

Focus

When you have found the focus for your investigation, you do not necessarily have a project title. It is the first step in finding the way into your material. What do we mean by this rather over-used word 'focus' anyway? Just that it provides a direction for your investigation. You may be faced with a lot of data and somehow you have to narrow down the scope of your approach. You must look closely at language, and if you attempt to cover all aspects of it you won't look closely enough. 'Focus' is a useful metaphor, because when you are focusing on something you are not totally unaware of surrounding features: you realise that they impinge on what you are looking at, yet you see in most depth and clarity what you are concentrating on. If you're fortunate – or inspired – you might see something no-one else has seen.

There are some projects which provide their own framework by the nature of the task. The most straightforward of these are those which deal with comparisons or developments.

Comparisons

We have already discussed the importance of comparing like with like. There might be some point in comparing a live python with a stuffed koala bear, but on the face of it there seem to be so many differences that the task seems laughably easy. If you were to undertake it at all, your first challenge would be to convince your audience that the exercise had any validity. In order for there to be any purpose in comparing one thing with another there must first be some points of similarity.

Normally the rule about comparing one stretch of language with another is to reduce the number of features you are comparing to the few which form the core of your investigation. Thus, if you are comparing transcripts of two three-year-olds on the basis of gender, make sure the boy and girl have similar backgrounds, and if possible are in the same position in the family, and that either both or neither attend playgroup regularly. You still will not be able confidently to attribute differences in language to gender alone and make large conclusions about child language acquisition on the basis of such a small sample, but you will be attempting to isolate the feature which most interests you. If, on the other hand, you are interested in the impact of playgroup attendance on language development you would limit the other variables and choose children of very similar age and background and of the same sex.

If you are comparing the styles of different newspapers, make certain you compare news items with news items, features with features and comment with comment. If you are comparing instruction manuals or guides, compare them describing the same or very similar processes or places. Don't take on too much. Comparing two, or at most three, different subjects is enough. By this we don't mean only look at two newspaper articles, one from each of your chosen papers: you can handle a bigger sample than that. But compare the *Daily Star* with the *Daily Telegraph* in news or features, not the styles of the *Daily Star*, the *Daily Mirror*, the *Daily Mail*, the *Daily Express*, the *Guardian* and the *Daily Telegraph* in news and features, or the finished product will be a survey not an investigation.

It will be obvious from these remarks that although a project which is comparison provides you with a framework, you will still have to decide which features to concentrate on. You can't compare everything.

Development

Another approach which provides you with a structure but not necessarily a focus, is to look at the development of a subject's language, or the language of a sequence of publications (such as a reading scheme). This usually takes forward planning, but not always. You could look at the progressive degrees of complexity in a reading scheme for example, and this would be fairly easily available. If, however, you wish to study the language development of a two-year-old over a period of six months it obviously takes a large commitment of time and a great deal of forethought. Another example of this might be to look at the changing language of a political or public information campaign as it responded to public opinion polls. This data would take more time to gather than an afternoon spent in the local reference library. However, time spent in data collection might be time saved in wondering how to structure your final project. What you would be looking for in your project is how the material changes, but within that large question you might very well have to narrow down the aspects you concentrate on.

Narrowing down – looking at the language

It is not possible to be endlessly specific about what you might start looking for when, having chosen your broad approach to the data, you begin to look in detail at the language. That will very much depend on what you're looking at, as well as the focus you've decided upon.

If you are looking at spoken language you may now be wishing to look at the phonological features of pronunciation, accent, stress, pitch and tone. On the other hand you may well have decided to minimise your reference to these and to concentrate on interactive features of a conversation, the dynamics of the exchange.

If you are working on journalism, news reporting or advertising, you may have decided to concentrate on semantic features, to classify and group together similar words and to discuss the effect of the choice of one word rather than another. Or you may be more interested in grammatical structures, the use of the passive, sentence types, major and minor sentences. Perhaps a combination of both is appropriate?

However, there are some approaches generally worth taking which would apply to most projects.

Patterns and repetitions

Do certain features – be they sounds, words, structures – recur, establishing the tone and coherence of the language? What is characteristic of this user's idiolect, or style of writing? There may be a preponderance of words from a particular register, or associated with a specific field. There may be a distinctive sentence pattern, a tendency to begin or end sentences in a certain way. There may be a particular way of pronouncing a vowel sound, or omitting consonants at the end of words. As you look harder at your material you are bound to see certain features recurring which may be attributable to an individual style or dictated by what the language is being used for – or a combination of the two. These are worth grouping together and examining further. The likelihood is, when you look a little harder, that within a group of features you thought were similar, there are some further groupings which could be made. If, for instance, looking at the style of a particular journalist, you have noticed that he often uses a form of direct address to the reader and you have collected all the examples of this in your data, you may find on closer examination that he does it for different effects – to sound familiar, to share references, to challenge his readers, to appear to attempt a dialogue. What you thought was going to be a fairly straightforward discussion of the use of one particular language 'trick', you now discover is more complex and varied than you first imagined. This is what should happen as you get further into your investigation. You discover much more than appeared at first sight. And that is why most students have no trouble in achieving the stipulated word length (if any).

Look for departures from the pattern. Once you've established what are the predominant features of language use within your data, you can examine variations from them. You won't have to look very hard for these, as they're probably some of the first things you noticed. Are there any sudden switches of tone or register, words used unexpectedly, departures from Standard English, or switches into it? Did that two-year-old, just once, use a construction you weren't expecting? The list is endless and will depend very much on the variety of language you are working with. These features which draw attention to themselves are easy to spot, but why are they there? How do they fit into the overall patterns?

Don't lose sight of the wood for the trees. Don't forget the overall structure of the language you are investigating as you become involved in looking at the details. It is particularly easy in a piece of stylistic analysis to forget that the article or passage may have a beginning, a middle and an end, or at least some progression within it from unit to unit. The questions posed in the introduction to your project and returned to at the end should ensure that you don't get side-tracked or bogged down in feature-spotting for its own sake, but try to bear a sense of the data in its entirety in mind as you proceed with the description of small sections of it, and to relate the parts to the whole. Your data may not be an example of a 'whole'. It might be just a part of a transcription of a long conversation, lesson or lecture. Or your data could comprise several 'wholes' in that it is a collection of letters, or articles or sets of song lyrics. If you keep a sense at all times of what the language is being used for and relate your descriptive points to that you shouldn't go far wrong.

Don't make unsubstantiated claims. When you reach the end of your project, it can be a temptation to make larger claims for your findings than are justified by the scope of the investigation. You may have shown that in your sample of a hundred customers who address you at work, men are more likely to call you 'love' than women are, but you have not proved that this is true of the male population of Britain as a whole. Your findings may well be affected by regional, class and age factors which you can only speculate about.

Similarly, you may have discovered that of the two-year-old twins whose language you have been observing, the girl has a larger vocabulary than the boy. However, you have only observed and recorded this in relation to those children, and cannot go on to make more general claims about gender difference in relation to language development.

It is legitimate to indulge in a little speculation, and to refer to other, more comprehensive surveys in the same field if you are familiar with their findings, but you must bear in mind the limited scope of your own project. This is not always easy to do, especially if it has absorbed you day and night for months! However, your conclusions are not weakened but are stronger if they are based solely on your examination of the data, and are no less interesting for that.

HOW CAN I PRESENT MY FINDINGS? – HOW TO SUBMIT YOUR INVESTIGATION

Deciding on the best way to set out your project is much more than a cosmetic exercise. We are not going to discuss here whether you should have an illustration on the cover, or what sort of typeface to use. The major concern is that you say as directly as possible what you intend to say. Presenting your work clearly is an indication that you have a definite idea of what you are doing, and the process of working this out is as useful to you as it will be helpful to your readers.

Consider your reader

Your reader(s) should be your first concern. They should not have to work hard to puzzle out what you are trying to say, nor should they have to wade through pages of the appendix to find the sentence you are discussing in detail. Your project provides you with an opportunity to show that you can write, and that the time you have spent looking at other people's language has taught you a few lessons about how to improve your own.

Start in good time

You must be prepared to write several versions of your project, so make sure you leave yourself time to do this. Your first attempt will probably reveal omissions, non-sequiturs in your argument, technical errors and patches where the writing is less than clear. It may be too long and repetitive, or it may be too skimpy, with obvious gaps in coverage. The best way to discover these flaws is to give it to someone else to read, probably your teacher or a fellow student, although a non-specialist reader might have some interesting comments too – over-reliance on jargon or unclear use of technical terms perhaps? You will almost certainly be too involved with the material to view it dispassionately, although this can sometimes be overcome by leaving time between finishing a draft and coming back to read it. (We are speaking of the ideal world here. Time constraints may well prevent this.)

Another reason not to delay the actual writing of your project too long, however much preparation and research have been involved, is that the process of writing aids thinking. You do not have to have your project planned to the last detail before setting pen to paper, or fingers to keyboard. It is surprising how many students are reluctant to stop making notes and start writing the 'real thing'. Writing the thoughts, findings and analysis down can help to clarify things in your mind. This will help you to get to grips with the possibilities and limitations of what you will be able to say in the finished version.

Don't be defensive about your first attempt. Criticism can be constructive in this case. You know your work isn't perfect – yet! Your most critical readers may be the ones who in the end provide the most help. However, it is *your* project, and after due consideration you might decide to reject some of the critical remarks, but weigh them up carefully first. To soften the blow you can ask your readers to tell you what they like about your work as well – there's bound to be something even in the most tentative first draft.

Title

The logical place to start a section on presentation is with the title – but this does not mean that the title need be the first thing you write. The safest sort of title, which is perfectly adequate, if not inspired, is descriptive: 'The language of sports commentaries: An analysis of the Radio 2 commentary on the football game between England and Scotland on 21st May 1988'. The opening part of this title indicates the general field of the investigation, the second is more specific about the data it is based on. Don't make it too long and complicated – the title should definitely be shorter than the project itself!

If the project has set out to answer a question, then make that question the title. This arouses curiosity in the age-old 'read-on' tradition, and indicates the direction the project will take. Questions make good titles: 'Do men and women speak the same language? An analysis of three conversations: men only, women only and a mixed group'.

Of course this raises expectations that you will have answered the question by the end of your investigation, whereas your findings may be inconclusive. Don't worry about this. Don't force a conclusion if there isn't one.

Some students are inspired to produce short, snappy titles followed by a more explicit description. They may even attempt wit. An investigation into common spelling mistakes by fifteen-year-olds, for example, was called 'The error of our weighs, waze, ways'. One which investigated the idiosyncratic style of Salvador Dali's diaries had the title 'Painting by letters' and looked at whether the painter was trying to use words in the same unsettling way he used images. This approach is fine, if it works, but it is not necessary. The most important aspect of a title is that it gives a clear idea of what is to follow.

Style

Which style is appropriate to project writing? You have been studying language, and a project is a writing exercise in its finished form. It is important to get this right. Is it advisable to make your style lively, humorous or original in order to make your project easily readable? On the whole, the answer to this is no. It is not the primary purpose of your project to entertain your readers. On the other hand, you do not want to bore them. A direct, clear style is best. Try to write as simply as possible and to convey your meaning accurately. You do not have to use a lot of technical or jargon words to sound impressive, but only where they are necessary and the most straightforward way to make your point. Wit should be confined to section headings and sub-titles, and in any case used only if you are good at it. Accept the advice of others on this point.

It is a good idea to break up your text into sections. It makes it more 'digestible' for the reader and shows you have a plan and a structure. If used correctly, they also help you to make your points more clearly: significant analysis or conclusions can easily get lost and be overlooked if the text is continuous. Structuring also makes reference back much easier. To make an obvious point, page numbers also help with this.

How to begin?

The best way to begin is with your hypothesis, the question you are asking of your data. This may be preceded or followed by some account of how you came to choose this topic and to formulate your approach. This is a personal investigation, and your reasons for choosing this area are interesting to the reader as well as relevant to your investigation. Describe the process by which you came to your general topic area, and to narrow down the focus of your project. By this we don't mean that you go into too much detail:

> Sitting on the top deck of the thirty-nine bus on my way home from the pictures wondering whether or not to get off a stop early and get some chips, I heard a woman behind me say 'She's a strange woman, that Mrs Reynolds.' I began to wonder about the frequency of delayed naming in the Bradford dialect...

(if there is such a phenomenon!) This would be including too much irrelevant personal detail. However, some indication of how you did decide on your topic can convey some of your interest and enthusiasm. Was the source of your topic personal observation, or did it come from your reading? Did the general area or the question come first? How did you then refine your ideas to give you the shape of your project? Start with the beginning and describe the process. If this is in fact your third project idea after two unrelated false starts, it is not necessary to describe your previous subjects. But if the area you began with was similar and it is as a direct result of a previous false start that you finally developed your current project, then it may well be relevant. It is part of the process.

Having introduced your topic and indicated the question you are asking of your data you can then outline how you are going to proceed and give your reader an idea of what to expect from your project and what the scope of it is. As with any good résumé or plot summary you should not give away the ending at this point. Don't arouse unreasonable expectations, but arouse some!

Explain your methods

Briefly explain how you collected your data, and the principles which underlie the collection of it. How did you make sure you were comparing like with like? How did you reduce variables which might have confused your findings? Did problems with data collection actually affect the subsequent direction of the project? Do you have reservations about the material you finally had to work with, or does it exactly serve your purposes? This is the place to explain this to your reader, although it is not necessary to include a blow-by-blow account.

Where should I present the data?

All the data which you have used and referred to should be submitted with your project, usually in the form of an appendix. However, when you are referring in detail to any part of your data within the body of your project you should include it at that point. The golden rule is to consider your reader. It should be easy for the reader to refer to the data you are analysing, without having to keep turning to the back.

You will probably have access to a photocopier, and it is useful to make several copies of your material, whether it is a transcript, newspaper articles, advertisements or poems, as a back-up in case you lose anything, as a copy you can scribble on, and as a sparc copy you can cut up and insert whole in the main part of the project when you are considering that part in detail.

In some types of project the decision about how and where to display your data is crucial, and solving the problem is an important step in the project's development. Consider an investigation which is comparing two different translations of a work in a foreign language. The whole point of the exercise is to make detailed comparisons of two texts. It is vital to display both texts, and probably the original, in a way which makes it easy for the reader, and for you, to make rapid reference from one to the other. You would have to decide what size 'chunks' of the text would be manageable – sentences or paragraphs? You might also wish to highlight certain features, such as lexical choice, to compare directly. Colour coding with highlighting pens can help here. A student of ours who was comparing two versions of Albert Camus's *L'Etranger* spent a long time evolving a consistent system which simplified data reference for the reader, but once she had, the whole method of procedure fell into place. Not all considerations of where to display data in your project are as complicated as this, but many do involve decisions about how much data to include at which points in the body

Male Labels

Label	Occupation/ position in society	Age	Appearance	Personality
Pub Boss	X			
Cheeky				X
Fire-eater	X			
Tory chief	X			
Party Chairman	X			
Opponent of Loose Morals				X
Thatcher's Key Supporter				X
BBC Interviewer	X			
Straight-Talking				X
Top Tory	X			
Manager	X			
Mid 30's		X		
Co-star	X			
Dentist	X			
55-year-old		X		
Prosecutor	X			
61-year-old		X		
Husband	X			
Killer				X
Heathrow Porter	X			
46		X		
Total 21	**12**	**4**	**0**	**5**
%	**57**	**19**	**0**	**24**

Framework for analysis

The main body of your project will be given over to a description and analysis of your data. It is important that this proceeds in a systematic, logical fashion. The simplest way, but not necessarily the best, is to 'talk us through it', concentrating on various language features as you work your way through the data. The problem with this is that it can lead to a lot of repetition, as the same pattern is observed at different points. This is a rather naïve approach and has the look of a first attempt. It probably is what you did when you first looked at the data, but by the time you reach the finished product you should be aiming to produce something rather more sophisticated. Having said this, it is just possible that this is the best way to proceed with your data – if it's a transcript of a conversation for example. If you are convinced, then do it this way. It is your project.

However, most projects gather together examples of one particular feature and discuss them together, as in the 'labelling' in the *Sun* articles mentioned above. Once you have decided what these clusters of features are, then your only problem is the order in which you discuss them. Do you look at the most prominent first? Do you keep what you regard as your most striking discovery and perceptive analysis until the end? Do you arrange your analysis along phonological/lexical/grammatical lines? It is up to you, but there must be some discernible organisation and system. This is the main part of the investigation and your project will stand or fall according to the quality of it. Display your hard work to best advantage.

The conclusion

Your conclusion should return to the question you asked of your data at the beginning. Have you answered it? You must be honest in your answer, which should be faithful to the analysis you have just undertaken in the main part of the investigation. It doesn't matter whether you are able to say 'My analysis of the evidence has indeed shown…' or 'I found to my surprise when I looked in detail…' or even 'Although this appears to bear out my hypothesis the sample is probably too small…'. This is the part of the project you were aiming towards, but the process of the investigation is more important than the originality of your conclusion. The quality of your conclusion, in that it arises directly from looking at the data, is crucial but don't force it.

You must not make greater claims for your investigation than the examination of the evidence can stand. You may have discovered that the language used in the sports section of the tabloid newspaper is more complex than that used in the news stories, as measured by sentence length and use of specialist terms. You will only have shown this to be the case for the edition(s) of the newspaper(s) you have looked at, not for all tabloid newspapers for all time. You may go on to speculate about why this difference exists, but you cannot say conclusively why it is so. You may have called your project 'The Language of Fantasy Literature', but you will certainly only have looked at a relatively small sample. You cannot make claims for the whole genre, and you would invalidate your conclusions if you did. You may believe that your findings hold good for a particular writer's entire oeuvre, but unless you've looked at it all (highly unlikely!) you must not state that they do. State clearly what you think you have discovered and don't be unduly modest, but don't make unrealistic claims which will weaken the whole enterprise. The time and words that are available to you inevitably limit the scale of your project, but if it is clear, original and it answers the questions it raised, you and your supervisor have every reason to be gratified.

Sources

At the end of your project you should acknowledge any books you have consulted which you have found useful in writing your project. You may have used the vocabulary and approach for discourse analysis which you read about in a specific volume, or you may have adapted it for your own purposes. Either way you should list the titles of any books which have given you ideas or inspiration, or which you have drawn on to improve your understanding of your topic area.

Presentation

How important is it to have your project presented in a professional manner? It is not vital to have your work word processed. Perhaps you yourself can't type and you certainly can't afford to pay for someone else to do it. You will definitely not be penalised for this. However, your final version should be presented with care. It should be legible, clear, and easy to read and follow. The quality of the work itself is the most important thing, but if you have not taken the trouble to consider your reader it may indicate that the whole process has been rushed and ill-thought-out. Leave yourself enough time to make sure that the final draft gives the impression that you have approached the whole enterprise with care and commitment.

INSIDE A MARKER'S HEAD – EXAMPLES OF GOOD AND BAD PRACTICE

We have discussed at some length what goes to make a good project, what topics, approaches and modes of presentation seem most appropriate and fruitful. It now seems a good idea to exemplify the points we've made with extracts from genuine projects. All were produced under the supervision of the writers, so we know how much they represent a triumph or disaster.

We do recognise that the project represents a difficult task for many students, but given guidance, sense and determination the worst horrors can be avoided. No-one expects everyone to be a genius, full of original ideas and talented as a writer, but we can expect you to ask yourself basic questions like

Is this really a project rather than an essay?

Have I displayed some relevant knowledge?

Does this project have a structure?

Does it make sense?

Is it as legible and as well written as I can make it?

Does it reach conclusions and prove something?

If the answer to any of these questions is no, do something about it!

First impressions

Clearly, presentation matters. No, it is not worth taking a course in word processing; yes, it is worth doing a genuinely neat final draft that looks as though someone cares about it. Your project ought to be the culmination of a lot of research, thought and writing – don't let yourself and your material down at the last hurdle. Why not put it in a plastic wallet at least, so that it doesn't get dog-eared? Trite trivia will still be trite trivia even if beautifully typed and bound, but you do yourself no favours by assuming that your intellect will shine through illegible scrawl. It will not.

Every cover sheet tells a story

Is your title hopelessly vague? 'Television adverts', 'Comparing popular and quality newspapers' or 'Child language acquisition' immediately give the impression of a poorly focused, probably entirely unoriginal project. Some A-level language students manage to come up with witty, striking titles; at least ensure that yours sounds considered and personal. One project which had a first draft title 'Analysis of songs' (subtext 'I can't think what the hell to do but I like pop songs so I'll have a bash at them') became, by final draft, 'A linguistic analysis of songwriting from the 1960s and 1970s commenting on difference, change and development'. The subtext of this is very different: 'This is not waffle, it is linguistic and I know exactly what I'm looking at.' The area still sounds rather large but the reader feels the writer is in control.

Your brief description of your project also speaks volumes. Does it actually say any more than the title? Notice the wording: 'outline of topic studied and sources consulted'. You are expected to write some of it at least after you have written the rest. Your outline ought to give the marker a clear and positive impression of what is to follow. Don't miss your chance!

Your supervisor's remarks may well accompany your project. It is silly for you to think that these have nothing to do with you: 'X has still not produced her data', 'Y failed to consult me' and 'Z insisted on including this against my advice' help no-one. 'Excellent in every way' and 'I wish every language project were as easy to supervise as this one' paint a very different and more encouraging picture. Your teacher is an important resource – and probably a bad enemy to make!

What do you get marks for?

Examination boards recommend a loose marking scheme to their markers. The names for the different elements vary a little from board to board but the same virtues – knowledge, clarity and wit – are bound to be appreciated. Of these elements, knowledge is the most vital at this level. The NEAB, for example, recommends its markers to give around half of the available marks for linguistic knowledge. This includes many possible aspects: grammar, phonetics, analytical skill and topic knowledge all come under the umbrella. As you prepare your project, ask yourself 'Where am I getting my linguistic knowledge marks from?' Have you proved that you can do discourse analysis, or understand difficult theories of child language acquisition, or transcribe phonetically, or discuss morphemes or syntax convincingly, for example? Look at what you have done and try to be objective. Do you sound as if you know what you're talking about? Is your approach rigorous? Are your comments precise and accurate?

To show what I mean by precise and accurate let's look at a couple of examples of analysis from projects. Read each one yourself. Both are from projects whose main task is to analyse literature linguistically. Ask yourself:

- Is the writer knowledgeable?
- Is she using specialist terms with confidence and appropriateness?
- Is she precise?
- Is she proving anything?

Candidate A

Catherine also uses colloquial phrases in letter number six – 'Well I never' is an expression not authentic to Brontë's writing, or indeed to letter writing, especially at the beginning of a correspondence. Catherine is writing letters to Heathcliff, but the style of writing is almost like a dialogue. These examples show a complete lack of formality, the formality inherent in letters written at that time. 'I don't know why I put up with you' is another modern phrase, as is 'How are you doing over there in New York?' (letters six and one respectively).

The reference to 'all that Wuthering on the moors' is a play on the title 'Wuthering Heights'. 'Wuthering' is an old dialect word used in Yorkshire to mean stormy or blustering. By re-collocating the word 'Wuthering', the connotation shifts from those suggesting something passionate and turbulent to something clearly disparaging. In the same letter (number one), there is a reference to Golgotha – the Aramaic word for Calvary which is the place where Jesus Christ was crucified. Biblical allusions were quite widely used at the time when 'Wuthering Heights' was written. This use of a Biblical term suggests that Edgar's sister is a cross which Catherine must bear, but she expresses this in an indirect and sophisticated way.

The writer does use some archaic lexis to emphasise that the theme of the story is a nineteenth-century novel. However, the letters contain a combination of lexis from the nineteenth century and the modern/late twentieth century. An example of the archaic lexis used to add to the humour can be seen in the third letter, 'Ah me alas, alackaday...' which are terms not in use today, neither would the archaic word for influenza – 'grippe' – be used in either speech or writing today. The writer uses the term 'New World' many times – this is an old word for America.

Not all of the lexis used is early nineteenth or late twentieth century. For example, in the first letter, Catherine says 'Edgar is sweet but a terrible stick.' 'Stick' is lexis most commonly found in the late nineteenth/early twentieth century. It is used in this context for humorous reasons; the connotations of 'stick' are highly inappropriate, and it creates a jar of registers which is characteristic of the humour of the story.

Catherine uses different terms to finish her letters such as 'Yours in ennui' (letter three) – a French word meaning boredom

– and a Latin phrase more likely to have been used in previous centuries, 'Yours in extremis' – meaning at the point of death. The use of these words is characteristic of pastiche, the style of the piece is exaggerated for humour. 'Yours in extremis' conjures up an image of a girl pining away, but here it is used in a semi-joking way. In the novel, the characters do not dramatise themselves so much.

In the second letter, Catherine says 'We Yorkshire lasses are not so dumb as you think!' The use of 'dumb' in this context is to mean stupid. This is an example of an Americanism which would not have been used in the nineteenth century, as the American influence would not have infiltrated the English language at that time. Such usage of Americanisms is only a recent happening.

The letters were obviously not written in the nineteenth century and they are not typical letters of any period. The letters are more like an actual conversation between Catherine and Heathcliff. The letters are accurate in that they contain questions, although most people would not begin to write a letter with a question (letters one and five), especially not during the period when 'Wuthering Heights' was written.

The letters are a cross between the original novel and a more up-to-date version. Certainly, a nineteenth century writer would not have begun a letter 'Dear Heathcliff, you Bastard...' as in letter number eleven, which is obviously a modern usage of the word.

Candidate B

Analysis of 'Gulliver's Travels'

The tone of the passage at first strikes me as humorous and quite dramatic as it is so unusual. When reading the passage it is very easy to get into the atmosphere and you can imagine yourself actually being there. You can see the story from two sides, as Gulliver himself being attended to and what the Lilliputians must have seen and felt like. Swift therefore seems most concerned with the atmosphere, although Gulliver himself is setting the story.

The language is formal, although Gulliver is telling the story himself it is not colloquial. All the responses are directed at the Lilliputians as Gulliver keeps mentioning what they are doing and what their lives are like. Nouns are mainly concrete but some proper nouns are used for effect, to make the piece more realistic e.g. 'Burgundy'. Adjectives are very frequently to do with the senses and to describe the situation such as 'small' and 'universal'. Verbs are mainly in the past tense e.g. 'descended', and they are showing the situation and what everybody is doing. The infinite form of the verb is used e.g. 'to stand', 'to mount'. There are some fictional words in the passage e.g. 'Hekinah Degul' and 'Borach Mivola'; this is supposed to be the language of Lilliput.

There is a semantic field in the passage to do with the meat which Gulliver was eating e.g. 'flesh of several animals – there were shoulders, legs and loins, shaped like those of mutton – very well dressed.' Collocation is used, e.g. 'half a pint'.

Personal pronouns are found frequently throughout the passage e.g. 'my sides', 'my mouth', 'my hand'. Demonstratives such as 'that hogshead' can be found and relative pronouns e.g. 'who durst venture', 'that several ladders', 'which I drank'.

Conjunctions which connect phrases together seem to be fairly frequent: 'and' is used a lot in the first sentence. Co-ordinating conjunctions can be found also, e.g. 'They slung up with great dexterity one of their largest hogsheads, then rolled it towards my hand.'

Candidate A

1 Ground thoroughly covered – a clear line of argument
2 Assertions backed by precise and valid examples
3 Technical terms in abundance, appropriately used
4 Comments precise and convincing
5 An intelligent, perceptive analysis – impressive.

Candidate B

1 No line of argument – no overall statement
2 Assertions rarely borne out by evidence
3 Technical terms absent or ill-understood
4 Comments vague and unconvincing
5 This is analysing by rote – no evidence that she understands why features are there.

These were my summative remarks of what I thought as I read them. Did we agree? For your interest the first extract came from a grade A project, the second from one which failed – so I hope you could tell the difference.

Phonetic transcription

Doing this accurately is a skill in itself and will impress. However, it should also be serving a useful purpose. The most likely such purpose is to clarify exactly what someone sounds like in order to comment on their accent. This is the purpose to which this candidate is putting it. First he transcribes his subjects' speech accurately:

Got up at quarter to seven this morning made myself a drink
gɒt ʊp æt kwɔrtə tə sevən ðs mɒrnin meɪd mɪself æ drɪnk

of tea sat down for half an hour while I came round went
ov ti sæt daʊn fʌ haːf ən aə waɪl æ keɪm raʊnd went

upstairs got dressed came back down washed the breakfast pots
ʊpsteəz gɒʔ drest keɪm bæk daʊn wɒʃd ðə brekfəst pɒts

Then he finds patterns within their speech in order to make specific points about their accent:

The Salford Accent

The Salford accent, or what is supposedly a Salford accent, has become familiar to many people around Britain through the programme 'Coronation Street'. Yet to many people unfamiliar with the area it is difficult to tell which of the accents on the programme most truly depicts the Salford one.

For example, Brian Tilsley seems to have more of a Geordie accent, Sally seems to have a Bolton/Bury accent, while Vera Duckworth has a very over-emphasised and exaggerated Salford accent, but someone unfamiliar with the area would find it difficult to tell the difference. Hopefully, my project will help to illustrate what is a true Salford accent.

1) The first feature I came across was the use of the 'schwa'. That is, instead of /ɜ/ for the 'er' sound at the end of or middle of a word, the schwa /ə/ sound is used.

   e.g. in /kwɔrtə/

2) The next feature is the dropping of the final consonant of a word, commonly the 'g'.

   e.g. instead of /lɪvɪŋ/ it is /lɪvɪn/

3) The dropped final consonant is a common feature of the Salford accent, as are the following vowel sounds:

   The 'a' sound is /æ/ for example in the word /bæk/. /bæθ/ would have been a better example, but this was not used in the transcript. The /æ/ sound is a typical Northern accent feature in comparison to Received Pronunciation which would be /aː/

   Also the deep North /ʊ/ was a common feature in words such as /ʊp/

4) Some vowel sounds were sounded in an unfamiliar way, for example, the /ɪ/ in /mɪself/

Then he gives his subjects a word list in order to check their pronunciation of certain, isolated phonemes against those of another speaker:

funny	/fʊnɪ/
book	/bʊk/
luck	/lʊk/
door	/dɔr/
butter	/bʊtə/
begin	/bɪḡɪn/
later	/leɪtə/
no	/nəʊ/
stay	/steɪ/
hanging	/haŋɪn/
birthday	/bəθdeɪ/
bus	/bus/
door	/dur/
tomatoes	/tɒmaːtəʊs/
potatoes	/pʌteɪtəʊs/
honour	/ɒnə/

The use of phonetic transcript has enabled this candidate to differentiate very clearly between the speakers. Without this system he would be reduced to saying things like 'The Bolton accent has much longer vowels.' This is far too vague to be of any linguistic value: precision is all when discussing vowels. It is far more helpful, in this case, to say 'Whereas the Salford speaker has the pure vowel /ʊ/, the Bolton speaker has the diphthongised vowel /ʊə/.'

If you has to ask you ain't got it: rhythm

Many projects are written about songs, the analysis of which inevitably leads to discussion of rhythm: weak candidates waffle about a song being 'rhythmic' and 'lines being drawn out'. The candidate quoted below has ensured that she is rigorous by looking at stress and syllabic structure. She has also used phonetics to clarify how the lines are sung.

Rhythm

Rhythm plays an important part in the way a song appeals to its audience, but its analysis depends largely upon its stress and syllabic structure.

In song writing rules can be broken; words can be 'moulded' to fit the rhythm or mispronounced to fit the rhyme. Also music can be written to suit the lyrics. One can often tell by the use of lexis and rhyme, whether the music or the lyrics was written first. It was the case with many songs of the 1960s that the music was written first and the lyrics were made to 'fit', hence the occurrence and in fact re-occurrence of cliché and metaphorical language.

One usually finds that the songs containing the simpler lexis have a steadier rhythm. This is the case with the songs chosen for this section of the project. Both songs have a steady rhythm, but when the lexis is written on paper one wouldn't think that this was the case as the lines are of unequal length in terms of the number of syllables that they contain. This comes back to an earlier point I made about 'words being moulded to fit the lyrics'.

For example, Song 1, Verse 1:

> As I walk this land of broken dreams, (9)
> I have visions of many things, (8)
> And happiness is just an illusion (10)
> Filled with sadness and confusion (8)

(The numbers in the brackets indicate the number of syllables in each line.)

Lines of random length are not very easily set to a 'fixed' rhythm, so to make things easier the verse is pronounced thus

> 'As I walked this land of broken /drɪ//ɪmz/ (10)
> I have visions of /ə/ many /θɪ/ɪŋz/ (10)
> And happiness is just an illusion (10)
> Filled with sadness and confus- /ə//ən/ (9)

As you can see, certain vowels have been diphthongised i.e. (/drɪmz/ becomes /drɪ//ɪmz/). Now the first three lines are decasyllabic and fit into the rhythm. The last line has only nine syllables, but the introductory 'Now' which starts the chorus each time makes up the tenth.

It is worth mentioning, perhaps, that in the first draft this candidate found this aspect of analysis difficult. Here is her first attempt at analysis:

In this first verse, the first line has nine syllables, the second is octosyllabic, as is the last, and the third is decasyllabic. Lines of random length are much more complex and cannot be easily set to music. Therefore rules are broken and the lines are put into much more simple form. This is where the steady rhythm enters. The verse therefore is pronounced thus:

> As I walk this land broken dre-eams
> I have visions of many thi-ings
> And happiness is just an illusion
> Filled with sadness and con-fu-usion

The first three lines become decasyllabic lines, due to lengthened vowels. The last line has nine syllables, which leads into the chorus which always begins 'Now...' This could, of course be making up the extra vowel, as the line containing nine syllables runs straight into the 'Now'.

No-one expects you to get everything right at first or ever, unaided. It is vital that you are self-critical and listen to advice, though!

Can you manage your grammar?

Where weak candidates go wrong here is by feeling that they must include some comment about sentence structure or parts of speech, but being, in fact, incapable of saying anything constructive. It is pointless saying 'verbs include the future tense and the past tense: future "there would be" and past "you lived", "it struck him"'. What does this prove? Why did the writer employ these tenses? Was the past gaining detachment, the future predicting, or what? The 'whats' of language are of limited value unless you make some intelligent remarks about the 'whys'.

Similarly, it is of no value to state that 'There are 73 simple, 22 compound and 7 complex sentences in this extract' or 'Many of the sentences are long and hard.' What does this mean? And what does this preponderance of simple sentences tell us about audience? Much more sensible is the following approach:

As children of the age of approximately five get confused if word order other than standard is used, adjectival and adverbial phrases are not common in the programme. This is because they would affect standard word order.

Sentences are mainly simple and compound. Simple sentences, for example 'Now have a look inside', 'You could use one of those um clothes drying racks.'

The compound sentences often use the simplest conjunction 'and'. Examples: 'And then I stuck bits of material for curtains, and here is the door and it's got a handle'; 'A piece of cardboard is stuck here to make an upstairs and a downstairs and the window and door have been cut in.'

There are very few complex sentences such as 'There's a tasty looking carrot. It wouldn't be though because this carrot is made out of cardboard and paper.'

About an even number of short and long sentences are used. Some long sentences are often still simple.

The programme contains sentences that are mostly statements, informing the audience. There are only a few commands, imperative ones, for example, 'Have a look at these children playing' and 'Now have a look inside.'

There are also polite commands, for example, 'You could have a go at making this' and 'Perhaps you could make a toy shop for your toys.'

The few imperatives and questions are for the child's involvement in the programme, but the tone is predominantly informative.

This says a good deal about structures: their complexity, function and type. The same candidate deals in a helpful way with parts of speech:

Lots of nouns are used, mainly concrete nouns. These often refer to objects shown and used in the programme. For example, 'Big Ted has got cushions and even a box television, books, cup and saucer.'

Plenty of adjectives are present, mostly simple ones such as in 'Put a big curtain over the top of it all', 'This bit is a great big box.' The adjectives are informative.

There are lots of verbs, for example, 'Look at these children playing,' as lots of action takes place in the programme.

Here the writer is not merely feature-spotting: she is able to label what is there in order to explicate why it is there.

Is the knowledge displayed relevant?

A warning note: do resist the temptation to add in anything linguistic that you happen to know in a desperate bid to get some linguistic-knowledge marks. It has to be relevant. If the purpose of the project is to compare two three-year-olds' language development, it is pointless to explain all the stages they've already gone through. In the first place, it is irrelevant; in the second place it looks like teacher's notes! You ought to be utilising your linguistic knowledge to shed light on your data, not wheeling out one more time half of an essay that once got you a good mark. Such stuff is useless padding and easily spotted as such by a marker.

Structure

Introductions

What about the rest of the marks? Something which is vital to a project is a good structure and line of argument. One of the most disastrous failures for a project is signalled by its looking and reading like an essay.

Your project will have an introduction in which you clarify for the reader what your hypothesis is and how you are going to test it. A good project ought, as we have said, to be seeking to discover something, not merely describing. Here is an introduction which, though brief, does its job:

Introduction

My aim in this project was to ascertain whether or not the language of romantic fiction differs in different women's magazines, and having defined the differences between them, I chose the three magazines which closely fitted my aims. The magazines I chose covered the range of women's papers – 'Cosmopolitan', 'Woman's Own' and 'The People's Friend'.

The Magazines

'Cosmopolitan' is published monthly. It is a glossy magazine, around two hundred pages in length. The style of the magazine tends to attract well educated readers and has a variety of features and articles which are of general interest, not purely for its female readers. 'Cosmopolitan' contains several fictional stories in each issue, which do not necessarily have happy endings, nor are they typical 'boy meets girl' romances as some magazine stories tend to be.

'Woman's Own', as its name suggests, is a magazine mostly for women. This weekly magazine has cookery articles and clothes features as well as articles of general interest. 'Woman's Own' features both weekly serials and short stories. The serials tend to be serialised books rather than stories written especially for the magazine, such as the novels 'Lace' or 'The Thorn Birds'. The short stories are generally light romantic fiction, and they would usually have happy endings.

'The People's Friend' is a Scottish magazine available throughout England. The style of the magazine tends to appeal to older ladies, containing clothes patterns and recipes every week. It has both serials and short stories. The serials tend to have a Scottish flavour and the short stories are light, romantic fiction which always have happy endings. 'The People's Friend' is published weekly.

Method

I took each magazine and read the short stories which I had chosen. Then I gave each story a full linguistic analysis, as for literary material.

Your introduction sets the tone for the test of your project. If it is derivative (i.e. reads as if it's been copied from a book), narrative or descriptive, it is setting the wrong tone. Look at this example and see if you agree with my remarks:

Introduction

The existence of the English language as a separate idiom began when Germanic tribes had occupied all the lowlands of Great Britain. When the invasions from the continent were discontinued, the settlers in their new homes were cut off from their continental relations which was an imperative condition of linguistic unity. The historical records of English do not go so far back as this, for the oldest written texts in the English Language (in Anglo Saxon) date from about 700 and are thus removed by three centuries from the beginnings of the language. Comparative philology is able to tell us something about the manner in which the ancestors of these settlers spoke centuries before that period, and to sketch the pre-historic development of what was to become the language of Chaucer and of Shakespeare. *copied*

There are more varieties of English in Britain than any other English speaking country. The diagram shows this and explains why this is the case. *point?*

The passages chosen to analyse are from Shakespeare's 'Hamlet', Jonathan Swift's 'Gulliver's Travels' and George Orwell's '1984', three very different books. *!!!*

The analysis hopes to show why these pieces are different and give the reader some idea of the change in language structures.

Narrative, derivative & largely irrelevant

As you will have noticed, the data used is secondary. This makes it doubly important that the project has an interesting and clear focus. This introduction does not encourage us to believe this project has that. To say that the writer 'hopes' to give the reader 'some idea' of the change in language does not augur well: you are not rewarded for diffidence! It may seem unkind to give examples of bad practice, but we hope by raking up forgotten disasters to avoid your going down the same blind alleys.

To prove the point that we don't expect brilliance on all fronts, take a look at another introduction and my comments on it. Yes, it has its limitations; parts of it are irrelevant and the style is nothing spectacular, but it has many virtues, too. It shows thought, it is not derivative, it clearly means well and is the beginning of a voyage of discovery. This represents a middle range C-grade candidate doing their best. Your personal best – whatever that may be – is as much as anyone can ask of you.

Introduction

When thinking of a project title I decided to do my project on changes in written language. I was going to use Shakespeare's writing to study, but decided against this, as Shakespeare's literary writing was not a 'natural' look at English from this period of time, as like any literary piece, it has been changed and perfected to make a classic piece of writing. **honest and clear**

I wanted writing from the nineteenth century that showed how most people would have used English. I decided to analyse the informal language that can be found in personal letters. Letters often express a style of writing that is the nearest to spoken language. When writing to somebody with whom you share a relationship, true feelings can be thought about and written down, as a permanent record of spoken-style English.

good point

I decided to use letters from the nineteenth century because this English is not too archaic, so that the lexis is totally different. I was not looking for the changes in spelling, which occurs in the seventeenth and eighteenth century, because the English language did not have a set mode. However I wanted to find differences between emotive language and how it is expressed, and the change in lexis and actual sentence structure. I expected to find some of the lexis to be different in context than it is today.

For example, the word 'nice' in the English language today is one of the most meaningless and corrupted words. We can use it for a variety of objects, like 'the nice girl', 'the nice house', 'the nice little business' and 'a nice sum of money'. The word 'nice' almost becomes an approving noise. However, nice was not always so vague, and its meaning has undergone drastic changes. It derives from the Latin word nescius, which means 'ignorant'. In 1560 it meant foolish, stupid, in 1606 it was used to mean wanton and also in the sixteenth century it was sometimes used to signify rare or strange, difficult to please, fastidious and thus precise or particular.

rather irrelevant

By analysing letters rather than literature we may also find more colloquial language, and it is more likely to find slang, blasphemy and possibly swearing, since letter writing is a natural intimate form of communication and it is spontaneous and tells us a lot about how people spoke.

a little repetitious

I have chosen to analyse two letters from the nineteenth century, and two letters from the early twentieth century. I will be looking for unusual sentence structures, colloquial lexis and also the individual style of writing people possess.

good

In my study of informal English I will be studying letters written by men, both of whom are writing to two different people, and so their style of writing can be seen to change according to audience. By using men, rather than men and women, we can narrow the reasons for language change, as men and women do tend to write in different styles.

sensible and genuine if not scintillating!

Some candidates don't feel confident enough to tackle an entirely new field but at least have the sense to put the old wine in new bottles. An introduction can point out to the reader what the 'angle' is:

Hypothesis

My hypothesis is that I would expect the child from the middle class family to be ahead of the child from the working class family in stages of language acquisition. I would also expect to find that she has a wider vocabulary. The reason for this difference would be that her parents would probably be better educated and therefore they would have a much more varied lexis and they would talk to her in a more adult way using this wide lexis.

Method

I took a child from a working class family and taped her talking while playing. I then took a child from a middle class family of the same age and taped her also at play. These two children were chosen because they have only one major difference and that is that they belong to a different class.

Conclusions

Following the introduction, most projects have the 'sandwich filling' – very often of detailed analysis. It is important that these analyses are somehow brought together at the end rather than standing in splendid isolation. The industrious and sensible candidate whose introduction we read earlier worked through her four analyses and then wrote a fair conclusion:

When I first analysed the two letters by John Keats I was surprised at the sophisticated lexis that was used. Even today, formal letters written to people who we do not know would not contain the sort of lexis that Keats' letters did. Keats was writing to a good friend, Benjamin Bailey, and his girlfriend Fanny Brawne, so this elaborate lexis was quite unusual.

The letters written by 'Ed' were totally different and did not contain the formal, sophisticated tone of Keats' letters. Ed's writing was much more colloquial and chatty. The most striking feature I found about the four letters I analysed was that of the two, Ed seemed to be in the most depressive situation, being at war, and despite this, Ed's letter was far more chatty and colloquial than Keats'.

The different styles of writing that Keats and Ed possess were quite dramatic. Keats' writing was definitely longer in quantity and contained a lot of hyperbolic and emotive lexis. Ed's writing however was a lot shorter in length, had a lot of abbreviated words, and was generally more colloquial and friendly.

It could be said that if Keats' writing is a good, fair look at typical written English of the nineteenth century, then we could say that letter writing may have been more of an 'art' or hobby, and this elaborate lexis may not have been a natural form of spoken language of this period. It seems that Keats has taken a lot of care and time when writing his letters, and his ideas in his writing to Fanny about his love for her are very expressive and provoke emotion:

'But if you fully love me, though there may be some fire, 'twill not be more than we can bear when moistened and bedewed with pleasures'.

We could say that Ed's writing is more like the style of letter writing we would read today. It contains the same sort of friendliness and colloquialism that is used today. Ed seems to use phrases that were probably popular at the time he writes the letter. 'Wind up': he uses this expression in both his letter to Jess and his mother. Ed also uses the word 'absolutely' which was also a popular word in this period. Today certain phrases and words are popular for limited periods, and then they often die out. It seems that the word 'absolutely' may have been an example of this.

Ed's writing is generally more factual than Keats' letters, which tend to contain more statements, especially in his letter to Fanny.

Keats' writing was definitely more philosophical and hyperbolic, and contained less factual information even though the letters are longer than Ed's.

It is a little repetitive and the style is nothing remarkable but it does round the project off.

Some conclusions, of course, are rather too much to believe from the data given. On the basis of two children only, one candidate's assertion that 'The hypothesis that a middle class child would acquire language more rapidly than a child of the working class is correct and must be accepted' is not really on, is it? Tact and diplomacy do matter: don't fail to mention what your project has proved but don't exaggerate its importance.

It can be very difficult to avoid being repetitive in conclusions. If you have chosen to analyse two programmes/stories/poems to see how they are similar and how they are different you have little choice but to do each on its own and then the two together. A very talented candidate might manage to discuss both at once, in detail, and also make general points. However, this would be difficult and no reasonable marker would object to your doing it the other way – as the following one has:

A comparison of the radio programme and the television programme

When comparing the two programmes, the most obvious difference is that the television programme makes full use of visual aids, which the radio programme cannot use. The television programme is based on the audience <u>watching</u> what is going on. It doesn't give instructions to make the audience join in. The contents of the programme rely on the audience watching the screen. Firstly there is a film. The audience are instructed to '<u>Have a look</u> at these children playing.' If the film is on the screen, a song is sung by the narrator. The words of the song correspond to certain actions in the film.

Features in the studio use visual aids, which are talked about and pointed to. Songs are sung and actions to go with them are performed by the narrators. For example, the song about sailing has the man pictured in a pretend ship.

When the second film is watched, there are only occasional words from the narrator. This is an example of the programme's reliance on the audience watching the screen. The whole of the programme would be hard to understand without the visual side.

The lexis is slightly more complicated and colloquial. The speech is also more chatty, less carefully spoken and less clear than the radio programmes. This is because the visual side makes it easier to understand.

The radio programme concentrates on getting the audience to join in, as they have nothing to watch to keep them interested. Obviously, the radio programme has no films like in 'Playschool' but it does have songs sung by the narrators. The difference is the songs on the radio include parts for the audience to join in with.

The television programme makes full use of the visual side, while the radio makes full use of sound effects. The noises animals make are used instead of pictures of animals, short tunes signal the beginning or the end of a piece in the programme, whereas on the television, the changes in the topics can be seen.

Both programmes have a male and a female narrator. In the radio programme, different sections appear to be spoken by Tony and Janet. This gives the audience a change of voice to listen to and helps distinguish between the different areas in the programme.

My Conclusion

The radio programme appears to have more of an educational element to it, because of the 'teacher like' speech and instructions and the clearness of the speech.

Although both radio and television programmes contain many different sections such as songs, stories, etc. in the short time they are on, the radio stays to the theme of the farm. I favour this, because I think once the children get used to the theme of the programme, they may be able to relate some of their own knowledge of farms, either from television or real life experiences, to the programme. If they have no idea what a farm is about, they should have some knowledge by the end of the programme. I also think the radio programme is more stimulating for the children, because of the way they are made to join in.

Sarah's response backs up some of what I've said. She was mostly interested in the parts of 'Playschool' that showed some involvement for the audience. They were not actually allowed to join in there and then, but the ideas were there for them to use afterwards. The least appealing parts were the footages of film. These had very little narrated parts. The only thing to do was watch. Perhaps the topic of the film (children playing) was not very interesting to the audience.

Of the two, the radio programme was obviously the one which Sarah preferred. I think this is because the programme got the audience to join in.

I would conclude that the radio programme fulfils its aim better than the television programme. It succeeds in entertaining and involving the *audience throughout. I think the audience like being involved in the programme and 'Playschool' did not provide much involvement.*

Keep your conclusion brief: one side of A4 typed ought to be enough.

The best candidates combine linguistic knowledge, a sense of direction in their writing and good style. A grade A conclusion will be stylishly expressed: 'Women no longer need to be carried off to harems by darkly handsome sheikhs' (in reference to the world of women's magazines). Such a conclusion will also offer genuine insights into language, will make suggestions and display perception:

There are conclusions already made in each section of the project, so there is little point in repeating how the accents and dialects of Bolton and Salford differ.

The project has proved that, within six miles, two very different accents exist. Also, there is a marked dialectal variation.

The origins of the two areas may provide an explanation as to why there are such differences.

Bolton was one of the main centres of the industrial revolution, in particular the cotton industry. During this period many people will have migrated into Bolton from the surrounding countryside. These people perhaps had broad accents which were picked up and spread around the town.

Salford has always held an important position on the outskirts of Manchester, and at the head of the Manchester Ship Canal. It has perhaps been influenced by Merseyside or the Irish from the canal, or by the traders and immigrants who came into Manchester, again during the Industrial Revolution.

These origins may appear to be too recent to be valid reasons for the development of regional accents. Some may argue that accents and dialects have taken more than one hundred and fifty to two hundred years to develop. Personally, I think that the Industrial Revolution has had a great deal to do with causing regional variations. Before this time, the population was much more spread around the country in very small settlements. An industry developed, towns and cities grew up and various separate regions and then conurbations could be identified. With this, a common accent and dialect may have developed, and even if there were other causes, this seems to have been a very important one.

Another theory is that of 'mee-mawing'. This is, during the Industrial Revolution, Bolton was one of the main centres. Therefore many people would work in the mills and would have to lip-read. To make themselves understood, they would have to exaggerate vowel sounds, and thus the accent would develop.

Hopefully, the work in this project has illustrated to you the variations in Salford and Bolton language.

I would like to thank both the subjects for their co-operation, and also my English teachers for their help.

Notice that this very good candidate does not go over the same ground in his conclusion. He also feels relaxed and confident enough to adopt a slightly more personal tone. For example, he writes

Comparing the Salford and Bolton Accents: the Similarity

The title is not a mistake: I could only find one!

A strong enough candidate can show a little more personality than a mediocre one could. However, bringing your personality into a project can be a dangerous thing. If in doubt, do as the following candidate who ended her project in a very clear, workmanlike way. It may not be exciting to read, but it's obviously intelligent and thorough!

Summary of results

Roman Catholic	Mormon
1 There is only one speaker through the sermon, the priest.	1 There can be a number of people speaking, which can be any of the members, not necessarily the bishop.
2 The sermon is more formal as it has been prepared.	2 The service is slightly informal as the speakers are sharing their own personal testimonies.
3 The priest uses formal modes of address but none which show any level of intimacy with any member of the congregation.	3 The speakers use formal modes of address but show intimacy with the congregation as specific names are used.
4 Uses the distinction between first and second person to create a sense of hierarchy.	4 There are frequent first person references as they are talking about personal experiences. Use of the third person plural only when the speaker is referring to the time when she wasn't a Mormon: she is distancing herself.

5 There is a progression from abstract nouns, when the priest begins by giving his spiritual message, to concrete nouns, as he tells the congregation how they should apply the message to their lives.

6 There is the use of proper nouns for those who are considered to be holy figures of worship.

7 There is a progression from active verbs in the syntactic sense but not the semantic sense, towards slightly more active nouns. The pattern is not as distinct as those found previously, e.g. nouns.

8 Lexis begins formal and ends slightly colloquial.

9 Speech is prepared, therefore it will be more formal, fluent and clear.

10 Pauses are planned for effect.

11 As the speech has been prepared, rhetorical questions occur.

12 The priest doesn't use any biblical quotations.

5 There is no progression from concrete nouns when the speaker is talking of personal experiences to abstract when she is relating her previous experience to how she feels now she is a member.

6 The proper nouns which are used are the names of the speakers' family.

7 There is a distinct progression from active verbs, when relating everyday experiences, to stative verbs to convey the spiritual level she has reached through her experiences.

8 Lexis begins colloquial and becomes slightly more formal.

9 Speech is not prepared as the speakers are relating past experiences, therefore disfluency will occur.

10 A lot of voiced and unvoiced pauses in this transcript.

11 No rhetorical questions.

12 The speakers use a lot of biblical quotations and back them up with one of their personal experiences that relate to them.

Conclusion

The language reflects the way in which the churches are organised, not simply in the kinds of language used but in the progressions which seem to occur within the extracts. All of which support the idea that the Roman Catholic sermon is more authoritarian and the Mormon services are egalitarian.

As any A-level language student knows, 'it ain't just what you say, it's the way that you say it': if your written style is unclear, vague or clumsy, if you can't spell for toffee or have no idea how to construct a sentence, it will have a decided impact upon your mark. Be prepared to re-draft your project till it says something reasonably original, says it clearly and says it correctly if not stylishly. The writer who handed in

> The results show that Sophie as a very good command of the english language. The non-fluency features show however, that although she is well advanced she still requires to think before talking some of the time. She does not have any more stages to learn

was doing her valid and original data a disservice.

Summary

In a nutshell, here are the thoughts which most often go through a marker's mind:

Scope/data

Am I reading something fresh?

Have they taken on too much?

Is this authentic?

Oh no? not TV ads again!

Crystal and Davie (or other textbook) chapter five one more time!

Structure

This proves nothing!

Why is this here?

I read this in the introduction (when reading the conclusion).

This is not what the data shows.

Knowledge

This is just a list.

Why use phonetic script if you can't get it right?

I recognise this but they don't admit sources.

They don't know an adverb from an adjective!

This transcription is as clear as mud.

Style

The teacher might at least have corrected all these spelling errors.

All these subheadings are boggling my mind!

The pie charts are very pretty but what do they prove?

Get to the point!

If this seems very negative, it is only to stop you making anyone think such things. Most of the examples included in this section are of good, not bad practice. Good luck!

Chapter 17
Language Investigation Under Exam Conditions

Just as the exams in English Language have moved away from a simplistic distinction between the literary and non-literary they have also blurred distinctions between 'coursework' and exam-based activities.

Whereas language investigation and original writing have, in the past, been perceived as activities requiring long gestation and much re-drafting, candidates now pursue these them in timed, controlled conditions. However, the skills are the same as discussed in the previous chapter; it's just that you are relieved of the responsibility of providing your own data.

A STUDENT'S GUIDE TO LANGUAGE INVESTIGATION EXAMS

In such an exam there are four key steps.

1   IDENTIFY what issues the material raises, CATEGORISING its element.

2   SELECT the focus(es) you want and the material that will be most relevant.

3   ANALYSE the material in some detail.

4   EXPAND from the specific, AMPLIFYING points about language topics and underpinning knowledge.

WHAT YOU NEED TO PROVE IN EACH OF THESE STEPS

1   That you know enough to see the possibilities of the material.
Consider the levels of language. Is there more to be said about sound, lexis or grammar for example? You could also consider what the material conveys about language and society issues like class and gender, or language-change ones like correctness and neologisms.

2   **That you can select on a rational basis and categorise in a linguistic way.**
For this you will need to prioritise the significant from the less significant rather than describing everything. Don't waste time re-writing huge lists: instead cut and paste, and annotate given data. You could also consider presenting findings diagrammatically.

3   **That you can go into a focused, detailed discussion using the correct terminology**.
Also that you can pursue a line of argument.

4   **That you can see the underlying importance of things.**
This necessitates reading between the lines and using your background knowledge, of Bruner, Bernstein or the way language is structured, for example.

Identification and selection are crucial steps toward good, detailed analysis but cannot be an end in themselves. Analysis needs to be rigorous and relevant and the best candidates will certainly link the microcosm to the macrocosm!

HOW TO PRESENT YOUR INVESTIGATION

Not as an essay, is the most vital thing to remember.

Start by clarifying what your assumption or question is. If you are not clear about your focus of interest the rest will inevitably be a shambles. You needn't limit yourself to one hypothesis but too many will make the focus diffuse. Two or three are probably the optimum.

Then you want a meaty but interestingly presented evidence and analysis section drawing on skills you've developed through other chapters of this book. Remember that much useful analysis is quantitative. Mean length of utterance; ratio of non-standard grammar and so on are far better communicated in bar charts or pie charts than in prose. Use continuous prose only where it is the best channel for communicating your ideas. This doesn't mean random jottings and notes are acceptable; they're not, because they won't seem coherent or developed.

Qualitative analysis is valid, too. You may feel summative statements are best made in sentences. Do consider a brief list of findings or conclusions. Subheadings are often poorly used but can break a text up and section it clearly.

At the end you may not need a conclusion; indeed given the time available to you it might seem impossible to reach any. You could instead use a sub-heading like 'Issues Arising' to indicate what you feel could be further explored. Again, consider using flow charts or spider diagrams if they would serve your purpose.

Many of the skills for an investigation exam are those you will have developed during a language course. The analysis of discourse, for example, which we discussed in Chapter 4, is likely to be of use. A firm grasp of a working technical terminology is vital, too. Most importantly of all, **show an ability to see how every language choice has a significance of which you have an informed knowledge**.

MATERIALS YOU MIGHT USE TO HONE YOUR SKILLS

....

ACTIVITY

Data from previous candidates' language coursework projects are an immediate and fruitful source. In pairs look at any stretch of data and ask yourselves the following questions.

Stage One: CATEGORISE

- What are its most striking aspects?
- Its context?
- Is it discourse? If so, most interesting interactively or idiolectically?
  Are participants of any 'Language and Society' interest?
  Gender? Region? Class? Status? Role?
  Or interesting in Language Change terms?
  Their age and thus preferred slang and code? Their preferred semantic fields?
  Or in Child Language Acquisition terms?
  Their stage of development?
  Carers' language? Evidence of Hallidayen functions?
  Or is the better focus the discourse itself? Non-fluency features?
  Turn taking and dominance?
  Topic drift and shift?
  Grice's Maxims? Remember: formality, domain, connotation.
- Its audience? e.g.
  Yellow Pages lists:
  Health clubs aimed at men or women?
  Nursing homes aimed at the elderly or their carers?
  Eating places appealing to the middle or working class?
  As you see, most investigation leads back to language and society!
- Its purpose?
  Persuasive is a firm favourite for exams.
  Using which techniques (terms)?
  Head or heart?
  Simple or subtle?
  Spoken or written?
- And so back to CONTEXT!

Health warning

When categorising, beware of doing so by life as opposed to language focus. Categorising bands by musical style uses extraneous, irrelevant knowledge. Far better to consider why bands of the 50s had cosy, family

names and those of the 80s anarchic ones. Linguists need to explore connotations not merely denotations.

••

Practice data

••

ACTIVITY ◼️◗ 💬

Three follow some specific examples of our students' data. In pairs, consider the two speakers below. Both are Pakistani but their ages are different. Consider whether you could have told us that and whether you can tell which is the younger man. Quickly go through Stage One of the process, deciding what avenues of exploration are possible in relation to this transcript.

••

TRANSCRIPTION A
(65-year-old male)

I came in this country in nineteen fifty seven

I learn this English in my college in Pakistan Because that was a compulsory subject

I use English when I go with er English people

Well the children who born in this country they they can speak English best (.3) who go in the school (.) and in this country

Well if you want to live in this country you must learn the English (.2) you must have a good English Well it's a easy for the child who born in this country because he playing with the children and he can learn the English just like the English boys children

Well it is a easy to learn (.) yes

Eh (.) what do you mean office of his just a minute where's stop off his trolley

OK I mean that er (.2) pissed off

Footy footy footy

This one is a mean (.) get off pissed off get off yes

What's that chap crap (.) mean bad crap mean bad

Footy footy (.3) these are only (.) you know (.) these youngsters (.)

TRANSCRIPTION B
(17-year-old male)

Er seven years ago (.) I don't exactly remember the date I think its nineteeen eighty… seven eighty eight

Well why I learnt it because its compulsory since I was only ten then (.) aand I learnt it at er a language centre first I went there for seven months and from there I went to second years in the er primary school in the fourth year

(,) Well erm Id use (.) English (.) when I HAVE to probably when I'm speaking to someone else in English at college or somewhere I'd prioritise Urdu since I have a better understanding of it

Er (.2) I think it would be people who got degrees in Pakistan (.) who came here (.) and improved their English here formally because erm (.) I think they have a better vocabulary and a word order and they makes less grammatical mistakes since grammar in there has to be learnt by heart rather than here its just taught you just take it as it is and learn it

Erm (.) I don't know whether I speak good English or not but people say erm in contrast in my situation since I only came seven years ago which is quite a long time I think I speak good English

(.) Er yes Id say that because it only took me seven months to get the basics

Once you've identified your linguistic avenues of exploration, you need to select several which are:

Manageable in terms of scope and time

Feasible in terms of your knowledge and skills

Presentable quantitatively and qualitatively

Useable as springboards to an amplification of your ideas.

Stage Two: SELECT AND CLASSIFY

....

ACTIVITY 🌚 💬

Still in your pairs, select two key focuses and discuss the features that will help you explore them. What can be usefully quantified? These aspects can be dealt with in this section of your investigation. Some possibilities with this particular data include:

Mean length of utterance

Ratio of non-standard usage

Examples of Bernstein's Restricted and Elaborated codes

Proportion of non-fluency features of participants.

Take twenty minutes and individually decide how best to present the evidence under these categories. Now compare notes and decide which of you seems to have communicated more clearly and shed more light.

....

Compare your first efforts with those of two of our students. What if anything could you learn from their work and which of the two do you consider more useful?

Sarah

Grammatical Mistakes

The number of mistakes found within both transcripts are shown in the graph below.

Number of grammatical mistakes

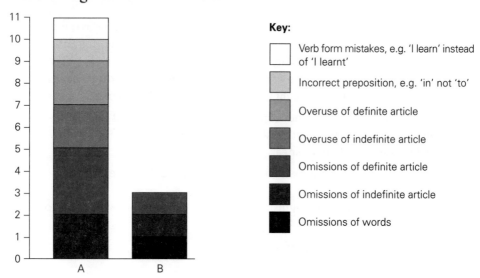

Key:

☐ Verb form mistakes, e.g. 'I learn' instead of 'I learnt'

▨ Incorrect preposition, e.g. 'in' not 'to'

▨ Overuse of definite article

▨ Overuse of indefinite article

▨ Omissions of definite article

▨ Omissions of indefinite article

■ Omissions of words

Kate

1 Total word count in whole conversation

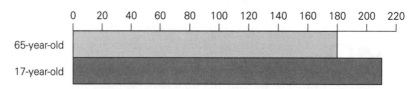

2 Mean length of utterance (not including fillers)

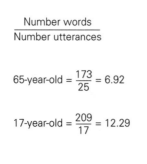

$$\frac{\text{Number words}}{\text{Number utterances}}$$

$$\text{65-year-old} = \frac{173}{25} = 6.92$$

$$\text{17-year-old} = \frac{209}{17} = 12.29$$

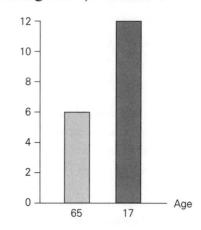

3 Number of fillers

	Fillers	% of total coversation	
65-year-old	6	$\frac{180}{6} = 30$	3.33%
17-year-old	10	$\frac{210}{10} = 21$	4.76%

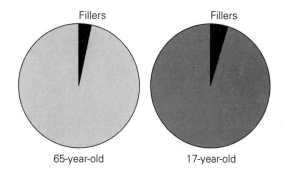

4 Number of pauses

	1 sec	2 sec	3 sec
65-year-old	8	2	2
17-year-old	10	1	0

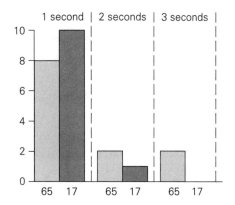

5 Number of non–standard features

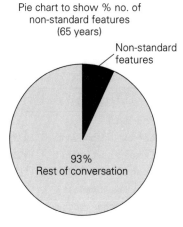

Pie chart to show % no. of non-standard features (65 years)

Non-standard features

93% Rest of conversation

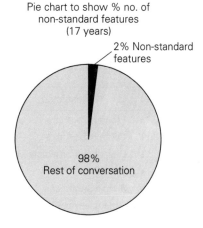

Pie chart to show % no. of non-standard features (17 years)

2% Non-standard features

98% Rest of conversation

As is probably apparent, Kate is very good at this sort of thing. You will see much more of her methodology.

Stage Three: DETAILED ANALYSIS

At this point you need to deepen your analysis. You need to return to the aspects you have so far explored. Have you given detailed examples of all the linguistic phenomena? For example, have you exemplified the difference between a filler and a pause in non-fluency features? Have you used linguistic terms appropriately and accurately – for example, detailing different non-standard features like omission of the indefinite article, or unmarked past tense. If you are satisfied that the detail and labelling are in place, are there other features that you have failed to discuss at all? When you are confident that you have covered sufficient ground sufficiently accurately, move on to summarising the significance of these features. What do they indicate about these language-users? Their background? First language? Education? Ensure that you raise these issues in clear prose and give evidence for all of your assertions. Complete your analysis section in not more than 45 minutes.

Now compare it with Kate's, who went on to get 80/80 in the exam. Note how she develops her point and gives a detailed breakdown of non-standard features.

Kate 2

Pie chart to show the % no. of the different non-standard features (65 years)

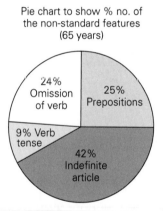

Pie chart to show % no. of the non-standard features (65 years)

- 24% Omission of verb
- 25% Prepositions
- 9% Verb tense
- 42% Indefinite article

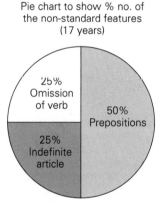

Pie chart to show % no. of the non-standard features (17 years)

- 25% Omission of verb
- 50% Prepositions
- 25% Indefinite article

7. Features of Bernstein's Restricted + Elaborated Code

Restricted	Elaborated
• Pronoun 'we' 'they'	✸ • Pronoun 'I'
• Context Bound	✸ • Context independent
• Describes Immediate situation	✸ • Explores past + future
• Anecdotal	• Generalisation abstract
• Simple sentences	• Complex sentences
• Little use modifiers	• Greater range modifiers
• Simple vocab.	• Latinate vocab.

If you placed examples from each speaker against each feature ✸ here this would have been more useful.

- The 65-year-old shows more tendency to use restricted code.
- The 17-year-old shows more tendency to use elaborated code.
- However, both use features from both codes.

You will notice from the marker's notes that even this candidate is not perfect; perfection is not required especially in exam circumstances!

What is required is a sense that the investigation is going somewhere; that you have identified useful avenues to explore and that you have presented detailed and linguistic evidence to back your ideas. Before you move on to the final stage, check that what you have written so far is relevant, accurate and well-presented.

Stage Four: AMPLIFICATION

··

ACTIVITY ▣ ▨

Return to your colleague and jointly make notes on issues arising and links across your data. Are you dealing broadly here –

with how language works: sound effects; lexical choices; structural choices linking to your analytical skills developed in stylistics work but deepening and refining them,

OR

with topic-related knowledge such as how language reflects society, looking at how language choice reflects individuality or group membership,

OR

with how language changes, looking at not only how words and structures are developed and borrowed over time and space but also how they are a reflection of their time culturally,

OR

with how language is acquired and used by children and how this impacts on our understanding of adult forms and the nature of language?

··

The Pakistani male data could be approached from at least three of the above directions.

> Non-standard useage could be analysed lexically and structurally.

> Status ascribed to non-standard language could be discussed and reasons suggested for why it is used by some speech communities.

> The critical learning period for the acquisition of grammar and the function of the LAD (Language Acquisition Device, see below) could be offered as an explanation for these differences.

A very ambitious candidate like the one we've quoted covered all this and added a discussion of Bernstein's codes, but remember: it is not necessary to discuss everything but it is important to do what you do focus on well. Amplification demands two abilities: to make connections and to go into depth.

Have a look at some of the final section of our model answer.

Kate 8

<u>General overview of the Data</u>

Even to a non-linguist, it is obvious that the 17-year-old speaker (B) is more fluent in English and has a better understanding of the language than the 65-year-old, speaker (A).

<u>Why have these conclusions been made?</u>

Looking at the total word count, B says 210 words as opposed to A who says 30 words fewer. This evidence may seem trivial until the mean length of utterance is considered. Each utterance of B's, on average, is almost twice as long as A's average. This indicates that B is more fluent than A.

<u>What does the study of Non-Standard features tell us?</u>

Non-standard features (NSF) means what its name implies. It is when something varies from the accepted norm — i.e. Standard English. NSF are usually associated with grammar.

7% of A's conversation has NSF in it whereas only 2% of B's speech involves NSF.

Some people believe that NSF are 'wrong' and indicate lack of education whereas others associate it with dialect.

However, these beliefs are associated with speakers whose first language is English. In this investigation we are considering people whose first language is Urdu and whose second language is English.

Because of this, the number of NSF in the speaker's conversation could perhaps imply the level of knowledge and understanding of the English language.

<u>Language acquisition</u>

However, these points are less significant than the fact that speaker B began learning English at an early age, whereas A was not exposed to English in his infancy.

Nativists such as Chomsky believe that children are born with an innate capacity for language development: that the human being is in some way structured towards the development of language, so that when a child is exposed to language, certain language-structuring principles automatically begin to operate. The model that is used to indicate what is going on is called the Language Acquisition Device (LAD).

A note on timing

If you are doing a Language Investigation exam as part of the NEAB A-level in English Language we suggest you divide the two and a half hours as follows:

30 minutes: select task and survey the material. Get a clear sense of its possibilities and categories.

45 minutes: write the meat in the sandwich. First classify the quantitative elements and present them clearly then deepen your analysis, identifying the significance of your selected language features and phenomena.

10 minutes: check your middle section. Is there a clarity of focus and presentation? Add subheads and diagrams if need be.

45 minutes: write your amplification.

10 minutes: re-read the lot! Have you completed all the stages, CATEGORISE, SELECT and CLASSIFY, ANALYSE, AMPLIFY as well as you can?

Having looked at one set of data in some detail we would now like you to attempt all or some stages of an investigation with the following data. You could use any page of *Yellow Pages* for more of these lists. Health Clubs, florists, eating places; all have proved fertile ground for investigation data!

1 Words and Phrases of the Eighties

Brill	501's	HIV	Lean Cuisine
Interface	Yo	High fibre	Dustbin of history
E Number	Lager lout	Blackadder	Giro
Fax	Young fogey	New man	Polyunsaturates
FTSE–100	Networking	Enterprise Zone	Infrastructure
Foodie	I've been clamped	NIMBY	Vorsprung durch
North South divide	User friendly	State of the art	technick
XR3i	Bimbo	Quality of life	Semtex
Hip hop	Loadsamoney	Loony left	Fossil fuel
Bad	Toyboy	Brat pack	Electronic tagging
Yuppy flu	Yuppy	Wrinkly	Cardboard City
AIDS	Dawn raid	Comic relief	Artificial intelligence
Naff off	Personal organiser	Crucial	First Grannie
MTV	Glasnost	Smart card	Wets
G.C.H.Q.	Computer virus	Niche marketing	Genetic engineering
SS-20	Big bang	Right on	Child abuse
Chill out	Tell Sid	Green	Walkabout
Glitterati	1992	Thirtysomething	Street cred
On yer bike!	Greenhouse effect	Hyper	Theme Park
Wicked	Ozone friendly	Nuclear free zone	Rustbelt
Sad	Chattering classes	Insider dealing	Televangelist
Filofax	Trivial Pursuit	Care in the	Dingo baby
Designer label	Artificial additive	community	Poll tax
Mega	Reaganomics	Bono	ECU
Go for it	OK Yah	Dream ticket	
Fast tracking	Compassion fatigue	Flexible friend	

A thought

If you are writing about Language Change, will you address how words have been formed as well as the fields of life they belong to? This will bring in analytical as well as topic-related skills.

2 Take-Away Food

(Selected extracts from *Yellow Pages*, Manchester North edition)

Adriana's Continental Sandwich Shop

Al-Fazal Kebab House

Andy's Hollywood Pizza Company

Asim Tandoori Centre

Babolli Pizza House

Barbara's Butty Shop

Bar-b-Q Land

Bent Burger, The

Betta Butties

Billy Bunter's

Bite to Eat

Bitz 'N' Pizzas

Butty Bar, The

Carol's Lunch Box

Carriageways Sandwich Shop

Cheng Yuen Kwan

Country Kitchen

Croissants Food Services

Crumbs

Da Mamia Mia

Dishy's Sandwich Bar

Eat your Heart Out

Fone-A-Feast

Gino's Dial-a-Pizza

Golden Moon

Goodies

Happy Valley Chinese Takeaway

Hungry Tums

Jade Garden

La Favorita

Mrs Muffin's Food Emporium

Munchers

Nip-In Butty Bar

Omar Sharif

Picnics

Pizza and Potato Factory, The

Raj-Mahal

Royton Tandoori Land

Rumble Tummies

Sandwich Express

Savouries

Scoffers Sandwich Bar

Silver River

Snacks 'N' Stuff

Spice of Life

Take A Break

Tandoori Nights

Tasty's Snax

Uppercrust Sandwich Bar

Wood's Speciality Sandwiches

Audience is an obvious option here but so is persuasive language. Niche marketing or what we have elsewhere called audiences within audiences is a good way to address both.

· ·

ACTIVITY ⊞ ▨

As a class, decide the audiences you will consider. You might consider class, or level of affluence; you might think about old people or their carers. Decide which homes are targeting which niches. Then analyse the texts to find how words, layout and selection of facts contribute to audience appeal.

· ·

Discourse

This often comes up as data in investigation exams.

Whichever specific example of discourse you are given you can approach it primarily as discourse, i.e. discussing how it follows the rules of spoken language, or you can use it as an example of children, middle-class women, gang members etc. showing what Skinner would call verbal behaviour. Most good investigators would deal with both, but which to give greater time to will depend very much upon the specific data.

Take a look at the following data.

CONVERSATION BETWEEN ANDREA AND SAM

ANDREA – Tell us who you are.
1. SAM – My name's Sam
ANDREA – Yeah

2. SAM – And I live at 33 Osborne Street, and I am seven years old and I like playing on my bike.
ANDREA – Is that because your Mummy and Daddy like cycling?

3. SAM – Yes
ANDREA – Hasn't your Mummy been to see the Queen, because of that?
SAM – Yes?
ANDREA – Why was that?

5. SAM – Er, because she is the world champion.
ANDREA – She's a what?

6. SAM – A world champion
ANDREA – What about your Daddy as well?

7. SAM – He's a cyclist too, both of my Dads, but they're not world champions like my Mum
ANDREA – Did she like seeing the Queen?

8. SAM – Yes.
ANDREA – What did she do?

9. SAM – She just got congratulated and saw erm all the flamingos.
ANDREA – Flamingos?

10. SAM – And animals, and I've got a new bike last night.
ANDREA – So are you going to be a world champion?

11. SAM – Yes.
ANDREA – Like Chris Boardman

12. SAM – Yes
ANDREA – What did he do this year?

12. SAM – Erm, in the Kellogs tour?
ANDREA – Yeah.

14. SAM – He packed in.
ANDREA – Why was that?

15. SAM – Because of the heat.
ANDREA – Heat?

16. SAM – He got a new helmet but erm the next day when it was the tour er, he felt sick so he packed in.
ANDREA – So he did not want to carry on?

17. SAM – No.
ANDREA – But he was only in France.

18. SAM – I know.

ANDREA – Are you going there?

19. SAM – Yeah.

ANDREA – So do you think that you'll get too hot?

20. SAM – I don't know because we will be at the seaside a lot.

ANDREA – Don't you like Batman?

21. SAM – Yeah but I don't know anything about him anymore.

ANDREA – What about when you are older, what do you want to be?

22. SAM – An archaeologist.

CONVERSATION BETWEEN AIMEE AND ANDREA

ANDREA – Have you seen one of these before?

1. AIMEE – Yeah

ANDREA – Where?

2. AIMEE – In your house.

ANDREA – So which school do you go to?

3. AIMEE – Ashfield Valley

ANDREA – What's it like?

4. AIMEE – Nice

ANDREA – Who is the there?

5. AIMEE – My friends

ANDREA – Is the one that comes to your house?

AIMEE – Mmm

ANDREA – What is she like?

6. AIMEE – She's nice.

ANDREA – Just nice?

AIMEE – Mmm

ANDREA – What do you play?

7. AIMEE – We play Mmm, we play that she's pretending that she's my dog.

ANDREA – How do you play that?

8. AIMEE – Just get Mmm a skipping rope and then put it round Natalie and then hold it.

ANDREA – Natalie, where does she live?

9. AIMEE – Don't know

ANDREA – You don't know?

10. AIMEE – I've forgot the street name.

ANDREA – So, is there a lot of boys at your school?

11. AIMEE – Don't know.

ANDREA – Do you not like boys?

12. AIMEE – No.

ANDREA – Why not?

13. AIMEE – They're too rough

ANDREA – Are you going to tell me a story?

AIMEE – Mmm

ANDREA – What about when you went on holiday with Lee and Emma?

14. AIMEE – We went on the beach, we went on the beach and we went in the water.

ANDREA – What was the water like, was it good?

15 AIMEE – It was cold.

ANDREA – What about your Mummy and Daddy?

16. AIMEE – Mmm… they stayed in the caravan.

ANDREA – What is that like?

17. AIMEE – Nice and we have bunkbeds.

ANDREA – How about what you want to be when you are older?

18. AIMEE – Be a nurse.

ANDREA – Why?

19. AIMEE – Cause I like it.

ANDREA – Do you?

ACTIVITY

Write down individually the two things that immediately occur to you.

Now compare notes with your colleague.

Possibilities for this data include:

Child language

Gender difference

Turntaking/discourse

Use of questions/interviewing techniques

The girl who collected this data intended to look at child language but decided that in this stretch of discourse the gender difference was actually more interesting. Would you agree? Her group members felt her interviewing technique was notable though she was unaware of it!

The point is that language is such a varied and complex business that there are always numerous options open to the exam candidate so don't be too limited in what you consider discussing or feel that some knowledge is worth more marks than other knowledge. The only basis on which to choose should be that there is enough to discuss and you have the necessary knowledge and terms to discuss it.

ACTIVITY

We will finish this section with two more stretches of discourse. We suggest that several individuals attack one in their own way using our method, then assess one another's work. Which avenue proved more fruitful? Can you perfect yours having read theirs? Perhaps you should now write your own guide to this exam?

OPTION 1

Transcription of interview by Sir David Frost of John Major

MAJOR: What they read in the newspapers, what they hear, about the concerns of everyday life. (½). They live in a world that is changing with bewildering speed (.) and they've seen most of the stable institutions, that they've known most of their lives for one reason or another under attack (.) The church, the Monarchy, the government (.) They've seen standards of behaviour that they've grown up with (½) in their eyes beginning to fall away. They're very worried about this insecurity (½), they want to know what is happening, what's happening to the rest of the world and why is it happening? And I found that concern echoed (½) in almost every part of the country over the last two or three years.

FROST: But at the same time in (½) if that's the origin of the campaign

MAJOR: mmm

FROST: and that's (½) er largely what you said in your speech and so on (½) it was soon (.) seen and perceived by people as a personal and sexual morality thing

MAJOR: No, it

FROST: But no, and so at the very least if it wasn't in your mind (1/2) then it was mis-interpreted (½) or as you bin quoted as saying off the record, highjacked by some of your (½) colleagues into becoming a personal morality

MAJOR: No

FROST: Michael

MAJOR: Well we're

FROST: Dear Michael, dear Michael Howard talked about the fact that we should look at New Jersey, where single parent (½) mothers er are infact

MAJOR: Well, well let

FROST: punished for having another child, for having another child

MAJOR: let me deal, let me deal directly with those points

FROST: So, it was hi. Either you started the sexual morality, or it was hijacked by other people.

MAJOR: Well, firstly it's much broader, it's much broader than that. And what

FROST: It was hijacked though wasn't it?

MAJOR: Well, I don't think it was hijacked, I think it has been misunderstood in some quarters and misinterpreted, but it wasn't I don't think hijacked in any sense. (.) The (½) Back to Basics policy (1½) i...t runs across the whole theme of government. Back to Basics in education, to make sure we deal with the basis of education. Children don't go to school for experience in my judgement, they go there to read, to write, to add-up and to learn decent values. (½) In terms of crime and punishment, (½) people think we've got out of kilter, the distinction between the criminal and the victim. I tend to agree, Michael Howard agrees.

OPTION 2

Interviewer: Miss. K. Williams (K)
Interviewee: Mr. F. Roberts (F)

F: Er (.) My name is Frank Roberts (1.0) un at the beginnin of the war a was eight years old (2.0) er I lived in Derker which is an estate a council Estate in Oldham (.) lived there since 1932 (1.0) er

K: Right erm (1.0) Did your parents tell you anything about the war (.) did they mention it to ya?

F: Erm well my Mother died (.) unfortunately died when I was five

K: ey

F: So eh (.) erm mi father worked in a local cotton mill just round the corner from ere (.) to Moss Inn (.) and er (3.0) I can't remember him telling me anything about (.) although he (.) must have done because he was in the first world war and er there was still the fear in men ere from that ere war which was only like twenty one years previous (.)

K: Yeah

F: So erm everyone saw the war memorial and er (1.0) er remembrance service every November Eleventh and er a lot like mi grandmother had her son killed and er she lived with it at the time

K: Yeah

F: So (1.0) er everyone was aware of war but er this new war which (.) which was coming er we were told about (.) say gas masks and things like that you see which (.) which put a sense of fear in us as little children

K: So (1.0) Did you feel excited about the war when it started or were you confused at all?

F: Well we were given some propaganda that the (.) er army was the er strongest army in Europe being told that er we believed it and er we thought we were safe actually that there was Poland and er France and er Britain against Germany

K: Yeah erm (1.0) Did you Father go to war?

EXAMPLES OF PRACTICE

Over the next few pages we have reproduced various sections referring to the words and phrases of the Eighties on page 318. See if you can tell whether each is an analysis or amplification, a survey or classification. We are not suggesting all these are best practice: all students are not geniuses. By the time you have got to here we hope every step of the exam and technique required will be tediously familiar!

Student's Work A

These I put into a graph so it could be seen more clearly the difference between the categories.

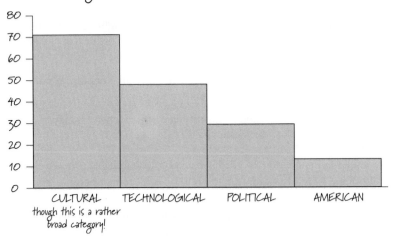

CULTURAL *though this is a rather broad category!*   TECHNOLOGICAL   POLITICAL   AMERICAN

Student's work B

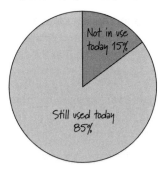

Not in use today 15%

Still used today 85%

Student's Work C

When looking at the list it shows that not all the words are understood by everyone. Many are only known to people in the business field or many are only known to the younger generation.

I wanted to then look at how many of the 144 words could be understood by a general audience, a young audience and a business audience.

	TALLY	TOTAL
Young	HHT HHT HHT IIII	19
Business	HHT HHT HHT HHT I	21
General	HHT HHT HHT HHT HHT	25

This shows there is a fairly equal amount of numbers between each group. It shows that only a small section of new words can be understood by everybody. It also shows that new words are being developed.

Student's Work D

Language Investigation — Language Change

Words and Phrases of the 80s — How does the language betray the attitude of the speaker

— What are the key influences in the 80s

— How have they been introduced/developed into society.

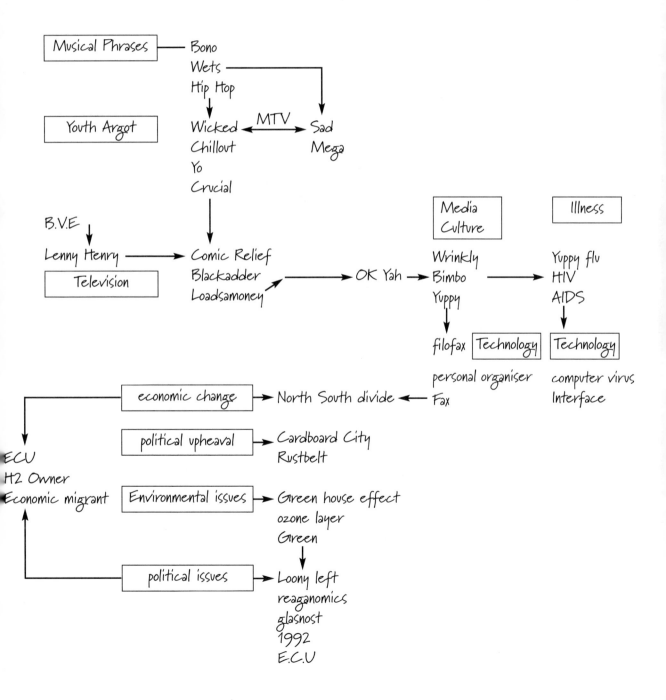

Formation of words associated with 80s Television

Blackadder — black — the colour + adder — a venomous type of snake.
— give the connotation of a dark + venomous character
cynical yet cunning. A compound

MTV — Music Television — made into an acronym for simple recognition

Loadsamoney — 2 words joined together by indefinite article, to make
a popular 80s phrase. Informal, speech-like word
unusual word order.

Tabloid Journalese — formation of phrases

Loony Left — Alliterative quality — gives amusing and dramatic quality +
connotation of neologism — newly coined phrase to describe left being
deranged. The socialist section of the Labour Party.
Word order with adjective in front of abstract noun give emphasis.

Yuppy — taken from 'yup' a variation of yes — by young business people.
denotation — young upwardly mobile professional — neologism as 'yuppies'
were not evident before the 1980's — informal + also harsh sounding.

Americanisms in Britains 80s phrases

Hip Hop — American slang adjective meaning fashionable
Word class shift to 'a noun' after compounding hip + hop together. Hip
Hop describes a new genre of music which crossed musical boundaries
— hop + was extremely fashionable in America — Hip

Yo — version of Black Vernacular English
used by young black americans to replace hello
interjection — used as a greeting

Chill Out — Black American English Word Class Shift
dictionary definition — sensation   feeling of coldness   Chill
relax   calm down
used to mean relax.

Bad — First seen in 80s as a Michael Jackson song — portrayed violent
gang of black American youths.
The black gangs then claimed the word so its class shifted +
mirrored the original meaning therefore Bad means good.

Wicked — another example of word class shift.
wicked was used by young black Americans to mean something
extremely good changed from extremely bad.

How did these Black American Words come to be key 80s words in Britain?

As the attitudes towards black people in America have always been a derogatory one, until more recent years, black people were always associated with being 'bad' and 'wicked' people. It is perhaps unsurprising that the Black youth argot also used these words but with different connotations so that bad meant good. This word shift phenomenon is also found in the youth argot of British children and youths. With the words 'sad' and to a certain extent 'mega'. Sad went from meaning upset and unhappy to stand for something or someone not up to standard.

The comedian Lenny Henry brought these words to the masses. Previously it was only the Black Youths in the inner city areas of London. He did a sketch of Dermot Wilkins, a Brixton black man who was 'wicked' and 'crucial' and as Henry's popularity grew more and more children copied his language and the Black American Youth Argot was transferred to the British Young Argot.

Candidate E

Semantic Fields of Key 80s phrases

MEDIA

Television — Blackadder — Situation comedy starring Rowan Atkinson, Tony Robinson +

Thirtysomething — American Situation Comedy for adult audience

Loadsamoney — 'Yuppie' characters created by Harry Enfield

MTV — 24hr music video, started in America

Tell Sid — Electricity privatisation advert slogan

Comic Relief — Comedy event on BBC fun for charity, started by Lenny Henry.

Music — Bono — Chosen name for vocalist or superstar

Hip Hop — Form of music originating from Black American ghettos.

Wets — Abbreviated name for Scottish band Wet Wet Wet.

Tabloid Journalese — Loony Left — term for the socialist wing of Labour Party

Yuppy — Name for young, upcoming business people

Lager lout — The stereotypical British hooligans

ost – European Currency Unit, a single european currency
Glasnost – Openness between Russia and the Western States, signalling ending of the cold war.

<u>Environment</u> – Greenhouse Effect – Used to describe the predicted warming of the Earth
Ozone Layer – Gaseous chemical protecting the earth from the Sun's rays

Candidate F

The media's attitude to the 80s Decade

The British media was in the position of being able to alter the attitude of the general public and to make them aware of aspects of life that were previously unknown. An example of this is the tabloids' use of 'Cardboard City' to highlight the problems of homelessness in London. The attractive quality of the phrase and also the fact that it used deviant collocation to emphasise the problem means that people notice it and therefore an issue is made out of the plight of the homeless in cardboard city. If the allusion of cardboard city was not used then homelessness would not have been such a major 80s issue.

The British tabloids were generally positive towards the Conservative government. Margaret Thatcher was in power throughout the whole of the decade. In order to convince the British public that the left wing Labour party were not capable of ruling the tabloids carried the phrase 'Looney Left' in order to portray socialists as deranged. However, this approach to degrade the Labour Party was an extremely cynical notion but this was typical of the British media. The 80s was a decade full of cynicism and pessimism which is perhaps why people who were successful were mocked and attacked by the press and the public.

Individuals in society who were previously respected by the public such as the elderly and business people were treated with contempt and cynicism and therefore the terms 'wrinkly' and 'yuppy' were coined by the media because the word 'wrinkly' gives the impression of being full of wrinkles – which is derisory and the elderly were viewed in this manner because it was the youthful business class who were successful but <u>they</u> were degraded for being young and stereotypically of wealthy backgrounds so the elderly could attack the people in society who attacked them.

Conclusions to be drawn from the 80s

The words and phrases echoed the general atmosphere of the decade's culture. A lot of 80s words are short, such as 'fax', 'hyper' and 'giro' and in the 80s quickening and shortening were key aspects of business and culture. Things such as fast food, supermarkets and huge shopping centres combined to supposedly make life more straightforward and even the vast continent Europe being made more accessible to the public with the relaxing of the Cold War and Glasnost plus the free market in the European Community being on the political horizon. However, the simplistic shrinking world had its serious drawbacks such as a growing cynicism through the nation emphasised by the tabloids' attitude to sensitive political economic issues like 'poll tax' and the 'greenhouse effect.' Plus the creation of 'lager louts', 'AIDS' and 'cardboard city' have served as a serious warning for the future.

Chapter 18
Original Writing

Throughout this edition of *Your Own Words* we have tried to integrate writing and analysis tasks. In this final chapter we consider the relationship between using language and studying language. Traditionally students have studied English Literature without having to try to write creatively themselves and have been asked to display their own writing skills mainly in the form of a well turned critical essay. Many aspiring writers often say how inhibiting they find the weight of the whole tradition of English Literature when they sit down to write themselves. However, language students study a far wider range of texts and consider them from the point of view of their appropriateness and their fitness for purpose rather than their excellence. They are asked to write in different styles for different audiences and come into contact with many different varieties they are keen to emulate. Many students study language precisely because they like to write, and several of the A-level syllabuses give equal weight to writing and to analysis. How are the two activities related?

The relationship between analysis and writing is complicated. We all speak and understand language without any explicit knowledge of the rules. We name things without knowing what a noun is and use verbs, prepositions and adjectives, to list but a few, without any conscious understanding of parts of speech. Similarly we write frequently; lists, cards, letters, reports, essays, stories, without thinking 'What are the characteristics of good narrative writing, or informative prose? That's how I must write this.' We're often particularly good at writing in a certain style when we have been reading a lot of it, without consciously imitating the features. Somehow it just gets into our heads. However, good writing, really good writing, does not usually just flow spontaneously from our, or anyone else's fingers. Writing is a craft. Anyone who writes for a living, be they tabloid journalist or poet laureate, knows a lot about using language, what works and what doesn't work for them, and this skill comes from practice. We may know pretty exactly what we want to say and the effect we want to have, but actually achieving such effects is difficult and takes a lot of hard work. This is where a consciousness of style and a familiarity with different structures can really help.

As part of your course you will be asked to write in a variety of styles for different audiences. You may be able to choose to do this as coursework, or as part of the exam. You may be writing with free choice from scratch or re-presenting source material in some different form. Most of these tasks will be as close to a 'real' writing task as possible and one of the main yardsticks for judging the success of the piece will be 'fitness for purpose'. Would it 'work' as a real script, pamphlet or speech? Once upon a time the only type of writing A-level English candidates would be asked to do would be essays, timed or otherwise. Writing essays does develop formal powers of expression and, hopefully, logical, well ordered presentation of argument and evidence. But where in the world outside education would you be asked to write an essay, even though you may be asked to demonstrate those skills? Now you have the opportunity to show a greater range of writing skills. An A-level English Language course raises your level of understanding of different varieties of language and asks you to display your ability as a language user through writing, which in turn increases your consciousness of the choices you make every time you yourself put pen to paper. And so the two parts of the course feed into each other. Or that's the theory.

WRITING COMMENTARIES

The activity which best brings together your skills as writer and as a student of language is the 'commentary' in which you are asked to comment as objectively as you can on your own work. You may be doing this as part of your coursework or in the original writing paper of an examination. In either situation you will be expected to make explicit the link between writing and analysis and apply the skills you have learnt in one part of the course to your own work. You will be asked to reflect and comment on your writing using some of the same approach and terminology you might use in textual analysis, but with the added advantage of actually knowing the process the writing has been through to achieve the finished product.

You have already seen an example of a commentary in Chapter 7 and another appears in a few pages' time. These students are attempting to explain what they set out to achieve in their pieces and the extent to which they have, or have not, succeeded. A good commentary will normally include some reference to the genesis of the piece of writing and mention any models or other examples of the particular genre you may have had in mind when you started the piece. The commentary later in this chapter is particularly strong in this area as it is a commentary on pastiche, which is a conscious imitation and exaggeration of a particular style, usually for comic effect. The student is better at describing at how she reproduced the style than she is at judging the effect, but she does show how much conscious craft went into the two pastiches.

Did you have to undertake any research and gather together any information to write your piece? If you did, this too should be referred to in the commentary along with your methods of transforming the material and making it your own, rather the way you might in a case study paper. Of course any direct quotation must be acknowledged.

How many drafts did your writing go through and what prompted the changes from one to the next? Hopefully one contributory factor will be the comments of your readers. Having given due consideration at the outset to the audience you are aiming for, it is then perfectly legitimate, indeed very sensible, to give your first attempts to some typical readers and to ask them what they think. If they think any parts are unclear or difficult or illogical (depending on the piece), go back and rework them. The candidate who comments on her children's stories in Chapter 7 is particularly good at this.

How did you try to appeal to that audience in the first place: through vocabulary, sentence structure, layout? All are worth discussing in the commentary, although it should not be too long or overelaborate, overshadowing the writing itself. We are occasionally presented with a rather average piece of writing but a brilliant commentary on what's not quite right about it. This prompts the obvious question 'Why didn't you have another go and put it right?' and of course there are more marks awarded to the writing itself than to the commentary, so in these cases the balance is clearly wrong. However, if the aim of the piece is ambitious (and this is particularly true of poetry or other literary forms), it doesn't do any harm at all to say that your work might have fallen rather short of your hopes for it. Some types of writing – the less formulaic ones – are more difficult than others and very few of us are going to achieve true success and originality every time.

What examiners are looking for in commentaries is your ability to reflect on yourself as a writer, evidence that you are conscious of the effects you are striving to achieve and the craft that went into the piece. Standing back and looking at your work will help you to improve as a writer. In the context of the English Language exam it might also help you to understand the writing process which others go through and therefore make you a better analyst of the work of others.

ORIGINAL WRITING IN EXAMINATIONS

Some people love pressure and need deadlines to produce their best work. In our opinion this is about the only advantage of being asked to produce a piece of original writing (and accompanying commentary) in exam conditions. However, in some syllabuses, candidates are now forced to choose between original writing and a project as their coursework option and if you want to write a more leisurely piece of language investigation in project form, then the original writing exam will have to be tackled. Both original writing and language investigation seem to us to be activities best undertaken over a period of time, but we do not live in a perfect world and so the choice will probably have to be faced. Your school or college may make the choice for you, or you may be able to decide where your own strengths lie. Either way, many of you may need to produce a piece of writing in exam conditions so we'll attempt some tips on how to approach this.

When faced with a choice of tasks in the exam situation you have little time to make up your mind, so our first piece of advice is to know yourself as a writer. Know which sort of writing you're best at and for which audiences, and if these options come up, go for them. During your course you will have been given opportunities to try your hand at different varieties of writing in different registers aimed at different groups. You know which ones you like doing best and achieve the best results at. Use this knowledge if you have the opportunity. You are unlikely suddenly to succeed at a variety you've found difficult before.

Read the options carefully and make sure that you pay attention to every requirement. If the audience is specified, then before you start consider the lexical levels and appropriate structures and length. If the task is informative or persuasive, think particularly carefully about ordering your facts or opinions and how to break up your text for maximum impact. Draw on the knowledge you have gained (hopefully in part from this book) about different varieties of language. In fact keeping in mind context, audience and purpose all the way through is as useful for writing as for analysis. Since you are also going to have to comment on your writing it is particularly useful to jot down some of these thoughts before you start. Then, when you look back over your piece after you've finished, you can compare it with what you set out to achieve. It may not matter if the match isn't perfect, as the writing may have taken on a life of its own rather than being wholly formulaic, but that gives you something to comment on too. There is very little time in the exam situation for drafting and redrafting as there is in the original writing coursework option, giving you less to draw on for your commentary. However, if you have sketched out a plan, then you can compare the finished version with that.

It may be easier to attempt a persuasive or an informative piece in the exam because the features of many varieties of these are rather more predictable than those of some entertaining forms. Identifiable features of persuasive writing, such as establishing a relationship to the audience, drawing them in, emotive lexis, possibly antithesis or contrast, are easier to include and to comment on at the end. You might in fact like to mark them in the text so that you can pick them out and refer to them with ease. However, the main part of the exam is the writing itself, not the commentary, so if you are really good at humour, for instance, and get the opportunity to do it, then take the opportunity to go for that, even if it is harder to comment on. In the end it's up to you. You will feel more relaxed and confident if you've practised different varieties beforehand, and practised them in timed conditions. Try to look on the time constraints as a challenge. The exam situation itself may seem artificial, but there may well be situations later in life when you have to produce an article, a summary, a written defence or argument in a very short space of time, and the exam will have been very good practice. And you *have* to produce something. Sometimes, sitting down with a blank piece of paper in front of you, when time is not of the essence, waiting for inspiration to strike can be even harder. In the rest of this chapter we try to give you some ideas for getting started with original writing, in individual and group situations.

SOME IDEAS TO GET YOU STARTED.

It clearly makes sense to look at varieties and models to give you ideas. But let us make one thing clear immediately. No-one is suggesting that you approach creative writing like a recipe:

> Mix two rhetorical questions, three parallel structures and plenty of emotive lexis.
>
> Blend well. Add a pinch of sarcasm and humour to audience's taste.
>
> Result: persuasive writing.

But there is much to be said for a little conscious craft. Writing is, as we've indicated, work, not a matter of sitting awaiting inspiration or a visit from the muse. Yes, you should be committed to what you are writing about; yes, you should know what you are talking about; but there is nothing wrong with thinking about useful techniques and appropriate register.

Your ultimate aim will be to find your own voice, Your Own Words indeed, but paradoxically this doesn't happen without a lot of practice because you have to be in control of your technique, and while you're developing this you might find that one of the best ways to get started is to use other writers or texts as models.

PASTICHE AND PARODY

This is a genre of writing in which you deliberately write in the style of someone or something else. It might be that, having steeped yourself in popular newspapers for a month, you know you can capture their tone perfectly. Do it! The best way to check if you have really grasped the style of a writer or genre is to try to emulate it. Even if you eventually decide that you prefer to write something more original, it will have been a useful exercise. If you want to attempt something a little more light-hearted (and harder, if we're frank) try a parody (such as poetic parody, at the end of Chapter 15). This is a deliberate exaggeration of a style. It has to be over the top, but it also has to have the hallmarks of the original – or no-one will see the joke.

· ·

ACTIVITY

Try to write the first paragraph of each of a love, science fiction, war and children's story. Don't make life easy for yourself by too direct a reference to the subject matter. Now ask a friend or relative what sort of writing they come from. Also ask them how they could tell. What were the giveaway clichés of situation and language? Which of the four did they think you wrote most convincingly?

Now write the rest of that story and ensure that the style is consistent, but consistently extreme. In the last page or so destroy the reader's expectations.

· ·

ACTIVITY ○ ◪

Look again at the second part of Chapter 9, which discusses genre writing. Romantic and horror fiction are both a lot of fun to do; children's fiction is another possibility. Try starting like a very traditional example of the genre and then subvert it. Give the story a twist in the tail: don't punish the baddy or kill the evil alien or have the hero or heroine live happily ever after. Of course this will only be funny and effective if you have convinced the reader in the first instance. And if you are going to convince them, you really need to know what you are sending up very well.

We include next, one student's parodied versions of newspaper styles. We have also included her commentary on her work. Read her writing analytically, underlining the typical features of news writing, marking exaggerations with asterisks and highlighting examples of parody. If, as we believe, analysis and commentary writing are very similar and mutually supportive, you should find that her comments flesh out your annotations.

No signs of agreement

The miners dispute, now into its tenth month, is showing no signs of ending.

DISCUSSIONS between N.U.M president Mr Arthur Scargill and N.C.B. leader Mr. Ian Macgregor, have so far proved to be ineffectual. It was disclosed that further negotiations would take place later on this week.

The majority of mine workers are still out on strike but large numbers of men are returning to work each day.

Mr Scargill said, 'We can win this dispute if we stick together. The figures of men returning to work, as released by the N.C.B. are unrealistic. Hopelessly unrealistic.'

It is believed that the high figures quoted by the N.C.B. are part of tactics currently being employed by the N.C.B. to dishearten the disputing miners.

Said Mr Scargill, 'They must not believe everything they hear.'

Mining families are finding it progressively more difficult to cope with the rising cost of living.

Many families are going hungry and there is much concern, particularly for the children of the miners.

An N.C.B. spokesman said 'There is no way we are going to alter our decision to close uneconomic pits. These men will return to work sooner or later. We know that most families are suffering due to low finances and we are fairly confident that many will return to work if only for the sake of their families.'

To close down collieries, in many areas, would be to take away the major, and in some cases the only, source of employment.

With already high unemployment figures, had the N.C.B. considered this aspect?

'Obviously we have considered this, but the decision, reached by us and the Government is still withstanding. To keep open many pits would not prove beneficial to the economy of the country and at the end of the day, that is what we have to consider.'

It has been alleged by the N.C.B. that the only reason why more men have not returned to work is because they fear that they will be victimised.

Mr Scargill vehemently denies this allegation. 'That is totally untrue, I find it hard to believe that even the N.C.B. could come up with a statement as incredible as that.

The reason these men are out on strike is because they value their jobs and value their whole way of life. Obviously the men would like to return, of course they are finding things hard, but I am not prepared to make any decisions concerning their future until the Government and N.C.B. are prepared to alter their plans to close the pits which they consider to be uneconomic.'

The amount of picket line violence is creating a cause for concern.

It is thought that the disturbing amounts of excess violence, as witnessed on the picket lines, towards working miners and towards the police is undermining the very valid cause the miners have.

However, it is claimed by Mr Scargill that many of the people responsible for the acts of violence are not mine workers but political agitators.

'Many of the picketers are merely agitators, not miners, who have come from all over the country. It is these people who are causing the trouble, not the miners. This began as a peaceful dispute but has accelerated into something much more.'

The N.C.B. and the Government have condemned the violence saying it is 'disgusting and barbaric' and that the pickets behaved 'like animals'.

An N.C.B. spokesman said 'We are not prepared to revoke any of our decisions; especially in the light of the uncivilised behaviour displayed by many of the picketers.'

The N.C.B. chairman, Mr Macgregor said, 'I am not prepared to comment on the strike at this moment in time.'

Negotiations will resume tomorrow and it is hoped that a compromise will be reached.

Mr Scargill said, 'I want this strike to be settled just as much as anyone else, but I want a secure future for my men guaranteed.'

The Daily Sprite

'I DEFIED THE PICKETS'

The Truth; The Passion; The Pain; The Heartbreak – Miner Reveals All! 34-year-old Jimmy Jones crossed the picket line today!

DESPITE INSULTS and abuse from so-called 'workmates', father of fourteen Jimmy, clocked on for the first time in over six months.

Heart-rending

Jimmy, who works at one of Yorkshire's largest collieries, agreed to tell us, your sizzling, sensational Sprite, his heart-rending saga of the strike and how it has affected him and his lovely family.

Poverty-stricken

It has been hard. For six long months they have had to endure an almost poverty-stricken lifestyle.

Said Jimmy, 'I didn't want to go back to work, but me and my wife have had to struggle on next to nothing. The kids, I've got fourteen kids, have had to make do.

They have had to take it in turns to go to school; we've only got one pair of shoes, between fourteen of them that is. It's worrying, I don't want my kids to miss out on their education, not when jobs are so hard to come by.'

'…sake of my family.'

What will Jimmy do when the strike is over?

'They probably won't talk to me,' Jimmy said of his workmates, 'But I don't care. I can take it. I returned to work for the sake of my family. They are the most important thing in my life.'

Invalid mother

Not only does large-hearted Jimmy have a wife and fourteen children to support but has his invalid mother to support too.

Said Jimmy, 'My mother, she's sixty-nine. She depends on me. She needs some new teeth and a heart transplant and she's got dry rot in her wooden leg… that's why I've gone back to work.'

Jimmy's mother, 69-year-old, silver haired Sarah Jones said 'He's a good lad.'

'Proud'

Jimmy's blonde, 38-24-36, 5'9" wife Sharon, aged 29, has been a great support to Jimmy.

Sharon said 'I'm so proud of my Jimmy, the kids are really proud of him and his mother, his poor old invalid mother, she's so proud of him.'

'Scab'

Until the strike breaks up, Jimmy will have to put up with shouts of 'scab' each day as he crosses the picket line to do an honest day's work.

'…old drinking mates… '

Even when the strike is over many of Jimmy's old drinking mates will not want to know him. How has this affected Jimmy?

Said Jimmy, 'Obviously my social life has been stripped down to a minimum.

'I can't go out to the pub anymore. Not that I could afford to go to the pub, not to drink anyway, but me and the lads used to go down to the Bull on a night, have a natter, a game of darts, play pool, have the odd 5 or 6 pints, you know. That's all in the past now.

None of them want anything to do with me now. But I am devoting my time to my wife and my children.'

Said blonde, bubbly Sharon, 'Jimmy hasn't got very many friends left, well he hasn't any at all actually, but he's coping really well. He doesn't mind having to work on his own.'

Return to work

But Jimmy won't be back on his own for long though!

Statistics show that thousands of miners are giving up the picket lines in return for work – and pay!

The N.C.B. revealed today that by next week, more than three-quarters of the striking miners will have returned to work and the whole Scargill saga will be over.

Talks

Talks between the N.C.B. and N.U.M. will take place today at a secret location at London's Hilton Hotel, away from the media.

'… continue working…'

And what will Jimmy do in the meantime?

'I'll continue working, I believe I'm doing the right thing. This strike has been going on for more than six months now. We can't win. The sooner Scargill realises that the better.'

Encouraging

Sharon and their fourteen children have all been a great encouragement to Jimmy.

Said Sharon, 'We are a family and we are all right behind Jimmy. The kids have been very understanding. They are terrific kids. I just hope all the others follow Jimmy's selfless example.'

Jimmy said of his family 'I couldn't have done it without them!'

On page 3 Jimmy poses with Samantha Fox.

Commentary

The two articles are a pastiche cum parody of two newspaper styles. The second article is written in the style of a 'gutter press' or popular tabloid newspaper such as 'The Sun'. The first article is written in the style of a quality press newspaper.

The primary function of a popular press newspaper is to entertain and appeal to emotions rather than to inform.

The aim of quality press newspapers is primarily to inform and educate people.

The distinction of the two styles is achieved by the use of features which are typical of newspapers.

The first noticeable feature of the tabloid parody is the large bold print headline. This is a graphetic feature employed frequently by the popular press newspapers. It is intended to be eyecatching and to obtain a reader's interest. The headline is sensationalistic and contains a highly emotive word 'defied'. 'Defied' has connotations of a heroic, courageous figure and creates interest.

Following the main headline is a sub-headline 'Exclusive story' – this is a feature used frequently by the popular press with the main function of selling newspapers. The 'Exclusive story' is a tactic used by newspapers who would like to convince the public that they should buy this newspaper because they won't find this story anywhere else.

The sub-headline contains a series of highly emotive words e.g. 'the pain'; 'the passion'; 'the heartbreak'. These words are intended to gain the interest of the reader and create intrigue; 'pain' and 'passion' are also alliterative which is eyecatching.

In contrast to the outstanding and eyecatching headline of the popular press article, the broadsheet version is much simpler and less eyecatching. The headline is more informative and contains no emotive words.

'No Signs of Agreement' is simply informative and does not appeal to the emotions or attempt to sell newspapers. The audience it is aimed at is a more educated one, who don't need enticing to buy the newspaper.

Popular press newspapers often use sub-headings. The sub-headings tend to be highly emotive words. For example 'Heart-rending' 'Poverty stricken'; 'Invalid mother', 'Proud'. These emotive words are used to evoke pity and sympathy.

The subject of the story is one of human interest, as is common in the popular press, and is not an informative news story as the first article is intended to be.

The lexis in the tabloid article is extreme. It is emotive and often hyperbolic. For example, words and phrases such as 'heart-rending saga', 'endure', 'struggle', 'honest day's work'.

As frequently appears in the popular press there is heavy pre-modification when referring to a person. This is often hyperbolic. For example 'Jimmy's blonde, 38-24-36, 5'9" wife Sharon, aged 29' and '69-year-old, silver haired Sarah Jones'; 'blonde, bubbly Sharon' and 'large-hearted Jimmy'.

There is use of alliteration in the popular press e.g. 'sizzling, sensational Sprite'; 'saga of the strike', 'Scargill saga' and 'blonde, bubbly'. The alliteration is eyecatching and sounds 'snappy' and is more entertaining.

The lexis in the broadsheet article is much more sophisticated. For example 'ineffectual', 'negotiations', 'vehemently denies this allegation'. These are not everyday words and are intended to appeal to a more educated audience.

There is a deviant collocation of the lexical item 'accelerated' in this version: 'This began as a peaceful dispute but has accelerated into something much more'. 'Accelerated' is usually associated with the speed of a car but is used here to emphasise the speed with which the dispute has developed.

There is alliteration used: 'creating a cause for concern' — this is emphatic.

A syntactical deviance is common to both styles of newspaper. For example, the placing of the verb in the subject position 'Said Mr Scargill' and 'Said Jimmy'. This is for purposes of emphasis.

Syntactical deviance also occurs in the tabloid piece in 'Despite insults and abuse from so-called "workmates" father of fourteen Jimmy clocked on for the first time in over six months'. Here the SV(c)A pattern is changed to A(C)SV. This is to bring emphasis onto the emotive word 'despite', which evokes sympathy.

The pre-modification 'father of fourteen' is alliterative and sounds entertaining. There is also post-modification: 'Jimmy, who works at one of Yorkshire's largest collieries, agreed...'

The sentence structures in both articles are complex and compound. Very few simple sentences occur due to the pre- and post-modification.

The broadsheet version is informative and the complex and compound sentence structures are needed to allow the information to be successfully conveyed.

The subject of the miners' strike, on which the articles were based, is treated in different ways by the two types of newspaper. The 'popular' press has a tendency to take one man's story and create news out of nothing, making a plea to the heart of the nation. The 'quality' press report the situation.

The truth of many popular press articles is often dubious, therefore there is deliberate hyperbole in the tabloid article, for example, '... The kids, I've got fourteen kids, have had to make do. They have had to take it in turns to go to school; we've only got one pair of shoes, between fourteen of them that is'; and '... She needs some new teeth and a heart transplant... and she's got dry rot in her wooden leg...'

There is very little emotion in the 'quality' article and many statements appear objective. For example: 'It was disclosed that...' and 'It is believed that...', 'It has been alleged...'

Though there is a slight political slant to the left, the broadsheet article does attempt to present both sides of the argument and not just one.

The tone of register of the tabloid version is informal and colloquial, this is in contrast to the more formal tone of register of the other.

It is lighthearted and entertaining as this is the way in which the popular press presents news articles. The final sentence 'On page 3, Jimmy poses with Samantha Fox' is hyperbolic to ridicule and parody popular press newspapers.

The broadsheet version presents the news in a more factual and informative way but tries to be interesting so that it is comprehensible and readable.

The differences occur in the two articles because they have a different aim, a different political slant and a different audience.

Having looked at one student's attempt, you might like to attempt a newspaper parody yourself. This exercise will also help you with the skills of re-presenting the same information for different audiences.

....

ACTIVITY

Find a story in the popular press and re-write it as it might appear in a quality paper. Ensure that it is a story that they would cover: a political story perhaps, or a major disaster, i.e. not just a 'human interest' story. If you buy two papers, one quality, one popular, you ought to be able to find the same stories in both. Do your translation and then see if you have caught the tone.

....

ADVERTS

Another easily accessible and familiar type of writing you might like to attempt, is the language of advertisements. Keep an eye open for advertisements for new products or companies. Guess where else they might advertise and try to design an appropriate advertisement for the alternative context. For example, if you've seen the poster, have a go at the Sunday supplement centre-spread. If you've seen the television commercial, design the poster. Again, chances are you'll get a chance to compare your effort with the professional job. Did you pick the right sort of layout and colours? Was your level of formality right – even if you didn't use the same words? Is your catchphrase better than theirs? If you produced one you're particularly pleased with you could ask a friend to see if they can tell the difference. If they can't, or think yours is better, perhaps you've discovered your future career!

Adverts do represent the most obvious examples of persuasive writing. Try to make life a little more difficult for yourself. Instead of changing format only, think carefully about target audience. There are many products which are used by a very wide-ranging group. However, within the group, different segments will be 'got at' by different adverts. Life insurance and charities are two good examples of this. You will find other examples in Chapter 7, 'Audience', and Chapter 8, 'Purpose'.

....

ACTIVITY

Look in magazines for different advertisements for the same product or service. Look at your examples and isolate the significant changes. Then find another product or service and try to write the yuppie advert, the family advert and the granny advert. If you are unclear what appeals to these groupings look at *Cosmopolitan* (career women/yuppies), the *Radio Times* (the ultimate family magazine) and *The People's Friend* (as read by my eighty-seven-year-old grandmother).

....

MORE PERSUASIVE LANGUAGE

You might want to stretch yourself farther by tackling more difficult varieties of persuasive language. The convenient thing about being a language student is that you can always check your efforts against the real thing: language is all around us.

....

ACTIVITY

If you want some examples of persuasive technique, a good way to start is by taping *Question Time* from television, or *Any Questions* from Radio 4. Tape it rather than watching or listening to it, though: this will enable you to watch it by instalments and do some prediction exercises. This is how to go about it:

Listen to a question put to the panel.

Switch off and ask yourself, writing down your reply:

- Which panel member will answer first?
- Will they adopt a very formal or fairly informal style?
- Will they allow their regional accent to come through or get as close to RP as they are able?
- Will their tone be emotional or factual?
- Will they use emotive or statistical lexis?
- Will they sound impassioned and sincere, eminently reasonable, sarcastic?
- Which speaker will disagree/oppose or support them?
- How will their speech style be different?

This probably sounds impossibly difficult. In fact the tactics and techniques of speakers on such programmes are almost depressingly predictable. Nor is their individual identity that important: they are usually the token 'government spokesperson', 'backbench rebel' or 'right-wing Conservative'. They do tend to conform to type!

If you are not in the habit of watching these programmes you might need to watch a few to 'tune in'. This is probably educational, in any case.

••

If you really do find that task too difficult, you can do a more straightforward jotting down of distinctive features as you listen. Or you could follow an individual – such as the Prime Minister or Leader of the Opposition – through several contexts and see how they vary their persuasive technique. Prediction is more fun, though. You should eventually be able to write the script for them.

INFORMATIVE AND INSTRUCTIVE WRITING

It may be, of course, that you do not want to find your voice as a journalist, advertising copy-writer or spin doctor; that you would prefer to acquire expertise in more everyday, functional language use. We are thinking here of informative and instructive writing. It is all too easy to assume that these are bread and butter and straightforward. In fact, they are, in their own way, very demanding. You may not be trying to move or persuade people so you may not be choosing individual lexical items with as much care, but you are trying to be precise and clear. This has two main impacts upon your language. The first is that you do not want to waste the reader's time in unnecessary words: you need to be very strict with yourself about keeping to the point. The second is that you need to sequence your material carefully. In instructive writing – for example recipes – it is disastrous to get something out of order. Nor is it acceptable to add 'a fair bit' of sugar or 'a good dollop' of milk. Precision is all.

The same is true when writing informatively. It is of no use to anyone to say that the First World War happened 'this century', or that water boils 'when it gets really hot'. If people did not write things as fatuous as this there would be no trade in exam howlers. Informative writing necessitates intelligent selection and ordering of appropriate material and is most certainly an examination skill. What are essay answers if not examples of informative writing? What are analyses if not informative commentaries on others' writing and speaking?

Many people find informative/instructive writing the least interesting sort of work to produce. One way to kill two birds with one stone is to write something about your exam subject. Perhaps you could make your fortune writing 'The Key to Success in A-Level English Language'.

Every time you decode a textbook and write your own notes you are producing informative writing for a specific audience. When you blend the material given to you by teachers with your own notes plus those from several different textbooks, you are doing the informative writer's job: that is, conveying a body of information as clearly, succinctly and appropriately as possible. You will probably need to think about layout: would subdivisions or numbered points help or simply distract? Have you prioritised material in order of importance, or chronologically or what? The main thing is that you do have a system and one which works for your material.

If you remain unclear about what the hallmarks of informative writing are, try using a body of material for different purposes, one informative, the other persuasive or entertaining. Refer back, too, to Chapter 8, 'Purpose', which looks at these varieties and how they overlap. Here are a few simple, useful exercises:

ACTIVITY

Collect some information on rape/child abuse/drug abuse (sorry if this sounds a gloomy task!). Any doctor's surgery will furnish you with material, so will any Citizens' Advice Bureau. The NSPCC and Rape Crisis Line are also very willing to supply information.

Using the material you obtain, produce two pamphlets for home delivery. One should be unbiased, factual and purely informative, the other should aim to persuade householders to do something about this terrible problem.

As you write and design your two pamphlets, think carefully about layout:

- What sort of graphics do you want?
- Are you going to use any subheadings?
- What tone are you attempting to convey?
- How much detail do you want and how will you make it accessible to your readership?

Think next about the sort of words you want to employ: should they be emotive, hyperbolic and extreme, or factual and unbiased? How colloquial or formal do you want to be?

This may, of course, lead you to a consideration of audience. Generally, a younger audience will prefer a less formal style. A very young audience will need a simple lexical and structural level.

ACTIVITY

Another useful exercise is to switch audience. Take an AIDS pamphlet aimed at the general public. Redraft it for high school students or trainee nurses. How will the material differ? How much specialist lexis will you use? How will you avoid patronising or confusing a relatively young audience?

The high school audience is a very useful target group for informative writing. Try putting together an information pack on a social or health issue for fourth formers. Or a unit in a GCSE Biology or History course. This will probably involve you in some instructive as well as informative writing since you will presumably want them to do something once they have read or while they are reading your material. Which of these two options seems better to you? Why?

ACTIVITY

If you would rather write for someone older – perhaps A-Level students – then think of a topic you might reasonably expect them to be interested in. Avoid the obvious: 'How to play football' or 'Making job applications' have both been done to death. They are about as original as doing a persuasive piece on abortion or capital punishment. So what might be valid? A guide to higher education? A guide to holiday jobs abroad? Some facts about drug and alcohol abuse (again a little well worn, but worthy)? A young visitor's guide to your city? If you live in a tiny village or in the middle of nowhere it may well be that you have no tourists to write for. Many seventeen-year-olds start driving lessons. Would a more informal version of the Department of Transport's *Driving Manual* be a good idea? Only, of course, if you know what you are talking about!

Knowing your subject is a vital prerequisite for any piece of informative writing. You have no right to mislead people about which hi-fi or camera to buy, what the significant differences are between the major religions of the world or how to perform Latin American dancing faultlessly. If you write about something, you must know your stuff, which does not mean copying out great chunks of previously completed History, Geography or Science projects. That sort of cheating always shows.

LITERARY MODELS

We have so far been looking at examples which, to a certain extent, follow a formula. To create good examples you need to practise and to hone your technique, but suppose you want to try something less predictable?

Poetry

Poetry and literary prose is a far harder nut to crack, but as we have said, they're only words – albeit fairly deviant and often sophisticated ones. It would increase your respect for the craft of poetry, if nothing else, to try and write something formally demanding, like a sonnet. Shakespeare makes it look easy. Believe us, it's not – and the surest way to discover this for yourself is to try. Making it rhyme, scan and say something sensible, never mind profound, is hard!

One quite entertaining and instructive way to produce a sonnet is to do a team effort. Six people each produce two lines of iambic pentameter. If that's pure jargon to you let us explain: all it means is that you want five iambs in each line, and an iamb is the name for two syllables – one unstressed, the other stressed (dee DUM). So an iambic pentameter has ten syllables which go 'dee DUM dee DUM dee DUM dee DUM dee DUM'. A famous example is the opening to Gray's *Elegy*: 'The curfew tolls the knell of parting day.' Another is the opening of Shakespeare's *Twelfth Night*: 'If music be the food of love, play on.'

To return to what we want you to do.

ACTIVITY ⊞ 🖋

All six of you write two lines of iambic pentameter. The lines must have the same final rhyme (e.g. 'cat' and 'mat') but need not otherwise link. For instance: 'The sun sinks slowly 'neath the chimney pots' and 'One dress was stripey; t'other one had spots.'

Everyone is now given all of the lines, and working in pairs you try to make a poem of them. The poem must rhyme ababcdcdefef. Then the sonnet needs completing with a heroic couplet (that is, a rhyming couplet of iambic pentameter). It should aim to conclude the poem with a generalised statement which sums it up. This is the hardest bit.

The surprising thing about this is that things which read remarkably like poems do arise, and six people given exactly the same lines come up with very different totalities – which tells you something about the several levels on which poems operate. Syntax is clearly very important.

If you find the idea preposterous take a look at these sonnets produced in half an hour by one of our A-level language groups:

> The lonely old man from Ridyard Estate,
> A broken down car parked up at his door
> No need to get up, no chance to be late,
> The wheels turn no more to do their tour.
>
> Birds at night fly high in the midnight sky
> As the trees rustled I heard a dog whine
> Something told me I was telling a lie
> Steps in the dark sent shivers up my spine

Moonlight across the sea shone bright at night
Footsteps in the white snow remind me of him
Though the blood dripping from him was an ugly sight
Killing him just didn't feel like a sin

A lonely man, a lonely girl hopeless
They got together but it was a mess.

Moonlight across the sea shone bright at night
The wheels turn no more to do their tours
Though the dripping blood was an ugly sight
Broken down cars parked at our doors.

Footsteps in the white snow remind me of him
The lonely old man from Ridyard Estate
Killing him just didn't seem like a sin
No need to get up no chance to be late

As the the trees rustled I hear a dog whine
Something told me I was telling a lie
Steps in the dark sent shivers up my spine
Birds at night fly high in the midnight sky

They also count, who only sit and cry
They mark the fact that all of us must die.

Another problem that some of us have with writing poetry is the very concentrated nature of its language. We are used to talking in longish units akin to sentences and we write in sentences, and suddenly to break grammatical rules and write a 'stream of consciousness' or metaphorically seems tough. It also (and I think this is crucial) seems pretentious. Something called *The Metaphor Game* is a great help in overcoming inhibitions about writing poetry. (Our thanks to the poet Gillian Clarke who introduced this game to us.)

ACTIVITY ▦ 💬

1   Someone is designated 'on' and thinks of a fairly famous person, alive or dead.
2   Everyone else asks questions such as what colour, type of food, tool, material, kind of transport, house does this person suggest to you? It is important that the person 'on' reacts quickly rather than pausing to consider. For example, if I were thinking of Marilyn Monroe I might come up with scarlet, hamburger (unglamorous but very American), hairdryer, black satin, red 'E' type and penthouse in answer to those questions.
3   The person 'on' gives the answers and also writes them down. Aim for about twelve.
4   Delete two which don't seem to go. (Of those I'd get rid of hamburger!)
5   Put the rest in alphabetical – and thus random – order. This stops you slipping into cliché.

6   Now, using the words given and exactly fifteen other words plus a title of up to eight words, write a poem.

....

Again, it is surprising what people come up with. It is also surprising how often people guess the mystery celebrity. This doesn't matter except that it does show how well their essence has been conveyed.

Once you've played the game a few times, you can actually manage it alone. You ask yourself the questions or simply write down a cluster of images. In this way you are trying to sum up 'Marilyn Monroeness' – not merely describe her. We hope you can see the distinction. Once again, even if what you create is not spectacularly good, it will have helped you to see how poetry can operate.

....

ACTIVITY ⬤ 🗇

Here are two sets of answers or images:

antique suitcase	Beethoven
a tent	brown and sage green
black hat and blue duffle coat	fairly large house
boarded with a family	larger than average family
piano	public schools
South America	roast beef and Yorkshire pud
visiting friends and cinema	Rolls Royce
very very hairy	*Neighbours*
	walking dogs

Go through stages 4, 5 and 6 above and see what you come up with.

....

Now take a look at what our students wrote. They quite enjoyed it; we hope you did too!

Beethoven filled every corner of this brown, sage green room
She was alone in this fairly large house which was, at the moment,
deserted by her
larger than average family

The lady, with her Margaret Thatcher hair style, sat at the piano,
on the polyester covered stool,
She recalls travelling to public schools in a Rolls Royce
and traditional dinners of Roast Beef and Yorkshire pud
Now, things have changed
She likes *Neighbours*, I've heard, and walking dogs.

He strolled, carrying his antique suitcase towards a tent on a camping site,
He wore a black hat and blue duffle coat, his face was brown
Previously, he boarded with a family
He loved his Aunty, and the sound of her playing the piano
whilst he was playing in the nursery
He remembered the South American holiday, visiting friends and cinema
He was now old and haggard, and very very hairy.

LITERARY PROSE

Perhaps the easiest way in is through first person writing. You might want to start with a story-telling voice which is quite like your own, drawing on your own experiences. There is nothing wrong with seeming to write someone else's autobiography, drawing on your own experiences perhaps but shaping and 'fictionalising' them. The effectiveness of first person writing is not judged in terms of its accuracy, but of its ability to draw the reader into the world it creates. This is the opening of the book which won the Guardian Fiction Prize in 1996, *Reading in the Dark* by Seamus Deane. It is fiction, but it certainly feels like autobiography. Perhaps it isn't always so easy to make the distinction since we draw on our own experiences for writing, however we choose to transmute them. This opening certainly has that whiff of authenticity about it.

STAIRS

February 1945

On the stairs, there was a clear, plain silence.

It was a short staircase, fourteen steps in all, covered in lino from which the original pattern had been polished away to the point where it had the look of a faint memory. Eleven steps took you to the turn of the stairs where the cathedral and the sky always hung in the window frame. Three more steps took you on to the landing, about six feet long.

'Don't move,' my mother said from the landing. 'Don't cross that window.'

I was on the tenth step, she was on the landing. I could have touched her.

'There's something there between us. A shadow. Don't move.'

I had no intention. I was enthralled. But I could see no shadow.

'There's somebody there. Somebody unhappy. Go back down the stairs, son.'

I retreated one step. 'How'll you get down?'

'I'll stay a while and it will go away.'

'How do you know?'

'I'll feel it gone.'

'What if it doesn't go?'

'It always does. I'll not be long.'

I stood there, looking up at her. I loved her then. She was small and anxious, but without real fear.

'I'm sure I could walk up there to you, in two skips.'

'No, no God knows. It's bad enough me feeling it; I don't want you to as well.'

'I don't mind feeling it. It's a bit like the smell of damp clothes, isn't it?

She laughed. 'No, nothing like that. Don't talk yourself into believing it. Just go downstairs.'

I went down, excited, and sat at the range with its red heart fire and black lead dust. We were haunted! We had a ghost, even in the middle of the afternoon. I heard her moving upstairs. The house was all cobweb tremors. No matter where I walked, it yielded before me and settled behind me. She came down after a bit, looking white.

'Did you see anything?'

'No, nothing, nothing at all. It's just your old mother with her nerves. All imagination. There's nothing there.'

I was up at the window before she could say anything more, but there was nothing there. I stared into the moiling darkness. I heard the clock in the bedroom clicking and the wind breathing through the chimney, and saw the neutral glimmer on the banister vanish into my hand as I slid my fingers down. Four steps before the kitchen door, I felt someone behind me and turned to see a darkness leaving the window.

My mother was crying quietly at the fireside. I went in and sat on the floor beside her and stared into the redness locked behind the bars of the range.

Seamus Deane: *Reading in the Dark*

To start with a mystery is one of the very best ways to start and this 'voice' sounds so real. It combines the world view of the child, counting the stairs and steps to the kitchen, with the perspective of distance 'I loved her then.'

Compare it with this piece of third person writing. It is in the third person, but it presents the scene from a very distinct point of view; one which, as you will discover, could not be strictly autobiographical, but definitely draws on close observation and empathy.

TAKING APART THE POCO POCO

Chapter 1

Raymond opened one eye, and then woke up. He could see when he was asleep, but saw more when he woke, as if you could open your eyes twice: the kitchen jumped several inches nearer. He knew without looking how it was outside. Dark, but with the palest breeze stirring. Long before the sun rose, a smidgen of light was borne in on the wind, not enough to dilute the generality of night, but sufficient to produce a faint silveriness as the breeze curved and twisted its way across the lawn.

He sniffed.

There was a chicken on the washing-machine, its smell icy and remote, as if a real chicken was managing to keep itself at a distance within a shell of polythene and stone. It made a howl rise to his throat but he tamped it down so that only a whimper came out. There were other smells too, a tedious assortment of vegetables, the gassy boiler, plastic tangy lino, bright metallic instalments of water (with an overlay of chlorine) from the drops that blipped out of the sink taps. From above, the prone sleepy odours of the humans, all in place. Stephen and Ann smelling separate, John and Margaret together, not so much tangled as striped, where they'd been lying close but still. The breeze slid under the back door like a sheet, hectic with outdoors, lawns, dirt, plants, trees, a distant but still heady bloom of crap.

Raymond's nose followed far-off possibilities and his heart thumped at what the day might offer. Then he brought his nostrils back home. Everything was in order except... there was a faint smell, previously unnoticed, by the flat cool odour of the window. It was black, malign. Raymond took a step towards it and then halted.

Richard Francis: *Taking Apart the Poco Poco*

At which point did you realise that Raymond is a dog? This particular novel is about one day in the life of a family and it is written from alternating viewpoints of its members, including Raymond. It is possible that the 'voice' of the narrator in *Reading in the Dark* is farther from the real voice of Seamus Deane than Raymond's is from Richard Francis. We mustn't assume too much. Both are convincing, that's what counts. We discussed some of the issues around choosing point of view in Chapter 11 and it might help to look at some of the extracts there. Deciding *how* you are going to tell a story is as important as deciding *what* the story is.

In fact many of the previous chapters provide you with ideas and examples to get you started. Chapters 9 and onwards might provide you with more variety, but many of the earlier examples will too, be they from textbooks, adverts, sports writing, fellow students' work, newspapers, press releases or poems. With so much writing around us how can we possibly hope to find something original to say? Do we have to find something original to say? Don't we just have to find the best words to express what we want to express in the best way we can (sounds familiar, see Chapter 10)? Even when we have correctly judged the context, audience and purpose of what we want to say, we still have to find a way to say it, and practice certainly helps us to find our own words.

GLOSSARY OF TERMS

The terms in this glossary are those whose first occurrences in the text are in capitals. They have been selected on two bases: either they seem to us to be words which may be unfamiliar to some readers, or they are well-known terms of which we would like you to have a working definition. They are listed in the glossary alphabetically.

In some cases we have felt the need to give two definitions – one which is as clear and simple as we can make it and one for those of you who want a rather more precise and linguistic definition.

Abstract nouns The names for ideas and emotions, things which exist notionally but not physically, e.g. 'love' and 'freedom'.

Accent The features of pronunciation which enable a listener to spot someone's regional and social derivation. Accent refers to sound only.

Active One of the two possible voices of verbs. In the active voice the subject of the sentence is the perpetrator of the verb. For example, in the sentence 'The dog bit the postman', 'The dog' is the subject of the verb part 'bit'.

The other voice for verbs is the **Passive** (see separate entry).

Addressee The person spoken to.

Addresser The person speaking.

Adjective Function: to modify or tell us more about nouns and pronouns. Distribution: before nouns and after determiners, e.g. 'the happy girl'; as complements, e.g. 'the girl is happy'; or after intensifiers, e.g. 'the girl is very happy'. Inflection: most adjectives can be made comparative by adding *er*, e.g. more happy = 'happier', or superlative by adding *est*, e.g. 'happiest'.

Adjunct The term used by some analysts for all the grammatically inessential elements in a sentence. The most common types of adjuncts are adjectives and adverbials.

Adverb Function: to modify or tell us more about a verb, adverb or adjective. Those modifying adverbs and adjectives, e.g. 'very', are often called intensifiers. Distribution: either before or after the word they modify – more usually after, more emphatically before. Inflection: how-adverbials are often the adjective plus *ly*.

Adverbial The general name for a word or group of words working as an adverb, i.e. modifying a verb, adverb or adjective.

Agent In passive structures, the person or thing which acted out the verb. It it is included, it follows the word 'by', e.g. 'The prisoner was interrogated by the Chief Inspector.' Here 'Chief Inspector' is the agent.

Anglo-Saxon More correctly, Old English.

Articles There are two articles: the definite 'the' used for particular nouns or ones already referred to, and the indefinite 'a' used for less specific nouns.

Audience The people to whom a stretch of language is addressed.

Back-channelling Referring things back to earlier, e.g. 'I should have mentioned this before'.

Clause A main clause (or simple sentence) must have a main finite verb and a subject.

Cohesion (as a term used in discourse analysis) That which causes separate conversational elements to make joint sense. Much of this is achieved by word order – that is, the distribution of items.

Collocated The term used to describe words which habitually go together, e.g. 'mad as a' will usually be followed by 'hatter'; 'might and' by 'main' and 'unaccustomed as I am to' by 'public speaking'. Sometimes a writer deliberately surprises our expectations by using deviant collocations such as 'happy funeral'.

Colloquial A term for language which is informal. Colloquialisms are usually spoken rather than written and change more rapidly than more standard forms.

Complement The element of a sentence which follows a subject and a being or stative verb. It can be a noun or an adjective; in either case it completes the sense of the sentence.

Complex The term for sentences which have two or more clauses, at least one of which is subordinate.

Compound The term for sentences which have two or more main clauses, each with its own subject. Subjects can also be referred to as compound when they involve two or more nouns, e.g. 'Jack and Jill'.

Concrete nouns The names for things which are visible and tangible (e.g. 'tables', 'sun') as opposed to things which exist notionally but not physically.

Conditional Verb forms and clauses which convey possibility. Conditional clauses are often introduced by 'if' or 'unless'.

Conjunctions Function words which link items in a list, the elements of a compound subject or object, or two or more clauses.

Connotation (cf **Denotation**) The emotional associations or links which a lexical unit or word has, e.g. 'Christmas' links to Santa Claus, snow, parties and presents – for most people it has positive connotations. On the other hand 'murder' links to death, criminality and violence and thus has negative connotations. The connotations of 'girl' could be positive – youthful – or negative – patronised.

Continuous The marked form of the verb which indicates the progressive by the use of the ending *ing*, e.g. 'talk' is simple and not progressive, 'talking' is continuous and progressive.

Conversion A word which shifts word class, e.g. 'a bonk', 'to bonk'.

Co-ordinating conjunctions These can link the parts of a compound subject or items of a list, and/or more importantly, the two or more main clauses of a compound sentence. There are only a few co-ordinating conjunctions: 'and', 'but', 'or', 'nor', 'either' and 'neither'.

Declarative The linguistic label for the sentence function of stating facts or opinions. Declarative sentences can also be referred to as statements or assertions.

Decode To interpret the full meaning of a stretch of language. This includes both its text and subtexts – the denotations and the connotations of the words.

Denotation (cf **Connotation**) The reference a word has to the thing, person or place it describes, i.e. its dictionary meaning; e.g. 'girl' = young female human being.

Determiners Function words which occur alongside and before nouns and specify quantity or significance. They include the two articles 'a' and 'the' and terms like 'some', 'this' and 'many'.

Dialect The elements of speech other than sound: words and grammar. When these are non-standard, i.e. not the same as Standard English, a speaker is regarded as having a localised dialect.

Diglossia Hierarchical subdivisions of language.

Direct object The thing or person receiving the action of the verb.

Discourse analysts Linguists who study stretches of spoken language (speech events) in order to generate rules about spoken language.

Domain An area or topic.

Dynamic The type or aspects of verbs which relate to action. Examples would be 'hit', 'wipe', 'frighten' or 'console'.

Elaborated code and variant (cf **Restricted code**) The sociologist Basil Bernstein suggested that this is used by more middle-class speakers. It is less context-bound than the restricted code and more generalised rather than anecdotal, but stresses personal opinion and role above group identity. It is advantageous in formal situations. Of course elaborated variant users also have access to restricted variant for more informal occasions.

(Bernstein's views are far from being uncriticised or proven. See Trudgill's book *Sociolinguistics* for a fuller discussion.)

Elucidation The sentence function in which a speaker clarifies what has been said. Elucidations can also support or oppose a previous remark.

Exclamatory The general name for sentences and utterances which convey surprise or other strong feeling.

False start The phenomenon of starting an utterance twice or re-phrasing.

Field Topic or subject of discourse.

Fillers Words added into discourse out of habit, or in order to gain thinking time. They are significant, but redundant in terms of meaning. Examples are 'well', 'sort of' and 'you know'.

Finite Verb forms which can occur alone in a main clause. They consist of all verb forms except the infinitive (e.g. 'to love', 'to take') and the participles ('loving', 'taken') which are referred to as **non-finite**.

Function Purpose.

Function words The small number of words whose main importance is grammatical rather than semantic. They have limited meaning alone but are significant in combination with other words. Function words include articles, determiners, pronouns, conjunctions and prepositions.

Habitual The term linguists use for actions which are regular. Habitual action is often signalled by verb form, e.g. 'I used to visit' rather than 'I visited'.

Idiolect The cluster of speech habits and sounds unique to an individual. It includes accent, pitch, word choice and style.

Imperative The more technical term for a command. As well as a sentence function it is a mood of verbs.

Indirect object In a sentence, the person or thing to or for whom the direct object is given/brought etc. In the sentence 'He bought her some flowers' the flowers are the direct object since they directly receive the action of the verb – the buying. He did not buy *her*, he bought *for* her, so she is the indirect object.

The indirect object can follow the verb but precedes the direct object.

Individuality The speech markers which allow you to recognise an individual. They include voice quality, volume/pitch and accent as well as pet words and phrases.

Initiating The first utterance in a conversation, important since it sets the tone for what follows and often indicates a dominant speaker.

Insider references References to people and places with a special meaning to insiders, e.g. Woodstock to cartoon readers or Sixties rock fans.

Interaction The term for the social element of discourse. It involves group dynamics: who is dominant? Who initiates conversation? What role do speakers adopt?

Interrogative The term describing the questioning sentence function.

Interrogative pronoun A question pronoun, such as 'which'.

Intonation The rise and fall of pitch of a speaker's voice. It is very important in decoding meaning and is often linked to function, e.g. questions have a rising intonation, statements a flat one. The difference between a true question where the form and function are interrogative (e.g. 'Would you like a banana?') and a rhetorical question where the form is a question but the function is a statement (e.g. 'Do you want a punch on the nose?') is highlighted by different intonations.

Intransitive Verbs which cannot take an object, e.g. 'go', 'be', 'seem'.

Latinate Words derived from Latin. They are often longer than the equivalent Old English word.

Lexical words The large group of words which have an ascribed, individual meaning. Syntax allows combinations of lexical and function words to create meaningful wholes.

Lexis The vocabulary of a language. Lexical items can be a group of words or a single word, e.g. 'around the bend' or 'mad'. All the lexical items or lexemes of a language make up its **lexicon**.

Minor sentence A sentence which lacks one of the two necessary elements – a main verb or a subject.

Mode The medium, usually spoken or written.

Modified A word is modified in meaning when an adverbial or adjectival is placed with it. We are usually given more information or told how to feel about the word by the modifiers which go with it. These can be post- or pre-modifiers.

Morpheme The smallest possible grammatical unit. It is smaller than the word and includes inflections with fixed meaning such as plural *s* and past tense *ed*. Prefixes such as *un* meaning 'not' are also morphemes.

Move The name for each turn in a discourse which a speaker has.

Non-finite Verb forms which cannot function as the main verb of a clause. There are only three non-finite verb forms: the infinitive ('to bite') and the present and past participles ('biting' and 'bitten').

Non-fluency features A general term for the normal pauses, errors and slips which occur when people talk spontaneously.

Noun Function: to name a person, place or thing. Nouns are very often the subject or object of a sentence. Distribution: after articles ('a', 'the'), prepositions or verbs. Inflection: nouns can be inflected for number (*s*/*es* for plural) or case ('*s* for the genitive, or possessive case).

Object The person, place or thing which receives the action of a verb in a sentence. In normal word order it follows the verb. Another name for it is the **direct object**.

Paralinguistic Features of conversation which are non-verbal but nevertheless convey meaning, for example shrugs or blown kisses. Non-verbal communication, involving gesture and facial expression, can be very important in decoding conversation.

Passive (cf **Active**) In the passive voice the subject of the sentence is the recipient of the action of the verb, e.g. in the sentence 'The postman was bitten by the dog', 'The postman' is the subject of the passive verb 'was bitten'.

Performative verbs Verbs which fulfil a function in being used, e.g. baptise.

Phatic communication The type of exchange which is redundant in terms of meaning but socially significant. It includes friendly noises like 'Morning', 'Nice sunny day' and 'How's things?'

Phrase A single element within a text which is longer than one word. It can be a verb such as 'look into', or a noun, adverbial or adjectival. It is differentiated from a clause because it lacks either the subject or predicate which a clause must have.

Idiomatic phrases have a fixed meaning which has little, if anything, to do with the meaning of the words within the phrase – for example, 'a wild goose chase' has nothing to do with terrorising birds. Colloquial expressions are also of fixed meaning and tend to be spoken rather

than written. Both idiomatic and colloquial expressions present non-native speakers with difficulty.

Pluperfect The tense which precedes the past and is signalled by 'had', e.g. 'When I had showered, I dressed.'

Post-modification This occurs after the noun or verb and often takes the form of a phrase or clause rather than a single word.

Pre-modification This occurs before the noun or verb and is more likely to consist of a single word or a list of single words.

Predicate The term for all elements in a sentence except the subject. A predicate can be a verb only or a verb, indirect object and object, for example.

Prepositions Function words which relate one word to another, often in space: 'in', 'on' and 'under' are examples. Sometimes they are used after verbs to alter their meaning.

Pronouns Words which stand in place of nouns, though they cannot do so after an adjective. Personal pronouns can be first, second or third person; subject or object. There are also possessive pronouns denoting ownership, e.g. 'his', and reflexive pronouns indicating action perpetrated on oneself, e.g. 'himself'. Pronouns can also be used as interrogatives, e.g. 'which?' and to relate one clause to another, e.g. 'who'.

Proper nouns The capitalised nouns which name particular people (Jane), places (London) or things (The Bible). Unlike common nouns, which are not individualised ('girl', 'city', 'book'), most proper nouns cannot follow determiners such as 'a' and 'the'.

Province Somebody's job, not region.

Received pronunciation The name for the most socially prestigious accent in Britain. It has no regional derivation, but is used by public school children, the Royal family and, traditionally, the BBC. It is more colloquially known as The Queen's English or BBC English.

Receiver The name for the recipient of a linguistic message, written or spoken. It includes both reader and listener.

Reformulation Saying the same thing in a different form of words.

Relative clause A post-modifying clause which is introduced by one of the relative pronouns. These are 'who', 'whom', 'whose', 'which' and 'that'.

Repetition The unnecessary repeating of a lexical unit.

Responses (as a term used in discourse analysis) The replies to **solicitations**. They are not exactly the same as answers to questions: there will be a link but it may be through the subtext rather than the text, e.g. 'Would you like to go to the park?' 'It's raining.'

Restricted code and variant A form of language use which the sociologist Basil Bernstein suggested was prevalent amongst some members of the working class. It is very context-dependent and clearly marks group membership. Some of its features include tag questions, heavy use of pronouns and anecdote. A speaker using only restricted variant, Bernstein argued, lacks stylistic range since this type of language use is only really meaningful to insiders and appropriate to relatively informal contexts. A speaker who only has access to this variant is thus disadvantaged in certain formal contexts like examinations, interviews and court cases.

Semantic field The grouping of words within areas of related meaning. Part of the meaning of each individual word is determined by the meanings of the other words in the same field, e.g. pink, crimson, red, magenta (colour); skirmish, battle, campaign (war); affection, passion, devotion, fondness (love).

Sender The name for the person communicating a linguistic message, whether written or spoken – it can therefore refer to either a writer or a speaker.

Sequencing The stylistic and linguistic ordering of words so that they make sense in terms of time. Tenses are particularly important in sequencing. In English we say 'If he comes, I will tell him'; in French the sequence is different, namely 'If he will come I will tell him.'

Simple The term for tenses which are unmarked, i.e. not progressive (ending in *ing*) and with no auxiliaries.

A sentence may be termed simple if it contains only one main clause and verb.

Solicitation The sentence function in which a speaker seeks information or clarification.

Specialist lexis Labels and verbs mutually agreed by specialists, e.g. camshaft, twitchers.

Speech Act Theory An explanation of the reasons for all utterances.

Standard English The form of English which is written and which most educated speakers use in formal contexts. It is more prestigious than non-standard English, though it must be stressed that this is for social and not linguistic reasons.

Stative A type of verb which expresses states of being and thought processes rather than actions. Examples are 'be', 'seem', 'know', 'realise' and 'mean'.

Stress What a speaker employs to foreground or highlight a word or morpheme. Greater volume and a rising intonation are both used. In transcription, stress is marked by capitalisation or by a mark before the stressed sound.

Subject The person, place or thing governing the verb – and, in normal word order, preceding it. The verb may be either stative or dynamic.

Subordinating conjunctions Conjunctions which link clauses but introduce a clause which is dependent on or subordinate to the other, main clause. They establish complex relationships: of time ('while'), result ('because') or condition ('if').

Subtext The implications of a text which are understood though not stated.

Syntax The arrangement of words into sentences, in accordance with the accepted rules for that language.

Tenor Another word for tone or style. Usually relates to formality.

Tense A category relating to verbs which marks when an action took place. The major tenses in English are the present, past and future, but further divisions can be made.

Text A stretch of language, written or spoken, which can be studied, analysed or described. It can be very short – 'One Way' on a traffic sign – or very long – *War and Peace* or the film *1900*.

Transitive The group of verbs which can be followed by a direct object, e.g. 'bite', 'kiss', 'buy'.

Turn-taking In conversation, people usually wait their turn to speak. Some, out of eagerness or rudeness, interrupt, but the norm is for one speaker to yield the floor by prolonging a pause or glancing at the elected next speaker who then takes her turn.

Unvoiced pause A silent gap in speech, marked in transcription by (.).

Utterance The normal unit of division for spoken as opposed to written language. Its end is marked by a pause or by a new speaker taking over.

Verb Function: words of doing or being. Distribution: between the subject and object or complement of the clause (the verb and object or complement are sometimes referred to as the predicate). Inflection: important for tense: *ed* for the past in many verbs, *ing* to show the continuous. Also for person: *s* for the third person singular, e.g. 'he likes'.

Voiced pause A gap in speech marked by a noise such as 'er' or 'erm'.

Word class The grammatical grouping of words according to their function. A more precise name for parts of speech. Words are often allocated to class according to their distribution (where they tend to occur) or their inflections (their word endings).

ACKNOWLEDGEMENTS

The authors and publishers wish to thank the following for permission to reproduce copyright material:

A House for Mr Biswas by V. S. Naipaul, Penguin UK

Extracts from *Midnight's Children* by Salman Rushdie, Jonathan Cape

'The bombing of the Pan Am flight 103...' from *The Militant*

Extracts from *The Life and Times of Michael K* by J.M.Coetzee, Secker and Warburg

'The health workers were eager...' from *New Internationalist* ©

Dinner at the Homesick Restaurant by Anne Tyler, Chatto and Windus

Waterland by Graham Swift, Random House UK Ltd, reproduced by permission of A. P. Watt Ltd.

Pedigree Chum advertisement, extract reproduced by permission of Pedigree Masterfoods

Women, Men and Language by Jennifer Coates, Pearson Education Ltd.

'villa@uefacup.win.uk' by David Moore from the *Daily Mirror*

'From the Serengeti to the Victoria Falls' advertisement, Voyages Jules Verne

Death of a Salesman by Arthur Miller, Methuen

'What's the Matter' by Michael Rosen, Heinemann Educational

'Don't Mention Tiffany...' from *Just Seventeen*, Emap Elan

Keelhaul from *Europe–A History* by Norman Davis

'EU chimp ruling...' from Sunday Sport 29/3/98

AIDS awareness advertisement, Health Education Authority

Extract from 1997 AGM agenda, Authors' Licensing & Collecting Society Ltd.

'Jurassic mark' and 'Pandora's début' from *BBC Wildlife Magazine*, Volume 14, Number 2

Birds magazine, extract reproduced by permission of the Royal Society for the Protection of Birds

'The cutting takes about 20 minutes...' by Ann McFerran, from *The Times Educational Supplement* 11/9/98

Memorandum extract, National Union of Teachers

All England Law Reports by Harris, extracts reproduced by permission of The Butterworths Division of Reed Elsevier (UK) Ltd

'Life and Times' © *BBC Music Magazine*, Volume 6 Number 4 (December 1997)

© *The Economist Style Guide*, published by Profile Books Ltd, London, 1998

'Play it again' from *The Big Issue*, February 1998

'Blowing in the Wind' by Gary Crossing, first published in *The Big Issue*

Extract from leaflet, by permission of Golden Charter

Extract from Dignity Plan advertisement, SCI Pre-arrangement Ltd.

'Yorkshire Words', series in *Dalesman* magazine, by Dr. Arnold Kellett of the Yorkshire Dialect Society

Extract from Christopher Bruce biography by Jane Pritchard, Archivist, Rambert Dance Company

Terence Rattigan biography, extract reproduced by kind permission of John Good Holbrook

'The choreography for *Airs*...' by Susan McGuire (restaged Paul Taylor's ballet *Airs* for Rambert Dance Company in 1997)

'I feel so sorry for those poor boys...' by Victoria Glendinning, first published in the *Daily Telegraph* 10/1/98

'What was it that departed...' from *London Review of Books* 30/10/97

'Fingers on Buzzers' by Simon Harvey, from University of Nottingham magazine Issue no. 3

Extracts from marketing literature, Direct Wines Ltd

Salopian Brewery extract from the *Good Beer Guide 1998*, Campaign for Real Ale (CAMRA)

'Cross-Channel ferry disaster' by David Usborne, Peter Dunn and Anne Spackman © *The Independent* 1987

'Britain and Japan must go forward together' from the *Sun* 14/1/98

'Argentina says sorry' from the *Sun* 23/10/98

'May we suggest...' extract from advertisement first published 1990, Saab Great Britain Ltd

Property details, George Wimpey plc Ad

'The Law is an Ass' from the *News of the World* 20/4/97

'April – Dubrovnik' by David Robson © *The Independent* 1998

'December – New York' by Hamish Mykura © Hamish Mykura / *The Independent* 1998

Notes from a Small Island by Bill Bryson © Bill Bryson, published by Black Swan, a division of Transworld Publishers Ltd. All rights reserved.

Holidays in Hell by P. J. O'Rourke, extract reproduced by permission of MacMillan

Photographs and Notebooks by Bruce Chatwin © 1993 Bruce Chatwin. Reprinted with the permission of Gillon Aitken Associates Ltd.

A Woman of Substance by Barbara Taylor Bradford, HarperCollins Publishers Ltd.

A Matter of Honour by Jeffrey Archer, HarperCollins Publishers Ltd.

The Exorcist by William Peter Blatty, extract reproduced by kind permission of William Morris Agency Inc.

Metamorphosis and Other Stories by Franz Kafka, Secker and Warburg

Watchwords by Roger McGough, Random House UK Ltd, reproduced by permission of the Peters Fraser and Dunlop Group Ltd

The Radiant Way by Margaret Drabble, Weidenfeld and Nicolson

The Diaries of Jane Somers by Doris Lessing, extract reproduced by kind permission of Jonathan Clowes Ltd.

Separate Tracks by Jane Rogers, Faber and Faber Ltd, extract reprinted by kind permission of the Peters Fraser and Dunlop Group Ltd

'An Irish Airman Foresees his Death' by W. B. Yeats, reproduced by permission of A. P. Watt Ltd. on behalf of Michael B. Yeats

'Not Waving but Drowning' by Stevie Smith, Andre Deutsch Ltd.

Saturday Night and Sunday Morning by Alan Sillitoe, © Alan Sillitoe 1958, 1986

'On Roofs of Terry Street' and 'A Removal from Terry Street' from *Selected Poems* by Douglas Dunn, Faber and Faber Ltd.

'Hay-making' from *Letter from a Far Country* (1982) by Gillian Clarke, reproduced by permission of Carcanet Press Ltd

The Blindfold Horse by Shusha Guppy © 1988 Shusha Guppy. Reprinted with the permission of Gillon Aitken Associates Ltd.

'Them & [uz]' by Tony Harrison © Tony Harrison

'Sonny's Lettah' from *Inglan is a Bitch* by Linton Kwesi Johnson © Linton Kwesi Johnson, reproduced by permission of LKJ Music Publishers Ltd.

Nottingham and the Mining Countryside by D. H. Lawrence, extract reproduced by permission of Laurence Pollinger Ltd and the Estate of Frieda Lawrence Ravagli

'Death of a Son' by Jon Silkin was first published in *The Peaceable Kingdom*, Chatto and Windus, 1954, and is reproduced by permission of the executors of the Literary Estate of Jon Silkin

'Song for Last Year's Wife' by Brian Patten, HarperCollins Publishers Ltd.

'Do Not Go Gentle Into That Good Night' from *Collected Poems* by Dylan Thomas, J. M. Dent

Staying On by Paul Scott, Heinemann

Walter by David Cook © 1978, David Cook. Reproduced by permission of the author c/o Rogers, Coleridge & White Ltd., 20 Powis Mews, London W11 1JN

Lake Wobegon Days by Garrison Keillor, Faber and Faber Ltd

Wilt by Tom Sharpe, Secker and Warburg

Weekend from *Watching Me, Watching You*, extract reproduced with permission of Curtis Brown Ltd., London on behalf of Fay Weldon. Copyright Fay Weldon

'Watch Your Step – I'm Drenched' by Adrian Mitchell © Adrian Mitchell. Available in *Balloon Lagoon and the Magic Islands of Poetry* (Orchard Books 1997). Reprinted by permission of the Peters Fraser and Dunlop Group Ltd on behalf of Adrian Mitchell. Educational health warning! Adrian Mitchell asks that none of his poems are used in connection with any examinations whatsoever.

'Hawk Roosting' from *Lupercal* by Ted Hughes, Faber and Faber Ltd.

'Crow Resting' by Edward Pygge, reproduced by permission of Cover Stories

Extract from *Breakfast with Frost* interview is reproduced with kind permission of the BBC. (The BBC does not vouch for the accuracy of the text, which was transcribed by a student.)

Taking Apart the Poco Poco by Richard Francis. Copyright © 1995 Richard Francis. Extract reprinted by permission of Fourth Estate Ltd.

Reading in the Dark by Seamus Deane, Random House UK Ltd., extract reproduced by permission of Sheil Land Associates Ltd

Every effort has been made to trace the copyright holders of the extracts reprinted in this book. The publishers apologise for any inadvertent inaccuracies or omissions, which they will be pleased to rectify in a subsequent reprint.